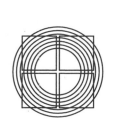

Integral Books publishes today's finest writers and thinkers addressing the full spectrum of human activity—from business to psychology, spirituality to medicine, education to politics, art to ecology—with a comprehensive approach that encompasses body, mind, and spirit in self, culture, and nature. Rooted in the pioneering work of series editor Ken Wilber and his Integral Institute, these works of scholarship, nonfiction, and literature are designed to awaken, inspire, and liberate.

SELECTED BOOKS BY KEN WILBER

The Spectrum of Consciousness (1977)

No Boundary: Eastern and Western Approaches to Personal Growth (1979)

The Atman Project: A Transpersonal View of Human Development (1980)

Up from Eden: A Transpersonal View of Human Evolution (1981)

A Sociable God: Toward a New Understanding of Religion (1983)

Eye to Eye: The Quest for the New Paradigm (1983)

Quantum Questions: Mystical Writings of the World's Great Physicists (1984)

Grace and Grit: Spirituality and Healing in the Life and Death of Treya Killam Wilber (1991)

Sex, Ecology, Spirituality: The Spirit of Evolution (1995)

A Brief History of Everything (1996)

The Eye of Spirit: An Integral Vision for a World Gone Slightly Mad (1997)

The Marriage of Sense and Soul: Integrating Science and Religion (1998)

The Essential Ken Wilber: An Introductory Reader (1998)

One Taste: The Journals of Ken Wilber (1999)

The Collected Works of Ken Wilber, vols. 1–8 (1999–2000)

Integral Psychology: Consciousness, Spirit, Psychology, Therapy (2000)

A Theory of Everything: An Integral Vision for Business, Politics, Science, and Spirituality (2000)

Boomeritis: A Novel That Will Set You Free (2002)

The Simple Feeling of Being: Visionary, Spiritual, and Poetic Writings (2004)

Integral Spirituality: A Startling New Role for Religion in the Modern and Postmodern World (2006)

The Integral Vision: A Very Short Introduction to the Revolutionary Integral Approach to Life, God, the Universe, and Everything (2007)

Integral Life Practice: A 21st-Century Blueprint for Physical Health, Emotional Balance, Mental Clarity, and Spiritual Awakening (2008, with Terry Patten, Adam Leonard, and Marco Morelli)

AVAILABLE ON AUDIO

A Brief History of Everything (2008)

INTEGRAL SPIRITUALITY

A Startling New Role for Religion in the Modern and Postmodern World

Ken Wilber

INTEGRAL BOOKS

Boston & London

2007

INTEGRAL BOOKS

An imprint of Shambhala Publications, Inc.

Horticultural Hall

300 Massachusetts Avenue

Boston, Massachusetts 02115

www.shambhala.com

Excerpts from *Mind at Ease: Self-Liberation through Mahamudra Meditation* by Traleg Kyabgon, © 2003, reprinted by arrangement with Shambhala Publications, Inc.

Table 3.1 by Daniel P. Brown and table 3.2 by John Chirban reprinted from *Transformations of Consciousness: Conventional and Contemplative Perspectives on Development* by Ken Wilber, Jack Engler, and Daniel P. Brown, © 1986, reprinted by arrangement with Shambhala Publications, Inc.

9 8 7 6 5 4 3

Printed in the United States of America

♾ This edition is printed on acid-free paper that meets the American National Standards Institute Z39.48 Standard.

♲ This book was printed on 30% postconsumer recycled paper. For more information please visit us at www.shambhala.com.

Distributed in the United States by Random House, Inc., and in Canada by Random House of Canada Ltd

The Library of Congress catalogues the previous edition of this book as follows:

Wilber, Ken.

Integral spirituality: a startling new role for religion in the modern and postmodern world / Ken Wilber.—1st ed.

    p.   cm.

Includes index.

ISBN 978-1-59030-346-7 (hardcover: alk. paper)

ISBN 978-1-59030-527-0 (paperback)

1. Spirituality. 2. Consciousness. I. Title.

BL624.W533 2006

204—dc22

2006001082

To Colin Bigelow
Manjushri to Vajrapani, some might say

Contents

A Note to the Reader

IN THE PAST TWO DECADES, a radically new theoretical framework for organizing the world and activities in it has started to achieve prominence and widespread recognition. Known as the Integral Approach, it has been used in everything from business to medicine, psychology to law, politics to sustainability, art to education. Because the Integral Framework claims to be comprehensive or inclusive, each discipline using it has been able to reorganize itself in more comprehensive, effective, efficient, and inclusive ways. The Integral Approach itself does not add any content to these disciplines; it simply shows them the areas of their own approaches that are less than integral or less than comprehensive, and this acts as a guide for reorganizing the disciplines in ways that are proving to be, in some cases, nothing less than revolutionary.

What if the Integral Approach were applied to **spirituality**? That is the topic of this book.

The very nature of this topic is so serious, so somber, and the ramifications so monumental in reach and scope, that I didn't want the tone of this book itself to suffocate in seriousness. I therefore chose a tenor that in some cases might appear to have gone too far in the other direction, toward lightness and even frivolity. But I think this is the only way to proceed with a topic that involves nothing less than ultimate concern about issues such as God and Spirit, redemption and release, sin and salvation, illusion and waking up. Lightness of touch is the wiser tone, and luminosity a grace.

One of the main difficulties in presenting the Integral Approach is that you have to explain it before you can apply it. So I have included, as a type of prologue or prelude, a 32-page overview called "Introduction: The Integral Approach." Those of you familiar with the Integral Approach can of course skim through this or skip it altogether.

After the Integral Approach is briefly introduced and explained, it is applied to spirituality. I won't give a summary of the conclusions this book reaches, but simply point out that it addresses perhaps 4 or 5 of the most pressing issues facing spirituality—such as applying spirituality in everyday life, proof of Spirit's existence, stages of spiritual development, the role of meditation or contemplation, Eastern and Western approaches to religion—and their relation to currents in the modern and postmodern world. The result is what amounts to a manifesto for an Integral Spirituality.

I do believe that an integral approach to spirituality discovers a role for religion in the modern and postmodern world that has been overlooked entirely, and this radically new role for religion not only works, it holds a very real type of salvation for humanity on the whole. Exactly what this role is will be explained as the discussion unfolds.

There are several footnotes in the book, and, for those who would like to go into these issues in more depth, on the www.kenwilber.com and wilber.shambhala.com websites, you will find hundreds of pages of endnotes. Throughout this book you will also notice mention of "Excerpts A–G." These are excerpts from volume 2 of the Kosmos Trilogy (vol. 1 of which is *Sex, Ecology, Spirituality*). These Excerpts are also posted on the www.kenwilber.com and wilber.shambhala.com sites.

In the following pages, when writing about the Integral Approach, I often use the pronoun "we" instead of "I." This "we" refers to the colleagues at Integral Institute (I-I), and I use "we" in describing this work because it really is a joint effort of hundreds of individuals who are immediately involved as staff at Integral Institute (and tens of thousands who are members of I-I), dedicated to bringing a more integral approach to all walks of life. Several times throughout this book you will be invited to join us (www.integralinstitute.org) if you would like to help with this extraordinary adventure.

It's a new day, it's a new dawn, it's a new man, it's a new woman. The new human is integral, and so is the spirituality.

K.W.
Denver, Colorado
Spring 2006

INTEGRAL SPIRITUALITY

Introduction

THE INTEGRAL APPROACH

OVERVIEW

During the last 30 years, we have witnessed a historical first: all of the world's cultures are now available to us. In the past, if you were born, say, a Chinese, you likely spent your entire life in one culture, often in one province, sometimes in one house, living and loving and dying on one small plot of land. But today, not only are people geographically mobile, but we can study, and have studied, virtually every known culture on the planet. In the global village, all cultures are exposed to each other.

Knowledge itself is now global. This means that, also for the first time, the sum total of human knowledge is available to us—the knowledge, experience, wisdom, and reflection of all major human civilizations—premodern, modern, and postmodern—are open to study by anyone.

What if we took literally everything that all the various cultures have to tell us about human potential—about spiritual growth, psychological growth, social growth—and put it all on the table? What if we attempted to find the critically essential keys to human growth, based on the sum total of human knowledge now open to us? What if we attempted, based on extensive cross-cultural study, to use all of the world's great traditions to create a composite map, a comprehensive map, an all-inclusive or *integral* map that included the best elements from all of them?

Sound complicated, complex, daunting? In a sense, it is. But in another sense, the results turn out to be surprisingly simple and elegant. Over the last several decades, there has indeed been an extensive search for a comprehensive map of human potentials. This map uses all the known systems and models of human growth—from the ancient shamans and sages to today's breakthroughs in cognitive science—and distills their major components into 5 simple factors, factors that are the essential elements or keys to unlocking and facilitating human evolution.

Welcome to the Integral Approach.

An Integral or Comprehensive Map

What are these 5 elements? We call them **quadrants, levels, lines, states,** and **types.** As you will see, all of these elements are, right now, *available in your own awareness.* These 5 elements are not merely theoretical concepts; they are aspects of your own experience, contours of your own consciousness, as you can easily verify for yourself as we proceed.

What is the point of using this Integral Map? First, whether you are working in business, medicine, psychotherapy, law, ecology, or simply everyday living and learning, the Integral Map helps make sure that you are "touching all the bases." If you are trying to fly over the Rocky Mountains, the more accurate a map you have, the less likely you will crash. An Integral Approach ensures that you are utilizing the full range of resources for any situation, with the greater likelihood of success.

Second, if you learn to spot these 5 elements in your own awareness—and because they are there in any event—then you can more easily appreciate them, exercise them, use them . . . and thereby vastly accelerate your own growth and development to higher, wider, deeper ways of being. A simple familiarity with the 5 elements in the Integral Model will help you orient yourself more easily and fully in this exciting journey of discovery and awakening.

In short, the Integral Approach helps you see both yourself and the world around you in more comprehensive and effective ways. But one thing is important to realize from the start. The Integral Map is just a map. It is not the territory. We certainly don't want to confuse the map with the territory—but neither do we want to be working with an inaccurate or faulty map. Do you want to fly over the Rockies with a bad map? The Integral Map is just a map, but it is the most complete and accurate map we have at this time.

What Is an IOS?

IOS simply means **Integral Operating System.** In an information network, an operating system is the infrastructure that allows various software programs to operate. We use **Integral Operating System** or **IOS** as another phrase for the Integral Map. The point is simply that, if you are running any "software" in your life—such as your business, work, play, or relationships—you want the best operating system you can find, and **IOS** fits that bill. In touching all the bases, it allows the most effective programs to be used. This is just another way of talking about the comprehensive and inclusive nature of the Integral Model.

We will also be exploring what is perhaps the most important use of the Integral Map or Operating System. Because an IOS can be used to help index any activity—from art to dance to business to psychology to politics to ecology to spirituality—it allows each of those domains to talk to the others. Using IOS, business has the terminology with which to communicate fully with ecology, which can communicate with art, which can communicate with law, which can communicate with poetry and education and medicine and spirituality. In the history of humankind, this has never really happened before.

By using the Integral Approach—by using an Integral Map or Integral Operating System—we are able to facilitate and dramatically accelerate cross-disciplinary and trans-disciplinary knowledge, thus creating the world's first truly integral learning community. And when it comes to religion and spirituality, using the Integral Approach has allowed the creation of Integral Spiritual Center, where some of the world's leading spiritual teachers from all major religions have come together not only to listen to each other but to "teach the teachers," resulting in one of the most extraordinary learning events imaginable. We will return to this important gathering, and ways you can join in this community if you wish.

But it all starts with these simple 5 elements in the contours of your own consciousness.

States of Consciousness

We said that all of the aspects of the 5 elements of the Integral Model are available, right now, in your own awareness. What follows is therefore, in a sense, a guided tour of your own experience. So why don't you come along and see if you can spot some of these features arising in your own awareness right now.

Some of these features refer to subjective realities in you, some refer to objective realities out there in the world, and others refer to collective or communal realities shared with others. Let's start with states of consciousness, which refer to subjective realities.

Everybody is familiar with major **states of consciousness**, such as waking, dreaming, and deep sleep. Right now, you are in a waking state of consciousness (or, if you are tired, perhaps a daydream state of consciousness). There are all sorts of different states of consciousness, including *meditative states* (induced by yoga, contemplative prayer, meditation, and so on), *altered states* (such as drug-induced), and a variety of *peak experiences*, many of which can be triggered by intense experiences like making love, walking in nature, or listening to exquisite music.

The great wisdom traditions (such as Christian mysticism, Vedanta Hinduism, Vajrayana Buddhism, and Jewish Kabbalah) maintain that the 3 *natural states* of consciousness—waking, dreaming, and deep formless sleep—actually contain a treasure trove of spiritual wisdom and spiritual awakening . . . if we know how to use them correctly. We usually think of the dream state as less real, but what if you could enter it while awake? And the same with deep sleep? How do you learn something extraordinary in those awakened states? In a special sense, which we will explore as we go along, the 3 great natural states of waking, dreaming, and deep sleep might contain an entire spectrum of spiritual enlightenment.

But on a much simpler, more mundane level, everybody experiences various states of consciousness, and these states often provide profound motivation, meaning, and drives, in both yourself and others. In any particular situation, states of consciousness may not be a very important factor, or they may be the determining factor, but no integral approach can afford to ignore them. Whenever you are using **IOS**, you will automatically be prompted to check and see if you are touching bases with these important subjective realities. This is an example of how a map—in this case, the IOS or Integral Map—can help you look for territory you might not have even suspected was there. . . .

STAGES OR LEVELS OF DEVELOPMENT

There's an interesting thing about states of consciousness: they come and they go. Even great peak experiences or altered states, no matter how profound, will come, stay a bit, then pass. No matter how wonderful their capacities, they are temporary.

Where states of consciousness are temporary, **stages of consciousness** are permanent. Stages represent the actual milestones of growth and development. Once you are at a stage, it is an enduring acquisition. For example, once a child develops through the linguistic stages of development, the child has permanent access to language. Language isn't present one minute and gone the next. The same thing happens with other types of growth. Once you stably reach a stage of growth and development, you can access the capacities of that stage—such as greater consciousness, more embracing love, higher ethical callings, greater intelligence and awareness—virtually any time you want. *Passing states have been converted to permanent traits.*

How many stages of development are there? Well, remember that in any map, the way you divide and represent the actual territory is somewhat arbitrary. For example, how many degrees are there between freezing and boiling water? If you use a Centigrade scale or "map," there are 100 degrees between freezing and boiling. But if you use a Fahrenheit scale, freezing is at 32 and boiling is at 212, so there are 180 degrees between them. Which is right? Both of them. It just depends upon how you want to slice that pie.

The same is true of stages. There are all sorts of ways to slice and dice development, and therefore there are all sorts of **stage conceptions.** All of them can be useful. In the *chakra* system, for example, there are 7 major stages or levels of consciousness. Jean Gebser, the famous anthropologist, uses 5: archaic, magic, mythic, rational, and integral. Certain Western psychological models have 8, 12, or more levels of development. Which is right? All of them; it just depends on what you want to keep track of in growth and development.

"Stages of development" are also referred to as **"levels** of development," the idea being that each stage represents a level of organization or a level of complexity. For example, in the sequence from atoms to molecules to cells to organisms, each of those stages of evolution involves a greater level of complexity. The word "level" is not meant in a rigid or exclusionary fashion, but simply to indicate that there are important *emergent* qualities that tend to come into being in a discrete or quantum-like fashion, and these developmental jumps or levels are important aspects of many natural phenomena.

Generally, in the Integral Model, we work with around 8 to 10 stages or levels of consciousness development. We have found, after years of field work, that more stages than that are too cumbersome, and less than that, too vague. Some of the stage conceptions we often use include those of self development pioneered by Jane Loevinger and Susann Cook-Greuter; Spiral Dynamics, by Don Beck and Chris Cowan; and orders of consciousness, researched by Robert Kegan. But there are many other useful stage conceptions available with the Integral Approach, and you can adopt any of them that are appropriate to your situation.

As we get into the specifics later in this book, you will see how incredibly important stages can be. But let's take a simple example now to show what is involved.

EGOCENTRIC, ETHNOCENTRIC, AND WORLDCENTRIC

To show what is involved with levels or stages, let's use a very simple model possessing only 3 of them. If we look at moral development, for example, we find that an infant at birth has not yet been socialized into the culture's ethics and conventions; this is called the **preconventional stage**. It is also called **egocentric**, in that the infant's awareness is largely self-absorbed. But as the young child begins to learn its culture's rules and norms, it grows into the **conventional stage** of morals. This stage is also called **ethnocentric**, in that it centers on the child's particular group, tribe, clan, or nation, and it therefore tends to exclude those not of one's group. But at the next major stage of moral development, the **postconventional stage**, the individual's identity expands once again, this time to include a care and concern for all peoples, regardless of race, color, sex, or creed, which is why this stage is also called **worldcentric**.

Thus, moral development tends to move from "me" (egocentric) to "us" (ethnocentric) to "all of us" (worldcentric)—a good example of the unfolding stages of consciousness.

Another way to picture these 3 stages is as **body, mind,** and **spirit.** Those words all have many valid meanings, but when used specifically to refer to stages, they mean:

Stage 1, which is dominated by my gross physical reality, is the "body" stage (using body in its typical meaning of physical body). Since you are identified merely with the separate bodily organism and its survival drives, this is also the "me" stage.

Stage 2 is the "mind" stage, where identity expands from the isolated gross body and starts to share relationships with many others, based perhaps on shared values, mutual interests, common ideals, or shared dreams. Because I can use the mind to take the role of others—to put myself in their shoes and feel what it is like to be them—my identity expands from "me" to "us" (the move from egocentric to ethnocentric).

With stage 3, my identity expands once again, this time from an identity with "us" to an identity with "all of us" (the move from ethnocentric to worldcentric). Here I begin to understand that, in addition to the wonderful diversity of humans and cultures, there are also similarities and shared commonalities. Discovering the commonwealth of all beings is the move from ethnocentric to worldcentric, and is "spiritual" in the sense of things common to all sentient beings.

That is one way to view the unfolding from body to mind to spirit, where each of them is considered as a stage, wave, or level of unfolding care and consciousness, moving from egocentric to ethnocentric to worldcentric.

We will be returning to stages of evolution and development, each time exploring them from a new angle. For now, all that is required is an understanding that by "stages" we mean progressive and permanent milestones along the evolutionary path of your own unfolding. Whether we talk stages of consciousness, stages of energy, stages of culture, stages of spiritual realization, stages of moral development, and so on, we are talking of these important and fundamental rungs in the unfolding of your higher, deeper, wider potentials.

Whenever you use IOS, you will automatically be prompted to check and see if you have included the important **stage aspects** of any situation, which will dramatically increase your likelihood of success, whether that success be measured in terms of personal transformation, social change, excellence in business, care for others, or simple satisfaction in life.

Lines of Development: I'm Good at Some Things, Not-So-Good at Others . . .

Have you ever noticed how unevenly developed virtually all of us are? Some people are highly developed in, say, logical thinking, but poorly developed in emotional feelings. Some people have highly advanced cognitive development (they're very smart) but poor moral development (they're mean and ruthless). Some people excel in emotional intelligence, but can't add 2 plus 2.

Howard Gardner made this concept fairly well known using the idea of **multiple intelligences**. Human beings have a variety of intelligences, such as cognitive intelligence, emotional intelligence, musical intelligence, kinesthetic intelligence, and so on. Most people excel in one or two of those, but do poorly in the others. This is not necessarily or even usually a bad thing; part of integral wisdom is finding where one excels and thus where one can best offer the world one's deepest gifts.

But this does mean that we need to be aware of our strengths (or the intelligences with which we can shine) as well as our weaknesses (where we do poorly or even pathologically). And this brings us to another of our 5 essential elements: our multiple intelligences or developmental lines. So far we have looked at **states** and **stages**; what are **lines** or multiple intelligences?

Various multiple intelligences include: cognitive, interpersonal, moral, emotional, and aesthetic. Why do we also call them **developmental lines**? Because those intelligences show growth and development. They unfold in progressive stages. What are those progressive stages? The stages we just outlined.

In other words, each multiple intelligence grows—or can grow—through the 3 major stages (or through any of the stages of any of the developmental models, whether 3 stages, 5 stages, 7 or more; remember, these are all like Centigrade and Fahrenheit). You can have cognitive development to stage 1, to stage 2, and to stage 3, for example.

Likewise with the other intelligences. Emotional development to stage 1 means that you have developed the capacity for emotions centering on "me," especially the emotions and drives of hunger, survival, and self-protection. If you continue to grow emotionally from stage 1 to stage 2—or from egocentric to ethnocentric—you will expand from "me" to "us," and begin to develop emotional commitments and attachments to loved ones, members of your family, close friends, perhaps your whole tribe or whole nation. If you grow into stage-3 emotions, you will develop the further capacity for a care and compassion that reaches beyond your own tribe or nation and attempts to include all human beings and even all sentient beings in a worldcentric care and compassion.

And remember, because these are stages, you have attained them in a permanent fashion. Before that happens, any of these capacities will be merely passing states: you will plug into some of them, if at all, in a temporary fashion—great peak experiences of expanded knowing and being, wondrous "aha!" experiences, profound altered glimpses into your own higher possibilities. But with practice, you will convert those states into stages, or permanent traits in the territory of you.

THE INTEGRAL PSYCHOGRAPH

There is a fairly easy way to represent these intelligences or multiple lines. In figure 1 (p. 10), we have drawn a simple graph showing the 3 major stages (or **levels** of development) and 5 of the most important intelligences (or lines of development). **Through the major stages or levels of development, the various lines unfold.** The 3 levels or stages can apply to any developmental line—sexual, cognitive, spiritual, emotional, moral, and so on. The level of a particular line simply means the "altitude" of that line in terms of its growth and consciousness. We often say, "That person is highly developed morally," or "That person is really advanced spiritually."

In figure 1, we have shown somebody who excels in cognitive development and is good at interpersonal development, but does poorly in moral and really poorly in emotional intelligence. Other individuals would, of course, have a different "psychograph."

The **psychograph** helps to spot where your greatest potentials are. You very likely already know what you excel in and what you don't. But part of the Integral Approach is learning to refine considerably this knowledge of your own contours, so that you can more confidently deal with your own strengths and weaknesses as well as those of others.

The psychograph also helps us spot the ways that virtually all of us are unevenly developed, and this helps prevent us from thinking that just because we are terrific in one area we must be terrific in all the others. In fact, usually the opposite. More than one leader, spiritual teacher, or politician has spectacularly crashed through lack of an understanding of these simple realities.

To be "integrally developed" does not mean that you have to excel in all the known intelligences, or that all of your lines have to be at level 3. But it does mean that you develop a very good sense of what your own psychograph is actually like, so that with a much more integral self-image you can plan your future development. For some people, this will indeed mean strengthening certain intelligences that are so weak they are causing problems. For others, this will mean clearing up a serious problem or pathology in one line (such as the psychosexual). And for others, simply recognizing where their strengths and weaknesses lie, and planning accordingly. Using an integral map, we can scope out our own psychographs with more assurance.

Thus, to be "**integrally informed**" does not mean you have to master all lines of development, just be aware of them. If you then choose to remedy any unbalances, that is part of Integral Life Practice (ILP), which actually helps to increase levels of consciousness and development through an integrated approach. (We will be discussing ILP in detail in chap. 10.)

Notice another very important point. In certain types of psychological and spiritual training, you can be introduced to a full spectrum of **states** of consciousness and bodily experiences right from the start—as a peak experience, meditative state, shamanic vision, altered state, and so on. The reason these peak experiences are possible is that many of the major states of consciousness (such as waking-gross, dreaming-subtle, and formless-causal) are ever-present possibilities. So you can very quickly be introduced to many **higher states** of consciousness.

You cannot, however, be introduced to all the qualities of **higher stages** without actual growth and practice. You can have a peak experience of higher *states* (like seeing an interior subtle light or having a feeling of oneness with all of nature), because many states are ever-present, and so they can be "peek"-experienced right now. But you can-

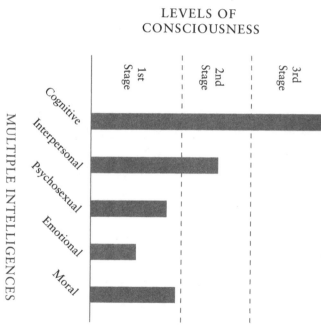

Figure 1. *Psychograph.*

MULTIPLE INTELLIGENCES

LEVELS OF CONSCIOUSNESS

3rd Stage

2nd Stage

1st Stage

Cognitive

Interpersonal

Psychosexual

Emotional

Moral

not have a peak experience of a higher *stage* (like being a concert-level pianist), because stages unfold sequentially and take considerable time to develop. Stages build upon their predecessors in very concrete ways, so they cannot be skipped: like atoms to molecules to cells to organisms, you can't go from atoms to cells and skip molecules. This is one of the many important differences between states and stages.

However, with repeated practice of contacting higher states, your own stages of development will tend to unfold in a much faster and easier way. There is, in fact, considerable experimental evidence demonstrating exactly that. The more you are plunged into authentic higher *states* of consciousness—such as meditative states—the *faster* you will grow and develop through any of the *stages* of consciousness. It is as if higher-states training acts as a lubricant on the spiral of development, helping you to disidentify with a lower stage so that the next higher stage can emerge, until you can stably remain at higher levels of awareness on an ongoing basis, whereupon a passing state has become a permanent trait. These types of higher-states training, such as meditation, are a part of any integral approach to transformation.

In short, you cannot skip actual *stages*, but you can accelerate your growth through them by using various types of *state*-practices, such as meditation, and these transformative practices are an important part of the Integral Approach.

WHAT TYPE: BOY OR GIRL?

The next component is easy: each of the previous components has a masculine and feminine type.

There are two basic ideas here: one has to do with the idea of *types* themselves; and the other, with masculine and feminine as one example of types.

Types simply refers to items that can be present at virtually any stage or state. One common typology, for example, is the Myers-Briggs (whose main types are feeling, thinking, sensing, and intuiting). **You can be any of those types at virtually any stage of development.** These kinds of "horizontal typologies" can be very useful, especially when combined with levels, lines, and states. To show what is involved, we can use "masculine" and "feminine."

Carol Gilligan, in her enormously influential book *In a Different Voice*, pointed out that both men and women tend to develop through

3 or 4 major levels or stages of moral development. Pointing to a great deal of research evidence, Gilligan noted that these 3 or 4 moral stages can be called *preconventional, conventional, postconventional,* and *integrated.* These are actually quite similar to the 3 simple developmental stages we are using, this time applied to moral intelligence.

Gilligan found that stage 1 is a morality centered entirely on "me" (hence this preconventional stage or level is also called **egocentric**). Stage-2 moral development is centered on "us," so that my identity has expanded from just me to include other human beings of my group (hence this conventional stage is often called **ethnocentric**, traditional, or conformist). With stage-3 moral development, my identity expands once again, this time from "us" to "all of us," or all human beings (or even all sentient beings)—and hence this stage is often called **world-centric**. I now have care and compassion, not just for me (egocentric), and not just for my family, my tribe, or my nation (ethnocentric), but for all of humanity, for all men and women everywhere, regardless of race, color, sex, or creed (worldcentric). And if I develop even further, at stage-4 moral development, which Gilligan calls **integrated**, then . . .

Well, before we look at the important conclusion of Gilligan's work, let's first note her major contribution. Gilligan strongly agreed that women, like men, develop through those 3 or 4 major hierarchical stages of growth. Gilligan herself correctly refers to these stages as *hierarchical* because each stage has a *higher* capacity for care and compassion. But she said that women progress through those stages using a different type of logic—they develop "in a different voice."

Male logic, or a man's voice, tends to be based on terms of autonomy, justice, and rights; whereas women's logic or voice tends to be based on terms of relationship, care, and responsibility. Men tend toward agency; women tend toward communion. Men follow rules; women follow connections. Men look; women touch. Men tend toward individualism, women toward relationship. One of Gilligan's favorite stories: A little boy and girl are playing. The boy says, "Let's play pirates!" The girl says, "Let's play like we live next door to each other." Boy: "No, I want to play pirates!" "Okay, you play the pirate who lives next door."

Little boys don't like girls around when they are playing games like baseball, because the two voices clash badly, and often hilariously. Some boys are playing baseball, a kid takes his third strike and is out, so he starts to cry. The other boys stand unmoved until the kid stops crying; after all, a rule is a rule, and the rule is: three strikes and you're out. Gilligan points out that if a girl is around, she will usually say, "Ah, come on, give him another try!" The girl sees him crying and wants to help, wants to connect, wants to heal. This, however, drives the boys nuts, who are doing this game as an initiation into the world of rules and male logic. Gilligan says that the boys will therefore hurt feelings in order to save the rules; the girls will break the rules in order to save the feelings.

In a different voice. Both the girls and boys will develop through the 3 or 4 developmental stages of moral growth (egocentric to ethnocentric to worldcentric to integrated), but they will do so in a different voice, using a different logic. Gilligan specifically calls these hierarchical stages in women **selfish** (which is egocentric), **care** (which is ethnocentric), **universal care** (which is worldcentric), and **integrated**. Again, why did Gilligan (who has been badly misunderstood on this topic) say that these stages were hierarchical? Because each stage has a higher capacity for care and compassion. (Not all hierarchies are bad, and this is a good example of why.)

So, integrated or stage 4—what is that? At the 4th and highest stage of moral development, according to Gilligan, the masculine and feminine voices in each of us tend to become integrated. This does not mean that a person at this stage starts to lose the distinctions between masculine and feminine, and hence become a kind of bland, androgynous, asexual being. In fact, masculine and feminine dimensions might become more intensified. But it does mean the individuals start to befriend both the masculine and feminine modes in themselves, even if they characteristically act predominantly from one or the other.

Have you ever seen a *caduceus* (the symbol of the medical profession)? It's a staff with two serpents crisscrossing it, and wings at the top of the staff (see fig. 2). The staff itself represents the central spinal column; where the serpents cross the staff represents the individual *chakras* moving up the spine from the lowest to the highest; and the two serpents themselves represent solar and lunar (or masculine and feminine) energies *at each of the chakras.*

That's the crucial point. The 7 *chakras*, which are simply a more complex version of the 3 simple levels or stages, represent 7 levels of consciousness and energy available to all human beings. (The first three *chakras*—food, sex, and power—are roughly stage 1; *chakras* 4 and 5— relational heart and communication—are basically stage 2; and *chakras* 6 and 7—psychic and spiritual—are the epitome of stage 3.) The important point here is that, according to the traditions, **each of those 7 levels has a masculine and feminine** aspect, type, or "voice." Neither masculine nor feminine is higher or better; they are two equivalent types at each of the levels of consciousness.

This means, for example, that with *chakra* 3 (the egocentric-power *chakra*), there is a masculine and feminine version of the same *chakra*: at that *chakra*-level, males tend toward power exercised autonomously ("My way or the highway!"), women tend toward power exercised communally or socially ("Do it this way or I won't talk to you"). And so on with the other major *chakras*, each of them having a solar and lunar, or masculine and feminine, dimension. Neither is more fundamental; neither can be ignored.

At the 7th *chakra*, however, notice that the masculine and feminine serpents both disappear into their ground or source. Masculine and feminine meet and unite at the crown—they literally become one. And that is what Gilligan found with her stage-4 moral development: the two voices in each person become integrated, so that there is a paradoxical union of autonomy and relationship, rights and responsibilities, agency and communion, wisdom and compassion, justice and mercy, masculine and feminine.

The important point is that whenever you use IOS, you are automatically checking any situation—in yourself, in others, in an organization, in a culture—and making sure that you include both the masculine and feminine types so as to be as comprehensive and inclusive as possible. If you believe that there are no major differences between masculine and feminine—or if you are suspicious of such differences—then that is fine, too, and you can treat them the same if you want. We are simply saying that, in either case, make sure you touch bases with both the masculine and feminine, however you view them.

But more than that, there are numerous other "horizontal typologies"

Figure 2. Caduceus.

that can be very helpful when part of a comprehensive IOS, and the Integral Approach draws on any or all of those typologies as appropriate. "Types" are as important as quadrants, levels, lines, and states.

SICK BOY, SICK GIRL

There's an interesting thing about types. You can have healthy and unhealthy versions of them. To say that somebody is caught in an unhealthy type is not a way to judge them but a way to understand and communicate more clearly and effectively with them.

For example, if each stage of development has a masculine and feminine dimension, each of those can be healthy or unhealthy, which we sometimes call "sick boy, sick girl." This is simply another kind of horizontal typing, but one that can be extremely useful.

If the healthy masculine principle tends toward autonomy, strength, independence, and freedom, when that principle becomes unhealthy or pathological, all of those positive virtues either over- or underfire. There is not just autonomy, but alienation; not just strength, but domination; not just independence, but morbid fear of relationship and commitment; not just a drive toward freedom, but a drive to destroy. The unhealthy masculine principle does not transcend in freedom, but dominates in fear.

If the healthy feminine principle tends toward flowing, relationship, care, and compassion, the unhealthy feminine flounders in each of those. Instead of being in relationship, she becomes lost in relationship. Instead of a healthy self in communion with others, she loses her self altogether and is dominated by the relationships she is in. Not a connection, but a fusion; not a flow state, but a panic state; not a communion, but a meltdown. The unhealthy feminine principle does not find fullness in connection, but chaos in fusion.

Using IOS, you will find ways to identify both the healthy and unhealthy masculine and feminine dimensions operating in yourself and in others. But the important point about this section is simple: various typologies have their usefulness in helping us to understand and communicate with others. And with any typology, there are healthy and unhealthy versions of a type. Pointing to an unhealthy type is not a way to judge people, but a way to understand and communicate with them more clearly and effectively.

THERE'S EVEN ROOM FOR MANY BODIES

Let's return now to states of consciousness in order to make a final point before bringing this all together in an integral conclusion.

States of consciousness do not hover in the air, dangling and disembodied. On the contrary, every mind has its body. For every state of consciousness, there is a felt energetic component, an embodied feeling, a concrete vehicle that provides the actual support for any state of awareness.

Let's use a simple example from the wisdom traditions. Because each of us has the 3 great states of consciousness—waking, dreaming, and formless sleep—the wisdom traditions maintain that each of us likewise has **3 bodies**, which are often called the **gross body**, the **subtle body**, and the **causal body**.

I have 3 bodies? Are you kidding me? Isn't one body enough? But keep in mind a few things. For the wisdom traditions, a "body" simply means a mode of experience or energetic feeling. So there is coarse or gross experience, subtle or refined experience, and very subtle or causal experience. These are what philosophers would call "phenomenological realities," or realities as they present themselves to our immediate awareness. Right now, you have access to a gross body and its gross energy, a subtle body and its subtle energy, and a causal body and its causal energy.

What's an example of these 3 bodies? Notice that, right now, you are in a *waking state* of awareness; as such, you are aware of your **gross body**—the physical, material, sensorimotor body. But when you dream at night, there is no gross physical body; it seems to have vanished. You are aware in the dream state, yet you don't have a gross body of dense matter but a **subtle body** of light, energy, emotional feelings, fluid and flowing images. In the dream state, the mind and soul are set free to create as they please, to imagine vast worlds not tied to gross sensory realities but reaching out, almost magically, to touch other souls, other people and far-off places, wild and radiant images cascading to the rhythm of the heart's desire. So what kind of body do you have in the dream? Well, a **subtle body** of feelings, images, even light. That's what you feel like in the dream. And dreams are not "just illusion." When somebody like Martin Luther King, Jr., says, "I have a dream," that is a good example of tapping into the great potential of visionary dreaming, where the subtle body and mind are set free to soar to their highest possibilities.

As you pass from the *dream state* with its subtle body into the deep-sleep or *formless state*, even thoughts and images drop away, and there is only a vast emptiness, a formless expanse beyond any individual "I" or ego or self. The great wisdom traditions maintain that in this state—which might seem like merely a blank or nothingness—we are actually plunged into a vast formless realm, a great Emptiness or Ground of Being, an expanse of consciousness that seems almost infinite. Along with this almost infinite expanse of consciousness there is an almost infinite body or energy—the **causal body**, the body of the finest, most subtle experience possible, a great formlessness out of which creative possibilities can arise.

Of course, many people do not experience that deep state in such a full fashion. But again, the traditions are unanimous that this *formless state* and its *causal body* can be entered in full awareness, whereupon they, too, yield their extraordinary potentials for growth and awareness.

The point, once again, is simply that whenever IOS is being utilized, it reminds us to check in with our waking-state realities, our subtle-state dreams and visions and innovative ideas, as well as our own open, formless ground of possibilities that is the source of so much creativity. The important point about the Integral Approach is that we want to touch bases with as many potentials as possible so as to miss nothing in terms of possible solutions, growth, and transformation.

Consciousness and Complexity

Perhaps 3 bodies are just too "far out"? Well, remember that these are phenomenological realities, or experiential realities, but there is a simpler, less far-out way to look at them, this time grounded in hard-headed science. It is this: *every level of interior consciousness is accompanied by a level of exterior physical complexity*. The greater the consciousness, the more complex the system housing it.

For example, in living organisms, the **reptilian brain stem** is accompanied by a rudimentary interior consciousness of basic drives such as food and hunger, physiological sensations, and sensorimotor actions (everything that we earlier called "gross," or centered on the "me"). By the time we get to the more complex **mammalian limbic system**, basic sensations have expanded and evolved to include quite sophisticated feelings, desires, emotional-sexual impulses, and needs (hence the beginning of what we called subtle experience or the subtle body, which can expand from "me" to "us"). As evolution proceeds to even more complex physical structures, such as the **triune brain** with its **neocortex**, consciousness once again expands to a worldcentric awareness of "all of us" (and thus even begins to tap into what we called the causal body).

That is a very simple example of the fact that increasing interior consciousness is accompanied by increasing exterior complexity of the systems housing it. When using **IOS**, we often look at both the **interior levels of consciousness** and the corresponding **exterior levels of physical complexity**, since including both of them results in a much more balanced and inclusive approach. We will see exactly what this means in a moment.

And Now: How Do They All Fit Together?

IOS—and the Integral Model—would be merely a "heap" if it did not suggest a way that all of these various components are related. How do they all fit together? It's one thing to simply lay all the pieces of the cross-cultural survey on the table and say, "They're all important," and quite another to spot the patterns that actually connect all the pieces. Discovering the profound **patterns that connect** is a major accomplishment of the Integral Approach.

In this concluding section, we will briefly outline these patterns, all of which together are sometimes referred to as **A-Q-A-L** (pronounced *ah-qwul*), which is shorthand for "all quadrants, all levels, all lines, all states, all types"—and those are simply the components that we have already outlined (except the quadrants, which we will get to momentarily). **AQAL** is just another term for **IOS** or the Integral Map, but one that is often used to specifically designate this particular approach.

At the beginning of this introduction, we said that all 5 components of the Integral Model were items that are *available to your awareness right now*, and this is true of the quadrants as well.

Did you ever notice that major languages have what are called 1st-person, 2nd-person, and 3rd-person pronouns? The **1st-person** perspective refers to "the person who is speaking," which includes pronouns like *I, me, mine* (in the singular) and *we, us, ours* (in the plural). The **2nd-person** perspective refers to "the person who is spoken to," which includes pronouns like *you and yours*. The **3rd-person** perspective refers to "the person or thing being spoken about," such as *he, him, she, her, they, them, it,* and *its*.

Thus, if I am speaking to you about my new car, "I" am 1st person, "you" are 2nd person, and the new car (or "it") is 3rd person. Now, if you and I are talking and communicating, we will indicate this by using, for example, the word "we," as in, "We understand each other." "We" is technically 1st-person plural, but if you and I are communicating, then your 2nd person and my 1st person are part of this extraordinary "we." Thus, 2nd person is sometimes indicated as "you/we," or "thou/we," or sometimes just "we."

So we can therefore simplify 1st-, 2nd-, and 3rd-person as "**I**," "**we**," and "**it**."

That all seems trivial, doesn't it? Boring, maybe? So let's try this. Instead of saying "I," "we," and "it," what if we said the **Beautiful**, the **Good**, and the **True**? And what if we said that the Beautiful, the Good, and the True are dimensions of your very own being at each and every moment, including each and every level of growth and development? And that through an integral practice, you can discover deeper and deeper dimensions of your own Goodness, your own Truth, and your own Beauty?

Hmm, definitely more interesting. The Beautiful, the Good, and the True are simply variations on 1st-, 2nd-, and 3rd-person pronouns found in all major languages, and they are found in all major languages because Beauty, Truth, and Goodness are very real dimensions of reality to which language has adapted. The 3rd person (or "it") refers to objective truth, which is best investigated by science. The 2nd person (or "you/we") refers to Goodness, or the ways that we—that you and I—treat each other, and whether we do so with decency, honesty, and respect. In other words, basic morality. And 1st person deals with the "I," with self and self-expression, art and aesthetics, and the beauty that is in the eye (or the "I") of the beholder.

So the "I," "we," and "it" dimensions of experience really refer to **art**, **morals**, and **science**. Or **self**, **culture**, and **nature**. Or the **Beautiful**, the **Good**, and the **True**. (For some reason, philosophers always refer to those in this order: the Good, the True, and the Beautiful. Which order do you prefer? Any order is fine.)

The point is that *every* event in the manifest world *has all 3 of those dimensions.* You can look at any event from the point of view of the "I" (or how I personally see and feel about the event); from the point of view of the "we" (how not just I but others see the event); and as an "it" (or the objective facts of the event).

Thus, an integrally informed path will take all of those dimensions into account, and thus arrive at a more comprehensive and effective approach—in the "I" and the "we" and the "it"—or in self and culture and nature.

If you leave out science, or leave out art, or leave out morals, something is going to be missing, something will get broken. Self and culture and nature are liberated together or not at all. So fundamental are these dimensions of "I," "we," and "it" that we call them the 4 quadrants, and we make them a foundation of the integral framework or IOS. (We arrive at "4" quadrants by subdividing "it" into singular "it" and plural "its.") A few diagrams will help clarify the basic points.

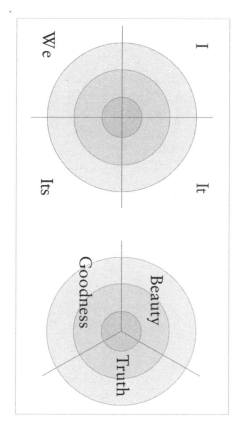

Figure 3. *The Quadrants.*

Figure 3 is a schematic of the 4 quadrants. It shows the **"I"** (the *inside* of the *individual*), the **"it"** (the *outside of the individual*), the **"we"** (the *inside* of the *collective*), and the **"its"** (the *outside of the collective*). In other words, the 4 quadrants—which are the 4 fundamental perspectives on any occasion (or the 4 basic ways of looking at anything)—turn out to be fairly simple: they are the **inside** and the **outside** of the **individual** and the **collective.**

Figures 4 and 5 show a few of the details of the 4 quadrants. (Some of these are technical terms that needn't be bothered with for this basic introduction; simply look at the diagrams and get a sense of the different types of items you might find in each of the quadrants.)

For example, in the **Upper-Left quadrant** (the interior of the individual), you find your own immediate thoughts, feelings, sensations, and so

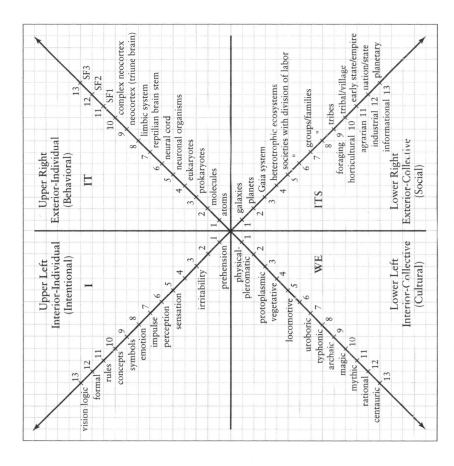

Figure 4. Some Details of the Quadrants.

on (all described in 1st-person terms). But if you look at your individual being *from the outside*, in the terms not of subjective awareness but objective science, you find neurotransmitters, a limbic system, the neo-cortex, complex molecular structures, cells, organ systems, DNA, and so on—all described in 3rd-person objective terms ("it" and "its"). The **Upper-Right quadrant** is therefore what any *individual* event looks like *from the outside*. This especially includes its physical behavior; its mate-rial components; its matter and energy; and its concrete body—for all those are items that can be referred to in some sort of objective, **3rd-person**, or "it" fashion.

That is what you or your organism looks like from the outside, in an objective-it stance, made of matter and energy and objects; whereas from the inside, you find not neurotransmitters but feelings, not limbic

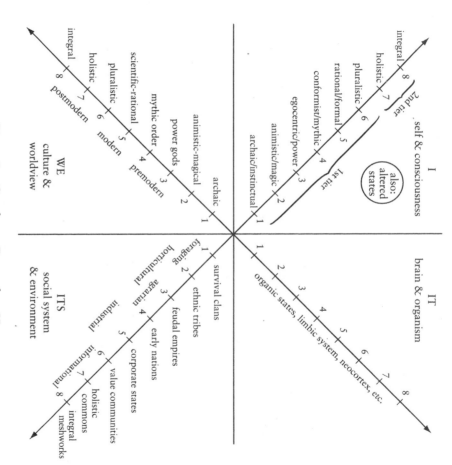

Figure 5. Quadrants Focused on Humans.

systems but intense desires, not a neocortex but inward visions, not matter-energy but consciousness, all described in **1st-person** immediateness. Which of those views is right? Both of them, according to the integral approach. They are two different views of the same occasion, namely you. The problems start when you try to deny or dismiss either of those perspectives. All 4 quadrants need to be included in any integral view.

The connections continue. Notice that every "I" is in relationship with other I's, which means that every "I" is a member of numerous we's. These "we's" represent not just *individual* but *group* (or *collective*) consciousness, not just subjective but intersubjective awareness—or **culture** in the broadest sense. This is indicated in the **Lower-Left quadrant**. Likewise, every "we" has an exterior, or what it looks like from the outside, and this is the **Lower-Right quadrant.** The Lower Left is often called the **cultural** dimension (or the inside awareness of the group—its worldview, its shared values, shared feelings, and so forth), and the Lower Right the **social** dimension (or the exterior forms and behaviors of the group, which are studied by 3rd-person sciences such as systems theory).

Again, the quadrants are simply the **inside** and the **outside** of the **individual** and the **collective,** and the point is that all 4 quadrants need to be included if we want to be as integral as possible.

We are now at a point where we can start to put all the integral pieces together: quadrants, levels, lines, states, and types. Let's start with **levels** or **stages.**

All 4 quadrants show growth, development, or evolution. That is, they all show some sort of stages or levels of development, not as rigid rungs in a ladder but as fluid and flowing waves of unfolding. This happens everywhere in the natural world, just as an oak unfolds from an acorn through stages of growth and development, or a Siberian tiger grows from a fertilized egg to an adult organism in well-defined stages of growth and development. Likewise with humans in certain important ways. We have already seen several of these stages as they apply to humans. In the Upper Left or "I," for example, the self unfolds from egocentric to ethnocentric to worldcentric, or *body* to *mind* to *spirit.* In the Upper Right, felt energy phenomenologically expands from *gross* to *subtle* to *causal.* In the Lower Left, the "we" expands from *egocentric* ("me") to *ethnocentric* ("us") to *worldcentric* ("all of us"). This expansion of group awareness allows social systems—in the Lower Right—to expand from simple groups to more complex systems like nations and eventually even to global systems. These 3 simple stages in each of the quadrants are represented in figure 6.

Let's move from **levels** to **lines.** Developmental lines occur in all 4 quadrants, but because we are focusing on personal development, we can look at how some of these lines appear in the Upper-Left quadrant. As we saw, there are over a dozen different multiple intelligences or developmental lines. Some of the more important include:

- the **cognitive** line (or awareness of what is)
- the **moral** line (awareness of what should be)
- **emotional** or **affective** line (the full spectrum of emotions)
- the **interpersonal** line (how I socially relate to others)
- the **needs** line (such as Maslow's needs hierarchy)

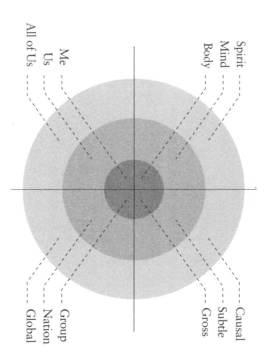

Spirit
Mind
Body

Causal
Subtle
Gross

Me
Us
All of Us

Group
Nation
Global

Figure 6.   AQAL.

- the **self-identity** line (or "who am I?," such as Loevinger's ego development)
- the **aesthetic** line (or the line of self-expression, beauty, art, and felt meaning)
- the **psychosexual** line, which in its broadest sense means the entire spectrum of Eros (gross to subtle to causal)
- the **spiritual** line (where "spirit" is viewed not just as Ground, and not just as the highest stage, but as its own line of unfolding)
- the **values** line (or what a person considers most important, a line studied by Clare Graves and made popular by Spiral Dynamics)

All of those developmental lines can move through the basic stages or levels. All of them can be included in the psychograph. If we use stage or level conceptions such as Robert Kegan's, Jane Loevinger's, or Clare Graves's, then we would have 5, 8, or even more levels of development with which we could follow the natural unfolding of developmental lines or streams. Again, it is not a matter of which of them is right or wrong; it is a matter of how much "granularity" or "complexity" you need to more adequately understand a given situation.

We already gave one diagram of a psychograph (fig. 1). Figure 7 is another, taken from a Notre Dame business school presentation that uses the AQAL model in business.

As noted, all of the quadrants have developmental lines. We just fo-

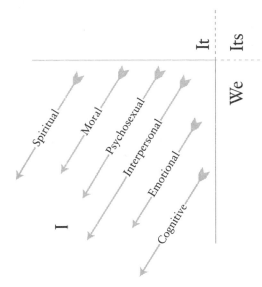

Spiritual

Moral

Psychosexual

Interpersonal

Emotional

Cognitive

I

It

We

Its

Figure 7. Another Version of the Psychograph.

cused on those in the Upper Left. In the Upper-Right quadrant, when it comes to humans, one of the most important is the bodily matter-energy line, which runs, as we saw, from gross energy to subtle energy to causal energy. As a developmental sequence, this refers to the permanent acquisition of a capacity to consciously master these energetic components of your being (otherwise, they appear merely as states). The Upper-Right quadrant also refers to all of the exterior **behavior**, actions, and movements of my objective body (gross, subtle, or causal).

In the Lower-Left quadrant, cultural development itself often unfolds in waves, moving from what the pioneering genius Jean Gebser called *archaic* to *magic* to *mythic* to *mental* to *integral* and higher. In the Lower-Right quadrant, systems theory investigates the collective social systems that evolve (and that, in humans, include stages such as *foraging* to *agrarian* to *industrial* to *informational* systems). In figure 6, we simplified this to "group, nation, and global," but the general idea is simply that of unfolding levels of greater social complexity that are integrated into wider systems.

Again, for this simple overview, details are not as important as a general grasp of the unfolding or *flowering nature of all 4 quadrants*, which can include expanding spheres of consciousness, care, culture, and nature. In short, the I and the we and it can evolve. Self and culture and nature can all develop and evolve.

We can now quickly finish with the other components. **States** occur in all quadrants (from weather states to states of consciousness). We focused on **states of consciousness** in the Upper Left (waking, dreaming, sleeping), and on **energetic states** in the Upper Right (gross, subtle, causal). Of course, if any of those become permanent acquisitions, they have become stages, not states.

There are **types** in all of the quadrants, too, but we focused on *masculine* and *feminine* types as they appear in individuals. The masculine principle identifies more with agency and the feminine identifies more with communion, but the point is that every person has both of these components. Finally, as we saw, there is an **unhealthy type** of masculine and feminine at all available stages—sick boy and sick girl at all stages.

Seem complicated? In a sense it is. But in another sense, the extraordinary complexity of humans and their relation to the universe can be simplified enormously by touching bases with the **quadrants** (the fact that every event can be looked at as an I, we, or it); **developmental lines** (or multiple intelligences), all of which move through **developmental levels** (from body to mind to spirit); with **states** and **types** at each of those levels.

That **Integral Model**—"all quadrants, all levels, all lines, all states, all types"—is the simplest model that can handle all of the truly essential items. We sometimes shorten all of that to simply "all quadrants, all levels"—or **AQAL**—where the quadrants are, for example, self, culture, and nature, and the levels are body, mind, and spirit, so we say that the Integral Approach involves **the cultivation of body, mind, and spirit in self, culture, and nature.** The simplest version of this is shown in figure 6, and if you have a general understanding of that diagram, the rest is fairly easy.

IOS Apps

Let's conclude what might be called this "Introduction to IOS Basic" by giving a few quick examples of its applications, or **"apps"**—in medicine, business, spirituality, and ecology.

Integral Medicine

Nowhere is the Integral Model more immediately applicable than in medicine, and it is being increasingly adopted by health-care practitioners around the world. A quick trip through the quadrants will show why the Integral Model can be helpful.

Orthodox or conventional medicine is a classic **Upper-Right quadrant** approach. It deals almost entirely with the physical organism using physical interventions: surgery, drugs, medication, and behavioral modification. Orthodox medicine believes essentially in the physical causes of physical illness, and therefore prescribes mostly physical interventions. But the Integral Model claims that every physical event (UR) has at least 4 dimensions (the quadrants), and thus even physical illness must be looked at from all 4 quadrants (not to mention levels, which we will address later). The integral model does not claim the Upper-Right quadrant is not important, only that it is, as it were, only one-fourth of the story.

The recent explosion of interest in alternative care—not to mention such disciplines as psychoneuroimmunology—has made it quite clear that the person's *interior states* (their emotions, psychological attitude, imagery, and intentions) play a crucial role in both the *cause* and the *cure* of even physical illness. In other words, the **Upper-Left quadrant** is a key ingredient in any comprehensive medical care. Visualization, affirmation, and conscious use of imagery have empirically been shown to play a significant role in the management of most illnesses, and outcomes have been shown to depend on emotional states and mental outlook.

But as important as those subjective factors are, individual consciousness does not exist in a vacuum; it exists inextricably embedded in shared cultural values, beliefs, and worldviews. How a culture (I.I.) views a particular illness—with care and compassion or derision and scorn—can have a profound impact on how an individual copes with that illness (UL), which can directly affect the course of the physical illness itself (UR). The **Lower-Left quadrant** includes all of the enormous number of *intersubjective* factors that are crucial in any human interaction—such as the shared communication between doctor and patient; the attitudes of family and friends and how they are conveyed to the patient; the cultural acceptance (or derogation) of the particular illness (e.g., AIDS); and the very values of the culture that the illness itself threatens. All of those factors are to some degree causative in any physical illness and cure (simply because *every* occasion has 4 quadrants).

Of course, in practice, this quadrant needs to be effectively engaged—perhaps doctor and patient communication skills, family and friends support groups, and a general understanding of cultural judgments and their effects on illness. Studies consistently show, for example, that cancer patients in support groups live longer than those without similar cultural support. Some of the more relevant factors from the Lower-Left quadrant are thus crucial in any comprehensive medical care.

The **Lower-Right quadrant** concerns all those material, economic, and social factors that are almost never counted as part of the disease entity, but in fact—like every other quadrant—are *causative* in both disease and cure. A social system that cannot deliver food will kill you (as famine-wracked countries demonstrate daily, alas). In the real world, where every entity has all 4 quadrants, a virus in the UR quadrant might be the focal issue, but without a social system (LR) that can deliver treatment, you will die. That is not a separate issue; it is central to the issue, because all occasions have 4 quadrants. The Lower-Right quadrant includes factors such as economics, insurance, social delivery systems, and even things as simple as how a hospital room is physically laid out (does it allow ease of movement, access to visitors, etc.?)—not to mention items like environmental toxins.

The foregoing items refer to the "all-quadrant" aspect of the cause and management of illness. The "all-level" part refers to the fact that individuals have—at least—physical, emotional, mental, and spiritual levels in each of those quadrants (see fig. 6). Some illnesses have largely physical causes and physical cures (get hit by a bus, break your leg). But most illnesses have causes and cures that include *emotional*, *mental*, and *spiritual* components. Literally hundreds of researchers from around the world have added immeasurably to our understanding of the "multi-level" nature of disease and cure (including invaluable additions from the great wisdom traditions, shamanic to Tibetan). The point is simply that by adding these levels to the quadrants, a much more comprehensive—and effective—medical model begins to emerge.

In short, a truly effective and comprehensive medical plan would be all-quadrant, all-level: the idea is simply that each quadrant or dimension (fig. 3)—I, we, and it—has physical, emotional, mental, and spiritual levels or waves (fig. 6), and a truly integral treatment would take all of these realities into account. Not only is this type of integral treatment more *effective*, it is for that reason more *cost-efficient*—which is why even organizational medicine is looking at it more closely.

(If you're more interested in this approach, see the Center for Integral Medicine at www.integraluniversity.org.)

Integral Business

Applications of the Integral Model have recently exploded in business, because the applications are so immediate and obvious. The quadrants give the 4 "environments" or "markets" in which a product must survive, and the levels give the types of values that will be both producing and buying the product. Research into the values hierarchy—such as Maslow's and Graves's (e.g., Spiral Dynamics), which have already had an enormous influence on business can be combined with the quadrants (which show how these levels of values appear in the 4 different environments)—to give a truly comprehensive map of the marketplace (which covers both traditional markets and cybermarkets).

Moreover, *Integral Leadership* training programs, based on an integral or AQAL model, have also begun to flourish. There are today 4 major theories of business management (Theory X, which stresses individual behavior; Theory Y, which focuses on psychological understanding; cultural management, which stresses organizational culture; and systems management, which emphasizes the social system and its governance). Those 4 management theories are in fact the 4 quadrants, and an Integral Approach would necessarily include all 4 approaches. Add levels and lines, and an incredibly rich and sophisticated model of leadership emerges, which is easily the most comprehensive available today.

(If you would like to pursue this approach, please see the Center for Integral Leadership and Business at www.integraluniversity.org.)

Relational and Socially Engaged Spirituality

The major implication of an AQAL approach to spirituality is that physical, emotional, mental, and spiritual levels of being should be simultaneously exercised in self, culture, and nature (i.e., in the I, we, and it domains). There are many variations on this theme, ranging from socially engaged spirituality to relationships as spiritual path, and we include all of those important contributions in Integral Life Practice (see below). The implications of an Integral Spirituality (www.integral spiritualcenter.org) are profound and widespread, and just beginning to have an impact.

Integral Ecology

Integral or AQAL ecology has already been pioneered by several associates at Integral Institute, and promises to revolutionize both how we think about environmental issues and how we pragmatically address and remedy them (See the Center for Integral Ecology at www.integral university.org).

The basic idea is simple: anything less than an integral or comprehensive approach to environmental issues is doomed to failure. Both the interior (or Left-Hand) and the exterior (or Right-Hand) quadrants need to be taken into account. **Exterior** environmental sustainability is clearly needed; but without a growth and development in the **interior** domains to worldcentric levels of values and consciousness, the environment remains gravely at risk. Those focusing only on exterior solutions are contributing to the problem. Self, culture, and nature must be liberated together or not at all. How to do so is the focus of Integral Ecology.

Integral Life Practice

The foregoing "IOS apps" tend to focus on some of the theoretical aspects of the Integral Approach. But what about the experiential and practical aspects of my own awareness, growth, transformation, and awakening?

Any map of the human being has an explicit or implicit practical approach, and the practical, 1st-person, experiential dimension of the Integral Approach is called **Integral Life Practice, or ILP.**

The basic nature of ILP is simple. I'll give a schematic summary: if you take body, mind, and spirit (as levels), and self, culture, and nature (as quadrants), and then you combine them, you get 9 possible areas of growth and awakening. Integral Life Practice is the first approach to cross-combine all of those for the most effective personal transformation possible (www.MyILP.com).

To give a slightly more expanded example: if you look at figure 6, you will notice that 3 levels in 4 quadrants actually gives you 12 zones. Integral Life Practice has created practical exercises for growth in all 12 zones, a radically unique and historically unprecedented approach to growth, development, and awakening. (We will return to ILP in chap. 10.)

Summary and Conclusion

Those are a few of the "applications" or apps of the Integral Model. We can now conclude with a brief summary of the main points of the model itself.

AQAL is short for **"all quadrants, all levels"**—which itself is short for "all quadrants, all levels, all lines, all states, all types," which are simply 5 of the most basic elements that need to be included in any truly integral or comprehensive approach.

When AQAL is used as a guiding framework to organize or understand any activity, we also call it an **Integral Operating System,** or simply **IOS.** More advanced forms of IOS are available, but IOS Basic has all of the essential elements (quadrants, levels, lines, states, types) to get anybody started toward a more comprehensive, inclusive, and effective approach.

Of course, **AQAL** or **IOS** itself is just a map, nothing more. It is not the territory. But, as far as we can tell, it is the most comprehensive map that we possess at this time. Moreover—and this is important—the Integral Map itself insists that we go to the real territory and not get caught in mere words, ideas, or concepts. Remember that the quadrants are just a version of 1st-, 2nd-, and 3rd-person realities? Well, the **Integral Map and IOS** are just 3rd-person words, they are abstractions, a series of "it" signs and symbols. But those 3rd-person words insist that we also include 1st-person direct feelings, experiences, and consciousness as well as 2nd-person dialogue, contact, and interpersonal care. The Integral Map itself says: *this map is just a 3rd-person map, so don't forget the other important realities, all of which should be included in any comprehensive approach.*

That's where things like Integral Life Practice come in. When AQAL or IOS is used for real-life personal growth and development, we speak of **Integral Life Practice,** which appears to be the most comprehensive and therefore effective path of transformation available.

Here's one other important conclusion. **IOS** is a neutral framework; it does not tell you what to think, or force any particular ideologies on you, or coerce your awareness in any fashion. For example, to say that human beings have waking, dreaming, and deep sleep states is not to say what you should think while awake or what you should see while dreaming. It simply says, if you want to be comprehensive, be sure and include waking and dreaming and formless states.

Likewise, to say that all occasions have 4 quadrants—or simply "I," "we," and "it" dimensions—is not to say what the "I" should do, or the "we" should do, or the "it" should do. It simply says, if you are trying to include all the important possibilities, be sure to include 1st- and 2nd- and 3rd-person perspectives, because they are present in all major languages the world over.

Precisely because **IOS** is a **neutral framework,** it can be used to bring more clarity, care, and comprehensiveness to virtually any situation, making success much more likely, whether that success be measured in terms of personal transformation, social change, excellence in business, care for others, or simple happiness in life.

But perhaps most important of all, because IOS can be used by any discipline—from medicine to art to business to spirituality to politics to ecology—then we can, for the first time in history, begin an extensive and fruitful dialogue between all of these disciplines. A person using IOS in business can talk easily and effectively with a person using IOS in poetry, dance, or the arts, simply because they now have a common language—or a common operating system—with which to communicate. When you are using IOS, not only can you run hundreds of different "software" programs on it, all of those programs can now communicate with each other and learn from each other, thus advancing an evolutionary unfolding to even greater dimensions of being and knowing and acting.

This is why thousands of scholars and teachers the world over came together and started Integral University, the world's first integral learning community. Because all of the various human activities, previously separated by incommensurate jargon and terminologies, can in fact begin to effectively communicate with each other by running an Integral Operating System, each of those disciplines can begin to converse with, and learn from, the others. This has never effectively happened anywhere in history, which is why, indeed, the Integral adventure is about to begin.

However we look at it, it all comes down to a few simple points. In your own growth and development, you have the capacity to take self, culture, and nature to increasingly higher, wider, and deeper modes of being, expanding from an isolated identity of "me" to a fuller identity of "us" to an even deeper identity with "all of us"—with all sentient beings everywhere—as your own capacity for Truth and Goodness and Beauty deepens and expands. Ever-greater consciousness with an ever-wider embrace, which is realized in self, embodied in nature, and expressed in culture.

Thus, **to cultivate body, mind, and spirit in self, culture, and nature.** This is the extraordinary aim and goal of the Integral Approach, and we would love to have you join us in this exciting adventure.

But if you think this is more of the typical "holistic" or "spiritual" or "new age" or "new paradigm" approach to these issues, that would be the first big mistake.

1

Integral Methodological Pluralism

WE START WITH THE SIMPLE OBSERVATION that the "metaphysics" of the spiritual traditions have been thoroughly critiqued—"trashed" is probably the better word—by both modernist and postmodernist epistemologies, and there has as yet arisen nothing compelling to take their place. So this chapter begins with an overview of the methodologies available that can be used to reconstruct the spiritual systems of the great wisdom traditions but with none of their metaphysical baggage.

Integral Methodological Pluralism (IMP) involves, among other things, at least 8 fundamental and apparently irreducible methodologies, injunctions, or paradigms for gaining reproducible knowledge (or verifiably repeatable experiences). The fundamental claim of AQAL Integral Theory is that any approach that leaves out any of these 8 paradigms is a less-than-adequate approach according to available and reliable human knowledge at this time.

The easiest way to understand IMP is to start with what are known as the **quadrants**, which suggest that any occasion possesses an inside and an outside, as well as an individual and a collective, dimension. Taken together, this gives us the inside and the outside of the individual and the collective. These are often represented as I, you/we, it, and its (a variation on 1st-, 2nd-, and 3rd-person pronouns; another variation is the Good, the True, and the Beautiful; or art, morals, and science, and so on—namely, the objective truth of exterior science, or it/its; the subjective truth of aesthetics, or I; and the collective truth of ethics, or thou/we).

Figure 1.1 is a schematic of some of the phenomena found in the quadrants according to reliable knowledge communities working with them. (Don't worry if some of the terms are unfamiliar; we will cover the important ones later.)*

We often refer to any event as a **holon**—a "whole/part," or a whole that is a part of other wholes—and thus each of the items labeled in the various quadrants can also be referred to as a holon (e.g., in the UR quadrant, a molecule is a holon that contains whole atoms and is contained by whole cells; in the UL, a concept is a holon that contains whole symbols and is contained by whole rules, and so on).

Now here, as they say, is where it gets interesting. If you imagine any of the phenomena (or holons) in the various quadrants, you can look at them from their own inside or outside. This gives you **8 primordial perspectives**—the inside and the outside view of a holon in any of the 4 quadrants.

These 8 primordial perspectives of any occasion are summarized in figure 1.2. The sum total of these 8 views we call **Integral Perspectivism.** We inhabit these 8 spaces, these zones, these lifeworlds, as practical realities. Each of these zones is not just a perspective, but an action, an injunction, a concrete set of actions in a real world zone. Each injunction *brings forth* or discloses the phenomena that are apprehended through the various perspectives. It is not that perspectives come first and actions or injunctions come later; they simultaneously co-arise (actually, tetra-arise). "Perspectives" simply locate the perceiving holon in AQAL space. To take such-and-such a perspective is to be arising in this particular area of the AQAL matrix. (In fact, we will soon give the "address" of a

---

* As introductory statements we say things like, "The quadrants are the inside and the outside view (or perspective) of the individual and the collective." More technically, with reference to these perspectives, we differentiate between the "view through" and the "view from." All individual (or sentient) holons HAVE or POSSESS 4 perspectives through which or with which they view or touch the world, and those are the quadrants (the view through). But anything can be *looked at* FROM those 4 perspectives—or there is a view of anything from those perspectives—and that is technically called a *quadrivium*. For example, a chair, as an artifact, does not possess 4 quadrants, but it can be looked at from those 4 quadrants or perspectives, which is then a quadrivium of views of or about the chair. An individual holon (like you or me) *has* an I, we, it, and its dimension-perspective (and hence a view through); an artifact does not, but I can look at the artifact from each of those perspectives or each quadrivium. Likewise, the 8 zones are "8 quadrants," and the 8 methodologies are "8 quadrivia." See appendix II.

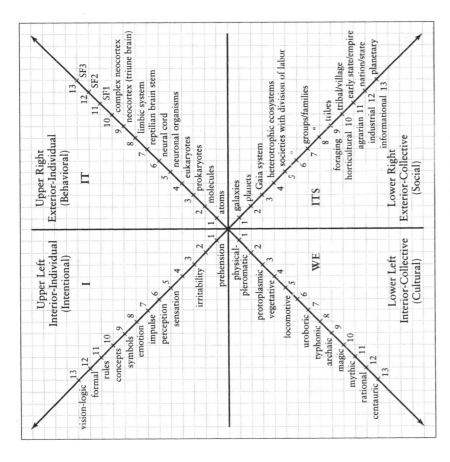

Figure 1.1. Some Details of the Quadrants.

holon in the AQAL matrix as: **address = altitude + perspective,** where *altitude* means degree of development and *perspective* means the perspective or quadrant it is in.)

We will come back to all that. The basic point is simply that these 8 fundamental perspectives also involve 8 fundamental methodologies. You not only can take a view, you can act from it. Some of the more well known of these methodologies are summarized in figure 1.3. These methodologies taken together are referred to as **Integral Methodological Pluralism.**

The idea is simple enough. Start with any phenomenon (or holon) in any of the quadrants—for example, the experience of an "I" in the UL quadrant. That "I" can be looked at from the inside or the outside. I can experience my own "I" *from the inside,* in this moment, as the felt experience of being a subject of my present experience, a 1st person having a 1st-person experience. If I do so, the results include such things as introspection, meditation, phenomenology, contemplation, and so on (all simply summarized as **phenomenology** in fig. 1.3).

But I can also approach this "I" *from the outside*, in a stance of an objective or "scientific" observer. I can do so in my own awareness (when I try to be "objective" about myself, or try to "see myself as others see me"), and I can also attempt to do this with other "I's" as well, attempting to be scientific in my study of how people experience their "I." The most famous of these scientific approaches to I-consciousness have included systems theory and **structuralism.**

Likewise, I can approach the study of a "we" from its inside or its outside. *From the inside*, this includes the attempts that you and I make to understand each other right now. How is it that you and I can reach

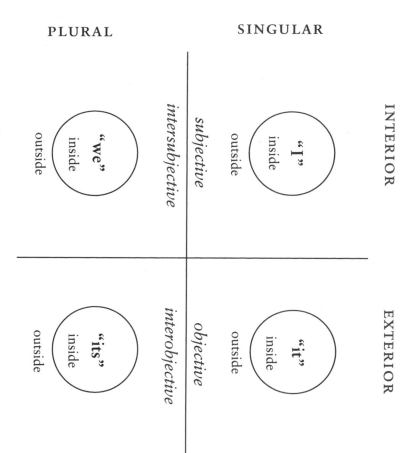

Figure 1.2. 8 Primordial Perspectives.

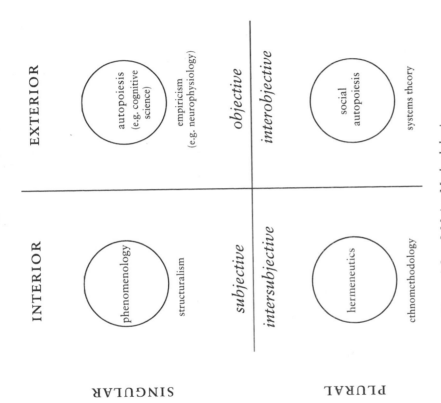

Figure 1.3. 8 Major Methodologies.

mutual understanding about anything, including when we simply talk to each other? How do your "I" and my "I" come together in something you and I both call "we" (as in, "Do you and I—do we—understand each other?")? The art and science of we-interpretation is typically called **hermeneutics.**

But I can also attempt to study this "we" *from the outside*, perhaps as a cultural anthropologist, or an ethnomethodologist, or a Foucauldian archaeologist, and so on (all of which are summarized in fig. 1.3 as **ethnomethodology**).

And so on around the quadrants. Thus, 8 basic *perspectives* and 8 basic *methodologies.*

Let me give a very quick indication of why this becomes crucially important for today's spirituality. Many of you are familiar with Spiral

Dynamics, a system of psychosocial development based upon Clare Graves's pioneering research on stages of value systems (if you're not familiar with SD, don't worry, we will summarize it later, at which point what I am about to say will make sense). SD is representative of the type of research that has been so valuable in understanding people's worldviews, values, and the stages of meaning-making that human beings go through. And many of you are aware of the profound meditative states of awareness referred to generally as *unio mystica*, *sahaj*, or *satori* (or illumination and awakening). These are states that are said by the great traditions to give knowledge or awareness of an ultimate reality. (Don't worry if you're not familiar with those terms either, we'll come back to them.)

Here's the point: you can sit on your meditation mat for decades, and you will NEVER see anything resembling the stages of Spiral Dynamics. And you can study Spiral Dynamics till the cows come home, and you will NEVER have a *satori*. And the integral point is, if you don't include both, you will likely never understand human beings or their relation to Reality, divine or otherwise.

Meditative understanding involves preeminently a methodology of looking at the "I" from the inside (using phenomenology); Spiral Dynamics involves studying it from the outside (using structuralism). Both of them are studying a person's consciousness, but they see very different things because they are inhabiting a different stance or perspective, using different methodologies. Further, a person could be quite advanced in one, and not in the other, or vice versa, and there is no way to tell using either of their yardsticks; they can't even see each other!

HORI-ZONES OF ARISING

Each view or perspective, with its actions and injunctions, brings forth a world of phenomena; a worldspace that (tetra-)arises as a result; a worldspace with a horizon. The sum total of all of that we simply call a **hori-zone,** or **zone** for short. A zone is a view with its actions, its injunctions, its lifeworld, and the whole shebang called forth at that address. You can think of it as a life-zone, or zone of awareness, or a living space—any number of terms will do.

But it is a definite location in the AQAL matrix: this actual holon living at this address, with these actions, bringing forth these phenomena. But all in very concrete terms. A zone is . . . actually going shopping.

And everything you might see and feel and do in the space that you inhabit doing so.

(We earlier briefly mentioned that a holon's address = its altitude + perspective. We will indeed come back to this in the next chapter and see how that relates to a zone. As we will discover, all of this is important because it relates to being able to "prove" the existence of anything, whether a rock, a proposition, or God. . . .)

Perspectives and methodologies are just subsets of hori-zones—they are some of the things that can happen in a zone of arising. This, too, will become clearer as we proceed. For now, simply think of a zone as everything that CAN arise in any of those 8 areas on figures 1.2 and 1.3. For convenience, we will label all of them (see fig. 1.4).

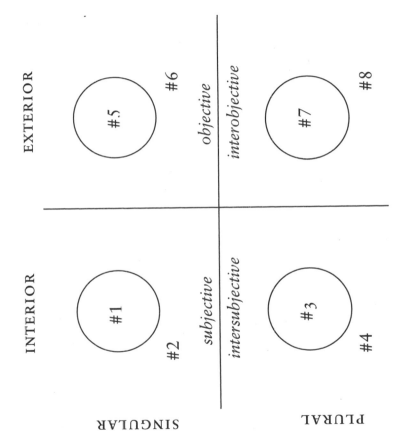

Figure 1.4. 8 Zones.

To return to Spiral Dynamics and meditation: when it comes to interior consciousness (the Upper-Left quadrant) both zone-#1 and zone-#2 methodologies are crucially important types of knowledge, and both complement each other wonderfully. (In case you're unfamiliar with them, we will give extensive examples of both in the next chapter.) Taking both into account is absolutely essential for making any sort of progress in understanding the role of religion and spirituality in the modern and postmodern world.

Once we acknowledge the research and importance of both, the trick is to then understand how they are related. How are zones #1 and #2 related—indeed, how are all 8 zones related?

This is a primary topic of this book. And, beyond that, what does all this have to do with religion in the modern and postmodern world?

An Integral Mathematics of Primordial Perspectives

For you advanced students out there, notice that the 8 methodologies are really giving us perspectives on perspectives on perspectives. For example, meditation involves the inside view of an interior view of an individual view. Francisco Varela's approach to biological phenomenology is the outside view of the inside view of the interior view. Hermeneutics is the inside view of the interior view of the collective view. And so on. Each **zone** actually involves at least **3 major perspectives** to locate it! (Don't worry, it's much simpler than it sounds!)

This leads to a new type of mathematical notation that we sometimes call **integral math**, which replaces traditional variables with perspectives. (For you not-so-advanced students, don't worry about this section; we'll pick up the fun again with the heading, "Integral Post-Metaphysics," and you don't need to even read this section if it seems unusually stupid to you.)

Using the shorthand of 1st person (for *the inside in general*) and 3rd person (for *the outside in general*), then **introspection**, let's say, which is a type of phenomenology (or zone-#1 activity), is when "I look into my mind"—or, I have a 1st-person experience of my 1st-person awareness, which we would write as **1-p × 1p**.

But I can also try to see myself "objectively," like others see me. So that would be a 3rd-person view of my own introspection, so let's write that as **3-p × 1-p × 1p**. Contrasted to that, pure meditation or introspection would be **1-p × 1-p × 1p**, which means a 1st-person view **(1-p)** of my 1st-person awareness **(1-p)** of me, or my 1st person **(1p)**. We will come back to Varela's view later, but for those of you following it now, Varela started with the objective organism in the Upper Right (or a 3rd person, **3p**). He then attempted to "see the world through the frog's eyes," or take a 1st-person view within that objective organism (**1-p × 3p**). And he then put that in scientific terms (**3-p**), so he had a **3-p × 1-p × 3p** (a 3rd-person conceptualization of a 1st-person view from within the 3rd person or "objective" organism).

That's a simple version of doing "integral math," which really means, *inhabiting as many perspectives of other sentient beings as you possibly can*. Get out of yourself and take the role of others, and take the roles of others yet again. . . . That's why the full name is an **integral mathematics of primordial perspectives**. Doing this type of integral math is actually what one person called **psychoactive**, because it's not really abstract math, but an actual putting yourself in somebody else's shoes, which forces your awareness to grow. (We will come back to that.)

Integral math can become enormously rich and complicated, with many more roles and terms and perspectives, but those are some examples for a start. (You can actually go on to build a type of real mathematics here, with the equal sign representing "mutual understanding or resonance." As far as we know, this is a radical new type of mathematics that replaces variables with perspectives and objects with sentient beings.)

But here's the main point we are following. Meditation, as we saw, is **1-p × 1-p × 1p** (or the inside view of the interior awareness of my 1st person). Spiral Dynamics, as it relates to an individual, is **3-p × 1-p × 1p**. It's a 3rd-person conceptual map of the interior awareness of a person.

With reference to Spiral Dynamics and meditation, you can see right in those equations that the first term in each phrase is different—very different—in Spiral Dynamics (**3-p × 1-p × 1p**) and in meditation (**1-p × 1-p × 1p**). As the underlined terms show, Zen and SD share two of the variables, but not the first: SD is a 3rd-<u>person</u> map of an interior territory, and Zen a 1st-<u>person</u> experience of an interior territory. There are some other important differences that we will get to in a minute, but you can start to see the useful distinctions that come from an Integral Methodological Pluralism and an integral mathematics of primordial perspectives.*

---

*In integral math, when we use 3 terms, such as **1p × 1-p × 3p**, those terms are usually: quadrant × quadrivium × domain (and "domain" can be a quadrant or a quadrivium). Of course, it can get much more complicated very quickly, but much

We will explore those differences in detail in a later chapter. And you *don't* have to know the math.

INTEGRAL POST-METAPHYSICS

The Integral view leads to an entirely new approach to metaphysics that is actually **post-metaphysics**, in that it requires none of the traditional baggage of metaphysics (such as postulating the existence of pre-existing ontological structures of a Platonic, archetypal, Patanjali, or Yogachara Buddhist variety), and yet it can generate those structures if needed (as I will try to demonstrate later).

This **Integral Post-Metaphysics** replaces *perceptions* with *perspectives*, and thus re-defines the manifest realm as the realm of perspectives, not things nor events nor structures nor processes nor systems nor *vasanas* nor archetypes nor *dharmas*, because all of those are perspectives before they are anything else, and cannot be adopted or even stated without first assuming a perspective.

Thus, for example, the Whiteheadian and Buddhist notion of each moment being a momentary, discrete, fleeting subject that apprehends *dharmas* or momentary occasions, is itself a 3rd-person generalization of a 1st-person view of the reality in a 1st person (3-p × 1-p × 1p). Each moment is *not* a subject prehending an object; it is a perspective prehending a perspective—with Whitehead's version being a truncated version of that multifaceted occasion, a version that actually has a hid-

---

of integral math is simply reiterations of those fundamental possibilities. As integral math gets more complex, we use 4 and 5 terms, not just 3 (e.g., **1p × 3-p × 1-p × 3p**). If we only use 3 of those terms, as I usually do in this book, then the definitions can look different from those given in the Excerpts, but they really aren't. For example, Varela's view using 4 terms is **3p × 1-p × 3-p × 3p**, and if you shorten that to 3 terms, it will look different depending on which 3 you choose. In the text, I am using the first 3 of those 4 terms (**3-p × 1-p × 3p**), but you could use the last 3 (**1-p × 3-p × 3p**).

Also, "the inside and outside of the singular and collective" technically are not the same as 1st, 2nd, and 3rd-person approaches or combinations thereof, and some severe theoretical problems result if this equation is made. We sometimes use 1-p and 3-p to represent inside and outsides views, but this is a concession to popular understanding and not the actual definitions. The quadrants (inside/outside × singular/plural) are much more fundamental and prior differentiations in Kosmogenesis than are 123p (and, in fact, generate them). Ditto for judgments such as aesthetic, moral, scientific.

den monological metaphysics. Integral Post-Metaphysics can thus generate the essentials of Whitehead's view but without assuming Whitehead's hidden metaphysics.

The same turns out to be true for the central assertions of the great wisdom traditions: an Integral Post-Metaphysics can generate their essential contours *without* assuming their extensive metaphysics. (If those examples are a bit too abstract, we will return to this topic shortly with some simpler ones.)

The problem with the Great Wisdom Traditions is that, heavy with metaphysics, their incredibly important truths could not easily withstand the critiques of either modernity or postmodernity. Modernist epistemologies subjected them to the demand for evidence, and because the premodern traditions were ill-prepared for this onslaught, they did not meet this challenge with a direct elucidation of the one area of their teachings that could have met the challenge: *the phenomenological core* of their contemplative traditions, which offered all the verifiable evidence one could want within a remarkably modern paradigm (contemplation was always a modern epistemology ahead of its time in a premodern world). Although both modernist contemplation and modernity itself were monological, they could provide legitimate proof *within their own exemplars*, which was a start.* But the Great Traditions failed to call on this one strong suit, and failing that, the premodern spiritual traditions, more or less in their entirety, were savaged and rejected by modernist epistemologies: modernity rejected premodernity altogether.

Not that it mattered much, because postmodernity rejected both. The important truth advanced by the postmodernist epistemologies is that all perceptions are actually perspectives, and *all perspectives are embedded in bodies and in cultures*, and not just in economic and social systems (which modernist epistemologies from Marx to systems theory had already spotted). Modernity flinched and then recoiled in the face of these postmodern critiques. If modern epistemologies had a hard time handling these postmodern critiques, you can imagine how the premodern traditions fared.

Integral Methodological Pluralism highlights an array of fundamental perspectives, some of which the postmodernist epistemologies would particularly come to emphasize (others they remained ignorant of, even while implicitly using them). In particular, AQAL insists that every occasion has 4 quadrants, including a Lower-Left quadrant (intersubjective,

*See Excerpt B from vol. 2, www.kenwilber.com, for a full treatment of that issue.

cultural, contextual), and the quadrants "go all the way down." In simpler terms, according to AQAL, all knowledge is embedded in cultural or intersubjective dimensions. Even transcendental knowledge is a 4-quadrant affair: the quadrants don't just go all the way down, they go all the way up as well. It's turtles all the way down, and it's turtles all the way up, too.

As we will see throughout this book, modernity tended to focus, not just on a particular level of development, but on the Right-Hand quadrants of objective exterior evidence; while postmodernity focused, not just on a particular level of development, but on the Lower-Left quadrant of intersubjective truth and the social construction of reality. The premodern wisdom traditions, which generally were not even explicitly aware of those 3 quadrants (they were not differentiated until modernity), were simply no match for the productions of modernity (e.g., modern science) and postmodernity (e.g., multiculturalism) in those domains. But there was one area that the Great Traditions still specialized in, an area forgotten, ignored, or sometimes even suppressed by modernity and postmodernity, and that was **the interior of the individual**—the Upper-Left quadrant with all its **states** and **stages** of consciousness, realization, and spiritual experiences. But by situating the great wisdom traditions in an integral framework—which accepts the enduring truths of premodern, modern, and postmodern realizations—their enduring insights can be salvaged to a remarkable degree.

For example, *virtually the entire Great Chain fits into the Upper-Left quadrant* (see appendix I, "From the Great Chain to Postmodernity in 3 Easy Steps"). The Great Chain, which, as Lovejoy pointed out, has been embraced by the vast majority of the greatest speculative and contemplative minds East and West for almost two-thousand years, and which represents the essence of those premodern traditions, is actually dealing with realities and phenomena that are almost *entirely* in the Upper-Left quadrant. This is not a negative put-down, but a positive address: these folks were consummate phenomenologists that would explore and master some of those realms with a genius and intensity often yet to be matched. But the Great Traditions did not—and could not at that time—really know about the contours of these other quadrants (e.g., serotonin, dopamine, neurosynapses, DNA, neocortex, triune brain, etc., in the UR; systems and complexity theories in the LR; multicultural hermeneutics in the LL, etc.). And thus they were bound to come under the harshest scrutiny because they claimed to have all-encompassing knowledge, or at least claimed to be complete paths, and yet discoveries in the other quadrants would decisively undercut that claim (but NOT undercut their claims in the UL, where they specialized—and that's the point: they have incredibly important if partial truths that need to be integrated in the larger picture).

Modernity, on the other hand, brought a breathtaking understanding to the Right-Hand quadrants, an understanding that, in that regard, blew the old Traditions out of the water. Under this modern onslaught, so badly did the Traditions fare, they all but retired from the scene of serious intelligentsia anywhere in the modern West (including theory and research). Modernity's triumphal march was deftly captured by Kant: "Modernity means that if one of your friends comes in and finds you praying, you would be embarrassed."

Indeed.

On the other hand, Postmodernity (these are just quick sketches, we will return to details later) focused on the other blind spot of the traditions—a blind spot shared by modernity—and that was the so-called *monological* nature of their knowledge (which means many things, but you can think of it as *not* being dialogical or not being intersubjective, or not realizing how culture molds individual perceptions of phenomena and *dharmas*, and then—having made that fundamental mistake—ascribing truth to what are, in part, merely cultural tastes).

Habermas calls monological knowledge by various names, particularly "the philosophy of the subject" and the "philosophy of consciousness"—both of which he and every postmodern theorist worth their salt completely savaged. The "philosophy of the subject" simply takes it that an individual subject is aware of phenomena, whereas that subject is actually set in cultural contexts of which the subject is totally unaware. For example, a Tibetan meditator in the 14th century would sit in his cave, meditating on an object of awareness—perhaps from the Zabmo Yangtig—and think he is dealing with given realities, whereas every single thing he is aware of is actually culturally molded to a significant (not total) degree. He thinks he is contemplating timeless truths, truths that hold for everybody, whereas a good number of them are Tibetan fashions.

"The philosophy of consciousness" is the similar assumption, namely, that there is consciousness and that phenomena present themselves to consciousness, either individual or a collective or store-house consciousness (e.g., *alaya-vijnana*). Every meditative and contemplative tradition makes this assumption. And it is simply wrong. It is profoundly mistaken and hence caught in what is often called *false consciousness* in several ways. The easiest way for now to state this unanimously agreed-upon postmodern criticism of the philosophy of consciousness is to simply say that the philosophy of consciousness is unaware of how the other 3 quadrants profoundly impact and mold consciousness in ways that are completely invisible to consciousness itself. (Again, the Great Holarchy of the wisdom traditions is almost entirely an Upper-Left quadrant affair.)

Therefore, introspection, meditation, and contemplation (and all of the exclusively zone-#1 methodologies) are caught in various types of illusion and ignorance that their own methodologies cannot get them out of. Postmodernity spotted this immediately (although it threw out the baby with the bathwater, as we will see), and proceeded to devastate the monological knowledge of both modernity and premodernity. Between the critiques of modernity and postmodernity, what was left of the Great Traditions could be put in a teaspoon.

The claim of Integral Post-Metaphysics is that the invaluable and profound truths of the premodern traditions can be salvaged by realizing that what they are saying and showing applies basically to the Upper-Left quadrant, so they needn't be held responsible for not knowing about the other 3 quadrants, and thus their own truths can be honored and included in the integral banquet. Likewise, Modernity was dealing largely with the Right-Hand quadrants, and Postmodernity with the Lower Left, all of which can be enthusiastically embraced.

Thus, shorn of their metaphysical baggage, the premodern wisdom traditions fit into an integral framework that allows modern and postmodern truths as well. This inclusive intent is genuine with AQAL, and the details of how to accomplish this integral embrace are spelled out in ways that are serious enough to merit further, sustained discussion and research. Failing to do so simply increases the alienation of the traditions from the modern and postmodern world.

THE GREAT TRADITIONS FLOUNDERED ON THE TABOO OF (INTER)SUBJECTIVITY

Here's an example of why taking these concerns into account is important for the contemplative traditions. B. Alan Wallace has written a wonderful book, The Taboo of Subjectivity, about the eventual domination of Western scientific materialism over interior introspection, resulting in a modern worldview hostile to contemplative and meditative traditions, East or West.

This is certainly true. Modernist epistemologies were generally defined by their empirical nature. But notice that empiricism—which means "experientialism" or "experience-based"—was *originally* big enough for interior experience, or introspection (UL phenomenology), as well as the more familiar exterior experience, or behaviorism (UR positivism). In fact, William James's *The Varieties of Religious Experience*, eulogized by Wallace, is a *quintessential modernist epistemology* (it replaces metaphysical postulates with experiential evidence, and it judges truth by its results, not its supposed ontological referents). In other words, it is a pure phenomenology, or as James preferred to call it, a "radical empiricism." But due to various currents, many skillfully elucidated in *The Taboo of Subjectivity*, interior empiricism was rejected in favor of exterior empiricism, and the contemplative traditions went down with that ship, at least in the eyes of late modernity.

But again, when it came to the fate of meditation and introspection in the West, having Modernity kill Premodernity was not the only problem, or even the major problem, which was that Postmodernity killed both. In fact, what the postmodernists attacked most vitriolically (and successfully) was the modernist phenomenology exemplified by a Husserl or a William James—or a Dogen or an Eckhart or a St. Teresa. Those were the objects of the postmodernist onslaught, and it was postmodernism that won the day in the Western humanities.

What all of these contemplative Traditions had in common is that they were, and still are, monological—they all subscribe to the philosophy of consciousness. The entire Buddhist psychology and great metaphysical systems of Theravada and Yogachara are built on monological consciousness, individual or collective, as are the great Neoplatonic systems in the West, including the contemplative traditions. In fact, all of the types of knowledge offered by both Premodernity (and Modernity) were *unaware of the constitutive nature of the Lower-Left quadrant*, and that is where Postmodernity leveled devastating (and accurate) critiques of both. Again, lots of babies were being thrown out with the bathwater, but by the same token, spiritual seekers were meditating on lots of bathwater and calling it dharma or gospel.

Thus, it wasn't just, or even especially, modern scientific materialism that killed meditative introspection and phenomenology, not in the humanities, anyway. It was the extensive and savage *postmodern attacks on phenomenology* (and all similar methodologies). Most postmodernists didn't even bother with science, they went straight after phenomenology. Foucault ignores the physical sciences and attacks Husserl. And the reason was as indicated: phenomenology failed to take into account the cultural embeddedness and the intersubjectivity of all awareness. The philosophy of the subject and subjectivity needs to be supplemented (not replaced) with the philosophy of intersubjectivity. The Upper Left needs its Lower Left (not to mention its UR and LR).

Postmodernity spotted this with a vengeance. Technically, the postmodernist critique of meditation would be: Meditative awareness is the quintessential type of monological awareness, which is not itself conducted in dialogue but in interior monologue of pure "presence" and "bare attention." But far from liberating somebody, that mode of awareness *merely cements their ignorance of their cultural embeddedness*, their intersubjectivity, and it is *that ignorance that allows social and cultural interests*—patriarchal, sexist, ethnocentric, androcentric—*to ride undetected into the awareness of a meditator even during satori. Satori is therefore just a big cement job on intersubjective ignorance*, allowing oppression and marginalization of dialogical realities: so much for the paths of liberation in the eyes of postmodernity.

Thus, it wasn't just the taboo of subjectivity that killed the contemplative traditions, it was the taboo of intersubjectivity *that the traditions themselves inherently contained and mindlessly continued to display*. Even if you remove the taboo of subjectivity, the traditions have not addressed the deepest of the postmodern critiques. And in that regard, offering more introspection and bare attention and vipassana and consciousness is NOT what the philosophy of consciousness needs—that is exactly more of the disease, not the cure. And while contemplative prayer or vipassana might free you from your ego, it will not free you from your culture, whose prejudices remain in the hidden intersubjective background never brought to consciousness and thus never transcended—a source of collective ignorance, false consciousness, and bondage in an island of egoic release.

In short, the double death suffered by the contemplative traditions in the last few centuries involved *the taboo (or ignorance) of subjectivity* or interiority that was **displayed by late modernity**, and *the taboo (or ignorance) of intersubjectivity* **displayed by the traditions themselves.** Thus the contemplative traditions were slammed by both Modernity and Postmodernity, and little survived that double onslaught, at least in the eyes of serious scholars and researchers. Modern science rejected the very real phenomena disclosed by contemplation, and so did the postmodern humanities. (If you would like to see a further discussion of this topic, please see appendix II. For a critique of two dozen of today's spiritual writers who have still not come to terms with the postmodern revolution, please see appendix III.)

GENERAL OUTLINES OF INTEGRAL EPISTEMOLOGY

Integral Methodological Pluralism is one way of handling those difficult issues. It explicitly finds room for premodern truths, modern truths, and postmodern truths, all in an integral framework not of conclusions, but of perspectives and methodologies. Moreover, it doesn't "cheat" by watering down the various truths in such a horrid way that they are hardly recognizable. *It takes all of those truths more or less as it finds them.* The only thing it alters is their claim to absoluteness, and any scaffolding (and metaphysics) meant to justify that unjustifiable claim.

Moreover, in ways we will return to later (when this will make more sense to an introductory reader), Integral Methodological Pluralism can *reconstruct* the important truths of the contemplative traditions but *without the metaphysical systems* that would not survive modernist and postmodernist critiques, elements it turns out they don't really need, anyway.

I am not saying that AQAL (or IMP) is the only solution to these problems, simply that AQAL has explicitly taken all of these problems into serious account, and thus it is one way to proceed to integrate the best elements of premodern, modern, and postmodern currents of humanity's and spirit's self-understanding. **An integral approach thus protects each of those currents from attacks by the other two.**

Let's see an example of that by focusing on interior realities, including meditative and contemplative realities, and exploring some of the major approaches to those interior occasions.

2

Stages of Consciousness

I N THIS CHAPTER we'll look at the startling, indeed revolutionary, discoveries made by the scientific studies of the interiors. We'll also see why introspection, meditation, and contemplation cannot spot these realities. And then we'll conclude with a more integral framework that acknowledges, honors, and believably includes them both.

Hori-Zone 2: The Scientific Study of the Interiors

Since we have mentioned Spiral Dynamics several times, let's start with that type of knowledge in the UL quadrant—namely, the inside of the interior, but looked at objectively or "scientifically" (**3-p × 1-p × 1p**). In other words, start with any occasion or event—in this example, a human being—then look at its **individual** form (a 1st person or 1p), then look at the **interior** or 1st-person view of that individual (**1-p × 1p**)—which means their own direct experiences and introspected realities—but do so from an objective, scientific, or 3rd-person stance (**3-p × 1-p × 1p**). How on earth can you possibly do that? Well, that was the great breakthrough discovery I just mentioned, which we will elaborate below. In figure 1.4, this is simplistically indicated as zone #2 in the Upper-Left quadrant, namely, looking at a holon in the UL *from the outside*, which is exactly what Spiral Dynamics does, for example.

This type of methodology has been central to some of the greatest discoveries of both the modern and postmodern Western approaches to consciousness. One of the most famous was that of Lawrence Kohlberg and moral development. One of his students, Carol Gilligan, used this zone-#2 methodology in an equally famous fashion, summarized in *In a Different Voice*. Gilligan took a group of women and asked them questions like, "Does a woman have a right to an abortion?" Gilligan found that they gave three different answers to that question: Yes, No, and Yes.

The first type of answer was, "Yes, she has a right to an abortion, because what I say is right, and fuck you," pardon her French. The second type of answer was, "No, she does not have a right to an abortion, because that is against the law/the Bible/my society, and so that would be horrible." The third type was, "Yes, under certain circumstances she can do so, because you have to weigh the overall impact on everybody, and sometimes an abortion is a lesser evil." These three responses are called **preconventional, conventional,** and **postconventional.**

When it specifically came to women's moral development, as presented in *In a Different Voice*, Gilligan called these three stages **selfish, care,** and **universal care** (depending on how many others were taken into consideration).

Generically, whether applied to men or women, I have suggested that we can also call these stages **egocentric, ethnocentric,** and **worldcentric.** All of the names for these stages convey useful information, and we will use all of them on occasion.

Notice that the *pre*-conventional (egocentric) and the *post*-conventional (worldcentric) answers are **both Yes,** and the conventional answer is No. If you are not familiar with this type of research, you might confuse pre-conventional and post-conventional simply because both give the same answer. You might assume that anybody saying, "Yes, I can break the conventional law," is somehow a post-conventional rebel attempting to subvert dominant hierarchies in the name of a higher freedom. Maybe; and maybe they are simply saying, "Fuck you, nobody tells me what to do!" Both **pre**-conventional and **post**-conventional are **non**-conventional, so they often look alike to the untutored eye.

For just that reason, they are often confused. Confusing pre and post—or confusing pre and trans—is called the **pre/post fallacy** or the **pre/trans fallacy** (PTF), and we will see that an understanding of this confusion is very helpful when it comes to the role of religion in today's world. In any developmental sequence—pre-rational to rational to trans-rational, or subconscious to self-conscious to superconscious, or pre-verbal to verbal to trans-verbal, or prepersonal to personal to transpersonal—the "pre" and "trans" components are often confused, and that confusion goes in both ways. Once they are confused, some researchers take all trans-rational realities and try to reduce them to pre-rational infantilisms (e.g., Freud), while others take some of the pre-rational infantile elements and elevate them to trans-rational glory (e.g., Jung). Both that **reductionism** and that **elevationism** follow from the same pre/post fallacy.

This is a constant problem with, and for, spirituality. Particularly when you deal with the meditative, contemplative, or mystical states of spiritual experience—most of which indeed are non-rational—it might seem that all of the non-rational states are spiritual, and all the rational states are not spiritual. The most common example is dividing the states into Dionysian (nonrational) and Apollonian (rational), and then identifying Dionysian with spiritual. But that conceals and hides the fact that there is not just "non-rational," but "pre-rational" and "trans-rational." Even Nietzsche came to see that there are *two drastically different* Dionysian states (pre and trans). But once the pre/trans fallacy is made, it appears that *anything* that is not rational, is Spirit. Instead of pre-rational, rational, and trans-rational, you only have rational and nonrational, and the trouble starts there.

If you do not believe in Spirit, then you will take every trans-rational event and reduce it to pre-rational impulses and preverbal twaddle, perhaps claiming it is regressive, nothing but a holdover from the oceanic fusion days of infancy. You are a grand reductionist, and your names are legion, and happily you go about the day, collapsing trans-rational to pre-rational—reducing any experience of Spirit to a bit of undigested meat, and God is something you can simply outgrow, if you just keep trying. With this sleight of hand, this intellectual bit of laziness, all genuine trans-rational realities are dismissed.

If, on the other hand, you believe in Spirit, and anything non-rational is Spirit, then it appears that *every* pre-rational twitch or twinge—no matter how infantile, childish, regressive, self-centered, irrational, or egocentric—is somehow deeply spiritual or religious, and so you go about reinforcing those areas in your awareness that will most fight maturity. Every Peter-Pan piety is gloriously elevated to trans-rational. This makes even my selfish, pre-rational, preconventional impulses appear especially spiritual—yet they are not beyond reason, but beneath it.

This also leads, perhaps most sadly, to a rampant *anti-intellectualism* (instead of trans-intellectualism, which transcends and includes). This anti-intellectualism and anti-rationalism (that quickly slides into pre-rationalism), unfortunately fosters and encourages a narcissistic approach to meditation and spiritual studies (as it slides from worldcentric to ethnocentric to egocentric). This anti-intellectual narcissism is extremely common in popular culture and in alternative colleges devoted to spirituality. Egocentric feelings are confused with worldcentric feelings, just because both are feelings, and under this pre/post confusion, anything is considered spiritual if I just feel it and emote it really hard. If I can just feel my narcissism with great gusto, I'm getting closer to God (or Goddess or Buddha-nature), and thus "universal care" slides to "selfish" quicker than you can say "the Me Generation." This fearless and exuberant embrace of shallowness has marked too many of the alternative approaches to spirituality.

(Incidentally, the pre/trans fallacy applies only to stages, not to states. The only criticism I have seen of the PTF makes that confusion. Apart from that invalid criticism, there has been a fairly widespread adoption of this concept among experts, since it helps enormously to sort out otherwise intractable confusions.)

To return to Gilligan. Once she found that the response to her question fell into three classes (A: Yes; B: No; and C: Yes), she (and others doing similar research) followed the groups of test subjects over several years. She found that if anybody started out with response B, they *always* moved to response C, never to response A. Thus, somebody at A moved to B, and then to C, but never the other way around. In other words, these **classes** of responses were actually **stages** of responses.

This is very interesting, to put it mildly. Why is there this *directionality* in the psyche? Why do the stages never go backward? Why is time's arrow found in the psyche so insistently? What are these sequential stages *actually made of*? So the next task was to determine "what they're made of," or the **structures** or **patterns** in the psyche that seemed to underlie these stages.

This type of research—which was actually discovered almost a century ago, as we will see—was the beginning of the incredibly influential approach known as **structuralism.** The basic research went essentially like this: Pose a series of **questions** to large groups of people. See if their **responses** fall into any **classes.** If so, follow those classes over time and see if they emerge in a sequential order of **stages.** If so, attempt to determine the **structure** or makeup of those stages.

Those are exactly the research steps in genuine structuralism, the discovery of which had a galvanizing effect on all of the humanities and many of the sciences. Virtually all of today's stage conceptions—from Maslow to Graves to Loevinger to Kohlberg to Gilligan to Torbert to Kegan—still follow essentially those research steps first outlined by the developmental structuralists. So **structuralism**, in general, is the search for these interior structures and stages in the psyche and in culture, exactly as, say, those found by Gilligan and Graves, among literally hundreds of other researchers.

Notice a few things right off. To begin with, if you are such a researcher, you are already dealing with the **interiors** of individuals, because *you cannot see these structures anywhere in the exterior world*. Interior realities—whether those of introspection, meditation, or phenomenology—can be seen nowhere in the exterior world. So this structural research already places you in the Left-Hand or interior quadrants (and is already enough to get you thrown out of the positivistic camps).

But even though you are working with interior realities **(1-p × 1p)**, you are taking an exterior, "scientific," or "3rd-person" view **(3-p)** of them. When you research them, you are looking at them "from without," you are not necessarily experiencing them from within. For example, when you interview somebody at, say, moral stage 1 (preconventional or egocentric), you yourself are NOT necessarily experiencing moral stage 1. So you do not (necessarily) have a 1st-person experiencing moral stage 1. So you do not (necessarily) have a 1st-person *experience of certain states or stages*. Thus, in figures 1.2 and 1.3, the Zen meditator is looking at the "I" holon **from within** (via phenomenology and introspection), the objective researcher, **from without** (via, e.g., structuralism). But each of them is investigating interior or Left-Hand or "invisible" realities (which would get both of them thrown out of the positivistic, exterior, or Right-Hand camps). But both of them will each see certain phenomena and patterns that *are invisible to the other*—which is the important point (a point we will return to momentarily).

The Historical (and Continuing) Importance of Structuralism

One of the major differences between phenomenology and structuralism (or zone #1 and zone #2) is that phenomenology looks at the contents (or the phenomena) of the mind that arise in immediate experience or awareness, whereas structuralism looks for the patterns that the phenomena or experiences follow. Phenomenology looks for the *direct experiences and phenomena*, structuralism looks for *the patterns that connect the phenomena*. These patterns or structures actually govern the phenomena, but without the phenomena ever knowing it.

A good analogy is a game of cards, say, poker. If you watch a game of poker, and you are a phenomenologist, then you will try to describe each card, each phenomena, with great accuracy and presence; you will note all the different face cards, the markings on each card, their colors, size, shapes, textures, and so on. You will experience all of the cards as intensely as you can. But the cards are actually following *rules*, and *these rules cannot be seen anywhere on the cards themselves*. The structuralist is looking for the rules—the patterns, the holistic structures—that the mental contents or cards are actually following. You can look into your mind, introspect your mind, and you will *never* see these rules anywhere—they are invisible to introspection, invisible to meditation, and invisible to phenomenology in general.

(This is why you can sit on your meditation mat for decades and never see anything resembling the stages of Spiral Dynamics. But vice versa: you can study Spiral Dynamics till the cows come home and never have a *satori* or enlightenment.)

Historically, the school of structuralism (in the narrow sense) began as a zone-#4 approach in the Lower-Left quadrant (e.g., Lévi-Strauss, Jakobson). That is, it attempted to do for a "we" the kinds of thing that Carol Gilligan did for an "I": investigate these interior realities using "objective," "scientific," "3rd-person" approaches (although it did so many decades before Gilligan, Graves, Kegan, etc.). It soon became obvious that the original approach of structuralism (which was ahistorical and collectivist) was unsatisfactory and needed to be modified. The first step was making it a historical and/or developmental structuralism (or genealogy); the second was differentiating it into those approaches dealing with individuals (UL) and those dealing with cultures (LL).

Developmental structuralism applied to individuals (zone #2) was given its first successful form by the pioneering genius of one of America's greatest psychologists, **James Mark Baldwin**, in the early 1900s (his students included, among others, Jean Piaget). Baldwin, in fact, preceded all of the more famous developmental structuralists, including **Jean Gebser** and **Sri Aurobindo**, and Baldwin had a much more sophisticated model than either of them. Baldwin, this unsung hero, is being rehabilitated by those who understand these things. Jean Gebser's structural model, coming 40 years after Baldwin and not nearly as sophisticated or adequate, nonetheless had a strong impact, probably because it was so simplistically conceived, a one-line model that is now fairly well known: his major stages are **archaic** to **magic** to **mythic** to **rational** to **integral-aperspectival.** We will include this model in some later figures.

Interestingly, while Baldwin was pioneering zone-#2 approaches, his contemporary William James was giving one of the most rigorous treatments of zone #1, or the phenomenology of interior consciousness and its experiences, including the phenomenology of religious experiences (*The Variety of Religious Experiences*). Where James was cementing a modernist approach, Baldwin was seeding a postmodernist approach, creating the structuralism that would drive early postmodernism and, in its wake, later **postmodern poststructuralism.**

Finally, one of the pioneering forms of this developmental structuralism (or **genealogy**) applied to the collective "we," and especially its linguistically-generated worldviews, was done by **Michel Foucault,** which helped usher in the more recent wave of postmodern currents that, in both their healthy and unhealthy (or wildly exaggerated) forms, would come to dominate the humanities in academia for the last 4 decades. And where modernist epistemologies were eating away at the Great Traditions from one end (finding them "not scientific"), postmodernist epistemologies were eating away at them from the other (finding them oppressive, marginalizing, patriarchal, monological). There are remedies for both of these critiques, as we will see, but they were quite damaging and often legitimate.

In the meantime, the point is that today, when anybody investigates the **stages of development** of various aspects of an individual's interiors, they are following in the footsteps of these great pioneers, starting with James Mark Baldwin. In the 1950s, there was a temporary relaxation of the UR-positivism that tends to dominate American (i.e., Anglo-Saxon) academia, and thus there was a renewed interest in these general zone-#2 methodologies, followed by an explosion of research and a whole new round of pioneering geniuses in developmental studies, including Erik Erikson, Abraham Maslow, Clare Graves, Lawrence Kohlberg, and Jane Loevinger.

Individual stage investigators continue to use variations on zone-#2 methodologies (including, but not limited to, structuralism) in the Upper-Left quadrant, and these include Robert Kegan, William Perry, Robert Selman, Susann Cook-Greuter, Carol Gilligan, Spiral Dynamics, Jenny Wade, Michael Basseches, William Torbert, Patricia Arlin, John

Broughton, Kurt Fischer, Howard Gardner, and a host of other important researchers. . . .

Notice the immediate relevance for the contemplative and meditative traditions: *these approaches are giving information about aspects of consciousness that are invisible to meditation, centering prayer, and contemplation.* **You simply cannot see these stages using meditation,** introspection, phenomenology, or any of the zone-#1 approaches, East or West. This is why you can sit on your meditation mat for years and never see Spiral Dynamics stages, and why you therefore find none of these types of stages in any spiritual or contemplative text anywhere in the world.

This turns out to be crucially important for the reception of the contemplative traditions in the modern and postmodern world. *There are at present no major schools of meditation, contemplation, or prayer that take these types of stages into account.* This has also turned out to be an agonizingly difficult problem for the alternative colleges and approaches, most ot which also seem unaware of these important zone-#2 discoveries, probably because, again, you cannot see them with meditation or feel them with direct sensations.

A further problem is that any of the hori-zones can have dysfunctions, and if you can't see the zone, you can't see the dys-ease. "Boomeritis" or "pluralitis" is a dysfunction in some of the zone-#2 stages, and these types of dyseases cannot be seen by meditation or phenomenology or feeling-awareness. Thus the contemplative traditions, which should free you from various chains, simply tighten these chains (a fact that is immediately noticed by the zone-#2 researchers). Thus, the practitioners of contemplation today turn out inadvertently to be some of its most effective saboteurs.

OTHER OUTSIDE APPROACHES TO THE UPPER LEFT

Let me very briefly mention that there have been other outside approaches to interior phenomena besides genealogy, structuralism, and their variants. The most common is perhaps **systems theory**, originally used most notably by researchers such as Charles Tart. For those interested, I will pursue the role of systems theory in a note, and here simply say that, while useful in the Upper Left, systems theory has proven most applicable to the Lower Right (i.e., for various reasons, systems theory applies best to social holons, not individual holons).* We will return to systems theory when we survey the communal quadrants (LL and LR) and their role in spiritual awareness.

LEVELS AND LINES OF CONSCIOUSNESS

Staying with our "outside" or "objective" or "scientific" view of the interiors—the zone-#2 view of the UL—one of the first things we notice is the enormous variety of research pointing to various **developmental lines and their levels.** We then face the thorny issue of how these various developmental lines or "multiple intelligences" are related. This turns out to be especially important in spiritual development, as we will see.

Early developmental theorists tended to assume that there was one thing called development, and they were getting at it. Their stages were conducted on American, white, middle-class college students and con- simply a map of "the" course of development. Piaget assumed that his cognitive line was the only fundamental line, and everything else hung off it like lights on his Christmas tree. Clare Graves assumed that his "values systems" were actually "levels of existence" into which every- thing could be plopped (despite the fact that his initial research was sisted in their responses to only one simple question—"Define the be- havior of a psychologically healthy human organism"—an overall reductionism that is rather astonishing). Still, the early researchers could hardly have assumed otherwise, given the unknown and uncharted na- ture of the territory they were traversing.

But after 4 decades of this pioneering research, we can put all of their results on the table and have a look, and if we do so, an unmistakable pattern emerges. There is not one line of development that the dozens of models are giving different maps of; rather, there are at least **a dozen different developmental lines**—cognitive, moral, interpersonal, emo- tional, psychosexual, kinesthetic, self, values, needs, and so on. Each of the great developmentalists tended to stumble onto a particular develop- mental line or stream and explore it in great detail. They then often assumed that this was the only fundamental stream and all others could easily be reduced to something happening within their stream, an as-

---

*Various extra material is found at www.kenwilber.com and wilber.shambhala.com: specifically endnotes to this book, but also outtakes (deleted material), feedback, discussion forums, etc.

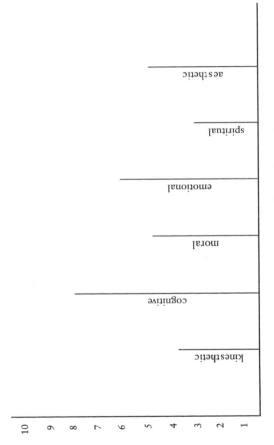

Figure 2.1.   Integral Psychograph.

sumption that only history and further research could disclose as unwarranted (we call this **stream** or **line absolutism**).

The idea of multiple developmental lines has become popular with the notion of multiple intelligences—cognitive intelligence, emotional intelligence, musical intelligence, kinesthetic intelligence, and so on. Research has continued to confirm that these multiple lines do indeed develop in a **relatively independent** fashion. A person can evidence very high development in some lines (e.g., cognitive), medium development in others (e.g., interpersonal), and low in yet still others (e.g., moral). AQAL introduced the **integral psychograph** as a representation of these multiple streams and their development (see fig. 2.1).

What are some of these developmental lines, and what do they mean? Among other things, it appears that the different lines (or multiple intelligences) are actually the different types of answers to the questions that life itself poses.

For example: **What am I aware of?** (The cognitive line or cognitive intelligence is the response to that life question; e.g., Piaget.) Of the things that I am aware of, **what do I need?** (Maslow's needs holarchy.) Of the things that I am aware of, what do I call my "**self**" or "**I/me**"? (Ego or self development line; e.g., Loevinger.) Of the things that I am aware of, which do I **value most**? ("Values systems"; e.g., Graves.) Of the things that I am aware of, how do I **feel** about them? (Emotional intelligence; e.g., Goleman.) Of the things that I am aware of, which are the most attractive or **beautiful**? (Aesthetic line; e.g., Housen.) Of the things that I am aware of, what is the **right** thing to do? (Moral intelligence; e.g., Kohlberg.) Of the things that I am aware of, what should I do in **relation** to you? (Interpersonal development; e.g., Selman.) Of the things that I am aware of, what holds **ultimate concern**? (Spiritual intelligence; e.g., James Fowler.)

Life poses those questions to us. We answer them. The structure and history of those answers is the great purview of genealogy and developmental structuralism. Each of those fundamental questions, precisely because they are presented to us by existence itself, seems to have evolved "organs" in the psyche that specialize in responding to them—multiple intelligences, if you will, devoted to being "smart" about how to answer life's questions. (See table 2.1.)

TABLE 2.1
DEVELOPMENTAL LINES, LIFE'S QUESTIONS,
AND RESEARCHERS

Line	Life's Question	Typical Researcher
Cognitive	*What am I aware of?*	Piaget, Kegan
Self	*Who am I?*	Loevinger
Values	*What is significant to me?*	Graves, Spiral Dynamics
Moral	*What should I do?*	Kohlberg
Interpersonal	*How should we interact?*	Selman, Perry
Spiritual	*What is of ultimate concern?*	Fowler
Needs	*What do I need?*	Maslow
Kinesthetic	*How should I physically do this?*	Gardner
Emotional	*How do I feel about this?*	Goleman
Aesthetic	*What is attractive to me?*	Housen

The great developmentalists simply watched those **questions** and their **answers**, noticed the **structure** of the answers, and **followed those over time**. Doing so (as we saw with Gilligan) allowed them to see that each of these developmental **lines** possesses **levels** (that unfold in **stages** or **waves**). Even referring to "highly developed" or "poorly developed" implies levels of development, and indeed, each of these developmental lines has been shown to have its own levels of accomplishment (and hence, stages of unfolding)—low to medium to high to very high (with no indication of an upper limit so far . . .). A "level of development" is always a "level in a particular line." We earlier noted an example of 3 general stages in the moral line: egocentric to ethnocentric to worldcentric.

Put the results of all of these researchers together—which is something none of them could have done in their early research—and the result is indeed something like the integral psychograph (fig. 2.1).

STREAMS AND SPIRALS EVERYWHERE

I hope I don't have to point out that developmental lines are not really lines in any strict sense. At most, they represent probabilities of behavior—and thus are something like probability clouds more than ruler-straight lines. Many researchers refer to developmental lines as **developmental streams** (and they call levels **waves**). Thus, "waves and streams" instead of "levels and lines." I like that and often use it.

Notice also that many developmental lines or streams often oscillate or spiral between various types of major polarities, each time covering the same ground but from a higher perspective. The notion of developmental lines occurring in spirals goes back at least to Erik Erikson (1963). For reference, I have included three diagrams that indicate this kind of spiraling behavior in some developmental lines: one based on Robert Kegan (1982), one on Susann Cook-Greuter (1990), and one on Spiral Dynamics (1996) (see figs. 2.2 a, b, and c on pp. 62–63).* The exact details of all these maps are not as important as the simple recognition that development is a wonderfully organic, streaming, and spiraling affair.

If you realize that the various levels or **waves** of development are holarchical (i.e., a series of nested spheres that transcend-and-include), and that developmental lines are often better depicted as streams or

*See Robert Kegan, *The Evolving Self: Problem and Process in Human Development* (Cambridge: Harvard University Press, 1982); Susann Cook-Greuter, "Maps for Living: Ego-Development Stages from Symbiosis to Conscious Universal Embeddedness," in Michael L. Commons et al. (eds.), *Adult Development*, vol. 2: *Models and Methods in the Study of Adolescent and Adult Thought* (New York: Praeger Publishers, 1990); and Don Edward Beck and Christopher C. Cowan, *Spiral Dynamics: Mastering Values, Leadership, and Change* (Cambridge, Mass.: Blackwell Publishers, 1996).

spirals, then the psychograph of figure 2.1 actually looks much more like that depicted in figure 2.3 on page 64 (although this one only has 4 levels and 5 lines, but you get the drift . . .).

THE RELATION OF THE DIFFERENT LINES TO EACH OTHER

So, what is the relation of the many developmental lines to each other? This is not nearly as simple a question as it might appear.

To begin with, the levels/stages in one line categorically cannot be used to refer to the levels/stages in another line. First, because there is no way to know exactly how they line up, and second, even if we did, the structures in the different lines are quite different from those in morality are described in terms quite different from those in Graves-ian values). This is why you cannot use Spiral Dynamics terms to describe, say, Piagetian cognition. Somebody can be at formal operational cognition and embrace orange values. But you can be at formal opera-

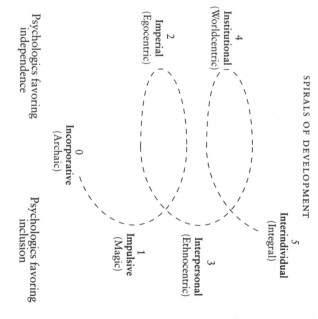

SPIRALS OF DEVELOPMENT

5
Interindividual
(Integral)

4
Institutional
(Worldcentric)

2
Imperial
(Egocentric)

3
Interpersonal
(Ethnocentric)

0
Incorporative
(Archaic)

1
Impulsive
(Magic)

Psychologics favoring
independence

Psychologics favoring
inclusion

2.2a.   Kegan (1982)

Figure 2.2.   Some Examples of the Spiraling Lines of Development.

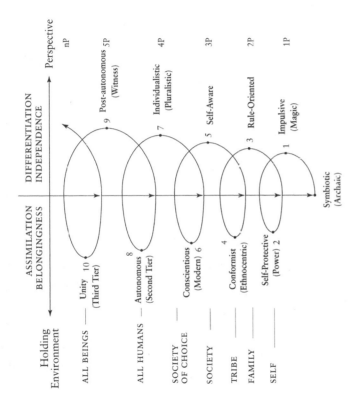

2.2b. Loevinger/Cook-Greuter (1990)

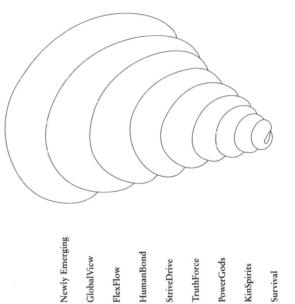

2.2c. Spiral Dynamics (1996)

tional cognition and also embrace blue values. Or red or purple. Thus, formal operational and orange are not the same thing. Evidence shows that a person, *in the same act and absolutely simultaneously*, can be at one level of cognition, another level of self-sense, and yet another level of morals, which cannot be explained by models like SD that draw primarily on one line. A ladder is still a ladder, even if you twist it into a spiral.

So the dozen or so different developmental lines are indeed different, as you might expect and as research confirms. But what is so striking is this: place the developmental models and lines next to each other, as in the psychograph, and all the lines seem to be growing in the same direction, which might be described as increasing complexity (to put it in **3-p** terms) and increasing consciousness (to put it in **1-p** terms). But what is the actual **gradient** here? *What is the vertical or y-axis in the psychograph?*

In other words, is there **one yardstick** that can be used to measure the height of all the developmental lines? That has been the great puzzle to developmentalists for the last several decades.

There are two theories available that attempt to explain this, and AQAL uses them both. One theory, accepted by most developmentalists, is that the basic yardstick is the cognitive line, because, alone of all the

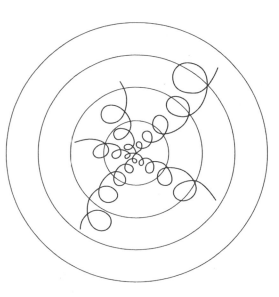

Figure 2.3.   Organic Waves and Spiraling Streams of Development.

lines, there does seem to be a mechanism relating it to the others. Namely, research has continued to demonstrate that growth in the cognitive line is necessary but not sufficient for the growth in the other lines. Thus, you can be highly developed in the cognitive line and poorly developed in the moral line (very smart but not very moral: Nazi doctors), but we don't find the reverse (low IQ, highly moral). This is why you can have formal operational cognition and orange values, but *not* preoperational cognition and orange values (again, something that cannot be explained if Spiral Dynamics vMEMEs were the only levels). So in this view, the altitude is the cognitive line, which is necessary but not sufficient for the other lines. The other lines are not variations on the cognitive, but they are dependent on it.

A major reason that the cognitive line is necessary but not sufficient for the other lines is that you have to be aware of something in order to act on it, feel it, identify with it, or need it. (This is why the questions are often worded like, "Of the things that I am aware of, what do I value?") Cognition delivers the phenomena with which the other lines operate. This is why it can serve as an altitude marker of sorts.

The other theory, which was introduced in *Integral Psychology* (and spelled out at length in the posted Excerpts), is that the y-axis is **consciousness per se.** Thus, "degree of consciousness" is itself the altitude: the more consciousness, the higher the altitude (subconscious to self-conscious to superconscious). In this view, all of the developmental lines move through the same altitude gradient—and that gradient is consciousness, which is the y-axis, or the "height" of any of the lines on the psychograph. So a level can be said to be "higher" in any line the greater the degree of consciousness in it. All of the lines can then indeed be aligned in the same psychograph, moving through the same altitude gradient (*as well as* moving through their own specific structures or stages, which still remain apples and oranges in that regard and cannot be reduced to each other—as, e.g., cognition cannot be reduced to values, or vice versa).

The analogy I use here is a dozen paths up a mountain: the different paths (representing developmental lines) all have very different views from the mountain, and these simply cannot be equated (the view up the north path and the south path are quite different), but there is a real sense in saying that both of the paths are now at 5000 feet, or the south-view path and the east-view path are now at 7000 feet, and so on. The altitude markers themselves (3000 feet, 8000 feet, etc.) are *without content*—they are "empty," just like consciousness per se—but each of the paths can be measured in terms of its altitude up the mountain. The "feet" or "altitude" means degree of development, which means degree of consciousness.

This happens to fit nicely with the Madhyamaka-Yogachara Buddhist view of consciousness as emptiness or openness. Consciousness is not anything itself, just the degree of openness or emptiness, the clearing in which the phenomena of the various lines appear (but consciousness is not itself a phenomenon—it is the space in which phenomena arise).*

(There is one more theory, a third contender, that explains altitude, and that is **the theory of basic structures**, also known as **ladder, climber, view**, a theory offered by AQAL. Suffice it to say that it is something of a combination of both of the above, and can be used with both fruitfully in the AQAL system. There is no need to pursue this theory in any detail, since its major points don't alter this discussion. Interested readers can follow up the references and the article, "Ladder, Climber, View" posted on www.kenwilber.com.)

Since consciousness itself is without specific contents, *how can we refer to its degrees or levels?* In other words, in the psyche, what shall we call 1000 meters up the mountain, 2000 meters up the mountain, 3000 meters up, and so on? We could *number* them, and often do (using anywhere from 3 to 16 basic levels of consciousness or general development). But this is less than satisfactory, because then different numbers are often used for the same level. Labeling or *naming* them is not the best idea, either, since names carry so many past associations; but we often end up using names anyway (usually by poaching terms from the levels in one line and making them apply to altitude in general, which is a theoretical disaster).

The great wisdom traditions hit upon a nice solution, starting with the *chakra* system about 3000 years ago, which was to use **the colors of the natural rainbow**, and when they did so, they always arranged them in the natural order—red to orange to yellow to green to turquoise to blue to indigo to violet. . . . The *chakras* themselves, for example, start at red, move up to yellow, then green, then blue, then purple, then clear light void. . . .

---

*This altitude view also accepts the previous (and widely held) view of cognition as necessary but not sufficient, because cognition is simply a qualified type of consciousness appearing as an actual developmental line (or path up the mountain) with its own structure and content. As such, the cognitive line is simply one line among other lines, with its altitude also measured by consciousness per se.

In addition to occasionally using numbers and names, I am going to follow that ancient tradition and simply use the rainbow as the y-axis, representing increasing levels of *development in general*, as "altitude-up-the-mountain." In figure 2.4 (opposite page 68) I have also included, as samples of particular developmental lines with their particular levels, the cognitive line (using a combination of Piaget for the lower, Michael Commons and Francis Richards for the intermediate, and Aurobindo for the higher stages in that line);* the Graves values line (I have also added its SD terms/colors); Kegan's orders of consciousness; and some of the major stages of the self-identity line most fruitfully elucidated by Loevinger/Cook-Greuter.

The nice point about this "altitude marker" of development is that it agrees with developmentalists that, indeed, the levels in a particular line cannot be used to refer to the levels in other lines. (With reference to fig. 2.4, for instance, you cannot speak of "StriveDrive cognition," as if they had the same structure, because the StriveDrive level can be embraced by several different levels of cognition.) But you can use "altitude" to refer to the same general level in all the various lines. (You *can* speak of amber cognition, amber values, amber self-sense, and so on.) We gave the analogy of paths up the mountain: if there are a dozen paths up a mountain, the view from each of the paths is somewhat different, and you cannot use the views or "structures" of any of the particular paths to refer to the views or structures in the other paths. In this aspect, it truly is apples and oranges. The views up the north side and the south side of the mountain simply cannot be treated identically, not without reductionism (of the line absolutism variety).

Moreover, the research that was used to justify the stage-levels in a particular line (e.g., Loevinger, Kohlberg, Graves) most definitely did not include the terms or structures from the other lines, let alone *all* of the other lines in existence (from kinesthetic to musical); hence, another reason the levels in one line cannot be used for the levels in the other lines. However, using "altitude" as a general marker of development

*For advanced students, notice that I have put in brackets "previously psychic, previously subtle, previously causal" for the higher levels. This is because we now use those terms strictly to refer to bodies and their corresponding states of consciousness, not to structures of consciousness. And, of course, the gross/psychic, subtle, causal, and nondual states of consciousness can occur at virtually any structure-stage of consciousness, not merely at the higher and highest (i.e., the Wilber-Combs Lattice).

allows us to refer to general similarities across the various lines, yet altitude as "meters" or "inches" or "yards" **itself has no content**; it is empty. "Inches" is a measure of wood, but nothing in itself. You do not go around saying, "I had to stop building my house today because I ran out of inches." Or, "I better go out and buy some meters." Meters is a measure or a marker of something, but itself is without content.

Likewise with "consciousness" when used in this fashion. It is not a thing or a content or a phenomenon. It has no description. It is not worldviews, it is not values, it is not morals, not cognition, not value-MEMEs, mathematico-logico structures, adaptive intelligences, or multiple intelligences. In particular, consciousness is not itself a line among other lines, but the space in which lines arise. Consciousness is the emptiness, the openness, the clearing in which phenomena arise, and if those phenomena develop in stages, they constitute a developmental line (cognitive, moral, self, values, needs, memes, etc.). The more phenomena in that line that *can* arise in consciousness, the higher the level in that line. Again, consciousness itself is not a phenomenon, but the space in which phenomena arise.

Thus, as indicated in figure 2.4, at *amber altitude*, the cognitive line (which is still necessary but not sufficient for the other lines) is at the concrete operational level (conop), the value-MEME is absolutistic (TruthForce/blue), the self level is conformist, the worldview level is traditional, and so on. At *turquoise altitude*, the cognitive level is late or mature vision-logic, value-MEME is systemic (GlobalView/turquoise), the self-sense is integrated (aka the "centaur"), the need is self-actualization, and so on. These are all relatively independent developmental lines, because one can be at vision-logic cognition and still have values at TruthForce, etc. (*Integral Psychology* contains tables with over 100 developmental models arrayed against levels in the cognitive line as an altitude marker, and you can consult that if you want.)

But in all of this, please remember one thing: these stages (and stage models) are just conceptual snapshots of the great and ever-flowing River of Life. There is simply nothing anywhere in the Kosmos called the blue vMeme (except in the conceptual space of theoreticians who believe it). This is *not* to say that stages are *mere* constructions or are socially constructed, which is the oppositely lopsided view. Stages are real in the sense that there is something actually existing that occurs in the real world and that we call development or growth. It's just that "stages" of that growth are indeed simply snapshots that we take at

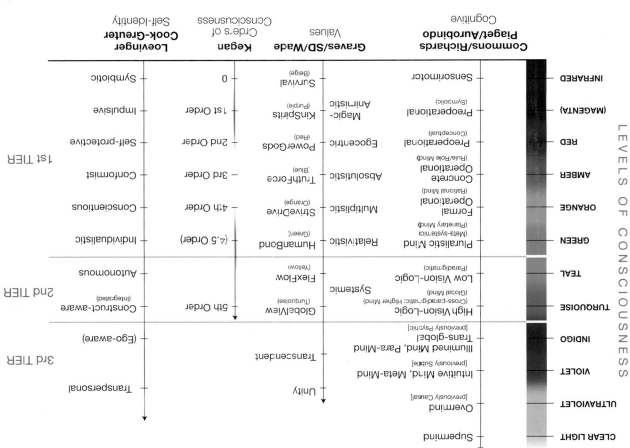

Figure 2.4. Some Major Developmental Lines.

	Commons/Richards Piaget/Aurobindo	Graves/SD/Wade	Kegan	Loevinger Cook-Greuter		LEVELS OF CONSCIOUSNESS
	Cognitive	Values	Crde's of Consciousness	Self-Identity		
INFRARED	Sensorimotor	Survival (Beige)	0	Symbiotic	1st TIER	
(MAGENTA)	Preoperational (Symbolic)	Magic-Animistic KinSpirits (Purple)	1st Order	Impulsive		
RED	Preoperational (Conceptual)	Egocentric PowerGods (Red)	2nd Order	Self-protective		
AMBER	Concrete Operational (Rule/Role Mind)	Absolutistic TruthForce (Blue)	3rd Order	Conformist		
ORANGE	Formal Operational (Rational Mind)	Multiplistic StriveDrive (Orange)	4th Order	Conscientious		
GREEN	Pluralistic Mind (Meta-systemic) (Planetary Mind)	Relativistic HumanBond (Green)	(4.5 Order)	Individualistic		
TEAL	Low Vision-Logic (Paradigmatic)	Systemic FlexFlow (Yellow)		Autonomous	2nd TIER	
TURQUOISE	High Vision-Logic (Cross-paradigmatic; Higher Mind) (Global Mind)	GlobalView (Turquoise)	5th Order	Construct-aware (Integrated)		
INDIGO	Illumined Mind, Para-Mind Trans-global [previously Psychic]			(Ego-aware)	3rd TIER	
VIOLET	Intuitive Mind, Meta-Mind [previously Subtle]	Transcendent				
ULTRAVIOLET	Overmind [previously Causal]	Unity		Transpersonal		
CLEAR LIGHT	Supermind					

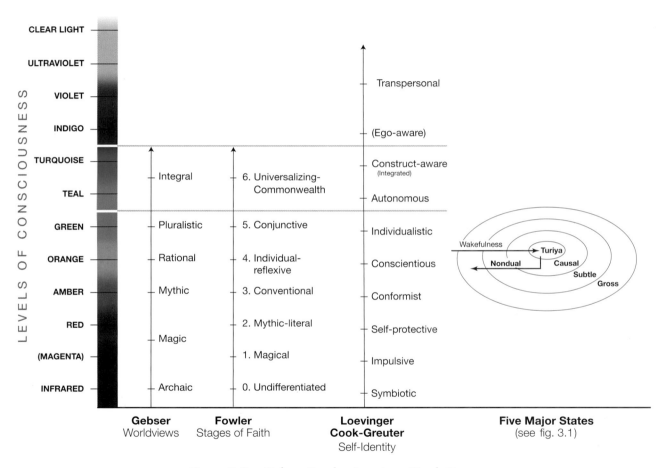

Figure 2.5.   Gebser, Fowler, Loevinger/Cook-Greuter.

particular points in time and from a particular perspective (*which itself grows and develops*).

Remember, we briefly mentioned the idea that: **Kosmic address = altitude + perspective.** We will circle back on this fascinating idea several times. The point here is that if we take a snapshot of something that is growing (e.g., an oak tree in zone #6, a society in zone #8, an individual's value systems in zone #2), the thing that is growing has an address, *but so does the photographer.* So we're not saying that stages don't exist in the real world, but simply that snapshots of them aren't the same as the real thing, and the real thing can be photographed in hundreds of equally useful and beautiful ways, each of which *brings forth* something new. Holding different photographs of a plant and arguing which are the only real photographs is just silly.

The address of the photographer (altitude + perspective) is just as important as that of the item being photographed. We always do well to remind ourselves that photographers can't see things that are over their heads, and thus wouldn't even think of photographing them.

James Fowler: Stages of Faith

Before we leave zone #2, I want to give one more very important developmental line that was discovered using this methodology, namely, that studied by James Fowler and reported in his influential *Stages of Faith* (and subsequent books). In figure 2.5, I have included Fowler's stages—which are **levels in the developmental line of faith**—along with Gebser, Loevinger/Cook-Greuter (for a point of reference), and a representation of *states of consciousness* that we will discuss shortly.

In regard to Fowler's work, it should be immediately emphasized that there are several different meanings of "faith" or "spirituality," only one of which is being investigated by Fowler. In chapter 4, we will cover several of these various meanings or aspects of spirituality—including spirituality as being the highest levels in any line, as a separate line itself, and as altered states. Fowler is researching the second meaning, spirituality as *a separate developmental line* itself. This meaning or aspect of spirituality is both *developmental* and *structural*—it is a classic zone-#2 approach, this time applied to questions having to do not with cognitive intelligence or emotional intelligence or musical intelligence, but with **spiritual intelligence.** This particular developmental line is an important aspect of overall spirituality, and its relation to the other dimensions or aspects of spirituality is something we will return to several times. (For those not familiar with Fowler's research, I will include a short summary of it later.) Henceforth, when I refer to the *stages of spiritual intelligence*, this specifically means Fowler's research findings.

All of the foregoing discussion of levels and lines of development is what interior holons (UL) look like from the outside (zone #2). What do they look like from the inside (zone #1)?

3

States of Consciousness

W HAT DO INTERIOR HOLONS look like from the inside? Whatever you happen to be feeling right now.

PHENOMENOLOGY, FELT EXPERIENCES, AND STATES OF CONSCIOUSNESS

But from there, it gets a little more complicated. One of the important distinctions that AQAL highlights is the difference between **structures** and **states**. **Structures**, which we began to explore in the previous chapter, is basically just another term for the **levels** in any line. Each level has a *structure*, or some sort of actual architecture or pattern. For example, if we speak of a level of complexity in a language, that level itself has some sort of structure or configuration or pattern, just as we would speak of the structure of a cell wall or the structure of the neocortex. What is notable about these structures is that, far from being fixed or rigid, they are literally whirlwinds. A language has a stable pattern or syntax, even though the words used for it are in motion constantly. Structures are extremely dynamic patterns that are often "autopoietic" or self-organizing. The parts of a cell are constantly being turned over, but the cell remains itself because it has a self-organizing, stable pattern. That **dynamic holistic pattern** is its structure.

That patterned wholeness, or stages of them, when viewed from without in an objective fashion, are exactly the "structures" studied by **structuralism** and **developmentalism**. Thus, with reference to Loevinger, "conformist," "conscientious," "individualistic," and so on, are some of the major structures (or levels) in the ego line of development.

(These *structures/levels* emerge in *sequential stages,* and so we often use **structures** and **stages** interchangeably, *but technically structures and stages are different*—other things emerge in stages, too—so for this part of the discussion, we will not equate them. Inelegant as it might be, if we want to refer to them together, we will refer to **structure-stages** when we mean the *sequential unfolding* of zone-#2 structures in the psyche. Loevinger, Kegan, Selman, Perry, Broughton, etc., are structure-stages. Despite the inelegant terminology, the point of all this will soon become obvious, I believe.)

In this chapter, we want to look at **states of consciousness** and compare and contrast them with **structures of consciousness.** Dry as it might initially seem, this relationship turns out to hold perhaps *the single most important key to understanding the nature of spiritual experiences* (and hence the very role of religion in the modern and postmodern world). With that modest and blushing introduction, let's begin.

We said that zone #1 in the UL (the inside of an "I") is simply whatever I happen to be thinking, feeling, and sensing right now. I could continue to describe my present, immediate, felt experiences and apprehensions in direct 1st-person terms ("There is a sensation of heaviness, heat, tension, lightness, luminosity, feelings of love, care, exaltation, momentary experiential flashes, etc.''), and many forms of **phenomenology,** by whatever label, do exactly that (fig. 1.3). Those are all variations on zone-#1 approaches, some of which investigate particular types of interior experiences known as **phenomenal states.**

That is, what I experience in an immediate, 1st-person fashion includes, in addition to specific "contents" or "immediate experiences" (a feeling, a thought, an impulse, an image, etc.), what are often called "phenomenal states." Notice that whereas I can experience states, I don't experience structures per se. *I never directly experience something* like "moral stage 3" or "the conscientious structure" or "stage-4 interpersonal relational capacity," even though that might be precisely the stage I am at, with all of my thoughts actually arising within that structure, unbeknownst to me. **Structures** can only be discovered by a zone-#2 methodology, which is why you cannot discover them using meditation or contemplation of any variety.* **States,** on the other hand,

*You can feel the insides of structures, so to speak, since they are the grooves in which your thinking and feeling run, but you can't see their actual structure, nor suspect their existence, using only phenomenology, meditation, introspection, etc.

are directly available to awareness, under various circumstances. I experience states, not structures.

Most of us are familiar with states of consciousness, and so are the great wisdom traditions. Vedanta, for example, gives 5 major **natural states** of consciousness: waking, dreaming, deep sleep, Witnessing (*turiya*), and Nondual (*turiyatita*). These 5 states are extremely important, so please take a moment to notice them.

In addition to natural or ordinary states, there are **altered** or **nonordinary states**, including **exogenous** states (e.g., drug-induced), and **endogenous** states (which include **trained states** such as **meditative states**).

Heightened states, ordinary or nonordinary, are often called **peak experiences.**

Most cultures, and certainly the great traditions, have a **cartography of states**, including natural, exogenous, and endogenous states.

Some of the **meditative cartographies** are extraordinarily elaborate, but all of them are based on zone-#1 methodologies and injunctions (such as zazen, centering prayer, shamanic voyaging, vipassana, ayahuasca, dervish whirling, contemplation, etc.), and can be confirmed as phenomenological experiences by those who wish to undertake the appropriate injunctions (e.g., sit on this mat, count your breaths from 1 to 10 until you don't lose count for at least an hour; follow this *mantram*; take this drug; dance like this; become one with the *koan*, etc.).

When you correctly follow those injunctions, you will have a series of phenomenological experiences. Whether those *phenomenological experiences* ("I see what feels like infinite light and love") have actual *ontological referents* ("There is a Divine Ground of Being") is, needless to say, an interesting question (which we will return to below, since that is one of the main purviews of Integral Post-Metaphysics).*

Many of the great traditions have created an elaborate psychology based on these states, and although the details needn't detain us, let me highlight a few features that are significant, because, at the very least, they are some of the greatest systems of interior phenomenology ever developed. The correlations I am about to summarize are in themselves contentious and difficult to prove. But we will simply assume them for the moment. I will use Vedanta and Vajrayana as an example (although

---

*For those interested, the psychedelic cartography of Stan Grof is likewise a zone-#1 cartography (which is why you can't find any zone-#2 stages in any of his cartographies, which severely limits them and their "cosmic game" and cosmology derivations).

Neoplatonism would do just as well), and we need to start by getting some complicated terminology out of the way.

According to both of them, meditative states are variations on natural states. For example, meditation with form (*savikalpa samadhi*)—such as *visualizing a deity* and repeating its name or *mantra*—is a variation on the **dream state**; and meditation without form (*nirvikalpa samadhi*)—such as focusing on awareness itself without any particular object—is a variation on **deep formless sleep.** Further, the 3 major natural states of consciousness (waking, dreaming, sleeping) are said to be supported by a particular energy or "body": the **gross body**, the **subtle body**, and the **causal body**, respectively (e.g., Nirmanakaya, Sambhogakaya, Dharmakaya; a fourth body, the Svabhavikakaya, is sometimes said to support the witnessing/nondual states). Although, technically speaking, *the terms "gross," "subtle," and "causal" refer ONLY to the bodies or energies (in the UR),* we also use those terms to refer to the corresponding general states of consciousness (in the UL). Thus, we can refer to the 5 major, natural, and/or meditative states of consciousness as: gross, subtle, causal, witnessing, and nondual states of consciousness. (As the traditions themselves often do, I will sometimes refer to 3, or 4, or 5 major states of consciousness—but all 5 are implied.)

For those of you who stopped trying to understand what I was saying somewhere in the middle of that paragraph, the upshot is simply that, according to the great wisdom traditions, all men and women have available to them at least 5 great natural **states of consciousness,** all of which can be directly experienced:

1. gross-waking states, such as what I might experience riding a bike or reading this page or doing bodywork;

2. subtle-dream states, such as I might experience in a vivid dream, or in a vivid daydream or visualization exercise, as well as in certain types of meditation with form;

3. causal-formless states, such as deep dreamless sleep and types of formless meditation and experiences of vast openness or emptiness;

4. witnessing states—or "the Witness"—which is a capacity to witness all of the other states; for example, the capacity for unbroken attention in the waking state and the capacity to lucid-dream;

5. ever-present Nondual awareness, which is not so much a state as the ever-present ground of all states (and can be "experienced" as such).

Vedanta and Vajrayana maintain that those states (and their corresponding bodies or realms of being) are available to all human beings by virtue of "the precious human body." What this means is that **these major states of being and consciousness are available, to some degree, to all humans at virtually any stage of growth**, including infants, simply because even infants wake, dream, and sleep.

That is a really, really, really important point, which we will come back to.

(As a sneak preview: because the essential contours of these major *states* are ever-present, then you can have a peak experience of a higher state, but not of a higher stage. If you are at Jane Loevinger's conscientious structure-stage of development, for example, research continues to demonstrate that you simply cannot have a peak experience of a higher structure, such as the autonomous—but you *can* have a peak experience of a gross, subtle, causal, witnessing, or nondual **state** of consciousness. Exactly how these two fit together is what we will want to return to.)

Although the general contours of these major states of being are available naturally and spontaneously to all humans, some of them can be intensely trained or investigated, and then these **trained states** hold some surprises, indeed.

TRAINED STATES: CONTEMPLATIVE AND MEDITATIVE STATES OF CONSCIOUSNESS

Even though the major natural states of being and consciousness are said to be available to all humans, at all stages, this doesn't mean that they can't be trained and exercised. **State training** is a particularly advanced zone-#1 technology brought to staggeringly advanced forms in the great meditative traditions East and West.

Generally speaking, *natural states do not show development*. Dream states occur, but they don't go anywhere. Natural states and most altered states do not show stages. They simply come and they go, as most states do—whether an emotional state or a weather state like a thunderstorm. Moreover, most states of consciousness are exclusive—you cannot be drunk and sober at the same time. And natural states persist even through advanced stages—even Buddhas wake, dream, and sleep (although they Witness them as Nondual).

But some states can be *trained*, and when this involves attention deployment—as many forms of meditation and contemplation do—then *these trained states tend to unfold in a sequential fashion.* And when they do so, they tend to follow the natural order of gross to subtle to causal to nondual states.

That means that in my *direct*, 1st*-person experience*, phenomenal states in many types of meditation are said to unfold from gross phenomena ("I see rocks") to subtle phenomena ("I see light and bliss, I feel expansive love"), to causal phenomena ("There is only vast emptiness, an infinite abyss") to nondual ("Divine Emptiness and relative Form are not two"). These are not 3rd*-person structures* (seen by zone #2), but 1st*-person states* (zone #1).

When states unfold in some sort of sequence (largely because they are trained), we call them **state-stages** (contrasted to **structure-stages**).

Because **states** by their very nature are much more amorphous and fluid than structures, this stage sequencing of states is very fluid and flowing—and, further, **you can peak-experience higher states.** (Although typically, without further training, they will be very transitory—merely altered states or temporary peak experiences. But with further training, "peak experiences" can be stabilized into so-called "plateau experiences.") Thus, if you are at a particular *state*-stage, you can often temporarily peak-experience a higher state-stage, but not stably hold it as a plateau experience.

On the other hand, research repeatedly shows that *structure*-stages, unlike state-stages, are fairly discrete levels or rungs in development; moreover, as research shows time and time again, *you cannot skip structure-stages, nor can you peak-experience higher structure-stages.* For example, if you are at preoperational in the cognitive line, you simply cannot have a formal operational experience—but you *can* have a subtle-state peak experience! (Again, we will return to the relation of states and structures shortly.)

As for these **state-stages**—which generically move from gross experience to subtle experience to causal experience to nondual—you can open virtually any manual of meditation or contemplation, East or West, and you will find a description of meditative or spiritual experiences unfolding in essentially that order, with quite specifically those general characteristics. One thinks immediately of St. Teresa's interior castles; the extraordinary cartographies of St. John of the Cross; the meditative cartography of Buddhaghosa's *Visuddhimagga*; the cartographies of the Church Fathers—such as St. Gregory of Nyssa, Origen, St. Dionysius (whose "way of purification," "way of illumination," and "way of unification" is as short and succinct a summary as you will find: purify the gross body via discipline and still the gross mind via concentration; find subtle interior illumination; surrender even illumination in a prayer of quietude and divine ignorance; thereby the soul and God find union in Godhead, one with the radiant All).

Perhaps the most sophisticated and careful study of any of the meditative traditions was that done by Daniel P. Brown (included in Wilber, Engler, and Brown, *Transformations of Consciousness: Conventional and Contemplative Perspectives on Development;* 1986). Brown conducted an extensive study of the root texts and the central commentaries in three major meditative traditions—the *Yoga Sutras* of Patanjali, the *Visuddhimagga* of Buddhaghosha, and the *Phyag chen zla ba'i 'od zer* (Moonbeams of Mahamudra) of Tashi Namgyal. These are, in a sense, the very pillars of both Hinduism and Buddhism.

Brown found that the meditative path in all of them traversed the same basic contemplative stages, which were all variations on gross preliminaries and training, then subtle experiences of light and luminosity, then variations on formless absorption or causal "black near-attainment," then breakthrough into nondual realization (and then possible further "post-enlightenment" refinements). This meticulous care and research, including reading the texts in their original languages, has made Brown's study an absolutely brilliant and enduring classic in meditative stages. (See table 3.1 for his short summary of the general stages of meditative states.)

In *Transformations of Consciousness,* coedited with Brown and Engler, we asked Harvard theologian John Chirban if we could carry a report of his own extensive work on the stages of contemplative states in the early Church Fathers, which we did. It showed the same essential organic sequence of stages, gross phenomena to subtle light to causal darkness and nondual union. (See table 3.2 for his summary. As with Brown's research, this is not to say that all contemplatives went through all of these stages, only that this is a synoptic composite.)

Probably one of the simplest and most accessible summaries of the generic stages of meditative states can be found in *The Varieties of Meditative Experience* by Daniel Goleman. Notice that the title of his book is deliberately modeled after William James's masterpiece, *The Varieties of Religious Experience.* This is entirely appropriate, in that both books are outlining zone–#1 phenomenology, and both of them are ignorant of zone #2. (In James's case, this was because the first great pioneer of zone–#2 methodology, James Mark Baldwin, was a contemporary of James's at the beginning of this century, and Baldwin's revolutionary

TABLE 3.1
STAGES OF MEDITATIVE STATES IN SOME PROMINENT EASTERN TRADITIONS
(Daniel P. Brown, in *Transformations of Consciousness*, 1986)

	THE STAGES OF MEDITATION	PERSPECTIVE	
		Buddhism	Yoga

Attitude, Affect Behavior	I. PRELIMINARY ETHICAL PRACTICES
	   A. Generation of Faith; Attitude Change
	   B. Formal Study; Intrapsychic Transformation
	   C. Sensory/Behavioral Regulation
	      Uninterrupted Awareness Training
		(photon-like)	mind-as-light
			
			(wave-like)

Thinking	II. PRELIMINARY MIND/BODY TRAINING
	   A. Body Awareness Training
	   B. Calming Breathing and Thinking
	   C. Re-arrangement of the Stream of
	      Consciousness
		discontinuous momentariness	continuous transformation of same thing

Perception	III. CONCENTRATION WITH SUPPORT
	   A.1. Concentration Training; Decategorizing
	   A.2. Internalization; Rearrangement of Image
	   B. Recognition of Various Patterns of all
	      Sense Modalities from the Seed
	   C. Stopping the Mind, i.e., Gross Perception
		discontinuously emanating seed	continuously transforming seed

Self	IV. CONCENTRATION WITHOUT SUPPORT
	   A. Tuning in Subtle Perception
	   B. Recognizing the Subtle Flow
	   C. Collapse of Ordinary Observer;
	      Restructuring of Perspective
		discontinuous immediate events
		
		Concomitant Perspective (Access)
			continuous vibration of *tanmātras*
			
			Reflection of *puruṣa* (*buddhi*)

Time/Space	V. INSIGHT PRACTICE
	  A. High-Speed Search of Subtle Flow;
	    Eradication of Self; Derealization
	  B. High-Speed Search of Gross Mental
	    Events; Shifts in Perceived Duration &
	    Frequency of Events of Subtle Flow;
	    Arising Only; Full Event in Slow Motion;
	    Quick Flashing Psychic Powers; Raptures;
	    White Light
	  C. Analysis of Mind-Moments and Their
	    Succession; The Problem of Perceived
	    Time-Space
	
	  Interconnectedness of all potential events
		emptiness
		non-entityness
		(*ngo bo nyid med*)
		
		discrete flashes
		
		Non-dissolution
		Co-dependent Origination
		of All Realms and Times
			cessation of
			sense-impressions
			
			sameness (*tulya*)
			
			transformation of one
			substratum (*dharmin*)
			
			Unity
			Unity of Manifest
			Cosmos (*prākrti*)

Cosmos	VI. ADVANCED INSIGHT
	  A. Equanimity of Interrelated Events;
	    Interaction of Specific Events
	  B. Stopping all Mental Activity/Reactivity
	    Enlightenment Moments:
	    Basis: Cessation of Mental Content; Vast
	    Awareness
	    Path: Return of Mental Content from
	       Changed Locus of Awareness
		
		Non-dissolution
			
			All Interactions of Manifest
			Cosmos
			Raincloud Samādhi

TABLE 3.2
STAGES OF CONTEMPLATIVE STATES IN SOME PROMINENT CHURCH SAINTS
(John Chirban, in *Transformations of Consciousness*, 1986)

APOPHATIC APPROACHES

STAGES	St. Isaac the Syrian	St. Seraphim of Sarov	St. Gregory Palamas	St. John Climacos	St. Maximos	St. Dionysios
V THEOSIS	(3) Perfection	Acquisition of the Holy Spirit	(3) Theosis	Step 30 Likening	(3) 'Αεί Είναι Eternal Being	(3) Unification Prayer of Union
		Kingdom Righteousness Peace				(Prayer of Quiet)
IV LIGHT		Illumination	(2) Divine Light Pure Hesychasm	Steps { 29 28 27 Hesychasm		(2) Illumination
						(Prayer of Recollection)

STAGES	St. Isaac the Syrian	St. Seraphim of Sarov	St. Gregory Palamas	St. John Climacos	St. Maximos	St. Dionysios
III APATHEIA	(2) Purification					(1) Purification
				Spiritual Development		(Prayer of Mind)
II METANOIA	(1) Repentance		(1) Prayer Labor	(2) Steps 1–26	(2) Εὐ Εἶναι (Well-Being)	
		Prayer Fasting Almsgiving				(Prayer of Simplicity)
I IMAGE					(1) Εἶναι (being)	

research had not yet entered the academic stream here and abroad; when it did, it helped fuel both structuralism and poststructuralism.)

In zone #1, William James tends to focus on naturally or spontaneously occurring states, and Goleman is further looking at trained states in zone #1, which therefore show some sort of sequentiality. And again, that sequence is more-or-less exactly as Daniel P. Brown outlined and as can be generically found in virtually any great meditative (or **trained-state**) system the world over.

To repeat, because these are *state*-stages, not structure-stages, there can be much fluidity, temporary skipping around, peak experiencing of higher states (not structures), and so on. But the general progression of states as they are mastered (from spontaneous to peak to plateau) was indeed gross to subtle to causal to nondual.

States are pictorially hard to depict; we'll settle for cloud-like spheres. Figure 3.1 is a summary of the typical progression of meditative states over a full course of meditative training, which may take anywhere from 5 to 20 years to master. What we see is a general progression of Wakefulness from gross to subtle to causal to nondual—a progression of Wakefulness from its typical confinement in the waking state, to a Wakefulness that persists into the dream state (at which point, lucid dreaming is common) and/or into the causal formless state (by whatever name), at which point states of advanced meditation, including cessation, are possible, and/or a very tacit awareness extending into the deep sleep state, so that a Wakefulness is experienced even in deep dreamless sleep (there is EEG confirmation of patterns in very advanced meditators consistent with this claim). At that point, all subjective states have been made object of the Witnessing presence, at which point Nondual union or even identity with a prior Ground is often reported. Exactly what a "divine Ground" means . . . well, you know exactly what it means, but we will return later and discuss this awakening in light of integral interpretations.

AND THE 64-THOUSAND-DOLLAR QUESTION IS . . .

We have examined *structures of consciousness* (which occur in stages) and *states of consciousness* (which, when trained, may occur in stages). The 64-thousand-dollar question is, how are they related? They are, respectively, perhaps the quintessential contributions of the **conventional approaches** to the Upper Left (zone-#2 structuralism and geneal-

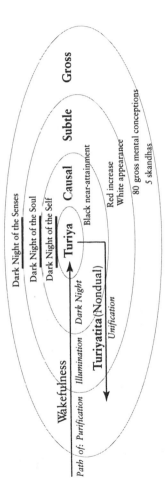

Figure 3.1.   Major Stages of Meditative States.

ogy) and the **contemplative approaches** to the Upper Left (zone-#1 meditation and contemplation). And this brings us back, indeed, to our original question: why can you sit on your meditation mat for decades and never see anything resembling the stages of Spiral Dynamics? And why can you study Spiral Dynamics till the cows come home and never get *satori*?

4

States and Stages

O NE OF THE THINGS I will try to do throughout this book is give very brief overviews of well-known methodologies, then suggest how they can fruitfully be integrated using an AQAL approach, something that needs to be done in any event if "integral spirituality" is to have any meaning. We start with Zen and Spiral Dynamics, and the aforementioned question: since they are clearly different, how are they related?

ZONES #1 AND #2: ZEN AND SPIRAL DYNAMICS

Spiral Dynamics is based on the work of Clare Graves, one of the great pioneers of zone-#2 developmental studies. His model is based on research originally done with college students presented with one simple question: "Describe the behavior of a psychologically healthy human organism." Following a standard zone-#2 methodology as old as Baldwin, Graves found responses to his question that eventually led him to formulate a system of development of what he and his students called levels in a **"values system."** Spiral Dynamics, based largely on Graves's work, refers to a **vMEME**, defined as "a systems or **values meme"** and also as "a core intelligence" (which I simply call values intelligence or the values line, one of the multiple intelligences).*

---

*SD claims that the vMEMES cover all intelligences, but that is categorically false: while vMEMES have their own types of cognition, morals, aesthetics, and so on, the vMEMES themselves do not structurally describe Piagetian cognition, Kohlberg morals, Loevinger self-sense, Torbert action-inquiry, Selman interaction, or Basseches dialectics, among many others—not in terms acceptable to those theorists,

Graves and SD speak of **8 levels/stages** of this adaptive intelligence, which briefly are (all following terms are directly from *Spiral Dynamics*):

Level 1 (A-N)—*Survivalistic*; staying alive; "SurvivalSense"

Level 2 (B-O)—*Magical*; safety and security; "KinSpirits"

Level 3 (C-P)—*Impulsive*; egocentric; power and action; "PowerGods"

Level 4 (D-Q)—*Purposeful*; absolutistic; stability and purposeful life; "TruthForce"

Level 5 (E-R)—*Achievist*; multiplistic; success and autonomy; "StriveDrive"

Level 6 (F-S)—*Communitarian*; relativistic; harmony and equality; "HumanBond"

Level 7 (G-T)—*Integrative*; systemic; "FlexFlow"

Level 8 (H-U)—*Holistic*; experiential; synthesis and renewal; "GlobalView"

Many people using Spiral Dynamics have difficulty understanding the essential nature of the knowledge that this system represents within a larger AQAL framework, so let me suggest this thought experiment and see if it helps:

Let's say you take a course in Spiral Dynamics at a university. For the sake of argument, let's say you are developmentally at Level 4, Purposeful. You read the textbook, you memorize the descriptions of the 8 levels or 8 vMEMES, you discuss them with the teacher and the class. You take the final exam, and it asks you to describe the 8 levels of values systems, and because you have memorized them, you do so perfectly. You get a perfect 100 on the exam.

The reason that you can describe Levels 5, 6, 7, and 8—*even though you are only at Level 4 yourself*—is that these are exterior or zone-#2 descriptions. They are the 3rd-person descriptions of various 1st-person realities. You can get a perfect 100 on the exam because you can memorize these 3rd-person descriptions, *even though you yourself are not at the higher levels*, whose descriptions you have memorized.

Now imagine a different exam. This one says: "Please describe Level-8 experience as it is directly felt, in immediate, 1st-person language," and this includes an oral exam with the same requirements. If your self-

anyway. Those are different lines with different structures. To the extent SD claims otherwise, it is caught in a demonstrable line absolutism.

sense is truly at Level 4, you will thoroughly flunk this exam. You can pass the 3rd-person exam, but you flunk the 1st-person exam.

In other words, studying the stages of SD can give you the outside (or 3rd-person) view of these stages, but cannot necessarily *transform you* to any stages higher than you are already at. This is not a fault of the system, this is exactly what zone-#2 descriptions are—namely, 3rd-person descriptions and structural formulations of 1st-person realities.

This is why studying Spiral Dynamics for years will not necessarily transform you. It engages 3rd-person cognition, not 1st-person self-identity. Again, this is NOT a fault of the model, it is EXACTLY what zone-#2 approaches do (or 3rd-person approaches to 1st-person realities). I am a big fan of the work of Clare Graves and the wonderfully accessible way that Spiral Dynamics, developed by Don Beck and Christopher Cowan, presents it. I continue to recommend SD as a good introductory model.* And Don, of course, is a founding member of Integral Institute;

---

*As for whether SD is a complete model of the psyche, I have already registered, in the previous footnote, my belief that it categorically is not; but Don strongly disagrees. Let's just say we firmly part ways here. It is one thing to claim SD covers all the important bases (itself disputable), but quite another to claim it *includes the actual structures-stages of*, e.g., Piaget, Kohlberg, Loevinger, etc., which it demonstrably does not, and which any truly integral model would.

A simple critique of SD involves the facts that it: does not cover states of consciousness (e.g., Tart); likewise does not cover state-stages; does not include higher, transpersonal structures (nor structure-stages) of consciousness; has no theory of the relation of states and stages/levels; confuses multiple levels with levels-and-lines; confuses enduring structures with transitional structures; has no developed notion of self-system nor therefore believable theory of repression and the unconscious; is bound up with the discredited notion of memes; does not include the actual structure-stages of Loevinger, Selman, Perry, Piaget, Kohlberg, etc. (and thus, in either dismissing them or claiming otherwise, is caught in a hidden but pervasive line absolutism); and confuses stages with multiple intelligences, which have stages. As a simple introductory tool, it's wonderful; as an actual psychological model, it's a disaster.

I have often been asked why I "changed my mind" about SD, but every one of those criticisms can be found in the footnotes to the first thing I ever wrote about SD (there are, in fact, *four full pages* of endnotes criticizing SD; see *A Theory of Everything*, endnotes 6, 9, and 10 to chap. 1). Likewise, every presentation of SD since then has included these criticisms directly or in footnotes—as this presentation does in this footnote. In other words, my position on SD has remained consistent from the very start, and the people who think I have changed my mind are folks who haven't read the footnotes. At the same time, and from the start, SD has not incorporated a single criticism, from me or anybody else that I can tell, largely, in my opinion, because it is not possible to have an academic discussion with individu-

and Chris Cowan and Natasha Todorovic have done a wonderful job of making much of the original Graves work available to a larger audience.

As for *transformation* itself: how and why individuals grow, develop, and transform is one of the great mysteries of human psychology. The truth is, nobody knows. There are lots of theories, lots of educated guesses, but few real explanations. Needless to say, this is an extraordinarily complex subject, which I will set aside for the moment as I finish this section.

So let's say that whatever zone-#2 level you are at, you decide to take up meditation. This is a 1st-person adventure, not a 3rd-person study. If you successfully take up any serious form of contemplation or meditation, you will begin to have a series of experiences. Because these are meditative experiences and states, they are not the fairly distinct structure-stages of most zone-#2 approaches. But they will tend to unfold in general waves of awareness, gross to subtle to causal to nondual—the major state-stages as in tables 3.1 and 3.2 and figure 3.1.

In Zen, the most famous version of these meditative stages is the **Ten Oxherding Pictures.** These are state-stages that depict both the overall course of Zen training and the moment-to-moment unfolding of any point of training. In one sense, as previously noted, they are stages in attention deployment and training, pushing Wakefulness from its typical confinement in the gross-waking state, and into a Wakefulness of subtle-dream phenomena (savikalpa, deity, illumination) and causal phenomena (nirvikalpa, formless, dark night)—by this point, we are at the 8th Oxherding Picture of an empty circle, and then to a realization of ever-

Nonetheless, when set in an AQAL context, I still recommend SD as a very useful introductory tool, and one that especially covers the stages of values systems or intelligence (after all, the "v" in vMEME stands for "values"; and "**a systems or values meme**" is a direct quote for their definition of a vMEME). That is the way "Graves/SD" is used in this chapter—for the levels of values adaptive intelligence, which can be mixed and matched to various life conditions, and exist in swirls and twirls and admixtures, but do not in themselves cover other intelligences *as defined and discovered* by other researchers (e.g., ask Bill Torbert if SD covers action-inquiry; ask Susann Cook-Greuter if SD covers self-development; ask Robert Kegan if SD covers orders of consciousness—they are all on record: the answer is a categorical no).

The 8 levels of vMEMES cover up to mature vision-logic cognition and centauric self-sense (turquoise altitude in fig. 2.4). Whatever else SD may or may not be, it is these 8 levels of value systems in zone-#2 that we will focus on this chapter.

als whose economic livelihood depends upon one model being the only correct model.

present nondual Big Mind/Big Heart (*sahaj*, Godhead, unity, Svabhavi-kakaya), which is the 10th Oxherding Picture, called "entering the mar-ketplace with open hands."

As noted, these are general variations on the same zone-#1 state-stages reported by Daniel P. Brown, as well as a simplified version given by Daniel Goleman in his *Varieties of Meditative Experience*.

Now, finally, the 64-thousand-dollar question: how are the Zen stages and the Spiral Dynamics stages related?

THE W-C LATTICE

At this point I am going to drag y'all through the convoluted mess that we had to go through in order to arrive at some sort of clarity on this issue. I'm going to do this because I had to slug through this rotten mess and I don't see any reason you shouldn't.

What was so confusing to us early researchers in this area is that we knew the stage conceptions of people like Loevinger and Graves were really important; moreover, some of these stages (e.g., Kohlberg) had been tested in a dozen or more cross-cultural studies; either you included these models or you had a painfully incomplete psychospiritual system.

But we also knew that equally important were the phenomenological traditions East and West (e.g., St. Teresa's *Interior Castle*, *Anu* and *Ati* Yoga), as well as the recent studies like Daniel P. Brown's on the com-monality of certain deep features in meditative stages. And so typically what we did was simply take the highest stage in Western psychological models—which was usually somewhere around SD's GlobalView, or Loevinger's integrated, or the centaur—and then take the 3 or 4 major stages of meditation (gross, subtle, causal, nondual—or initiation, puri-fication, illumination, unification), and stack those stages *on top of* the other stages. Thus you would go from Loevinger's integrated level (cen-taur) to psychic level to subtle level to causal level to nondual level. Bam bam bam bam. . . . East and West integrated!

It was a start—at least some people were taking both Western and Eastern approaches seriously—but problems immediately arose. Do you really have to progress through all of Loevinger's stages to have a spiri-tual experience? If you have an illumination experience as described by St. John of the Cross, does that mean you have passed through all 8 Graves value levels? Doesn't sound quite right.

A second problem quickly compounded that one. If "enlightenment" (or any sort of *unio mystica*) really meant going through all of those 8 stages, then how could somebody 2000 years ago be enlightened, since some of the stages, like systemic GlobalView, are *recent* emergents?

All of our early attempts at integration were stalling around this issue of how to relate the meditative stages and the Western developmental stages, and there it sat stalled for about two decades.

Part of the problem centered around: what is "enlightenment," anyway? In an evolving world, what did "enlightenment" mean? What *could* "enlightenment" mean?—and how could it be defined in a way that would satisfy all the evidence, both from those claiming it and those studying it? Any definition of "enlightenment" would have to explain what it meant to be enlightened today but also explain how the same definition could meaningfully be operative in earlier eras, when some of today's stages were not present. If we can't do that, then it would mean that *only* a person alive today could be fully enlightened or spiritually awakened, and that makes no sense at all.

The test case became: in whatever way that we define enlightenment today, can somebody 2000 years ago—say, Buddha or Christ Jesus or Padmasambhava—still be said to be "enlightened" or "fully realized" or "spiritually awakened" by any meaningful definition?

This complex of problems formed something of a Gordian knot for, as I said, the better part of two decades. The first real break came in understanding the difference between states and structures, and then how they might be related (once you figured out that you had to stop equating them). A few years after I introduced a suggested solution, my friend Allan Combs, working independently, hit upon an essentially similar idea, and so, in a painfully transparent bid for history, we named this the "Wilber-Combs Lattice" (after months of me having to explain to Allan how silly the "Combs-Wilber Lattice" sounded).

Here is the general idea. The essential key is to begin by realizing that, as we earlier noted (and emphasized), because most meditative *states* are variations on the natural states of gross-waking, subtle-dreaming, and causal-formlessness, then they are present, or can be present, at virtually all *stages* of growth, because even the earliest stages wake, dream, and sleep.

Accordingly, if you take any structure-stage sequence (we will use Gebser's—archaic, magic, mythic, rational, pluralistic, integral) and put those sequentially developing structure-stages (which we will again simply call *stages* unless otherwise noted) running up the left side of the grid or lattice, and then put the major *states* across the top (gross, subtle, causal, nondual), you get a simple version of the W–C Lattice (see fig. 4.1). There are many variations on this general idea, and I do not want to imply that Allan agrees with all of mine; but the general idea that structures and states overlap in complex ways is indeed the point. Most of these diagrams and the following discussion are my particular take on that general notion, and I think Allan agrees with these, but, again, I don't want to speak for him in these details, since we have each developed the germinal idea in various directions.

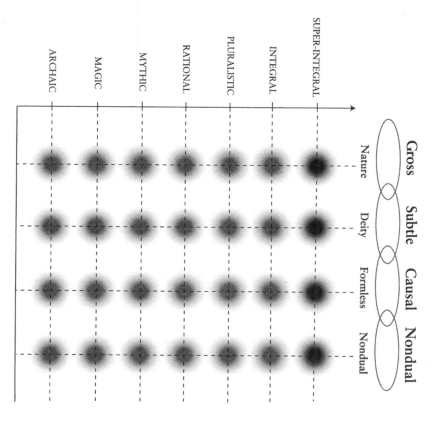

	Gross	Subtle	Causal	Nondual
	Nature	Deity	Formless	Nondual

Figure 4.1. The Wilber-Combs Lattice.

What you can see in figure 4.1 is that a person at any *stage* can have a peak experience of a gross, subtle, causal, or nondual *state*. **But a person will interpret that state according to the stage they are at.** If we are using a Gebser-like model of 7 stages, then we have 7 stages × 4 states = 28 stage-interpreted / state experiences, if that makes sense.

(And, as we'll see, we have evidence for all of these "structure-state" experiences).

That bold sentence was for us early researchers the breakthrough and real turning point. It allowed us to see how individuals at even some of the lower stages of development—such as magic or mythic—could still have profound religious, spiritual, and meditative state experiences. Thus, gross/psychic, subtle, causal, and nondual were no longer stages *stacked on top of* the Western conventional stages, but were states (including altered states and peak experiences) that can and did occur *alongside* any of those stages. This is suggested in figure 2.5 by placing the 3 major state/clouds to the right of the stages.

(What was doubly confusing to us is the fact that, as indicated in fig. 2.4, there are also 3 or 4 higher *structures* beyond the centaur and its vision-logic, and because these structures have characteristics that appear similar to those of the 3 or 4 higher states, it was almost impossible to spot the differences. So we kept stacking *zone-#1* higher states on top of *zone-#2* structures—and calling them higher structures—and we could not for the life of us figure out why that didn't work. This really drove us nuts. The W-C Lattice was so hard to see, even though the data were right in front of our eyes, because of this overlap.)

The point is that a person can have a profound peak, religious, spiritual, or meditative experience of, say, a subtle light or causal emptiness, but they will interpret that experience with the only equipment they have, namely, the tools of the stage of development they are at. A person at magic will interpret them magically, a person at mythic will interpret them mythically, a person at pluralistic will interpret them pluralistically, and so on. But a person at mythic will *not* interpret them pluralistically, because that structure-stage of consciousness has not yet emerged or developed.

But the 5 major states of consciousness are available more or less from the start, because everybody wakes, dreams, and sleeps, no matter what stage they are at. Putting those together immediately gives us something like a W-C Lattice.

Let me give one simple series to show what is involved. Take a subtle-**state** experience of intense interior luminosity accompanied by a sense of universal love. Let's say this person is Western and Christian, so that the Lower-Left quadrant (which is also intimately involved in providing the contexts for interpretation) has primed this experience of interior luminosity to be interpreted as an encounter with Jesus Christ (or the Holy Spirit). That subtle-realm religious experience *can occur at virtu-*

ally any stage—the magic, mythic, rational, pluralistic, or integral—but in each case, it will be interpreted according to the basic limiting principles of that stage.

Thus (to give some quick and stylized examples), at the **magic** stage, Jesus is experienced as a personal savior who can miraculously alter the world in order to satisfy my every desire and whim: Jesus as Magician, turning water into wine, multiplying loaves and fishes, walking on water, and so on (we are not talking about the ontological content, if any, of the interpretation; Jesus may or may not have walked on water, but at this stage, this is the thing that would mean the most to me). This stage is preconventional and egocentric, so this Jesus cares only about me.

At the next stage, the **mythic**, the same kind of subtle-state experience might be interpreted as communion with Jesus the Eternal Truth bringer. This stage is *absolutistic* in its beliefs, so you will either believe the Word exactly as written, or you will burn in hell forever. This stage is also *ethnocentric*, so *only* those who believe in Jesus Christ as their personal savior can be saved.

At the next stage, the **mental-rational**, Jesus Christ becomes a humanized figure, still fully Divine and fully human, but now fully human in a more believable way, as a teacher of the universal love of a deistic God (who has read *Principia Mathematica* and knows where to draw the line). Because this stage is the beginning of the postconventional and *worldcentric* stages, this is also the first of the stages of development that can find salvation through Christ Jesus but also allow that others might find equal salvation through a different path. You will be moving in a Vatican II fashion.

Have a series of profound spiritual experiences at the **pluralistic stage** and you will likely find yourself one of the authors of *The Postmodern Bible*, a wonderful example—out of thousands that have sprung up—of interpreting Jesus Christ and the Christ-experience through the lens of the green stage of development.

The **integral stage** for Gebser was one stage, but for us is simply the opening to at least 4 higher structure-stages of development (see figs. 2.4 and 2.5), any of which will insist on integrating its experience of Christ-consciousness with other expressions of the Holy Spirit around the world, and if so in your case, you might likely find yourself reading a book like this. (Frankly, any earlier/lower stages would simply not find this topic interesting. But if we do pat ourselves on the back, let it still be with humility: whatever stage we might be at, there are always higher stages; and somewhere, someplace, in some universe or dimension, somebody is writing a text that is over our heads. . . .)

TYPES OF MYSTICISM AND STATES OF CONSCIOUSNESS

Notice in figure 4.1 I have written *Nature, Deity, Formless,* and *Nondual* mysticism under their respective states. These are very loose assignations, but nonetheless quite useful (something I have added to the original W-C Lattice). The basic idea is that in each of the 4 major natural states, you can have a peak experience or intensification of that state. One of the ultimate peak experiences in any realm is to be *one with* the phenomena in that realm. To experience a oneness with all phenomena in the gross-waking state is a typical **nature mysticism**. To experience a oneness with all phenomena in the subtle-dream state is a typical **deity mysticism**. To experience a oneness with all phenomena (or lack thereof) in the causal-unmanifest state is a typical **formless mysticism**. To experience a oneness with all phenomena arising in gross, subtle, and causal states is a typical **nondual mysticism.**

That is one suggested explanatory classification (or typology) that I believe is quite valid. It is by no means the only possible typology, but it is quite useful. If we add that to the W-C Lattice, it helps us see that individuals might have an experience of oneness with nature—and hence be "nature mystics"—but they will interpret that oneness quite differently depending on the stage they are at. You can have a profound experience of oneness with nature and still be at a red level, an amber level, an orange level, a green level, and so on.

So there is not simply a "variety" of religious, meditative, or spiritual experiences provided by zone-#1 experiences (e.g., William James), there is a "variety of *interpreted*" religious, meditative, or spiritual experiences, because those experiences are *always already* set in contextuality and interpretation, which includes a sequence of *interpretative* capacities as revealed by zone-#2 methods (e.g., James Baldwin)—for example, Zen and SD, respectively.

Putting zone-#1 and zone-#2 research together gives us the W-C Lattice.

We will come back to that particular issue, but this whole topic becomes quite important, I believe, in watching how various nondual paths, East and West, have been interpreted in America in the last three decades, particularly with postmodernist currents (and their downsides, "boomeritis").

But quite apart from all of that, and quite apart from whether or not we can correlate those 4 major types of mysticism with those 4 states, the general contours of the W–C Lattice remain quite useful and valid, I believe. It gives us the first way of relating the structure-stages of developmental psychology with the states and stages of the spiritual/meditative traditions.

INTERPRETATION AND THE AQAL MATRIX

Let me make a simple technical clarification here, just once but with emphasis: when I say that a person will interpret a particular state or experience "according to the stage they are at," the more fleshed-out version is "according to the entire AQAL matrix" operative at that time. As always, interpretation is an AQAL affair.

This particularly includes "levels and lines" in the UL—a person will interpret an experience based on their psychograph (which means a multitude of intelligences all operating at once, clamoring for recognition by the self). In the LL, cultural backgrounds and intersubjective contexts are decisive (and almost entirely preconscious). In the UR, neurophysiological parameters set an enormous number of interpretive frames. In the LR, social systems have almost as strong an influence as Marx claimed. None of these factors can be overlooked; all of them have a hand in how an individual will interpret any moment of his or her experience. It is the entire AQAL matrix, in every moment, that speaks in and through an individual.

THE SLIDING SCALE OF ENLIGHTENMENT

Now, in a sense, "states and stages" was the easy part of the Gordian knot. The hard part of the problem can be stated in several different ways.

- If **evolution** occurs, how can **enlightenment** have any meaning? Enlightenment is supposed to mean something like being one with *everything*, but if *everything is evolving*, and I get enlightened today, then won't my enlightenment be partial when tomorrow arrives? Do I become unenlightened with the sun's dawn? Is there any definition of enlightenment today that will not rob me of it tomorrow?

- A typical response is to say that enlightenment is being one with that which is *Timeless* and *Eternal* and *Unborn*, but all that does is create a massive duality in Spirit—the timeless and eternal versus the temporal and evolving—and so what I am really saying is that enlightenment is being one with half of Spirit.

- We saw that a "nondual mysticism" was a "union with *everything* in the gross, subtle, and causal realms." But, as we have often seen, you can have a nondual state experience at virtually any stage, including magic and mythic, and these stages do not contain phenomena from the higher stages. So at the mythic stage, for example, you can have a realization of nondual, ever-present, Big-Mind awareness that is a pure unity experience with everything in your world, but that experience leaves out a great deal of the universe. Thus *satori* can actually be unity with a partial reality. Generally speaking, this is not good.

This is the part of the relation of states and stages that has proven the most difficult, and the solution I have suggested is also rather intricate. But every spiritual teacher I have discussed this proposed solution with agrees that it works, or at least is plausible. (How can we define Enlightenment with all these subtle difficulties in mind? Suggested answer: Enlightenment is the realization of oneness with **all states** and **all stages** that have evolved so far and that are in existence at any given time.) As for carefully going through all the steps that are involved in reaching that conclusion, I don't want to inflict that on any unsuspecting souls, so I will reserve it for appendix II ("Integral Post-Metaphysics"). We will pick up the discussion here with some more examples of zone #1 and zone #2 as applied to meditation/contemplation, which can be followed without any reference to that appendix.

Zones #1 and #2: Evelyn Underhill and James Fowler

As another zone #1 and #2 comparison, take what are perhaps two of the most famous and influential of all spiritual maps, those of Evelyn Underhill and James Fowler. They are almost perfect representatives not only of zones #1 and #2, but of developmental approaches to zones #1 and #2.

Underhill's work is so highly regarded because it is a survey and summary of the stages of the spiritual path based on a study of some of the world's most highly revered saints and sages. Conducted at the turn of the century, it has stood the test of time because it draws on material that doesn't date easily. In fact, it is essentially quite similar to the first great Western version presented by Dionysius, and down to today with comparisons like Daniel P. Brown's survey of the great Eastern paths. Underhill was a contemporary of William James, and they were both mining the zone-#1 approaches to empiricism from within. James conducted primarily a phenomenological description and classification of zone-#1 religious and spiritual state experiences, while Underhill conducted a developmental study of zone-#1 trained spiritual and meditative state experiences. Underhill focused particularly on **the phenomenological stages of the spiritual path**—in other words, *state-stages*—or the stages of felt experiences and *conscious events in the "I" space*, as apprehended and seen from within, as it unfolds over time under the discipline of spiritual practice (or *meditative states training*). These are things that you can see from your prayer cushion or your meditation mat over time.

Fowler studied those things that *you cannot see*, no matter how long you sit on your mat. In other words, he is taking a zone-#2 approach to unfolding spiritual awareness, which yields phenomena that can only be seen from without, in an objective stance, usually in large groups of people over long stretches of time. That's why you can find something like Underhill's stages in the contemplative texts the world over, but can find none of Fowler's stages in any contemplative or meditative system anywhere (and no Loevinger stages, and no SD stages, and so on).

Briefly, Underhill's stages of spiritual development are:

1. awakening/initiation
2. purification/pacification
3. illumination
4. dark night
5. unification

Fowler's are:

0. preverbal predifferentiated
1. projective-magical
2. mythic-literal
3. conventional

4. individual reflexive
5. conjunctive, beginning postconventional
6. postconventional commonwealth

Now it has long been recognized that both of them are onto something incredibly important, but their stages don't match up. Moreover, various scholars have commented that they seem to actually overlap in a way disallowed by each of them.

So what's going on here? Perhaps it is evident that Underhill is presenting the data from figure 3.1 (*state*-stages), and Fowler, from figure 2.4 (*structure*-stages)—both of which are represented in figure 2.5. By now, their respective sequences of stages are so familiar, so obvious, they simply jump out at you: Underhill's is a version of gross, subtle, and causal, and Fowler's is a version of preconventional, conventional, and postconventional.

Moreover, put those together and you have a grid of 9 types (the W-C Lattice), and all 9 of those types are abundantly in evidence. (Using Underhill's and Fowler's actual stages, you have around 4 × 6 cells.) Underhill is presenting the sequence of *states* across the top of the Wilber-Combs Lattice (fig. 4.1), while Fowler is presenting the sequence of vertical *structures* up the left-hand column. And that is precisely why somebody at *any* of Fowler's stages can experience *all* of Underhill's states. (And, of course, their relationship is identical to that of Zen and SD.)

To clarify this, you can simply imagine a W-C Lattice using Fowler and Underhill. Somebody at, for example, Fowler's stage 3—the conventional stage—can take up meditation practice or contemplative prayer, and proceed to delve into illumination, dark night, and unification *states*, but they will interpret each of those experiences according to their *stage* (in this case, conventional and conformist). Anybody familiar with the monastic traditions, East and West, from Zen to Benedictine, will recognize those souls who might be quite spiritually advanced in Underhill's sense (very advanced in contemplative illumination and unification) and yet might still have a very conformist and conventional mentality—sometimes shockingly xenophobic and ethnocentric—and this goes, unfortunately, for many Tibetan and Japanese meditation masters. Although they are very advanced in meditative *states* training, their *structures* are amber-to-orange, and thus their available interpretive repertoire is loaded by the Lower-Left quadrant with very ethnocentric and parochial ideas that pass for timeless Buddha-dharma.

(E.g., according to his secretary, the Dalai Lama believes homosexuality is a sin, anal sex is a sin, oral sex is bad karma, etc.—when everybody knows that oral sex is not bad karma, only bad oral sex is bad karma. But these sadly are typical mythic-amber beliefs.)

Not that Westerners necessarily fare any better: the typical Western teacher has a structure that houses its own dysfunction commonly known as "boomeritis" or "pluralitis," which is green pluralism opened to rampant red narcissism (the "me" generation). More about that later.

Because these structure-stages (amber, orange, green, turquoise, etc.) **cannot be seen with any amount of meditation**, they can be loaded with invisible pathologies lodged in the heart of Buddha-dharma in the West.

(American Buddhist teachers just shake their heads at mention of this, and recommend more meditation, which further intensifies the problem in most cases. As I said, we will return to this unfortunate scenario later. In the meantime, Asian meditation teachers, with a LL-quadrant that is heavily amber, or mythic-membership, and hence "non-egoic" in the sense of PRE-individualistic, and therefore used to having students simply obey them unhesitatingly and in a conformist-stage fashion, don't quite know what to do with individualistic-stage Westerners, whose LL-quadrant is loaded orange-to-green. Herein lies a three-decade tale of quadrant-clash and **AQAL clash**. At Integral Institute, we are preparing overviews of this AQAL clash, not with a view to blame but with a view to begin integral spiritual practice with as little hidden dysfunction as possible.)

On the other side of the lattice, you can have somebody *quite advanced* in Fowler's dimension *but not very advanced* in Underhill's contemplative dimension. This is not a case of "levels and lines" (i.e., you can be at different *levels* in various developmental *lines*), but a case of "states and levels" (each of those *levels* can experience the same general *states*; i.e., different *states* of consciousness can occur at different *levels/stages/structures* of consciousness—a comparison we call "states and levels," or more commonly—same thing—"states and stages"). These are two relatively independent elements in the AQAL matrix, and mapping the overlap of these two particular elements (states and stages/levels) is the W-C Lattice. But, of course, you can map other overlaps in the AQAL matrix as well, and all of them are telling (e.g., the integral psychograph maps "levels and lines," and you can also map types and levels, types and states, quadrants and levels, levels and types and states, etc.).

DARK NIGHT

In figure 3.1 (p. 83), I have added three "dark nights": the dark night of the (gross) senses, the dark night of the (subtle) soul, and the dark night of the (causal) self. A "dark night" is a generic term representing many things in different traditions, but in general it represents a passing through, or a letting go, of attachment or addiction to a particular realm (gross, subtle, causal), and/or sometimes the pain that comes from peak-experiencing a higher state that is already free of the particular addiction, and then being plunged back into the lower state, generating a profound sense of loss and suffering. Generally these dark nights occur in the transition phases between states, or the passing of Wakefulness (and hence identity) from gross-body waking to subtle-soul dream to causal-self formless to radical nondual.

That is, dark nights tend to appear at the boundary between those general states as *attachment to*, or *identity with*, those states is let-go of or surrendered. The states themselves (and their general realms of being and knowing) remain and continue to arise, but identity with them is stripped, and that "stripping" constitutes the respective dark nights of senses, soul, and self—causing a dark night of the senses, a dark night of the soul, and a dark night of the self. The causal/self dark night appears as, e.g., the 8th Zen Oxherding Picture, Teresa's 7th castle, *Anu* Yoga's "black near-attainment," and so on.

Again, because these are state-stages, not structure-stages, they are very fluid and open, not discrete and linear. Further, they are experienced and interpreted, as we just saw, according to the AQAL matrix of the individual (and the lineage) experiencing them. Some traditions emphasize them, others pass over them more quickly. And some traditions, it must be said, go further than others in the general state progression. This is a delicate and difficult issue, but many traditions push through the dark night of the soul (into causal oneness) but not the dark night of the self (into nondual suchness). Some, such as Teresa's 7th castle, take you right into causal emptiness and either leave you there, or leave you in silence as to what lies further. Others, like of course Eckhart, succeed in pushing through the dark night of self, which totally uproots the subject/object duality and self-contraction in any form, including its causal remnants (but even Eckhart remains vague on details, whereas something like *anuttara-tantra* is rich in them). The point, however, is simply that however far they push in the sequence, the overall composite sequence is as indicated in figure 3.1, which is a simple summary of the overall stages of meditative/contemplative states.

Such are some common *state*-stages. As for Fowler's *structure*-stages, notice that Fowler is presenting the objective results of only a few studies, and hence his data thin out at the top very quickly. It's not that there aren't any higher stages up there, but that there aren't many people up there. If Fowler continued to refine his research with those higher structure-stages in mind (as Cook-Greuter has done on the Loevinger line, for example), we would expect such research to reveal that, at this time, there are somewhere around 3 or 4 *stages of faith* beyond his stage 6 (which is roughly a **turquoise-level faith**), so we would expect to find that, being laid down now only thinly as Kosmic habits but still discernible (although less so the higher up you go in altitude on a mountain that is being co-created by its climbers), some version of **indigo faith** (at the same altitude as the trans-global mind), then **violet faith** (metamind), then **ultraviolet faith** (overmind) . . . , then faith itself becomes Fuller and Fuller and Fuller . . . , grounded in a Freedom and an Emptiness that never changes, that is timeless and eternal, the great Ground and Openness of the entire evolving display, that nonetheless is Witness to its own display evolving. . . .

FOUR MEANINGS OF THE WORD "SPIRITUAL"

This is the last major topic I would like to address in this general area, and it can be done fairly quickly by virtue of the terms we have already covered.

If you analyze the way that people use the word "spiritual"—both scholars and laypeople alike—you will find at least 4 major meanings given to that word. Although individuals themselves do not use these technical terms, it is apparent that "spiritual" is being used to mean: (1) the highest levels in any of the lines; (2) a separate line itself; (3) an extraordinary peak experience or state; (4) a particular attitude. My point is all of those are legitimate uses (and I think all of them point to actual realities), but we absolutely MUST identify which of those we mean, or the conversation goes nowhere fast, with the added burden that one thinks ground has actually been covered. In my entire life, I personally have never heard more people utter more words with less meaning.

Briefly, here are the 4 important uses, all of which I believe should be honored:

1. If you take any developmental line—cognitive to affective/emotional to needs to values—people do not usually think of the lower or middle levels in those lines as spiritual, but they do describe the higher and highest levels as spiritual (you can look at any of the developmental lines in figs. 2.4 and 2.5 and see this). The word "transpersonal," for example, was adopted with that usage in mind: spiritual is not usually thought of as pre-rational or prepersonal, and it is not usually thought of as personal or rational, it is thought of as profoundly trans-rational and transpersonal—it is *the highest levels in any of the lines.* (Following Maslow's data pool, we often use **third tier** as a very loose term to describe these developmental aspects of transpersonal structure-stages. See fig. 2.4.)

2. Sometimes people speak of something like "spiritual intelligence," which not only is available at the highest levels in any of the lines, but is *its own developmental line,* going all the way down to the earliest of years. James Fowler is one example of this. As you can see in figures 2.1 and 2.5, in this usage, "spiritual" is not something that refers only to the highest, transpersonal, and transrational levels in the various lines (which is usage #1), but is something that has its own first, second, and third tiers (or structure-stages), and these stages reach all the way down (like Fowler's stage 0). Put similarly, this spiritual line has its own prepersonal, personal, and transpersonal levels/stages. This is one of the reasons you have to follow usage extremely closely, because juxtaposing usages #2 and #1, we would say that only the highest levels of the spiritual line are spiritual. This, needless to say, has caused enormous confusion. (The AQAL position is that both usages—actually, all 4 usages—are correct; you just have to specify which or you get endlessly lost.)

3. Sometimes people speak of spirituality in the sense of a *religious or spiritual experience,* meditative experience, or peak experience (which may, or may not, involve stages). Virtually the entire corpus of shamanic traditions fit in this category (see Roger Walsh, *The Spirit of Shamanism*). William James, Daniel P. Brown, Evelyn Underhill, and Daniel Goleman are also examples of spirituality as a state experience (often trained). State experience is another important usage and is, of course, the horizontal axis in the W-C Lattice.

4. Sometimes people simply speak of "spiritual" as involving a *special attitude* that can be present at *any* stage or state: perhaps love, or compassion, or wisdom (i.e., it is a *type*). This is a very common usage, but in fine detail, it usually reverts to one of the first 3 usages, because there are actually stages of love, compassion, and wisdom (a fact missed by almost all green-wave writers on the need for love and compassion). Still, we always list it separately just in case.

I won't elaborate further on those 4 meanings. They are pursued at length in *Integral Psychology.* My point is simply that all 4 of those are valid meanings of the word "spiritual," but people usually mush them all together in their discussions, and the result is . . . well, more mush.

Speaking of usage #4, I've got a pretty bad attitude on this myself, so forgive a 15-second rant. You can take virtually 99% of the discussions of "the relation of science and religion" and put them in the mush category. I'm sorry, but that's how it seems to me. These discussions never get very far because the definitions that the discussants are using contain these 4 hidden variables, and the variables keep sliding all over the place without anybody being able to figure out why, and the discussions slide with them.

Especially when you realize that usage #3, which is a valid usage, contains—by its own account—**levels** of religion or **levels/stages of spirituality**, then things spin totally out of control (there is archaic spirituality, magical spirituality, mythic spirituality, rational spirituality, pluralistic spirituality, integral spirituality, transpersonal spirituality . . .). Somebody says, "Religion or spirituality tells us about deep connections and eternal values," and I have no bloody idea which religion or spirituality they mean, and all I'm sure is, they don't either. There are at least 5 or 6 major **levels/stages** of religion—from magic to mythic to rational to pluralistic to integral and higher—across **4 states** (gross, subtle, causal, nondual), which are also types or classes (**nature, deity, formless, nondual**), not to mention the four usages or **meanings** we are outlining in this chapter. And we didn't even get to the **quadrants** (spirituality as great Self or I, spirituality as great You or Thou, spirituality as great It or Other).

Before you tell me about science and religion, or religion and anything, please tell me which religion you mean. Even using just the W-C Lattice, there are some **two dozen** different religious or **spiritual truth-claims**. Which of those two dozen do you mean, and on what grounds are you excluding the others?

This is NOT an overly complicated scheme. It is the MINIMAL scheme you need to be able to say anything coherent on the topic.

5

Boomeritis Buddhism

WE COME NOW TO THE NOTION of **pathologies** or **dysfunctions** in any of the elements in the AQAL matrix. I will use boomeritis as an example. And then turn to what we might call "Boomeritis Buddhism" as a specific example of how this can affect—or infect—spirituality in general. That we are using Buddhism as an example should not detract from the fact that the same type of thing can happen—and is happening right now—to every form of religion and spirituality in today's world, with literally no exceptions that I can see. So if you are on a spiritual path other than Buddhism, then as we go along, you can make the appropriate translations and see how this might apply to your path as well. At the end of the chapter, I will have some resources, for all paths and faiths, that can help address this widespread problem.

BOOMERITIS

Boomeritis is important in itself, but it is indicative of a much broader and more important issue, in this case, stream or line pathology. More technically, **developmental-line dysfunction**, or DLD. I like "DLD" because it sounds like something that could land you on Oprah.

Any aspect of the psyche—or of reality, for that matter—can become dysfunctional. I can have a pathology or "un-wellness" in any quadrant, in any level, in any line, in any state, in any type . . . , and so on. Anything with a moving part can break down.

But in order to spot pathology, you have to be able to know where to look. We have seen that the meditative traditions are using predominately zone-#1 methodologies. As such, they have no real understanding or inclusion of the structure-stages of development in zone #2. Boomeritis is a significant dysfunction that can occur in the developmental structuration of an individual (zone #2), a dysfunction that cannot be seen or diagnosed by the meditation traditions, Christian to Jewish to Buddhist. This is NOT a fault of zone-#1 methodologies, which cannot be expected to spot zone-#2 issues. But it is a fault of the spiritual teachers who only use one of them.

Pluralitis or boomeritis itself was first noticeable in areas like the student protests of the 1960s against the Vietnam War (and is equally noticeable today in protests against the war in the Middle East). The students all claimed that they were protesting the war because it was immoral. Tests of moral development found that some of the students were indeed quite morally developed. In some studies, many of the protesters were saying "No!" to a war that they felt was wrong, and moreover, they were doing so from *post*-conventional levels of moral cognition using worldcentric reasoning. But many of the war protesters were *pre*-conventional, and they were saying "No!" from an egocentric, narcissistic level: basically, go fuck yourself, nobody tells me what to do!

So at the same peace rally, under the same tent, mouthing the same slogans, all saying "Hell, no, we won't go!," were both **pre**-conventional and **post**-conventional protests, and unless you knew what was going on, it looked like the protesters were all saying the same thing and coming from the same place. The war protest—which strongly protested the conventional stance—therefore attracted both very low and very high responses, and all were using the same high-level rhetoric, so that under the *postconventional* tent, *preconventional flourished*. Confusing these and treating them the same—which almost everybody did—is a classic **pre/post fallacy**.

Boomeritis is a particular version of that pre/post confusion.

Specifically, the Boomer generation was the first to have a significant percentage of its population be at the green waves of development—pluralistic, relativistic, postmodern. It was "I do my thing, you do yours," but coming in many cases from a fairly high developmental altitude—postconventional, worldcentric, green, global. But that pluralistic openness and nonjudmentalism *re-activated* and *encouraged* very egocentric and narcissistic impulses, and thus into the postconventional tent came the preconventional parade, with every low narcissism impulse relabeled high pluralism. The Me generation was born.

"Boomeritis" is a general term for post-conventional/worldcentric levels infected with pre-conventional/egocentric levels, or simply and most often, green infected with red (using those colors to mean altitude in any of the lines). This green/red complex would often involve taking rather low-level, narcissistic, self-centered feelings and impulses and re-labeling them with high-level, postconventional, worldcentric, and even spiritual names—and actually coming to think of its own egocentric and narcissistic feelings as being very high indeed. And thus, the harder you could feel your ego, emote your ego, and express your ego with real immediate feelings, the more spiritual you were thought to be.

Boomeritis Buddhism

Into this atmosphere came Buddhism, and therefore very quickly Buddhism—known as "the religion of no-ego"—often became "the religion of express your ego." Quite a feat, but welcome to America, boomeritis style.

Many American Buddhists of this generation were, as Boomers, pioneers in the green-pluralistic *stage* or wave of development, which, in itself, is actually a rather extraordinary achievement. Some of them also took up meditative practices, and could indeed attain very genuine and profound meditative *states* (because all of the states are available at pretty much every stage). But, as always, these meditative states would be interpreted according to the stage one was at. And thus, meditative states were quickly used to support the green-level pluralistic worldview.

(And in actual practice, too. For example, all of the pointing-out instructions for realizing the **nature of the mind**—which is one's own Buddha-mind—or an **ever-present, natural, self-knowing aware emptiness that is not other than its display**—can be realized at the green wave, precisely because the nature of the mind is compatible with all stages of the mind. From pointers such as "All is mind, mind is empty, empty is spontaneously present, spontaneously present is self-liberating" to ones such as "Allow your mind to be as it naturally is, and let thoughts dissolve in themselves. This is your innate mind, which is empty, self-knowing, natural awareness. Your mind is an intangible, aware emptiness. Look directly into the nature of this naked state!"—*all of those state realizations can be fully recognized at any number of stages, including green*. The same is true of Tozan's "5 ranks" in Zen, and so on. Thus everything from Dzogchen and Mahamudra to Zen was, and is, being used to support and encourage green, which is to say, ever-present Spirit is being used to reinforce and cement the green level.)

This is bad enough—in fact, something of a catastrophe—but there are two further, potential problems. The first is that many of the great contemplative texts, sutras, and tantras were written in the cognitive line from at least the turquoise and often indigo or violet levels. So **indigo** texts were being *translated downward* into **green** texts simply because both of them could be supported by similar meditative states and attainments. As we have seen, I can come out of a nondual state of awareness, and if I am green, *I will interpret Nonduality in green terms;* if I am ultraviolet, then in ultraviolet terms. The same authentic **state** can be used to support any number of **stages.** This **translation-downward** of great spiritual treatises is a significant problem.

The second problem is that, because I can use those authentic meditative states to support green, and because green pluralism can support and activate red narcissism, the entire meditative corpus can be used to support and prop up green/red personality structures. In other words, meditation can reinforce boomeritis. Hence, **Boomeritis Buddhism** was born. This is the translation downward of Buddhism not just into green but dysfunctional green, or pathological pluralism, or green/red. And the use of Buddhism to support and encourage "the narcissism of feelings" is one of the truly unfortunate situations now fairly rampant as the Dharma struggles to be rooted in the West. Very advanced meditative-state training is being used to prop up dysfunctional structures or DLD (one example of which is boomeritis, or green/red).

When nondual states in particular—which, to the extent they can be described, are a type of "all in one, one in all, one in one, all in all" (e.g., Hua Yen's 4 principles, Tozan's 5 ranks)—are translated into words, they can sound very like the green pluralistic wave itself, of "everything is mutually interpenetrating," with the odd and somewhat alarming result that *Ati* is being used to prop up Ego, Spirit is being used to cement the self-contraction.

The real problem is that *none of this can be seen with the tools of Buddhism.* Buddhism specializes in zone-#1 techniques, **but this is a zone-#2 illness,** it is an illness in the stages of development seen in zone #2. It is an illness that simply cannot be seen or detected in a Buddhist state of mind.

As the self-sense grows and develops from red egocentrism to amber conformity to orange rationalism to green pluralism to turquoise integralism to indigo and higher, something can go wrong at any of those stages—there are potential pathologies at any and all of those stages. But if you can't see those stages, you can't see the pathologies.

American Buddhists (indeed, the practitioners of any contemplative path—Buddhist, Christian, Jewish, etc.), bless every one of them (and us), have no idea that these zone-#2 stages exist; that individuals are interpreting their meditative experiences from a particular stage; that any of these stages can be dysfunctional; that this pathology is therefore invisible on their radar screens but is actually infecting their entire system of training. And this invisible pathology has crept into American Buddhism because it cannot be seen by Buddhism. In short, there is a **silent virus** in the operating system that can and often does crash the entire system. And the same thing is happening to the other contemplative traditions, and for the very same reasons.

Even advanced meditators run into this virus all the time without knowing it, and the advice they are given is to intensify their meditation, which intensifies the problem—which is blamed on the individual, which causes the individual's whole system to crash, sooner or later. And into therapy go the wounded. *Those who survive simply transmit the zone-#2 virus to their students.* And thus boomeritis spirituality is passed on, even by those considered enlightened by the criteria, the states (or zone-#1) criteria, of the contemplative traditions. And thus indigo (or higher) teachings and meditative-states training crash down into a pluralistic-green self that is home to a cultural narcissism it cannot spot but only embody.

And so it is that a system virus has entered the contemplative traditions and is eating its way through practitioners. . . .

Stay tuned. So far, the virus seems to be winning, but we shall see. Buddhists (among others) are intensifying their efforts—and have been for 20 years—but can't figure out why something is just not quite right, and most of those considered enlightened or realized *are demonstrably not integral.* As several critics have started to point out, you can actually get a degree in Boomeritis Buddhism from some alternative colleges, although a few of them are starting to shake their heads and wonder about it all.

But problematic as that is, it is simply indicative of a larger point: if any system is based on specializing in one of the 8 methodologies, then as a practitioner of that system I might not be able to spot any dysfunctions in the other 7 dimensions of *my own being.*

That's the main point. An integrally-informed approach can help with exactly this difficult situation, and an AQAL analysis can help the system begin to self-correct and self-organize and self-liberate in a more deeply comprehensive and inclusive fashion. Quite simply, the "View" can no longer be anything less than integral if enlightenment is to be not only Free but Full.

EMPTINESS AND VIEW ARE NOT-TWO

When one is in deep meditation or contemplation, touching even that which is formless and unmanifest—the purest emptiness of cessation—there are of course no conceptual forms arising. This pure "nonconceptual" mind—a causal state of formlessness—is an essential part of our liberation, realization, and enlightenment.

In the Theravada, or early Buddhism, this formless state of cessation (e.g., *nirvikalpa, nirvana, nirodh*), is taken to be an end in itself, a nirvana that is free from samsara or manifestation. Mahayana Buddhism went further and maintained that such a view is true but partial, and promptly dubbed Theravada "Hinayana Buddhism" ("Small Vehicle Buddhism"). Mahayana Buddhism maintained that while the realization of nirvana or emptiness is important, there is a deeper realization, where nirvana and samsara, or Emptiness and the entire world of Form, are one, or more technically, Emptiness and Form are "not-two." As the most famous sutra on this topic—*The Heart Sutra*—puts it: "That which is Emptiness is not other than Form, that which is Form is not other than Emptiness." This realization of Nonduality is the cornerstone of both Mahayana ("Great Vehicle") and Vajrayana ("Diamond Vehicle") Buddhism.

When it comes to the nature of enlightenment or realization, this means that a complete, full, or nondual realization has two components: absolute (emptiness) and relative (form). The "nonconceptual mind" gives us the former, and the "conceptual mind" gives us the latter. Put it this way: when you come out of nonconceptual meditation, what conceptual forms will you embrace? If you are going to enter the manifest realm—if you are going to embrace not just nonconceptual nirvana but also conceptual samsara—then what conceptual forms will you use? By definition, a nondual realization demands both "no views" in emptiness and "views" in the world of form. Meditation in particular is designed to plunge us into the world of emptiness; and what is designed to give us "correct form"? That is, what **conceptual view** or **framework** does nondual Buddhism recommend?

Traleg Kyabgon Rinpoche, one of the Tibetan masters who is as at home in the Western tradition as he is in the Eastern, is uniquely situated to comment on this (all following quotes are from *Mind at Ease: Self-Liberation through Mahamudra Meditation;* emphasis added). He starts by pointing out that **correct views** are just as important as **correct meditation;** indeed, the two are inseparable:

Buddhist meditation practices and experiences are always discussed from a particular viewpoint that is always taken to be valid and true—this cannot be otherwise. **Correct views have the ability to lead us to liberation,** while incorrect views increase the delusions of our mind. . . .

That is why we need a proper orientation or correct view when we embark on the path. Correct view is in fact our spiritual vehicle, the transport we use to journey from the bondage of samsara to the liberation of nirvana. Conversely, incorrect views have the potential to lead us off course and, like a poorly constructed raft, will cast us adrift and deposit us on the shores of misery. *There is no separation between the vehicle that transports us to our spiritual destination and the views that we hold in our mind.*

Unfortunately, Boomeritis ("nobody tells me what to do!") Buddhism was used in the whole spirit of "Dharma bums," where preconventional license was confused with postconventional liberation. Hence Buddhism was thought to be all about nothing but cultivating "no views," which is true only on the emptiness or Hinayana side of the street, but not true on the Mahayana side, which demands the union of emptiness and views, not the trashing of one of them. But this "no views at all" notion was uniquely suited to "nobody tells me what to do!" Traleg comments on this strange Westernized Buddhism:

Buddhism states that our normal views inhibit us and chain us to the limited condition of samsara, whereas the correct view can lead us to our ultimate spiritual destination. We should not conclude from this—although modern Western Buddhists often do—that meditation is all about getting rid of views, or that all views will hinder us from attaining our spiritual goal. This assumption is based on the legitimate premise that Buddhist teachings emphatically identify the need to develop a nonconceptual wisdom mind in order to attain liberation and enlightenment. However, many people mistakenly think that this implies that we do not need to believe in anything [Nobody tells me what to do!] and that all forms of conceptuality must be dispensed with right from the beginning. It is only incorrect views that we need to overcome. **The correct and noble view is to be cultivated with great diligence.**

What is this "correct and noble view"? It is simply the Buddhist view itself, or the central ideas, concepts, and framework that is Buddhism, counting its basic philosophy and psychology—including the Four Noble Truths, the Eightfold Path, the Twelvefold Chain of Dependent Origination, the central recognition of Emptiness, the Nonduality of absolute Emptiness and relative Form, the luminous identity of unqualifiable or empty Spirit and all of its manifest Forms in a radiant, natural, spontaneously present display, and the central linkage of: right ethics and right views > leading to right meditation (*dhyana*) > leading to right awareness (*prajna*) > leading to right compassion (*karuna*) > leading to right action and skillful means (*upaya*) on behalf of all sentient beings. *

*For those not familiar with Buddhism, it might be put this way, in a very free and liberal summary, if I were asked to put it in one (long) paragraph:

Life as normally lived is one of fragmentation and suffering. The cause of this suffering is the attachment and grasping of the separate-self sense. We can overcome suffering by overcoming this grasping and the identification with the separate self. There is a way, a path, that can overcome the separate-self sense and issue in complete liberation. This path includes right view, right meditation, and right awareness. **Right view** is something like the view being expressed in this paragraph. **Right meditation** includes focused concentration and insight training, which leads to right awareness. **Right awareness** is nondual awareness, which unites subject and object, emptiness and form. Repeated exposure to nondual awareness leads my identity to "deconstruct" and shift from gross forms (Nirmanakaya) to subtle forms (Sambhogakaya) to causal formlessness (Dharmakaya), a pure emptiness that can be referred to as a "no-self Self" or a "no-mind Big Mind"—no small mind, but all-encompassing Big Mind or nondual awareness, which finally undoes the separate-self sense and releases it in infinite openness. My identity then freely embraces gross (Nirmanakaya) and subtle (Sambhogakaya) and causal (Dharmakaya) realms in a fully integrated fashion (Svabhavikakaya)—a nondual realization that is the ground, path, and fruition of the way. Desire and thoughts and perceptions can (and do) still arise, but they instantaneously self-liberate in the vast emptiness and spaciousness that is their true nature. Because emptiness and form are not-two, then not only is desire not an impediment to realization, it is a vehicle of realization; not only is thought not an impediment to realization, it is a vehicle of realization; not only is action not an impediment to realization, it is a vehicle of realization. Fundamental nondual awareness therefore involves nothing less than a joyous playing with the

Buddhist training does many things, but it is particularly a *state-training* that deconstructs one's identity from mere gross ego, to subtle soul (or the root of the self-contraction), and finally to no-self Self. But as Traleg emphasizes, those experiences depend, at every point, on a correct interpretation or Right View in order to make sense of them. After all, many of those experiences are completely formless, and when you come out of them, you could just as well interpret them as an experience of Godhead, or Shiva, or *nirguna Brahman*, or Ayin, or Tao, or the Holy Spirit.

This was Daniel P. Brown's point, so badly misunderstood at the time, but brilliant and right on the money, as Traleg independently agrees. Brown said that there were the same basic stages on the spiritual paths of the sophisticated contemplative traditions, but these same stages were experienced differently depending on the interpretation they were given. Hindus and Buddhists and Christians follow the same general stages (gross to subtle to causal), but one of them experiences these stages as "absolute Self," one as "no-self," and one as "Godhead," depending on the different texts, culture, and interpretations given the experiences. In other words, depending on the Framework, the View.

Those individuals who assume otherwise are simply assuming a pre-modernist epistemology, that there is a single pregiven reality that I can know, and that meditation will show me this independently existing reality, which therefore must be the same for everybody who discovers it; instead of realizing that the subject of knowing co-creates the reality it

union of emptiness and luminous form, realizing the countless ways that the world of form, just as it is, is the Great Perfection in all its wonderment, and that the nature of the ordinary mind, just as it is, is the fully enlightened Buddha-mind. Hence simply resting in this ever-present, natural, effortless, easy, and spontaneously present aware emptiness, which is not other than the entire world of luminous form, is the Buddha's unsurpassed way. Because this nondual awareness embraces the entire world of thought and desire and form, this nondual awareness leads to right compassion for all sentient beings. Right compassion leads to skillful means in helping all sentient beings. Skillful means, like all relative action, is completely paradoxical: just as I vow to gain realization, even though there is no realization (or even though I am already realized), skillful means recognizes that there are no others to liberate, therefore I vow to liberate them all. Buddhist nondual realization accordingly leads to a radiantly joyous embrace of the entire world of form, a deep compassion for all sentient beings, and a skillful means for helping all beings cross the ocean of suffering to the shore of ever-present and never-lost liberation.

knows, and that therefore some aspects of reality will literally be created by the subject and the interpretation it gives to that reality.* American Buddhists at the time were particularly upset with Brown because his work showed similar stages for Christians, Buddhists, and Hindus (gross, subtle, causal, nondual)—even though they experienced them quite differently—and this implied that Buddhism wasn't the only real way. But time and experience have vindicated Brown's extraordinary work.

And Brown's work is an example of what we are talking about here, namely, there isn't just meditative experience per se—that simply does not exist. There is meditative experience plus the interpretations you give it. And this means, among other things, that we should choose our interpretations, view, and framework *very carefully*. Traleg Rinpoche:

In the Buddha's early discourses on the Four Noble Truths, the Noble Eightfold Path begins with the cultivation of the correct view. . . . Without a conceptual framework, meditative experiences would be totally incomprehensible. What we experience in meditation has to be properly interpreted, and its significance—or lack thereof—has to be understood. This interpretative act requires appropriate conceptual categories and the correct use of those categories. . . .

While we are often told that meditation is about emptying the mind, that it is the discursive, agitated thoughts of our mind that keeps us trapped in false appearances, meditative experiences are in fact impossible without the use of conceptual formulations. . . .

As the Kagyu master Jamgön Kongtrül Lodrö Thaye sang:

The one who meditates without the view
Is like a blind man wandering the plains.
There is no reference point for where the true path is.
The one who does not meditate, but merely holds the view
Is like a rich man tethered by stinginess.
He is unable to bring appropriate fruition to himself and
   others.
Joining the view and meditation is the holy tradition.

---

*Emptiness itself is not created or co-created, but Form is, and Emptiness is co-emergent with Form, therefore Nondual realization is in part interpretive.

As for the typical modern Western Buddhist that Traleg is criticizing, who so often sees Buddhism as a "no concepts" and "no intellect" stance, it is unfortunately true that, among other things, this anti-intellectualism has often turned Buddhism into a type of "feelings only" school. **Cognition** is the great dirty word for these individuals. "That's too cognitive" means "that is not spiritual." In reality, it's almost exactly the opposite, as Traleg is indicating. In that regard, notice that "cognition" is actually derived from the root gni (co-gni-tion), and this gni is the same as gno, which is the same root as gno-sis, or gnosis. Thus, **cognition is really co-gnosis,** or that which is the co-element of gnosis and nondual awareness. This is why Traleg is saying that cognition or co-gnosis is indeed the vehicle of our spiritual path. (Incidentally, this is why, as we saw, developmentalists repeatedly have found that the **cognitive line** is necessary but not sufficient for ALL of the other developmental lines, including feelings, emotions, art, and spiritual intelligence — exactly the opposite you would expect if the anti-intellectualist and anti-cognitive stance were right.)*

In Sanskrit, this gno appears as jna, which we find in both *prajna* and *jnana*. Prajna is supreme discriminating awareness necessary for full awakening of gnosis (*pra-jna* = pro-gnosis), and jnana is pure gnosis itself. Once again, cognition as co-gnosis is the root of the development that is necessary for the full awakening of gnosis, of *jnana*, of nondual liberating awareness. So the next time you hear the word "cognitive," you might hesitate before labeling it anti-spiritual.

As a short sidebar, it particularly helps when we realize that developmentalists view cognition as **the capacity to take perspectives.** Role-taking, or taking the view of another person, is something you can only do mentally or cognitively. You can *feel* only your own feelings, but you can cognitively take the role of others or *mentally* put yourself in their shoes (and *then* you can feel *their* feelings or empathize with *their* point of view). So **cognitive development** is defined as an **increase in the number of others with whom you can identify** and **an increase in the number of perspectives you can take.**†

Thus, for example, preoperational cognition means you can take a

---

*With regard to cognitive development, this stance confuses "necessary but not sufficient" with "not necessary at all," an unfortunate confusion common in the "feelings only" school of American Buddhism, itself a boomeritis twist on *chittamatra*.
†See fig. 2.2 (and 2.4) for one example of increasing perspectives using the Loevinger scale.

1st-person perspective (egocentric); concrete operational cognition means you can also take a 2nd-person perspective (ethnocentric); formal operational cognition means you can also take a 3rd-person perspective (worldcentric); early vision-logic means you can also take a 4th-person perspective (beginning Kosmocentric); mature vision-logic means you can also take a 5th-person perspective (mature Kosmocentric). That is why research shows that your feelings, your art, your ethics, and your emotions, all will follow behind the cognitive line, because in order to feel something, you have to be able to see it.

Traleg Rinpoche finishes by skillfully pointing out that what is particularly needed is not just any view, but a truly integral or comprehensive view.

In the Mahamudra tradition, we have to acquire a correct conceptual understanding of emptiness, or the nature of the mind. We cannot simply practice meditation and hope for the best; we need a conceptual framework that is based on a correct view....

If we are going to practice Buddhist meditation *we need to have a comprehensive view of our human nature, our place in the scheme of things, and our relationship to the world in which we live and to our fellow sentient beings.* Instead of thinking that all concepts are defiling in their nature and thus need to be overcome, we have to realize that it is only by developing an understanding of certain truths that we can gain insight. All of these considerations have to be taken into account when we do meditation, and our practice has to be informed by them. Otherwise, *our worldview may become increasingly fragmented and incommensurate with our own experience;* developing "nonconceptuality" then becomes an additional conceptual burden that leads inevitably to confusion.

Which brings us back to where we began: there is emptiness (and the formless mind), and then there is the manifest world (and the conceptual mind), and so the question is: what form in the mind will help both realize and express emptiness? Some form or view is there, like it or not, and so **correct view** has always been maintained as absolutely necessary for enlightenment. As Traleg says, it is the vehicle of realization, without which even meditation is blind.

But, as Traleg indicates, it's even more than that. The deepest Buddhist teachings—Mahamudra and Dzogchen—maintain that the nature of the mind is not in any way different from the forms arising in it. It is not just that there is Emptiness and View, but that Emptiness and View are not-two—exactly as *The Heart Sutra* maintained, when Form now means Forms in the mind, or View: *That which is Emptiness is not other than View; that which is View is not other than Emptiness.*

Therefore, choose your View carefully. And make your View or Framework as comprehensive or integral as possible, because your View—your cognitive system, your co-gnosis, your conceptual understanding, your implicit or explicit Framework—will help determine the very form of your enlightenment.

WHAT SHOULD I DO IF I AM ON A SPIRITUAL PATH?

So what is the recommendation here? Particularly if I am on a spiritual path—Christian, Buddhist, Jewish, New Age—how does all that affect me?

The recommendation is simple: **Supplement!** I'll expand that in 3 parts:

1. Since we have been discussing Buddhism, we'll use that as an example. Buddhism is a superb understanding of zone-#1 states (and trained states). Buddhist psychology and philosophy is staggeringly sophisticated in this regard. NOTHING NEEDS TO BE CHANGED HERE. You can continue to practice Buddhism, just as you are. A few things can be added, but nothing is going to be subtracted.

You might recall our definition of Enlightenment from the preceding chapter: Enlightenment is becoming one with **all states** and **all stages** at any given time. Thus, moving through the major *states of consciousness* (gross, subtle, causal, nondual) is a crucial aspect of Enlightenment, and this is exactly what Buddhist meditation will help you do. The same is true if you are on any developed contemplative path (Christian, Jewish, Vedanta, etc.). Your path, just as it is, is fine! So you can renew your faith, devotion, and practice with confidence. They all cover the basic necessities in zone #1 quite well!

2. But Buddhism, like all spiritual and contemplative traditions, has no real understanding of zone-#2 stages. None of the great wisdom traditions could be expected to have access to zone-#2 methodologies, any more than they could be expected to know about DNA or serotonin. But Enlightenment is becoming one not only with all states, but all stages, and this means that you can **supplement** your understanding of your own interior awareness, your own Upper-Left quadrant, by using

zone-#2 research and models to help you recognize where you are on the vertical scale of unfolding stages and capacity to take perspectives (even as you continue to practice, and should continue to practice, your zone-#1 spiritual path).* In your practice, and in your daily life, *using any of the stage models we have discussed*, are you at red, amber, orange, green, teal, turquoise, indigo, violet, ultraviolet?

We *already* saw that you will interpret your meditative *state* experiences according to whatever *stage* you are at. Likewise, **how you hold a View will itself be largely determined by whatever stage you are at.** For example, we already saw indigo Views being translated downward into green-stage terms! So what stage (or stages in different lines) are you at? What's your integral psychograph?

As we will see, an **Integral Life Practice** will help not only with states, but with these stages, and *you can do an Integral Life Practice while fully embracing and practicing your own spiritual path*. In fact, a spiritual path is an intrinsic part of Integral Life Practice, and if you didn't have one, we would suggest that you seriously consider taking one up. But we will return to this in chapter 10.

The overall point is very simple: the highest stages that have evolved to date, in any sort of substantial way, are right around turquoise/indigo. So in addition to being able to move your awareness through the major states (gross, subtle, causal, and nondual), **you need to vertically transform to around the indigo stage.**

3. In order to be able to do that, you need—among other things—a View or Framework that itself includes (or makes room for) both states and stages, or else you won't even begin to notice what is required. Thus, if you are on a spiritual path, you can keep your path basically just as it is, but begin to situate it in an integral or AQAL Framework.

This is relatively easy. The great contemplative spiritual traditions are dealing primarily with various realities in zone-#1. So continue your practice as you are now, but begin to notice, using any of the stage models we have discussed, just where your center of gravity is (red, amber, green, indigo, ultraviolet . . .). And then notice, in addition to zones #1 and #2, the other 6 zones as well, and notice that your contemplative path does not access those zones either, nor was it meant to. Nothing is wrong with your path! It just needs to be situated in relation to more recent discoveries from the modern and postmodern turns.

---

*See figs. 2.2 and 2.4 for examples of increasing perspectives using the Loevinger scale.

Put it this way: any integral path would at least make room for all 8 zones of my own being. I need a zone-#1 practice, and that can be supplied by my own spiritual path. Zone-#2 understanding can come from studying any of the stage models mentioned in this book. The other 6 zones are not as directly relevant for my personal practice, but I do need a general understanding of them, and we will return to this in the next chapter. An Integral Life Practice will exercise all of these, but even then, my own spiritual path can serve as the zone-#1 practice. So it is true that nothing is subtracted from my path, but a few things can be added: **Supplement!**

RESOURCES

If you keep your spiritual path just as it is, and simply plug it into an AQAL framework, the result is an "integral Christianity," "integral Buddhism," "integral Kabbalah," "integral Judaism," and so on. See www.integraltraining.com for many examples of this, and for how to do this with your own spiritual path if you wish—including Integral Christianity with Father Thomas Keating, and Integral Kabbalah with Rabbi Zalman Schachter-Shalomi and advisors such as Moshe Idel. You can affirm your faith *as it is*, and make it integral, all at the same time, with no worries, truly.

You can also check out the Department of Religious Studies at www.integraluniversity.org, where you can find Integral Christianity, Integral Kabbalah, Integral Buddhism, and Integral Judaism, among others. Incidentally, Traleg Rinpoche, the rather extraordinary spiritual teacher we have been quoting in this chapter, is an advisor at Integral Buddhism.

Finally, you might like to look at www.integralspiritualcenter.org, where you will find teachers working with exactly this issue, including (alphabetically): Saniel Bonder, Lama Surya Das, David Deida, Genpo Roshi, Linda Groves, Diane Hamilton, Father Thomas Keating, Sally Kempton (Swami Durgananda), John Kesler, Fred Kofman, Elizabeth Lesser, Jim Marion, Rabbi Zalman Schachter-Shalomi, Brother David Steindl-Rast, Patrick Sweeney, Frances Vaughan, Vidyuddeva, Roger Walsh, and Ken Wilber.

In short, a very workable integral View is AQAL, which can easily be used as the context of your own path. But please, find some sort of truly comprehensive View that integrates premodern, modern, and postmodern, because otherwise your practices and experiences will be interpreted in narrow and partial ways, and thus your practice can actually narrow your mind and fragment your awareness, so that you become *deeper* and *narrower* at the same time.

Notice individuals who have been practicing one path for a decade or more, and you will often see a gradual closing of their minds, a narrowing of their interests, as they go deeper into spiritual state experiences but don't have an integral Framework to complement their plunge into Emptiness, or Ayin, or Godhead, or Holy Spirit. The result is that they become closed off to more and more parts of the world, which can actually lead to a regression to amber or fundamentalism or absolutism. They become both deep mystics and narrow fundamentalists at the same time.

You know exactly what I mean, yes?

And the cure for that part is so easy: supplement! Just expand the Framework, widen the View—include Spirit's premodern and modern and postmodern turns—and simply make it integral.

This is not hard to do, particularly if you realize that the modern and postmodern turns are simply Spirit's continuing evolution of its own Form, the continuing revelation of the Word made a Flesh that happens to be evolving, the Eros that is the Logos of the growing Kosmos, the Dharmakaya manifesting in an evolutionary Nirmanakaya, the Tao of nature autopoietically unfolding. . . .

What did you think modernity and postmodernity involved? Something Spirit had no idea was coming? Something that caught the Dharmakaya off guard? Something that surprised the Holy Spirit? Something outside the Tao?

Then why not include them in your integral View?

6

The Shadow and the Disowned Self

IT's ASTONISHING THAT I CAN DENY I. That I can take parts of my self, my I-ness, and push them on the other side of the self-boundary, attempting to deny ownership of those aspects of my self that are perhaps too negative, or perhaps too positive, to accept. Yet pushing them away does not actually get rid of them, but simply converts them into painful neurotic symptoms, shadows of a disowned self come back to haunt me, as I look in the mirror of that which most disturbs me about the world out there, and see only the shadow of my disowned self. . . .

This chapter is about that shadow, what it is, how it got started, and how to take it back. But one thing is certain: the great wisdom traditions, for all their wisdom, have absolutely nothing like this. I know, I've spent thirty years checking with students and teachers, and the conclusion is unanimous: an understanding of psychodynamic repression, as well as ways to cure it, is something contributed exclusively by modern Western psychology. Many meditation teachers claim that they offer something similar, but when you look closely at what they mean, it really isn't this. Consequently, even advanced meditators and spiritual teachers are often haunted by psychopathology, as their shadows chase them to Enlightenment and back, leaving roadkill all along the way.

The good news is that this is fairly easily remedied.

THE SHADOW: DYNAMICALLY DISSOCIATED 1ST-PERSON IMPULSES

One of the great discoveries of modern Western psychology is the fact that, under certain circumstances, 1st-person impulses, feelings, and qualities can become repressed, disowned, or dissociated, and when they do, they appear as *2nd*-person or even *3rd*-person events in my own 1st-person awareness. This is one of the half-dozen truly great discoveries of all time in zone-#1 psychology, East or West, ancient or modern.

Shadow-Hugging and Shadow-Boxing

To give a highly stylized example—and for this example, remember that **1st** person is defined as the person speaking (e.g., "I"); **2nd person** is the person being spoken to (e.g., "you"); and **3rd** person is the person or thing being spoken about (e.g., "him," "her," "it"). There is also "case," such as subjective, objective, and possessive case, so that, for example, **1st-person subjective** is "I," **1st-person objective** is "me," and **1st-person possessive** is "my" or "mine." So here's the stylized example of how repression or dissociation occurs:

If I become angry at my boss, but that feeling of anger is a threat to my self-sense ("I'm a nice person; nice people don't get angry"), then I might dissociate or repress the anger. But simply denying the anger doesn't get rid of it, it merely makes the angry feelings appear alien in my own awareness: I might be feeling anger, *but it is not my anger.* The angry feelings are put on the other side of the self-boundary (on the other side of the I-boundary), at which point they appear as alien or foreign events in my own awareness, in my own self.

I might, for example, project the anger. The anger continues to arise, but since it cannot be me who is angry, it must be somebody else. All of a sudden, the world appears full of people who seem to be very angry . . . , and usually at me! In fact, I think my boss wants to fire me. And this completely depresses me. Through the projection of my own anger, "mad" has become "sad." And I'm never going to get over that depression without first owning that anger.

Whenever I disown and project my own qualities, they appear "out there," where they frighten me, irritate me, depress me, obsess me. And conversely, in 9 out of 10 cases, **those things in the world that most disturb and upset me about others are actually my own shadow qualities,** which are now perceived as "out there."

You might have seen the recent studies where men who were anti-gay-pornography crusaders, and who had dedicated a large portion of their lives to aggressively fighting homosexual porn, were tested for their levels of sexual arousal when shown photos of gay sexual scenes. The crusaders evidenced substantially more sexual arousal than other males.

In other words, they themselves were attracted to gay sex but, finding that unacceptable in themselves, spent their lives trying to eradicate it in others, while claiming they had no such nasty desires themselves. Yet all they were really doing was projecting their own despised shadows onto others, then scapegoating them.

This is why we are upset by those things, and only those things, that are reflections of our own shadows. This doesn't mean that others do not possess the qualities that I happen to despise. My neighbor really is a control freak! But why does it *bother me*? It doesn't seem to drive my wife nuts, or my other neighbors. Ah, but if they could just see what a total control freak this guy is, they would loathe him too, like I do! But it's my own shadow I loathe, my own shadow I crusade against. I myself am a little bit more of a control freak than I care to admit, and not acknowledging this despised quality in myself, I deny it and project it onto my neighbor—or any other hook I can find. I know *somebody* is a control freak, and since it simply cannot be me, it must be him, or her, or them, or it. If the despised person happens to actually possess the projected quality or drive, then that will act as a "hook" for my projected shadow, an inviting receptacle for my own similar, projected qualities. I'm not saying those other people aren't those things; I'm saying that if you project your own shadow onto them, you will have two things you hate.

It's that double dose of hatred that shows up as neurotic symptoms, the shadows of a disowned self. If the negative qualities of another person merely inform me, that's one thing; but if they obsess me, infuriate me, inflame me, disturb me, then chances are that I am caught in a serious case of shadow-boxing, pure and simple.

Those shadow elements can be positive as well as negative. We are not only a little bit nastier, but a little bit greater, than we often allow, and projecting our own positive virtues, potentials, and capacities onto others, we shadow-hug ourselves through life. Both shadow-boxing and shadow-hugging are classic examples of zone-#1 dyseases. . . .

So here is what is happening when I dissociate and alienate my own shadow, such as my own anger. The moment I push the anger away from me, the moment I push the anger on the other side of my I-boundary, it becomes a 2nd-*person occasion* in my own 1st person. That is, as I actively push the anger away from me, I am aware of the anger, but it has become a type of "you," in my own self. (As we said, "2nd person" means the person I am talking to, so 2nd-person anger means *anger that I am still on speaking terms with*, but it is *no longer I or me or mine*, it is no longer 1st-person). I might sense the angry feelings arising, but they arise in my awareness as if an angry neighbor were knocking on my door. I feel the anger, but I in effect say to the anger: "What do *you* want?"—not "I am angry," but "Somebody else is angry, not me."

If I continue to deny my anger, it can be completely dissociated or repressed into a *3rd-person occasion*, which means **I am no longer on speaking terms with it**: my anger has finally become an "it" or a complete stranger in my own awareness, perhaps arising as the symptom of depression, perhaps displaced onto other people, perhaps projected onto my boss himself. My own "I"-anger has become a disowned "it," haunting the halls of my own interiors, the ghost in the machine of my contracted self.

In short, in the course of a typical dissociation, when my angry feelings arise, they are converted from my **1st-person** anger into a 2nd- or even 3rd-person **other** in my own awareness: aspects of my "I" now appear as an "it" in my own "I," and these "it" feelings and objects completely baffle me: this depression, IT just comes over me. This anxiety, IT's driving me crazy. These headaches, I don't know where THEY come from, but I get them when I'm around my boss. Anything except "I am very angry," because this anger, it is no longer mine. I am a nice person, I would never have anger—but these headaches are killing me.

That highly stylized example is meant to highlight a **phenomenological** train of events: certain "I-subjects" can arise in awareness ("I am angry!"), be pushed away or denied, and the alienated feelings, impulses, or qualities *put on the other side* of the I-boundary: I now *feel* them as *other* ("I'm a nice person, I'm not angry, but I know *somebody* is angry, and since it can't be me, it must be him!") Once that happens, the feeling or quality does not cease to exist, but *ownership* of it does. These **disowned** feelings or qualities can then appear as painful and baffling neurotic symptoms—as "**shadow**" elements in my own awareness.

The goal of psychotherapy, in this case, is to convert these "it feelings" into "I feelings," and thus **re-own the shadow**. The act of re-owning the shadow (converting 3rd-person to 1st-person) removes the root cause of the painful symptoms. The goal of psychotherapy, if you will, is to convert "it" into "I."

WILL THE REAL FREUD PLEASE STAND UP?

The entire notion of the psychodynamic unconscious actually comes from this type of *experiential evidence and inquiry*—it is a thoroughly zone-#1 discovery. It is not usually remembered that Freud, for example, was a brilliant phenomenologist who, in many of his works, was doing exactly this type of interior phenomenology and hermeneutics (*phenomenology* in my own 1st person, and *hermeneutics* when my own 1st-person impulses become 2nd- or 3rd-person impulses and symbols in my own awareness that require hermeneutic interpretation as if I were talking to somebody else: *These symptoms, what do they mean?*).

This is not a far-fetched reading of Freud, but it is a reading obscured by the standard James Strachey English translations of Freud. Not many people know that Freud never—not once—used the terms "ego" or "id." When Freud wrote, he used the actual pronouns "the I" and "the it." The original German is literally "the I" and "the it" (*das Ich*, "the I," and *das Es*, "the it"). Strachey decided to use the Latin words "ego" and "id" to make Freud sound more scientific. In the Strachey translations, a sentence might be: "Thus, looking into awareness, I see that the ego has certain id impulses that distress and upset it." Translated that way, it sounds like a bunch of theoretical speculation. But Freud's actual sentence is: "Looking into my awareness, I find that my I has certain it impulses that distress and upset the I." As I said, Strachey used the Latin terms "ego" or "id" instead of "I" and "it" because he thought it made Freud look more scientific, whereas all it really did is completely obscure Freud, the brilliant phenomenologist of the disowned self.

Perhaps Freud's best-known summary of the goal of psychotherapy is: "Where id was, there ego shall be." What Freud actually said was: "Where it was, there I shall become."

Isn't that beautiful? "Where it was, there I shall become." I must find the alienated parts of myself—the its—and re-own them into I. It's hard to find a better summary, even to this day, of what psychotherapeutic shadow work is all about.

The approach we use in Integral Training is not specifically Freudian or Jungian—we don't use "psychodynamic" exactly the way Freud did, and we don't use "shadow" the way Jung did—but I want to briefly touch bases with what that original psychodynamic research was doing, because that methodology itself is still as valid today as ever, even more so, now that it is rapidly being forgotten in the rush to take a pill instead (in the UR), or try to meditate the shadow away (in the UL), neither of which will get at it.

So let's take a quick tour here, and then I'll share with you how we have updated this absolutely essential practice of **finding**, **facing**, and **re-owning** the most feared and resisted aspects of ourselves. . . .

PSYCHODYNAMIC PHENOMENOLOGY: THE SHADOW LURKING IN ZONE #1

There are a million interesting ways to go with the discussion, but I would like to emphasize just a few short summary points.

The essential discovery of Freud and an entire lineage of what might be called *psychodynamic phenomenology* is that certain *experiential* I-occasions can become you, he, she, they, them, it, or its *within my own I-space*. Certain I-impulses can be dis-owned, and there is a felt resistance to re-owning these feelings ("All of psychoanalysis is built upon the fact of resistance"). In other words, *feelings and resistance to feelings* are the central realities here, and they all arise within zone #1—they are 1st-person *experiential realities* about "I" and "it," not theoretical speculations about egos and ids, whatever those are.

The discovery of this specific type of **resistance** to certain present feelings of my I-sense—a resistance to my own shadow in zone #1—is indeed one of the great discoveries of the modern West. As we will continue to see, there is really nothing like this particular shadow-understanding anywhere else.

Around those experiential phenomena (zone #1), various theoretical (zone #2) scaffoldings can be built. Freud, of course, had his own theories about why his patients *resisted their own feelings*. Today, not many of his theoretical speculations hold up well, but his zone-#2 theories should not obscure the central zone-#1 issue, which Freud absolutely nailed: I can deny my own feelings, impulses, thoughts, and desires. There is a phenomenology about all of that—about how I resist my own feelings and deny my own self—a phenomenology that needs to be continually refined and included in any integral psychology.

HISTORY AND THE SHADOW

"Not through introspection but only through history do we come to know ourselves." This quote from Dilthey is a superb summary of the West's second great contribution to self-understanding—namely, **geneal-ogy** (or historical consciousness), by whatever name. Freud is also in this general lineage. He points out that although we may discover shadow-resistance by introspecting in a certain way our own present experience, this gives way very soon to the further secrets unmasked by genealogy. Freud is only one of a very large number of Western researchers who attempted not only a phenomenology of *present* I-symptoms, but a rather extraordinary type of phenomenology of the *early stages of* I-development—the first weeks, months, and years of life. These investigators were looking at how these early stages of I-development might be conceptualized and researched from without (zone-#1): how, in the early stages of the I, various aspects of my felt-I might actually be pushed away and denied—alienated, dissociated, broken, and fractured—leaving an entire developmental trail of tears. Viewed from *without*, this is the standard, psychodynamic, **developmental hierarchy of defenses** (e.g., Vaillant), which is certainly important. But viewed *from within*, it is also the story of the self's journey—the *felt story* of my I's journey—its hopes and fears and self-contractions during the course of my I's growth and development.*

Both of those views—from within and from without—need to be kept in mind for an integral approach, and although few theorists would see it in exactly those terms (which is how an AQAL perspective discloses it), that development includes the essential *inside story* of the growth—and dysfunctions—of my "I." The essential point here is that, especially in its early stages, the 1st-person I can be damaged, showing up later as 3rd-person symptoms and shadows within my 1st-person awareness.

This view of the early stages of I formation—this **phenomenological history of the damaged-I** (especially during the first few years of life)—is part of the entire movement to understand the shadow, to understand the disowned self, to understand false consciousness in its many forms (and in this case, it is the shadow that is created in the history or the genealogy of my own self). This overall shadow-understanding is indeed one of the great contributions of Western psychology, a specific contribution we find nowhere else in the world.

---

*This highlights the importance of tracking individual interior, or UL, phenomena, both from within—zone #1, or **1p × 1-p × 1p**—and without—zone #2, or **1p × 3-p × 1p**. *From without*, defenses can indeed be conceptualized as a **hierarchy of defenses**, running vertically and developmentally from fusion to splitting to displacement to repression to inauthenticity to systematization to the repression of the sublime and so on. But *from within*, this is felt as a **threat zone**, a defensive boundary **that is experienced as fear**, not as a hierarchy of defenses. From within, the hierarchy of defenses is just the many ways that fear can be felt, the many ways that I can contract in the face of that fear, and the many aspects of my felt-self that I can consequently deny, displace, repress, project, alienate, resulting in psychological miscarriages, malformations, pain, and suffering.

HEALTHY TRANSCENDENCE: I INTO ME

Here is where that story collides with meditation and contemplation. What these Western "shadow researchers" discovered, as we began to note, is that in the early stages of development, parts of the self (parts of the "I") can be split off or dissociated, whereupon parts of the self appear as shadow and symptom, both of which are "its" (i.e., aspects of I appear as "it"). Once the repression occurs, it is still possible to experience the anger, but no longer the *ownership* of the anger.

The anger, starting as an "I," is now an "it" in my awareness, and I can practice vipassana meditation on that it-anger as long as I want, where I use "bare attention" in my meditation and simply notice that "there is anger arising, there is anger arising, there is anger arising"—but all that will do is refine and heighten my awareness of anger *as an it*. Meditative and contemplative endeavors simply do not get at the original problem, which is that there is a fundamental *ownership-boundary problem*. Getting rid of the boundary, as meditation might, simply denies and suspends the problem on the plane that it is real. Painful experience has demonstrated time and again that **meditation simply will not get at the original shadow**, and can, in fact, often exacerbate it.

Amidst all the wonderful benefits of meditation and contemplation, it is still hard to miss the fact that even long-time meditators still have considerable shadow elements. And after 20 years of meditation, they still have those shadow elements. Maybe it is, as they claim, that they just haven't meditated long enough. Perhaps another 20 years? Maybe it's that meditation just doesn't get at this problem. . . .

Here is how AQAL conceptualizes this important issue. Start with normal or healthy development. Robert Kegan, echoing developmentalists in general, has pointed out that the fundamental process of development itself can be stated as: *the subject of one stage becomes the object of the subject of the next stage.*

Thus, for example (and to speak in very generalized terms), if I am at the red stage of development, that means that my I—that my subject—is completely identified with red, so much so that I cannot see red as object, but instead use it as subject *with which* and *through which* I see the world. But when I move to the next stage, the amber stage, then the red-self becomes an object in my awareness, which itself is now identified with amber—thus, my amber-subject now sees red objects, but cannot itself be seen. If red thoughts or red impulses arise in my I-space, I will see them as the objects of my (now amber) self. Thus, the subject of one stage becomes the object of the subject of the next stage, and that is indeed the fundamental process of development. As Gebser puts it, **the self of one stage becomes the tool of the next.**

As generically true as that is, it doesn't yet tell the whole story. That is a 3rd-person way of conceptualizing the process; but in direct 1st-person terms, it is not simply that the subject of one stage becomes the object of the subject of the next stage, but that the I of one stage becomes the me of the I of the next stage.

That is, with each stage of healthy I-development, *1st-person subjective* becomes *1st-person objective (or possessive)* in my I-space: "I" becomes "me" (or "mine"). The red subject becomes object of the amber subject, which in turn becomes object of the orange subject, which in turn becomes object of the green subject, and so on—**but objects that are owned**—not just objective, but **1st-person objective or possessive.** Not just "objects of a subject," but my objects of *my* subject (i.e., I become me or mine).

Thus, for example, a person might say, "I *have* thoughts, but I am *not* my thoughts, I *have* feelings, but I am *not* my feelings"—the person is no longer *identified* with them as a subject, but still owns them as an object—which is indeed healthy, because they are still *owned* as "*my* thoughts.*" That ownership is crucial. If I actually felt that the thoughts in my head were *somebody else's thoughts*, that is not transcendence, but severe pathology. So healthy development is the conversion of 1st-person subjective ("I") to 1st-person objective or possessive ("me"/ "mine") within the I-stream. This is the very form of healthy transcendence and transformation: the I of one stage becomes the me of the I of the next.

Unhealthy Transcendence: I into It

Whereas healthy development converts I into me, unhealthy development converts I into it. This is one of the most significant disclosures of an AQAL perspective. Those studying the psychology of meditation have long been aware of two important facts that appeared completely contradictory. The first is that in meditation, the goal is to **detach or dis-identify** from whatever arises. Transcendence has long been defined **as a process of dis-identification.** And meditation students were actually taught to dis-identify with any I or me or mine that showed up.

But the second fact is that in *pathology*, there is a dis-identification or dissociation of parts of the self, so **dis-identify is the problem**, not the cure. So, should I identify with my anger, or disidentify with it?

Both, but timing is everything—developmental timing, in this case. If my anger arises in awareness, and is authentically experienced and owned as *my* anger, *then* the goal is to continue dis-identification (let go of the anger and the self experiencing it—thus converting that "I" into a "me," which is healthy). But if *my* anger arises in awareness and is experienced as *your* anger or *his* anger or an *it* anger—but not *my* anger—the goal is to first identify with and re-own the anger (converting that 3rd-person "it anger" or "his anger" or "her anger" to 1st-person "my anger"—and REALLY own the goddam anger)—and *then* one can dis-identify with the anger and the self experiencing it (converting 1st-person subjective "I" into 1st-person objective "me"—which is the definition of healthy "transcend and include"). But **if that re-ownership of the shadow is not first undertaken**, then meditation on anger simply *increases the alienation*—meditation becomes "transcend and deny," which is exactly the definition of pathological development.

This is indeed why even advanced meditators often have so much shadow material that just won't seem to go away. And absolutely everybody can see this except them. The recent twist in the Oprahization of America is that meditation teachers get together and talk endlessly about all their shadow issues, demonstrating that they can bring enormous mindfulness to their shadows, just not cure them.

The point is that those two facts about "detachment" or "dis-identification" that were so puzzling can be fairly succinctly stated in AQAL terms: **Healthy development converts I into me; pathological development converts I into it.** The former is healthy dis-identification or healthy detachment or healthy transcendence, the latter is unhealthy dis-identification or pathological dissociation or pathological transcendence or repression.

It thus appears—if we may summarize the discussion this way—that healthy development and healthy transcendence are the same thing, since development is "transcend and include." The subject of one stage becomes the object of the subject of the next, thus owning but transcending that subject, until—in an idealized sequence—all relative subjects and selves have been transcended and there is only the Pure Witness or the Pure Self, the empty opening in which Spirit speaks.

More specifically, we saw that in each stage of self development, the I of one stage becomes the me of the I of the next stage. As each I becomes me, a new and higher I takes its place, until there is only I-I, or the pure Witness, pure Self, pure Spirit or Big Mind. When all I's have been converted to me's, experientially nothing but "I-I" remains (as Ramana Maharshi called it—the I that is aware of the I), the pure Witness that is never a seen object but always the pure Seer, the pure Atman that is no-atman, the pure Self that is no-self. I becomes me until there is only I-I, and the entire manifest world is "mine" in I-I.

But, at any point in that development, **if aspects of the I are denied ownership, they appear as an it,** and that is not transcendence, that is pathology. Denying ownership is not dis-identification but denial. **It is trying to dis-identify with an impulse BEFORE ownership is acknowledged and felt,** and that dis-ownership produces symptoms, not liberation. And once that prior dis-ownership has occurred, the dis-identification and detachment process of meditation *will likely make it worse,* but in any event will not get at the root cause.

HORIZONTAL AND VERTICAL ENLIGHTENMENT

Let's pause at this point to interject a very important point to which we will return in a moment, but which deserves mentioning now. We have seen that the most adequate way to summarize Enlightenment is **becoming one with all available states and stages.** That definition includes what might be called **vertical Enlightenment**—or becoming one with all stages (at any given time in history)—and **horizontal Enlightenment**—or becoming one with all states (gross, subtle, causal, nondual).

Let's simply notice that our refined definition (or "double definition") of Enlightenment fits perfectly with everything that we just saw about development. To be fully Enlightened means to be one with—*to transcend and include*—all states and stages, and that means: All states and stages have been made object of your subject, all I's have been made me of the next I until there is only I-I, and the entire world is your object resting easily in the palm of your hand. You have dis-identified with everything and become one with everything, transcending and including the entire Kosmos.

If you have realized a horizontal Enlightenment—if you have made all gross, subtle, and causal states the object of your Witness—that is, so to speak, half of Enlightenment. But if your vertical development is only at, say, orange, then *you are one with all of the stages up to orange* (you have already transcended and included magenta, red, amber, and orange), but there lie ahead of you, or above you, the structures of green and teal and turquoise and indigo and violet. . . . Those are *actual structures of the Kosmos* that exist at this time in history but that you have not yet traversed, that you have *not* yet become one with (or not yet transcended and included), and thus there are aspects of the universe itself that you simply have not yet become one with. Those structures (in this case, from green to violet) are rather literally "over my head," and if my development does not yet include those Kosmic structures, those levels of consciousness, those layers of Spirit's own emanation, then I am not truly one with *all* of Spirit's manifestations at this time in history—which are actually aspects of my own deepest Self—and thus I cannot claim to be fully Self-Realized. . . .

Thus, full Self-Realization or full Enlightenment requires both vertical/stages and horizontal/states Enlightenment—transcending all states and stages (they become objects of my infinite subject, or me's of the I-I or Witness), and including all states and stages (the entire Kosmos becomes "mine" in nondual awareness), so that all subjects and all objects arise in the great play of the Supreme Self that is the I-I of this and every moment.

MEDITATION AND THE SHADOW

We will return to that important issue, but now to finish with our shadow saga:

Meditation, for all its wonders, cannot get directly at the original shadow damage, which is a boundary ownership problem. In the course of development and transcendence—whether horizontal or vertical—when the I of one stage becomes the me of the I of the next stage, if at any point in that ongoing sequence, aspects of the I are dis-identified with prematurely—as a defensive denial and dis-ownership and dissociation (which happens in the I *before* they become me, or truly transcended)—then they are split off from the I and appear as a "you" or even an "it" in my awareness (not as a me/mine in my awareness), and thus *my object world now contains two entirely different types of objects*: those that were once owned correctly, and those that were not.

And those two objects are *phenomenologically indistinguishable*. But one of those objects is actually a *hidden subject*, a hidden I, a sub-agency (or in progressed cases, a subpersonality) that was split off from my I, and thus that hidden-I can never truly be transcended because it is an **unconscious identification** or an **unconscious attachment** (it can never

Making sense of everything.™

www.IntegralLife.com

An **integral life** is **total freedom** to be who you already are.

A life where **peace** and **passion** come alive.

Providing a place for **everything** in your life.

Better relationships, sex, career and health.

More **effectiveness**, more **purpose**.

Less confusion, less fear.

In order to **be**. And to **become**.

Welcome to Integral Life.

Where growth enthusiasts make sense of everything.

be truly transcended because it cannot become a me of my I, because *my I no longer owns it*). Thus, when I witness this anger, it is your anger or it-anger or his anger, but not my anger. This shadow-anger, which arises as an object like any other *object* in my awareness, is actually a hidden-*subject* that was split off, and simply witnessing it as an object again and again and again only reinforces the dissociation.

This shadow-anger is therefore a fixation that I will never be able to properly transcend. In order to transcend shadow-anger, that "it" must first be made back into an "I," and *then* that "I" can become "me/mine," or truly and actually dis-identified with, let go of, and transcended. Getting at this damage, and re-owning the dis-owned facets of the self, is the crux of **therapia**, or therapy, and is a central part of any integral approach to psychology and spirituality.*

*For more advanced students, I will run through the same example with a little more detail.

- Healthy development converts 1st-person subjective to 1st-person objective or possessive (I to me or mine) *within the I-stream*, whereas unhealthy development converts 1st-person subjective to 2nd- or 3rd-person (I to yours, his, theirs, it) *within the I-stream*. The former is healthy dis-identification, the latter is pathological dissociation. Meditation can do both.

- In more detail, and from a slightly different angle, healthy development and transcendence converts events in my subjective-I (which I am completely "identified with" so much so that I cannot see them) into me or mine (which can be seen as an object of my next higher subject—I have transcended and included them: **owned** them AND **transcended** them), whereas pathological development converts my 1st-person I into a 2nd- or 3rd-person experience within my own I-space ("I am not angry, but I experience anger in my boss!"), so that I appear to have transcended them when I have actually dissociated them. Healthy dis-identification has become pathological dissociation.

Thus, healthy dis-identification (or detachment or nonattachment) is transcend and include: "I have anger, but I am not my anger" (just as the person would say, "I have thoughts, but I am not my thoughts"). Pathological transcendence or development is, "I am not this anger, and I do not have this anger." Healthy development converts I into me, pathological development converts I into it.

- The central point is that when one takes up meditation, **anger will appear as an object of awareness in both cases**. But one of them is shadow anger, and one of them is authentic or owned anger, and meditation not only *cannot tell the difference*, it can exacerbate the dis-identifying and dissociating tendency that created the problem in the first place. "There is anger arising, there is anger arising, there is anger arising . . ." (In plain English: "I am pathologically

This can be summarized very succinctly: dis-identifying with an owned self is transcendence; dis-identifying with a disowned self is double dissociation. Meditation does both.

TWO MAJOR CONTRIBUTIONS OF WESTERN PSYCHOLOGY TO SPIRITUAL AND TRANSFORMATIONAL DEVELOPMENT

We have been highlighting the fact that Western psychology has made two especially unique and fundamental contributions to a more integral

dissociating, I am pathologically dissociating, I am pathologically dissociating. . . ." And after years and years of pathologically dissociating, I wonder why I'm not getting anywhere on my spiritual path. . . .)

The problem is, by the time anger arises as a phenomenological object, the damage has already been done. And meditation cannot get at the damage because the prior 1st-person identity with the shadow is unconscious—the *hidden identification* with the shadow exists in the fact that the shadow is nevertheless and still my own 1st-person impulse, no matter how much I try to deny it, repress it, disown it, and see it as an object. And thus when my shadow-anger shows up as an object or a feeling that I can witness, then the dissociating self feels that this is fantastic!, because that is exactly what I am trying to do, see my anger not as mine but simply as something impersonal that I can witness or contemplate or transmute. "Letting go of anger" is exactly what meditation does—and what repression is trying to do! And the repressing self will do everything except own the anger as mine, at which point, but not before, I can begin to let go of it.

Both psychotherapy and contemplative spirituality are essentially zone-1 endeavors, and in their own ways, both of them are interested in converting I to me. But, as we saw, Western psychotherapy made one colossally important discovery: in the early stages of that development, parts of the "I" might be converted not into a *subjective* impulse that now appears not just as **object**, but as an **other**. The other is not just an object, but an object that frightens you, compels you, obsesses you, annoys you, infuriates you. This is not healthy transcendence but pathological dissociation, and meditation treats both of them—both object and other—equally, as phenomena that arise in awareness and are to be witnessed with bare attention. But by the time they appear in awareness as phenomena, the damage has occurred, and meditation simply seals the otherness of the alienated and inauthentic feelings. But meditation does get you in touch with these inauthentic feelings, so you become incredibly, exuberantly, selflessly and lovingly inauthentic.

The point is that whereas the contemplative traditions specialize in some of the

psychology. The first is the general **zone-#2 approach** to the development and evolution of consciousness, an approach that shows us aspects of the development of our own consciousness that we cannot get at from within, that we cannot get at in our own immediate feelings, experience, and awareness, but rather must stand back from far enough to have them come into focus. When we do so, we can start to see **genealogy**—or the whole wonderful series of developmental discoveries—from Nietzsche to Baldwin to Piaget to Foucault to Maslow to Graves to Loevinger—which is one of the modern West's greatest contributions to Spirit's own self-unfolding and self-understanding.* "Not through introspection but only through history do we come to know ourselves"—and some of that history unfolds in structure-stages or waves. **You find none of these particular types of stages of consciousness evolution in any of the contemplative or meditative traditions anywhere in the world.**

We saw, further, that something can go wrong with any of these zone #2 stages. And we saw that a classic example of a zone-#2 pathology or dysfunction is **boomeritis**. And the cure for that DLD (developmental-line dysfunction) is, for starters, developing a historical consciousness about the rise of my own boomeritis, understanding the stages and their dysfunctions that lead to my own pathological-green stance. "Not merely through introspection but history do I gain understanding," and from that understanding I can work toward a more integral consciousness (which can certainly be helped with an AQAL framework and an ILP).

The second uniquely Western contribution is that, if we do use introspection and look at zone #1—our own immediate awareness and now-available states and stages of zone #1, the psychodynamic traditions offer us invaluable lessons about damage in some of its earliest and most formative phases.

*Zone-#2 stages are, among other things, stages that individuals in a common group have in common—and that is why they are so very hard, if not impossible, to see (for the same reason fish can't see water). As individuals pass through these zone-#2 stages, the stages are indeed experienced from within—e.g., individuals at the amber wave experience "amber feelings," "amber thoughts," and "amber goals," *they just don't know they are amber.* Unless you can stand back from your group and study lots of other individuals in your group, you can't spot the structures your group have in common.

One way to do so is to study the history of your group. A few geniuses—Nietzsche, Gebser, Foucault—did so and managed to spot some of these structure-stages in an intuitive fashion. Another, more precise, way is actual systematic research with large numbers and groups of people over time to really spot and eluci-

feelings—and begin to explore them in a direct, experiential, phenomenological fashion, giving awareness to this present moment, then sooner or later we find various feelings that we are uncomfortable with. If we don't just feel them or witness them or do vipassana on them, but explore their actual origins, we find that certain of these feelings can be veils for hidden realities in my I-space, and an exploration of those feelings leads to the discovery that this contracting and dis-owning process begins early in the career of my I-stream.* Meditation's attempt to dissolve or deconstruct this "I" is not the solution to dis-owning but simply *the intensification of the original irresponsibility*. This is why meditation does not get at the shadow, only the symptoms.

That is the second major contribution of the modern West, namely, an understanding that, in the early stages of a psychological development that should convert each I into a me, some of those I's get dis-owned as its—as shadow elements in my own awareness, shadow elements that appear as an "object" (or an "other") but are actually **hidden-subjects**, *hidden faces of my own I*. Once dissociated, these hidden-subjects or shadow-its show up as an "other" in my awareness (and as painful neurotic symptoms and dyseases). In those cases, therapy is indeed: Where it was, there I shall become.

Where id was, there ego shall be—*and then, once that happens, you can transcend the ego*. But try transcending the ego before properly owning it, and watch the shadow grow. But if that identification has *first* occurred in a healthy fashion, *then* dis-identification can occur; if not, then dis-identifying leads to more dissociation.

SUMMARY

By way of summary, I will walk through the dis-owning process one more time. If this is already clear to you, please forgive the repetition.

---

date some of these common structures. The real beginning of this, as noted, was with James Mark Baldwin in the early 1900s.

*This second major discovery began as a zone-#1 investigation of present felt-resistance, which quickly involved a *reconstruction* of the early history of the I both from within (zone #1), as the feelings of the I and its threats, and without (zone #2), as a hierarchy of defense mechanisms—a type of genealogy from within and without, in both their healthy and unhealthy forms. The enduring idea was that an understanding of the genesis of my resistance can help me overcome it and befriend my own shadow. Psychoanalytic consciousness was always historical consciousness. *Curing shadow symptoms does not necessarily involve grasping their history, but understanding them does.*

We began with anger as a sample shadow-impulse. The anger starts out as a 1st-person reality (my anger; I am angry, I have anger). For various reasons—fear, self-restriction, super-ego judgments, past trauma, etc.—I contract away from my anger and push it on the other side of the I-boundary, hoping thereby not to get punished for having this horrible emotion. "My anger" has now become "anger that I am looking at, or talking to, or experiencing, but it is not my anger!" In that moment of *pushing away*—that moment of resisting or contracting—in that moment of pushing away, 1st-person anger has become a 2nd-person presence in my own 1st-person I-stream. If I push further, that anger becomes 3rd-person: I am no longer even on speaking terms with my own anger. I might still feel this anger somehow—I know *somebody* is angry as hell, but since it simply cannot be me, it must be you, or him, or her, or it. Come to think of it, John is always mad at me! Which is such a shame, since I myself never get angry at him, or at anybody, really.

When I push the anger on the other side of my I-boundary, it appears as a 2nd- or 3rd-person feeling that is nonetheless *still within my I-stream. I can still feel* "his" anger or "her" anger or the "it" anger. If the projection actually worked, after all, I would never feel it again and I would not have any problems. I would throw the anger out, and that would be that. It would be like amputating a leg—it would be totally gone, and it would really work—painful as it might be, I'd actually get rid of the leg-anger. But I am *connected* to my projection by the *secret ownership* of the anger (it is not really an object, it is my own hidden-subject). It would be like not cutting my leg off, just claiming that it is really your leg. It's not my leg, it's your leg! It's not my anger, it's your anger! (Now that's a major dysfunction, isn't it?)

So the hidden attachment or *hidden-subjective identity* of the "other's feeling" always connects the projection to its owner by a series of painful neurotic symptoms. Every time I push the anger on the other side of my I-boundary, what remains in its place *on this side* of the I-boundary is a painful *symptom*, a pretend lack of the alienated feeling that leaves, in its place, psychological pain. **Subject** has become **shadow** has become **symptom.**

So now we have dissociated or dis-owned anger within my own I-stream. This anger might indeed be projected onto others "out there." Or it might be dissociated and projected into parts of my own psyche, perhaps showing up as a monster in my dreams, a monster that always hates me and wants to kill me. And I wake up sweating from these nightmares.

Let's say I am doing a very sophisticated meditation practice such as Tibetan Buddhism (Vajrayana Buddhism), and I am working with "transmuting emotions." This is a very powerful technique in which one contacts a present negative emotion, feels into it with ever-present nondual awareness and brilliant clarity, and then allows the negative emotion to transmute into its corresponding transcendental wisdom.

So I start with my nightmare, and I notice that I have fear because of this monster. In the face of this monster, I feel a great deal of fear. So to transmute this emotion, I am instructed to **feel into the fear**, relax into the fear, and then let it uncoil and self-liberate into its corresponding wisdom of transparency.

Fine. Except that the fear itself is an *inauthentic* and *false* emotion (i.e., the product of repression), and transmuting inauthentic emotions not only presumes and reinforces the inauthenticity, it converts it into what might be called inauthentic wisdom, which is wisdom resting on a false base. And the repression is still in place! You haven't done a thing for that. So each time you experience anger, it will be projected to create monsters all around you, which will bring up fear in you (which is really fear of your own anger, not fear of that monster), and you will get in touch with that fear and transmute that fear—NEVER getting at the real and authentic emotion of anger. You will own the inauthentic emotion of fear, not the authentic emotion of anger.

THE 3-2-1 PROCESS OF (RE)OWNING THE SELF BEFORE TRANSCENDING IT

The therapeutic "3-2-1" process that Integral Institute has developed to help in these cases consists in turning those 3rd-person monsters (or "its") back into 2nd-person dialogue voices ("you")—which is very important—and then going even further and re-identifying with those voices as 1st-person realities that you re-own and re-inhabit using, at that point, "I" monologues, not voice dialogues. You end up with, "I am a very angry monster that wants to kill you!"

Doing so, you are *now* in touch with an authentic emotion, and it is anger, not fear. *Now* you can practice transmuting authentic emotions, and you will be transmuting authentic emotions, not inauthentic emotions. You will be moving 1st-person subjective into 1st-person objective/possessive—NOT into 2nd- or 3rd-person—and then you can let go of it, transmute it, or self-liberate it—and that is now *true* nonattachment and *healthy* dis-identification.

Doing so, you will have worked with the **repression barrier** that first converts anger into fear—you will not simply do vipassana on fear, or witness fear, or dialogue with fear, or transmute fear, or take the role of fear, or get in touch with fear, or directly experience fear—all of which seal the shadow and ensure that it will remain with you all the way to Enlightenment and beyond. Failing to work with the actual mechanism of dissociation (1 to 2 to 3) and therapeutic ownership (3 to 2 to 1), meditation becomes a way to get in touch with your infinite Self, while reinforcing the inauthenticity in your everyday finite self, which has broken itself into fragments and projected some of them onto others, where there the disowned fragments hide, even from the sun of contemplation, shadow-weeds in the basement that will sabotage every move you make from here to eternity. . . .

MEDITATION: HORIZONTAL AND VERTICAL EFFECTS

It has always been hard to define exactly what meditation was doing in the long haul. Clearly, a central component is *trained states*, and that involves, by whatever names, the movement of one's identity from gross ego to subtle soul to causal Self to nondual Spirit—what we are thinking of as "horizontal" state-stages or **horizontal development**—"horizontal" because it can be done at any of the vertical stages (as suggested in figs. 2.5 and 4.1). We saw, in fact, that if you are at amber, you will interpret your realization and experience of ego, soul, and Self in amber terms; if you are at green, you will interpret all of them in green terms, and so on.

But in the long haul, research indicates, meditation can engage **vertical development** (or the unfolding of vertical stages in the self line). In fact, meditation can help move you *an average of 2 vertical stages in four years*. That is just a very general finding, but it is illustrative. Thus, for example, if you are at red, meditation can help move you 2 stages to orange; if you are at amber, it can help move you to green, and so on.

You can actually create a W-C Lattice with gross ego, subtle soul, causal Self, and nondual Spirit across the top, and magenta, red, amber, orange, green, teal, turquoise, indigo, and violet up the side. You can then chart your likely progress in four years of contemplative prayer or meditation. Let's say you start as an orange ego: **horizontally**, you would be expected to move through several states, perhaps having your first *satori* into causal no-self Self (which would amount to an insight 3 states over). And then **vertically**, the average of 2 stages up. So in the Lattice, **3 states over, 2 stages up.**

Of course, it's much messier than all that, but in very general terms, you would expect that vertically, your center of gravity, which started at orange, would be permanently moving into teal; and horizontally, no longer would you interpret yourself merely as a gross ego, but would experience yourself as a subtle soul and even occasionally as a causal selfless Self—all of *which you would be interpreting from the stage you are at (in this case, it is now teal)*, and **within that stage**, whatever Framework you have.*

FRAMEWORK, AGAIN

That's important, because if your Framework doesn't explicitly make room for vertical transformation, then your View can actually hinder your growth and transformation. If your View is green, for example, you can start meditation and you will indeed begin bringing awareness to bear on gross states, which will give way to subtle states, which might continue into causal and nondual states. But you will interpret all of those through the green stage. Your consciousness is struggling to move not only horizontally through states but vertically through stages. In this case, your consciousness is struggling to move from green (and a green-interpreted ego, a green-interpreted soul, a green-interpreted Self) into teal and turquoise (and a turquoise-interpreted ego, a turquoise-interpreted soul, a turquoise-interpreted Self), but since those higher levels involve nested hierarchies and holarchies, and since green deeply

---

*This is a very interesting and ironic research finding, in that the contemplative traditions themselves, because they cannot see or register zone #2, have little in their teachings that register this shift in vertical stages (they have horizontal state-stages, not vertical structure-stages). So this is something you have to look for yourself (i.e., is this tradition coming primarily from red, amber, green, indigo, etc.?). In fact, the Framework of some traditions strongly discourages vertical stage development and actively encourages only horizontal states development (precisely because the former, not the latter, threatens the dogma and their own Framework). For example, some traditions are strongly amber (mythic-membership), and it is possible to go through gross-subtle-causal *state training and yet still remain at amber*, because the LL culture and the UL Framework create a groove, a Kosmic habit, so strong that it is extremely difficult to move out of.

distrusts all hierarchies, then your own View will cripple your higher development. Therefore, as always, choose your View carefully.

The Shadow Knows

Two loose ends, quickly:

1. Meditation might help you move 2 or more stages during a certain period, but *the shadow moves with you*. Unless resistance itself is dealt with, the specific shadow-repressions can and usually will remain in place.*

2. Although meditation can help vertical growth, because the traditions have no explicit concept or understanding of vertical structure-stages, their Frameworks might help—or hinder—vertical growth itself. That half of "double Enlightenment" is a hit-and-miss affair with the great contemplative traditions.† Integral Life Practice makes this vertical component explicit, both with the AQAL Framework and with actual transformative practices. Research already indicates that an integral practice that includes meditation accelerates vertical growth faster than meditation alone. See chapter 10.

Putting It All Together: The 3 S's

We have seen that, in the Upper-Left quadrant—the felt experiences of my present awareness—the contemplative and meditative traditions (both East and West) lack any clear presentation of at least two essential realities. First, the contemplative traditions lack any clear understanding

---

*We're not saying that meditation or prayer has no effect on the shadow, because it can relax the repression barrier to some degree, but that, *in and of itself*, does not guarantee ownership of the shadow, only increased access to it. This is also an empirical observation: after 20 years of meditation, people still have their shadows. . . .
†The simple fact that you meditate does not *guarantee* you will move 2 stages in four years, or that you will move vertically at all. Other factors include the cognitive components and the view or framework one holds. Many traditions—and individuals—have mindsets that actually hinder vertical transformation from meditation and allow only horizontal transformation (or trained-state progression), precisely because the latter does not necessarily threaten one's fundamental worldview or structure-stage.

of **zone-#2 stages**. Second, although they are working with zone #1, they lack any clear grasp of the early pathologies of that zone and how they distort present feelings and experience—namely, **the zone-#1 shadow**.

Where the contemplative traditions do excel—and where orthodox and conventional approaches fail miserably—is in **trained states of consciousness** that push into the outer limits of zone-#1 realities . . . literally into states of divine union and nondual realization. Obviously, if forced to choose between the two, one would take the revelations of the contemplative over the conventional. But why, if not forced, would one want to?

A simple one-sentence summary of what we have seen would be this: putting East and West (or rather, contemplative and conventional) together, we arrive at "**the 3 S's**" in the Upper-Left quadrant: **shadow, states**, and **stages**. These are perhaps the 3 most important facets of interior (or Upper-Left) awareness.*

Conventional researchers have discovered the zone-#2 **structure-stages** of consciousness development and the early zone-#1 **shadow** casualties, whereas the contemplative traditions East and West have plumbed the depths of the major zone-#1 **trained states** of consciousness and how to follow them to their apparent source, gross to subtle to causal to nondual. Moving **horizontally** through those major zone-#1 states of consciousness can also help **vertical** or zone-#2 development (but in ways not consciously grasped by the traditions themselves, blind as they are to zone #2 in general). The reason that state-meditation can help with vertical stage-development is that every time you experience a nonordinary state of consciousness that you cannot interpret within your present structure, it acts as a micro-disidentification—it helps "I" become "me" (or the subject of one state-stage becomes the object of the subject of the next)—and therefore helps with vertical development in the self line. But notice that the simple fact that you meditate does not guarantee vertical growth, let alone Enlightenment. Whether individuals or the traditions themselves encourage or discourage this vertical development depends largely on the center of gravity of their View or Framework—so again, choose your Framework carefully.

---

*In this regard, it is disappointing to see how even the most recent attempts at integrating East and West (from *Psychoanalysis and Buddhism* to the Mind and Life Institute to *The Sacred Mirror* to the Shambhala Institute to *Thoughts without a Thinker*) have failed to include all of the 3 S's, and how much an integral or AQAL approach could be useful here.

Enlightenment or Realization has at least 2 crucial components. Enlightenment is being one with—or transcending and including—all **states** and all **stages** at any given time in history (the former is "horizontal Enlightenment," the latter, "vertical Enlightenment"). In both cases, the *subject* of one (state or stage) becomes the *object* of the subject of the next—the I of one state or stage becomes the me of the I of the next, until all states and stages are object of your subject, all I's have become me and mine of the great I-I, the open Emptiness in which Spirit speaks, the nondual suchness of the Godhead of this and every moment, the Supreme Self that owns the Kosmos arising as One Taste. If at any point in that development (of I becoming me until there is only I-I), aspects of the I or finite self are alienated and repressed, they appear not as me or mine but as a shadow it. Healthy development converts I into me; unhealthy development converts I into me; an unowned and disowned subject hiding out in my painful symptoms. Re-owning my its converts them into me and mine, and then they can be released, let go of, and set free in the vast spaciousness of the great I-I embracing the entire Kosmos in the palm of its hand.

And so we can see the importance of all 3 S's: **shadow, states,** and **stages.** Combining all 3 is the challenge of an integral psychology and integral spirituality. And the rule again is: **supplement!** This is true for individuals and for traditions. Nothing needs to be subtracted from your spiritual path (except, perhaps, any claims for exclusivity); all that is required is adding or supplementing with information generated by Spirit's continuing evolution and unfolding. If you are interested in joining others who are helping to pioneer these integral approaches, please visit www.integralinstitute.org. We'd love to have you add your voice to this integral adventure.

7

A Miracle Called "We"

MANY PEOPLE HAVE a hard time grasping the exact relation of an individual and a group. Or an individual and a collective of any sort: a tribe, a nation, a planet, a biosphere—in short, what we call the relation between an **individual holon** and a **social holon**. It's easy to understand the confusion around this topic, because it is one of perhaps a dozen major but recalcitrant issues that thinkers have been grappling with for millennia. So let's start there.

GAIA AND THE WEB OF LIFE

The problem can be stated in all sorts of ways. The briefest is: "Is society itself an individual?" Or, "If the individual is an organism, is society an organism also?" A little more technically: "Is society made of individual organisms in the same way individual organisms are made of cells and molecules?" A popular version today is: "Is Gaia an organism?" Or, "Is Gaia a single giant organism, made of all living beings?"

Is society itself a type of super-organism, or just a bunch of individual organisms? At one end are the *atomists*, who believe that there are only individuals, and that societies are just a collection of individuals, a collection that has no independent reality whatsoever. At the other end are the *organicists*, who maintain that society is a Leviathan, a single super-organism that is the only reality, and of which individuals are parts. A popular version of this is the notion of the Web of Life, of which all organisms are strands.

Most sophisticated theorists, as you might imagine, have come down somewhere in between those extremes, granting a real reality to both individual and social holons. The question has always really been, "Now, what exactly is that relationship?"

One of the most popular responses has continued to be the idea of a Great Web of Life, or a series of holistic Webs, which basically postulates a sequence of nested spheres of relational being, with each higher sphere enveloping the lower, until you have the entire universe. The idea of a Great Nested Hierarchy of Being is a very old idea indeed, but it has hung around, like a cliché, for a reason. Most ecologists today, for example, use a version of a Great Nest of Being, with each higher level holistically subsuming the lower. Here is one version of the relationship of human beings to the universe from a popular book on eco-holism:

Sub-quantum vacuum
Quantum events
Atoms
Molecules
Cells
Organisms
Families
Communities
Nations
Species
Ecosystems
Biosphere
Universe

You find variations on that scheme everywhere. Alwyn Scott's *Stairway to the Mind* is highly regarded as a systems view of consciousness, and here is his holistic sequence as it relates to humans:

Quantum events
Atoms
Molecules
Biochemical structures
Nerve impulses
Neurons
Assemblies of neurons
Brain
Consciousness
Culture

That kind of holistic sequence is found in most systems thinking. It is central to Ervin Laszlo's "theory of everything," which Deepak Chopra endorses as "the most brilliant and comprehensive theory of everything imaginable." It is central to deep ecology. It is a crucial part of all New Paradigm thinking. Virtually all forms of eco-holism and Web-of-Life theories use it. And all of them are deeply, deeply, deeply confused.

The more I grappled with this intractable issue of individual and social, the more it seemed to me that all these approaches were caught in the same basic confusion. They were stacking apples on top of oranges (and then calling the whole sequence oranges, or calling the whole sequence apples). This did not solve the issue, but hid it.

It's a very subtle issue, but you can see it in any of the Web-of-Life series, including the two I just gave; and once you see it, I don't think you'll ever go back. Let's start by remembering that, in any of those holistic sequences, each senior level is built on, and includes, its junior levels as actual ingredients. For example, cells include molecules, which include atoms, which include quarks, and so on. You can't have a senior level, such as molecules, without having the junior level first—if there are no atoms, there categorically will be no molecules—and that is the rule that governs these holistic series. Everything on a genuine systems list has to follow that rule. Thus, in any holistic sequence or list—like the two I gave—each senior level can appear only *after* its junior levels have appeared (just like you can't have cells until after you have molecules).

So let's try it. Read down the first list and see how long that rule holds. It definitely holds true for atoms, molecules, cells, organisms. . . . But keep reading. If that list is correct, you can't have ecosystems until after you have nations.

And that's just the start of the problems. In Alwyn's hierarchy, for example, culture is something that just pops out at the top, as if it were icing on a layer cake, and consciousness and culture have to be the same kind of "stuff" as molecules and atoms, since they are in the same sequence. As I said, these systems series all look good at first blush, but the more you ponder them, the more ridiculous they become, pardon my French.

The first thing to notice does indeed revolve around the difficult issue of individual and social. I would come to advance a view that, if nothing else, is unique (i.e., the quadrants); and when it comes to individual and social, this solution, if that's what it is, has two main parts: (1) individual and social are not stacked on top of each other, *they are equivalent dimensions of each other*; and (2) individual and social each have *interior and exterior dimensions*. Hence, the 4 quadrants, or quadratic view, which suggests that each occasion, as it arises, has these 4 fundamental dimensions (the inside and outside of the individual and collective, or intentional, behavioral, social, cultural; or subjective, objective, inter-objective, intersubjective). They are not stacked on top of each other, nor stacked separately alongside of each other, nor interrelated in a great systems sequence. They are, quite literally, equivalent (but not identical) dimensions of each occasion. Each occasion tetra-arises and tetra-evolves.

Many theorists had realized that you can't stack social on top of individual (which is the first mistake both of those two earlier lists make), as if social holons were composed of individual holons. The example I usually give, of why individual holons are not the same as social holons (or, why the Great Web is greatly confused), is that of my dog Isaac, who is definitely a single organism on most days. Single organisms have what Whitehead called a *dominant monad*, which simply means that it has an organizing or governing capacity that all of its subcomponents follow. For example, when Isaac gets up and walks across the room, *all* of his cells, molecules, and atoms get up and go with him. This isn't a democracy. Half of his cells don't go one way and the other half go another way. 100% of them get right up and follow the dominant monad. It doesn't matter whether we think this dominant monad is bio-chemistry or consciousness or a mini-soul or a material mechanism—or whether that nasty "dominant" part wouldn't be there if we were just all friends and cooperated—whatever it is, that dominant monad is there, and 100% of Isaac's cells and molecules and atoms get right up and move.

And there is not a single society or group or collective anywhere in the world that does that. A social holon simply does not have a domi-nant monad. If you and I are talking, we form a "we," or social holon, but that "we" does not have a central "I," or dominant monad, that commands you and me to do things, so that you and I will 100% obey, as Isaac's cells do. That just doesn't happen in social holons, anywhere. You and I are definitely *not* related to this "we" in the same way Isaac's cells are related to Isaac.

Whitehead is not the only one to notice this. This was the type of criticism that Niklas Luhmann, the world's greatest systems theorist, leveled at Maturana and Varela, or rather, the part of their theory that was trying to make society a bigger organism. We'll come back to this and explain why, but Luhmann simply devastated that view. It just doesn't work. It massively does not work. Societies are not made of organisms. Societies are made of cells.

Go back to the first eco-holism list. The holons up to "organisms" are all individual holons; but the holons from "families" up are all social holons. But social holons should not be stacked on top of individual holons; rather, they exist as correlative realities. "Alongside" them. For example, cells have ecosystems—ecosystems don't pop into existence only *after* families and communities and species. Every individual holon has a social holon. But in both of those lists, all of the individual holons evolve, and then all of the social holons evolve, which is deeply confused indeed. Rather, individual and social arise correlatively. Atoms form galaxies, molecules form planets, cells form ecosystems, organisms form families, and so on. So let's line individual and social up correctly, and we have not one long list, but 2 correlative lists, as in figure 7.1.

Look familiar? Indeed, those are 2 of the 4 quadrants. So that's part 1 of the suggested solution. The AQAL suggestion is that social and individual are simply different dimensions *of the same arising*. Looked at one way, or from one perspective, the occasion appears as individual; looked at another way, from another perspective, it appears as collective (which we summarize by saying that individual and social are the upper and lower quadrants of the same thing). The upper quadrants are **singular** (individual), the lower quadrants are **plural** (social, collective), the left-hand quadrants are **interior** (consciousness), the right-hand quadrants are **exterior** (material), and all four arise together, they are coemergent tetra-arisings, if you want a technical mouthful. Not on top of each other in a single holistic sequence, and not even alongside of each other as separate things, but as *correlative dimensions of the same thing*. **You can't have singular without plural, nor exterior without interior**—it makes no sense whatsoever. Rather, all holons have 4 quadrants. *

"All holons have 4 quadrants" brings up part 2 of the suggested solution, namely, that societies (in this case like individuals) have an **interior** and an **exterior** (they have a Lower-Left quadrant and a Lower-Right quadrant). Add these interiors, and you move from figure 7.1 to figure 1.1. Again, the issues are very subtle until you see them, and then I think they tend to make a great deal of sense. Here's part 2; see what you think:

*There are individual holons, social holons, artifacts, and heaps. Only individual holons POSSESS 4 quadrants; the others can be looked at FROM 4 quadrants (i.e., quadrivia). See appendix II.

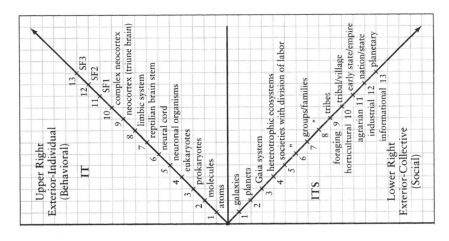

Figure 7.1.

We saw that most of the confused systems views, such as Laszlo's, maintain that, as he proudly puts it, "The difference between a swarm of bees and a dog is one of degree, not of kind." (Shall we say that Laszlo said that, or that a swarm of bees called Laszlo managed to say that?) As Niklas Luhmann pointed out, once you get over that simplistic "stack them on top of each other" approach, then you are faced with the really difficult issues. As we will see in the next chapter, Luhmann made a pioneering leap of genius in spotting the difference between zones #7 and #8—or what systems themselves, once you stop confusing them with degrees of individuality, look like from within. This was an extraordinary contribution, and we'll come back to it.

But the more you look at these issues, the more you realize that there is a difference—to start using these terms technically—between *inside* and *interior*, just as there is a difference between *outside* and *exterior*. For example, **inside the brain** is a limbic system, a neocortex, tissue systems, cells, molecules, and atoms—but **interior to the brain** is subjectivity and consciousness and what you are feeling right now, which includes sensations, impulses, ideas, emotions, thoughts, and so on. And these two realities—inside the brain and interior to the brain—are simply not the same thing! If you think about your brain, and then think about your mind, you *know* they are different, don't you? Your brain looks like a crumpled pink grapefruit. Your mind looks like your present experience right now. . . . Two different dimensions, indeed. The UR is your brain, the UL is your mind. And your feelings and consciousness and experience. Materialists want to get rid of consciousness by claiming it is just something *inside* the brain, but consciousness is not inside the brain, it is *interior* to the brain—inside the brain is just serotonin and neural synapses and digital data and limbic systems and a prefrontal cortex and shit like that. And that ain't interior!

Likewise with social systems or social holons. There is a difference between inside and interior (which is Luhmann's point), just as there is a difference between outside and exterior. I'll give some concrete examples of all these in a moment, but for now, simply notice that putting them all together gives us 4 quadrants on the large view—the interior and the exterior of the individual and the collective—and *each of those* has an inside and an outside, for 8 zones, or 8 fundamental perspectives (figs. 1.2, 1.3, 1.4). Thus, there is an inside and outside to each "we," to each "it," and so on.*

The quadrants offer us a way to integrate individual and social without trying to reduce social to individual nor make individuals merely parts in a web or cogs in a wheel, but members in a social system that is a dimension of their own being-in-the-world. Individual and social are each fully themselves, as themselves, *and they are inextricably intercon-

---

* Let's also note that in AQAL, the word *social* has a broad and a narrow meaning. The broad meaning is any collective system, communal holon, group, or society (or the lower 2 quadrants taken together). When we say "social holon" with no further ado, that broader meaning is intended. But "social holon" can also mean the *exterior* of any collective, as contrasted with its interior, and then "social" means *only* the Lower-Right quadrant, and "cultural" is then used for the Lower-Left quadrant. So whenever I say "social holon" in general, I mean "sociocultural holon," and **cultural holon** and **social holon** then refer specifically to the LL and LR, respectively. This is just another little fun bit of technical jargon that we designed to deliberately confuse folks, since we like to leave people thinking, "What the hell did he say?"

nected: they tetra-arise and tetra-mesh as mutual dimensions of every occasion, all the way up, all the way down.

So let's look at this in a little more detail and see what you think—and let's start with the Lower-Left quadrant, with this extraordinary thing called a "we." I've said it many times, but I do believe it is true: Spirit surely manifests itself in everything that arises, but it especially manifests itself in this miracle called a "we." If you want to know Spirit directly, one of the ways to do so is to simply and deeply feel what you are feeling right now whenever you use the word "we."

What on earth is this miracle called a "we"?

Entering Zones #3 and #4: The We Is Not a Super-I

We just saw that, although they are interconnected, there are also significant differences between individual and social. Among other things, individuals have a dominant monad, societies don't. Rather, where individual holons have a **dominant monad**, social holons have a **dominant mode of discourse**. Or, as AQAL puts it in more general terms, where individual holons have a dominant monad, social holons have a **pre-dominant mode of mutual resonance.**

A few quick examples. A flock of geese communicate with each other by, among other things, quacking at the same pitch (or whatever it is they quack at). If a goose is quacking at a completely different register, not understood by the others, then they won't be able to hear or interpret it correctly. That goose, for all its adventurous individuality, would be left behind the flock or, at any rate, would not be able to fly in V-formation very well, because it is not communicating adequately with its fellows. For any individual to fit into the group of which it is a member, it must be able to resonate with the basic communication that the group is using. In some cases, the very survival of the individual—depends upon having a dominant mode of resonance so that everybody can get on the same page when it comes to survival actions, among other things. A goose not willing or able to get on the same wavelength might be left behind or even attacked by the other geese themselves.

In order to fly in an adequate V-formation (LR, or "its"), the geese need to be on the same wavelength. According to AQAL, "being on the same wavelength" involves not only an exchange between the geese of material *signifiers* ("quacks") that are on the same material wavelength of Lower-Right "its," but also shared *signifieds*, or meaning, or an interior *mutual resonance* for the geese—in other words, a corresponding Lower-Left "we," however rudimentary.

If you acknowledge any sort of *interiors* for individual holons, then something like this is surely happening with *collective* interiors. The interior "we" is NOT a higher "I"—the group does not have a dominant monad or "I"—there is not a single, higher entity that directly controls and dominates all group members in a 100% fashion. There is rather a shared communication and resonance among members of the group—a predominant mode of resonance—that allows them to tightly coordinate, but never fully control, their behavior. This is the wonder of social holons.

The way you become a member of the group or social holon is, among other things, by mastering this mutual resonance. Those not willing or able to do so are indeed often "marginalized." But for the most part, this is not the "oppression" pictured by the postmodernists, who have understood only the smallest part of why mutual modes of resonance must occur in groups in order to survive.*

Often the dominant mode of resonance is a simple matter of expediency; sometimes of deeper meaning; sometimes of survival; sometimes of simple games and pastimes. A group of men have a Friday night poker card game. Let's say that there are 6 men, and, for the sake of argument, let's say that in the values line, they are all orange. Naturally, then, the dominant mode of discourse would be orange. Let's say that 1 man drops out, and a new man, who is green, joins the group. The dominant mode of discourse would still be orange—there are 5 orange and only 1 green—and so this new member would have to "bite his tongue" on many occasions if he doesn't want to be ostracized. He will either "talk orange" and thus fit in with the group, or he will speak his mind—which is green—and find himself getting into lots and lots of arguments, possibly even being asked to leave the group. He is surely being "marginalized," but if the orange men want everybody to be on the same wavelength as they have their recreational poker game and bull session, that is certainly their right.

---

*The dominant mode of resonance can indeed become oppressive under certain circumstances, but the cure for that oppression is moving to a higher level in the nested holarchy of increasing care and compassion, not trying to recapture an imagined past—and lower level—where this oppression supposedly did not exist. This is a long and complex topic, about which I have written considerably, but we will set it aside to finish the general point of this section.

Now let's suppose that 3 more men leave the group and 3 new men—all green—join. There are now 4 green, 2 orange—and the dominant mode of discourse slowly switches to green. Now the orange men will find themselves outnumbered, and they will have a hard time fitting into the group as a whole. They might even decide to leave, or possibly be asked to leave.

The point of these examples is that a dominant mode of resonance is simply how groups often operate. It is not merely or even usually a bad thing. It is usually either a necessity—as we saw, survival often depends on it—or sometimes a choice of preference—red humans and amber humans and orange humans and green humans usually hang out with their own types, simply to be on the same wavelength.

Let's return to the poker game and make one more point. Let's say that the group starts out with 6 red men. Let's say that 4 quit, and 4 new men—all green—join. Because there are now 4 green and 2 red, the dominant mode of discourse will quickly switch from red to green. Now let's say 2 green men and the 2 red men quit, and 4 turquoise men join. The dominant mode of discourse will switch from green to turquoise. Turquoise will not marginalize any other values, and precisely because it won't marginalize, e.g., orange business or amber traditions, the 2 green men will probably quit the integral group in huffy protest.

Notice the center of gravity (or the dominant mode of resonance) of the stages of the development of the group. *The group went from red, to green, to turquoise.* In other words, the group skipped all sorts of stages (it went straight from red to green, and then green to turquoise), something that no individual holon can do. Thus we arrive at yet another major difference between individual and social holons: **individual holons go through mandatory stages, social holons don't.**

There are simply no invariant structure-stages for groups, collectives, or societies. This is why you can't really use individual structure-stage theories—like Loevinger, Graves, Maslow, Kohlberg, etc.—to describe groups or social holons. I realize that some of the followers of those theorists say that you can. The reason it superficially appears that you can is that the group has a dominant mode of discourse, and the *structure of that discourse* is basically following the *structure of the dominant monad* of the individuals who run the discourse in the social holon. Hence, you can loosely speak of the poker game as a "green group" if the dominant mode of discourse is structurally green. But, as we saw, the group can jump those stages if the individual members change, and hence no group necessarily goes through those individual structure-stages. The *group itself* is following all sorts of patterns and all sorts of very different rules.

Among other things, individual holons have 4 quadrants, and the so-cial dimension of those individual holons unfolds in stages correlative with the other quadrants *in that individual*, but collectives or **social holons do not have 4 quadrants**, so they do not necessarily unfold in those types of vertical stages. It is only the confused notion that a collective is a giant organism that makes it appear that groups must go through the same invariant stages that individuals do. The "I" goes through a relatively fixed series of vertical stages; the "we" does not.

(There are phases and cycles in the development of collectives, but those are very loose and generic, and they usually apply to horizontal development. For example, there have been attempts—the most famous of which are those of Oswald Spengler, Arnold Toynbee, and Pitirim Sorokin—to show that societies go through invariant cycles, such as inception, growth, maturity, and decline; or sensate, idealistic, and ideal. But all of those stages/cycles can apply equally to "red" societies and "amber" societies and "orange" societies and "green" societies—that is, they are horizontal phases, not vertical stages. The same is true of things like Adizes business stages/cycles: they are horizontal collective cycles, not individual vertical stages. We include many of those cycles and phases in AQAL, we just don't confuse them with individual stages.)*

*On the long view—over long stretches of thousands of years of history—societies will appear to go from things like red to amber to orange, and that is true; true to the extent that the dominant mode of discourse is following the dominant monads of the leading edge of certain groups of individuals in that society, and those dominant monads definitely unfold in stages; and true also that individuals are molded by whatever stages/cycles the collective itself might be going through (e.g., Marx, Lenski). *But once a society has developed to a particular level, then groups in that society do not have to repeat those stages, but individuals do.* Thus, e.g., if the center of gravity of a society is, let's say, orange, then *individuals* born in that society *must* develop from magenta to red to amber to orange; but *groups* in that society can be formed at *any* of those levels, and groups in that society can jump those levels if individual dominant monads in those groups change (as we saw in the poker game). That is what I mean when I say that individual holons go through mandatory stages, social holons don't.

Whether a social holon goes through mandatory stages of its own development depends on what level, type, and line of social holon is meant: a family, a town, a nation, a corporation, an organization, a romantic relationship, etc., and then in the LL or LR? Each case is different depending on the AQAL matrix involved. Many of those social holons show cycles or phases. But groups or collectives do not go through stages in the same way that individuals do. However—and this is an entirely

There are many ways to talk about these important differences between individual and social, but perhaps the most significant (and easiest to grasp) is indeed the fact that **the we is not a super-I.** When you and I come together, and we begin talking, resonating, sharing, and understanding each other, a "we" forms—but that we is not another I. There is no I that is 100% controlling you and me, so that when it pulls the strings, you and I both do exactly what it says.

And yet this we does exist, and you and I do come together, and we do understand each other, and we can't help but understand each other, at least on occasion.

Interesting, isn't it? The richness and complexity of this "we" is simply staggering . . .

. . . **and yet it exists.** And we *can* understand each other—*you and I can understand each other!* But how on earth do you get in my mind, and I get in your mind, enough that **we are in each other** to the point that we both agree that we can each see what the other sees? However this happens, it is a miracle, an absolute, stunning, staggering miracle. . . .

And yet it does indeed exist. If we defined God as "the nexus of a we," right there we would have proof of God's existence. But let's explore this miracle a little bit more before we reach some integral conclusions. . . .

---

different issue—whatever the social holon is, or whatever the lower quadrants of any occasion, they exert a profound influence on their members—they are, in fact, the social dimensions of each member's being-in-the-world. Sociocultural holons do have a history, a genealogy, a semiotics, and a system—but those developments are not stages in the same way individual development is, because there is no dominant monad to unfold in a tight unity, only a collective of members mutually interacting: nexus-agency, not agency, and those two do not necessarily follow the same stages, if they show stages at all. What we do find is that factors in all 4 quadrants are involved: e.g., in the UR, evolutionary forces; in the LL, linguistic developments; in the LR, technology stages. Cultural stages are repeated in individuals, artifactual stages are not. That is, if society has moved through various stages in artifacts, individuals do not necessarily have to repeat them: if I am in a social system that has developed to, say, informational, I myself do not have to take up hunting, and then farming, and then industry, and then I can use my informational computer. All of this is explainable with AQAL, but not with simple stage or cycle theories (which AQAL uses but contextualizes).

Many of these differences are pursued at length in "Excerpts A–E" if you're interested, but they needn't detain us further. The simple point is that the stages that individual holons go through are not necessarily the stages, nor the types of stages, that social holons go through.

THE LOOK AND FEEL OF A WE

Think of any relationship that you are in. Imagine that we, or think about that we, or feel that we. Please try to keep that "we" in mind as we proceed....

Now, as with any holon anywhere, we can look at a "we" (or cultural holon) *from within* and *from without*—from the inside and from the outside.

Here is a wonderfully simple way to think of the difference between the inside and outside of an interior holon, whether an "I" or a "we." The outside view is how it **looks**, the inside view is how it **feels.**

The outside view is a type of **3rd-person** view—or how it looks from a distance—and the inside view is an intimate or **1st-person** view—or how it feels from within. *Structuralism* is one example of how an interior holon looks from the outside—it is a green holon, or a postconventional ethic, or a formal operational thought, or a stage-3 moral structure, or a blue vMeme, or a worldcentric ideal; and *phenomenology* is one example of how it feels from within—my immediate experiences, direct feelings, 1st-person impulses, desires, sensations, images, and so on.

We already spent some time on the look and feel of an "I"—or some of its outer (e.g., SD) and inner (e.g., Zen) contours. **So what does a "we" (1) look like from without and (2) feel like from within?**

SEMIOTICS: THE LOOK OF A WE

From without, *structuralism* began as an approach to cultural holons and linguistic systems; in that arena, it gave way to *post-structuralism* (Lacan, Derrida, Lyotard, Baudrillard) and *neo-structuralism* (Foucault)—all of which were, and are, attempts especially to understand a cultural holon. But for all their important differences, we can summarize the approaches to the outward forms of cultural holons as **zone #4.**

Of course, there is a great deal of overlap between zones, and we categorically do not wish to pigeonhole any discipline. But those approaches that focus predominantly on zone #4 include **semiology, gene-alogy, archaeology, grammatology, cultural studies, poststructuralism, neostructuralism,** and perhaps most importantly, **semiotics.** A more obvious and mundane example is **ethnomethodology,** which deals with the underlying codes, conventions, and rules of social interactions, and which is listed in figure 1.3 as representative of zone #4, as long as it is understood that all sentient beings, not just humans, have an ethnos or social grouping.*

HERMENEUTICS: THE FEEL OF A WE

That's a short overview of the outside of a we (or zone #4). And the inside of a we? Whenever you are together with a friend and you experi-

---

*Along with the general similarities of the zone-#4 approaches, there are, of course, significant differences. A major difference is their stance on the relation of signifier and signified. For Saussure, the relation is arbitrary, but once there, is a very tight, more-or-less unbreakable unit or sign in a system of differences held together by a unified structure—and the investigation of the rules, grammar, or deep structure of this linguistic or symbolic system is **semiology** (Saussure) or **semiotics** (Peirce). For a general integration of those two approaches, see K. Wilber, *The Eye of Spirit*, chaps. 4 and 5. For Saussure, the sign is dyadic (signifier, signified); for Peirce, the sign is triadic (sign, object, interpretant); for AQAL, the sign is quadratic (signifier, signified, semantic, syntax), each with several major levels. I will, for simplicity, refer only to sign, signifier, signified, and referent, but the fully AQAL nature of semiotics should be kept in mind. Again, see *The Eye of Spirit* for a summary, and volume 2 of the Kosmos Trilogy for a full account.

For the **poststructuralists**, from Lacan to Derrida to Lyotard, the relation of the signifier and signified is not so unified. *Structure* is replaced by *chains of sliding signifiers*. There is a fundamental gap between signifier (symbol) and signified (meaning), and those gaps are usually filled with ideology/ism—patriarchy, androcentrism, racism, sexism, etc. There is a *sliding relativism* between the signifier and signified, and an *unending deferral of meaning* (a failure to grasp the indeterminacy of meaning is called presence and metaphysics). But these sliding chains of signifiers can be studied by approaches such as grammatology (which are zone-#4 approaches, or $1p \times 3\text{-}p \times 1p*pl$, where $1p*pl$ means "1st person plural"; this is why zone #2 and zone #4 are similar, in that both are the outside view of an interior holon, the major difference being 1p singular of zone #2 and 1p*plural of zone #4).

Although poststructuralism has many important, enduring, and universal truths, its rabid denial of universal truths landed it in the first of many performative contradictions. Hilary Putnam, Donald Davidson, Jürgen Habermas, Karl-Otto Apel, and Charles Taylor, among many others, simply slaughtered them on this, and that part of poststructuralism just isn't taken seriously outside of the boomeritis narcissism of Lyotard and his American boomeritis (nobody tells me what to do!) followers—an admittedly large segment of academia, sadly. But, in any event, that rather complete relativism ended with Derrida's admission, in *Positions*, of a transcendental signifier—there is a reality to which signifiers must refer in order get a conversation going. Without a transcendental signifier, Derrida said, we couldn't even translate languages—and there ended the extreme poststructuralist stance. (Leaving behind

ence a shared feeling, or you believe that you understand each other, or see eye to eye, or share an emotion, the actual texture of those experiences, thoughts, shared insights, emotions, feelings—the *actual felt texture* of that shared space—is an example of the inside of a we.

Remember that a "we" in general is formed when a 1st-person singular ("I") is converted to a **2nd-person** ("you"). That is, **I + you = we.** (This is why AQAL often lists 2nd-person as "you/we.") *From the outside,* that we has a structure, a code, a system of rules, **chains of signifiers,** a grammar, a syntax, a grammatology, a semiotics. But *from the inside,* that we is a felt meaning, **a conglomerate of signifieds,** not a syntax but a semantics, not a structure but a yearning, not a grammar but a space of shared feelings and visions and desires and conflicts, a vortex of love and disappointment, obligations and broken promises, mutual understanding and devastating betrayals, the ups and downs of almost everything you call "important" in life, these webs of felt relationships.

Welcome to zone #3.

The discipline most concerned with how I can understand you, so that you and I can form a we, is **hermeneutics,** which is the art and science of interpretation. Among other things, for you and I to understand each other, we have to be on the same wavelength. Doing so, we will form a nexus of shared interpretations and understandings. That **nexus** (or the shared fabric of the we) will have an agency (hence, **nexus-agency** set in various types of **nexus-communions**), and thus have something of a life of its own (but will not form an independent "I" or

---

its very important, but very partial, truths. Many of those partial truths of post-structuralism—contextualism, constructivism, and aperspectivism—are fully incorporated in AQAL (see *The Marriage of Sense and Soul*).

Michel Foucault—a more sophisticated thinker—always retained his roots in structuralism (and hence utilized many of its enduring truths), even as he pioneered **neostructuralism.** Looking at overall Foucault (i.e., combining all three of his main phases), there is a developmental archaeology (of knowledge/epistemes), a genealogy of "neo-structures" of knowledge/power, and a continuity of self moving through them. With Habermas, I agree that Foucault is the postmodern poststructuralist that one simply must come to terms with; his neostructuralism is of course one of the sources of zone #4 orienting generalizations in AQAL.

Overall, then, we might note that AQAL includes **signifiers** *and* **signifieds** *and* **referents,** including both their sliding (or relativistic, culturally-specific) and their non-sliding (universal) aspects. (For the relation of signifiers and signifieds, see the next footnote, page 157.)

governing capacity all its own). That nexus will have a grammar, code, structure, or some sort of pattern (zone #4), and that structure will in some instances consist of the shared structures of the I's who are its members; and hence those structures/grammars will be similar to the structure-stages in zone #2, as we said.* But in so many other ways, it's a different beast, this magnificent "we" that forms as you and I understand each other, and love each other, and hate each other, and in so many ways **feel** each other's existence as **part of our own being**, which indeed it is. . . . .

Hermeneutics has many different forms, but its essence is exactly what you are doing right now, namely, trying to understand me. (Of course, if I were there with you, you and I would engage in actual dialogue. But even in the printed form, you must resonate with these words, and these words must resonate with you, or find a *reception* in your subject.) This activity of mutual resonance—which converts two "I's," each of which is a "you" to the other, into a "we"—is hermeneutics. Of course this process can be studied more objectively (introducing another 3-p term), and that is often what the discipline of hermeneutics does. But the subject matter is this actual we of understanding. From its more objectivist forms, such as **Wilhelm Dilthey**, to its more subjectivist forms, such as **Martin Heidegger**, to its more holistic forms, such as **Hans-Georg Gadamer**, the essential subject matter of hermeneutics is the activity of understanding, the activity of joining *subjects* into *intersubjects*, which brings forth a world perceived by neither alone.

It is—yes?—a miracle.

The world of intersubjectivity changes both the subject and the ob-

---

*In integral semiotics, if we use just the 4 quadrants as a quadrivium, a signifier (or material mark) is the UR, the signified (or what comes to mind) is the UL, chains of signifiers, or syntax, is the LR, and chains of signifieds, or semantics, is the LL. The referent exists or ex-ists (or is brought forth) in a worldspace, which we loosely identify with the LL to emphasize its cultural character, but a worldspace technically means the total AQAL configuration at the specified moment. (If we use 8 perspectives, syntax is 7/4, semantic is 8/3, signifier is 5/2, signified is 6/1.)

Perhaps the most important idea highlighted by integral semiotics is that of the developmental signified, or the idea that "what comes to mind" is in part determined by the developmental level or worldspace of the recipient of the message. For example, the **referent** of the **signifier** "Godhead" exists at the ultraviolet worldspace, and cannot be seen (or will not bring forth the correct **signified**) if one's consciousness has not developed to that level. Trying to prove Godhead's existence to those who are not established at ultraviolet or higher levels is a waste of time.

ject. The texture of intersubjectivity brings forth worlds that can be seen and felt neither as merely subjective (and hence merely relative) nor merely objective (and hence merely universal). Herein lies the entire world of the Lower-Left quadrant, an intersubjectivity that is an indelible dimension or inescapable contour of my being-in-the-world at every level of my existence, constitutive of one-fourth of the phenomena at any level, to put it crudely. But we neither absolutize this quadrant (as do the postmodernists) nor fail to understand its constitutive nature (as do the modernists)—and so of course we are rather loathed, or at least misunderstood, by both camps.

There is plenty of ignorance to go around. The hermeneuticists (zone #3) don't grasp how syntactical structures (zones #4) actually govern (and set limits to) their shared feelings and meanings. Phenomenologists (zone #1) fail to grasp how structure-stages (zone #2) govern the phenomena that CAN arise in any introspected space (not to mention the constitutive nature of the LL quadrant itself, especially the cultural background). Empiricists and behaviorists ignore the entire Left-Hand quadrants (a sort of gold standard for ignorance). Systems theorists don't ignore the interior quadrants so much as try to reduce them to exterior holistic systems (subtle reductionism).

But of all the dimensions that are easy to miss—or hard to spot—intersubjectivity is surely at or near the top of the list. If the postmodern poststructuralists did nothing more than simply put the spotlight on this dimension, that alone would forgive their otherwise insufferable rants—and so forgiven they are, at least in my book.

Most of us are familiar with Martin Buber's seminal concept of **I-Thou,** that the most significant realities are to be found in the relationship of my 1st person "I" to your 2nd person "Thou," and your 1st person "I" to my 2nd person "Thou"—and most especially, my relation to God as the Great Thou. So let's briefly explore this aspect of the Lower-Left quadrant.

Spirit in 2nd-Person

For AQAL, the quadrants, or simply the Big 3 (I, You/We, It), go all the way down and all the way up. As soon as there is any sort of manifestation, even causal, or as soon as Spirit itself first manifests in existence, there is Spirit in 1st-person, Spirit in 2nd-person, and Spirit in 3rd-person.

Spirit in 1st-person is the great I, the I-I, the Maha-Atman, the Over-mind—Spirit as that great Witness in you, the I-I of this and every moment. The very Witness *in which* this page is arising, and this room, and this universe, this Witness or I-I in you is Spirit in its 1st-person mode.

Spirit in 2nd-person is the great You, the great Thou, the radiant, living, all-giving God before whom I must surrender in love and devotion and sacrifice and release. In the face of Spirit in 2nd-person, in the face of the God who is All Love, I can have only one response: to find God in this moment, I must love until it hurts, love to infinity, love until there is no me left anywhere, only this radiant living Thou who bestows all glory, all goods, all knowledge, all grace, and forgives me deeply for my own manifestation, which inherently brings suffering to others, but which the loving God of the Thou-ness of this moment can and does release, forgive, heal, and make whole, but only if I can surrender in the core of my being, surrender the self-contraction through love and devotion and care and consciousness, surrender to the great Thou, as God or Goddess, but here and now, radiant and always, this something-that-is-always-greater-than-me, and which discloses the depths of this moment that are beyond the I and me and mine, beyond the self altogether, and given to me by the Thou-ness of this moment, but only if I can deeply and radically surrender in love and devotion to the Great-Thou dimension of this now. This Great God/dess that *faces me* right now, that is *talking to me* right now, that is *revealing* Him/Herself to me as a communion with Thou in a sacred we, is Spirit in its 2nd-person mode.

Spirit in 3rd-person is the Great It, or Great System, or Great Web of Life, the Great Perfection of existence itself, the Is-ness, the Thusness, the very Suchness of this and every moment. Spirit arises in its 3rd-person mode as this vast impersonal evolutionary System, the great Interlocking Order, the Great Holarchy of Being, of interconnected planes and levels and spheres and orders, stretching from dust to Deity, from dirt to Divinity, but all nonetheless in the Great Perfection of the unfolding suchness of this moment, and this moment, and this. All of those conceptions are 3rd-person conceptions, or Spirit in its 3rd-person mode.

Many people are comfortable with one of these 3 faces of Spirit, but get a little bit stuck in acknowledging the others. The theistic traditions, of course, are very comfortable with Spirit in 2nd-person, but often have a great deal of trouble feeling into the dimension of this moment that is Spirit in 1st-person, or the great I-I in their own awareness. And, of course, starting with Jesus of Nazareth and running through al-Hallaj and Giordano Bruno (to name a very few), as soon as somebody claimed to have realized Spirit in 1st-person mode, they were crucified, hanged, or burned. ("Why do you stone me? Is it for bad works?" "No, not for bad works, but because you, being a man, make yourself out to be God.")

In today's "new paradigm" spiritual movements, we usually see the opposite problem: *a complete loss of Spirit in 2nd-person*. What we find instead are extensive descriptions of Spirit in its 3rd-person mode, such as Gaia, the Web of Life, systems theory, akashic fields, chaos theory, and so on. This is coupled, to the extent there is a practice, with Spirit in 1st-person modes: meditation, contemplation, Big Mind, Big Self, Big Me. But no conceptions of a Great Thou, to whom surrender and devotion is the only response.

This amounts to nothing less than the repression of Spirit in 2nd-person. Remember, all 3 faces of Spirit are simply faces of your deepest formless Self, or the 3 faces of Primordial Self/Spirit as it first manifests. The 4 quadrants, or simply the Big 3 (I, We/Thou, It), are the 3 fundamental dimensions of your Primordial Unmanifest Self's being-in-the-world. In short, failing to acknowledge your own Spirit in 2nd-person is a repression of a dimension of your very being-in-the-world.

In today's America, the repression of Spirit in 2nd-person goes hand in hand with boomeritis. By emphasizing either a 3rd-person conception of Spirit as a great Web of Life, or a 1st-person conception of Spirit as Big Mind or Big Self, there is nothing before which the "I" must bow and surrender. The ego can actually hide out in 1st- and 3rd-person approaches. I simply go from I to I-I, never having to surrender to You.

Spirit in 2nd-person is the great devotional leveler, the great ego killer, that before which the ego is humbled into Emptiness. Vipassana, Zen, *shikan-taza*, Vedanta, TM, and so on, simply do not confront my interior with something greater than me, only higher levels of me. But without higher levels of Thou as well—the quadrants go all the way up!—then one remains subtly or not-so-subtly fixated to variations on I-ness and 1st-person.* That is why the merely 1st-person approaches often retain a deep-seated arrogance.

It's understandable why so many individuals abandoned the mythic-amber God, usually when they reached college and switched to orange and green worldviews. Abandon the mythic God they should—but not abandon Spirit in 2nd-person! Find, instead, the turquoise God, the in-

---

* Let me point out that this categorically is not referring to Genpo Roshi (and his Big Mind Process), a valued member of I-I who is working with us to help overcome this problem in American Buddhism.

digo God, all the way up to the ultraviolet God, which is the Great Thou that is the 2nd-person face of Spirit alongside the ultraviolet I-I and the Great It of the Dharmadhatu (or realm of Reality). These are the 3 dimensions of your own formless primordial Spirit as it manifests in the world of Form, and repressing any of them is repressing your own deepest realities.

The connection of this repression with boomeritis is borne out by many commentaries, such as the following from Tulku Thondup. He points out that Tibetan Buddhism actually has a central place for devotion. And yet Western Buddhists balk. They accept the aspects of Buddhism that point to Spirit as Big Mind (1st) and Spirit as Dharma Gaia (3rd), but not devotional Spirit. "So when some Westerners become interested in Buddhism, they could be disappointed to learn about the practice of devotion. They say something like: 'This is what we wanted to leave behind, praying to a higher authority outside ourselves.' What a funny situation, to run away from devotion, only to find belief and prayer waiting around the next corner!"

It's very simple: the point about the 3 faces of Spirit is that all 3 of them are vitally important, as dimensions of this very moment, or Spirit in 4 quadrants, all the way up, all the way down.

(At Integral Institute, we have developed a series of guided meditations—called **The 1-2-3 of God**—designed to help people move through all 3 dimensions of their own deepest Spirit. If you are interested, please check out www.integraltraining.com, ILP Starter Kit. You can also see *The One Two Three of God* CD set from Sounds True.)

The Postmodern Revolution Is Still Not Seen . . .

The ignoring of intersubjectivity—if we can return to the Lower-Left quadrant in general—can be found even in otherwise wonderfully expansive epistemologies, marring their important contributions and getting them rather abruptly dismissed by the postmodernists. In the next chapter, we will look at many of these, including Edward Morin, Michael Murphy, Deepak Chopra, Francisco Varela, Margaret Wheatley, Erwin Laszlo, Rupert Sheldrake. . . . The list, I'm sorry to say, seems endless. The tragedy is that this ignoring of intersubjectivity is so easily remedied with an integral framework. . . .

What is it about intersubjectivity that makes it so hard to see? The inside of a we can be felt, but the outside of a we has to be seen from a distance, and then over time, in order to grasp its full significance and structure. The same thing that makes zone #2 hard to grasp makes zone #4 hard to grasp. It cannot be seen with introspection, contemplation, feelings, or meditation—it cannot be seen by looking within, no matter how long you look.

Without the methodologies of zones #2 and #4, an entire dimension of our being-in-the-world, at literally all levels of our manifestation, goes silent into the night of our own ignorance. The discovery of zones #2 and #4 is a staggeringly important contribution of the modern and postmodern West.

This thing called a we. Not only between you and me, but between the highest I and the highest Thou of this and every moment. If I may, I would like to close this chapter with a meditation on one version of Spirit in 2nd-person, which is part of a foreword I wrote for a book called *Eyes of the Soul*. It seems as fitting as anything I could say on the subject.

I am sitting quietly in front of the computer, typing mundane words into a mundane keyboard on a mundane Monday morning. Slowly I begin to notice something unusual in the air, in the atmosphere around me, a soft, incredibly fine flickering of rain, a gold-dust twinkling, a wistful mist sprinkling and shining everywhere, a quiet riot of psychedelic platinum enlivening every direction I look, the world becomes alive with the articulate beating souls of every single raindrop, each being a small opening, all of them small apertures, into a radiant infinity that slowly invades my mind and soul as well, my heart begins to fill with that radiance, to spill gratefully out of itself and gracefully back into the world, an ecstatic painful radiant bliss that touches each with wonderment, the yearning of love and the dreadful tears of tender embrace, each shimmering raindrop a hidden soul reaching out to me and then, suddenly, a collective cacophony of Gods and Goddesses all singing as loud as they possibly can, looking at me and calling to me and urging me louder and louder, more and more thunderous, and me to them, and then spontaneously, uncontrollably, we all start shouting and crying and singing in unison, lord what a sound, what a thunder there was, as we all sobbed and we all shouted: is not this simple, present moment the very face of Spirit itself? And a total revelation that could never be improved in any way at all?

And with that, with the utter obviousness of it all, the rain simply stopped. I type the next mundane word into the mundane keyboard on this mundane Monday morning. But then, somehow, just a little, the world will never be the same.

8

The World of the Terribly Obvious

THE RIGHT-HAND WORLD

We can finish our general Integral overview by simply mentioning the Right-Hand (exterior) quadrants and their relation to spirituality in the modern and postmodern world. Because this book focuses especially on the interior or Left-Hand quadrants, I won't go into many details about the Right-Hand quadrants, so forgive the high-level abstract summaries.

We can start with the Upper-Right quadrant, or the study of the objective organism, and then move to the Lower-Right quadrant, or the study of objective groups of organisms. In the Upper Right, the objective or "it-organism" can be viewed from within or without, which we simply term zone #5 and zone #6, respectively. Let's take them in reverse order and begin with the outside view of the exterior organism.

ZONE #6: BEHAVIORISM AND EMPIRICISM, FOR EXAMPLE

The **zone-#6 approach** to the organism is the most common (**3-p × 3-p × 3p**), and is generally given the pejorative term "naive empiricism" by those who resent the fact that a triply abstracted 3rd-person view of anything could actually be called "naive," but who use the term anyway as an academic putdown. This outside view of an exterior object is the "view from nowhere," as Thomas Nagel wonderfully called it, in another semi-putdown. But it's not really the view from absolutely nowhere, just a 3rd-person view taken again and again and again, so that the homeopathic amounts of 1st-person realities remaining in the approach make it appear like a view from bloody nowhere. Other semi-putdowns include scientific materialism, mindless behaviorism, and monological positivism. (We will soon see why "monological" is a put-down for any postmodernist; "mono-logical" basically means "mono-subjective," which means *ignoring* the "inter-subjective," which is very bad—and integralism agrees.)

We have spent so much time on the interior or Left-Hand realities, we need to remind ourselves that interior realities are not taken as reali-ties by those of the aforementioned naive disposition. The worldview of "scientific materialism" takes the UR-quadrant as the only real quad-rant, and proceeds to attempt to explain the universe as if objects in the UR were its only constitutive elements. This curious homeopathic dilu-tion of human consciousness and spirituality, leaving the universe com-posed of nothing but frisky dirt, might seem an extremely odd thing to do, and it most certainly is, but that is not my fault.

There are two mistakes we can make in regard to this quadrant. One is to absolutize it, the other is to deny it. Modernity does the former, postmodernity the latter.

The point from an AQAL stance is that both Left Hand and Right Hand are equally real and equally important. While consciousness events are occurring in the Upper Left, they have correlates in the Upper Right. (They have correlates in all 4 quadrants, but we are focusing on the individual.) Every **state of consciousness** (including every *medita-tive state*) has a corresponding **brain state**, for example—they occur together, they are equally real dimensions of the same occasion, and cannot be reduced to the other.

The problem is that most conventional scientific approaches are locked into UR-quadrant absolutism and thus dismiss interior (UL) real-ities as being at best "epi-phenomena," or secondary productions of the real reality in the materialistic world (e.g., brain). This approach main-tains that the brain produces thoughts the way the eye produces tears. But the brain does not produce thoughts. There is simply an occasion that, when looked at in one way (1-p × 1p), looks like thoughts (or mind), and when looked at in another perspective (3-p × 3p), looks like a brain. But thoughts cannot be reduced to brain (materialism), nor can brain be reduced to thoughts (idealism), nor is this an identity thesis (rather, it is a tetra-interactive thesis). But that, needless to say, is an-other can of worms we needn't open here (for those worms, please see *Integral Psychology*, chap. 14, "The 1-2-3 of Consciousness Studies," and especially the section headed "The Mind-Body Problem").

The point at hand is simply that research into brain physiology and brain states in the UR is a very important item on an integral agenda, especially as regards contemplation and meditative states. Even better is to correlate those phenomena with phenomena in the other quadrants, which we call **simul-tracking**. Early simultracking research (at least in the individual quadrants) was first seriously done by Robert Keith Wallace and reported in *Science* journal in 1970, indicating that meditation involved a fourth, distinct state of consciousness with distinct physiological footprints. *This UR research into UL consciousness* initially had an electrifying effect: Meditation is real! Maybe even Spirit is real! You can measure it physiologically!

Richard Davidson and other researchers have continued this important general line of research into the UR brain-**states** that are correlates of UL **states of consciousness** (including meditative states). **Stages of consciousness** have not yet received attention in this particular research, probably because this research is done in conjunction with Buddhism and merely zone-#1 approaches, but hopefully in the future these neglected zones will find their way onto the research agenda.

Unfortunately, one can only fear for how this research is being interpreted at this time by the scientific culture. Scientific materialism is eating this research alive. Spirit is nothing but the brain! *God reduced to a brain state* is now the most common result of this research, sadly. There is a God-spot—a new G-spot!—in the organism, this time in the brain. Tickle this G-spot and you get a supernatural orgasm as the brain shoots its load. But that's the scientific materialist claim: all that meditation does is activate certain areas in the material brain. Meditation doesn't give any sort of insight into something real outside of the organism, it simply lights up a spot in the brain (or several of them), which causes, for example, a blurring or absence of self boundaries and a loss or diminishment of cognitive faculties, so that a subjective sense of "oneness" with the world results.

In short, scientific materialism does not take this research as evidence that Spirit is real, but just the opposite: as proof that spiritual realities are nothing but brain physiology, nothing but that darned ole G-spot activated. Divinity reduced to dopamine, and everybody can relax. And so would go quadrant absolutism yet again. . . . .

Quite apart from the abuses and reductionism involved with these Upper-Right approaches, an integral approach takes this quadrant and its phenomena very seriously. As related to consciousness studies, the general disciplines in zone #6 include **neurophysiology, brain biochemistry,** genetic research, **brainwave** and **brain-state research** (EEG, fMRI, PET, etc.), and **evolutionary biology.** These phenomena, and their AQAL correlations, are of crucial importance and deserve to be seriously investigated.

BRAIN STATES (UR) AND MIND STATES (UL)

I don't want to spend a great deal of time on this (because it is so straightforward, relatively speaking), but it is important to note that research in various brain states (brain-wave patterns, PET distributions, fMRI patterns) is slowly but surely drawing various brain signatures (or matter-energy UR fingerprints) of corresponding mind or consciousness states (UL)—what we have somewhat facetiously been calling a G-spot in reference to the meditative or spiritual forms of these signatures. The earliest types of correspondences focused on brain-wave patterns and

TABLE 8.1

BRAIN STATE SIGNATURES OF SOME COMMON MIND

(OR CONSCIOUSNESS) STATES

Mind State (Upper Left) (Or State of Consciousness)	Brain State (Upper Right) (Or State of Physiology)
Deep Sleep	Delta waves (1–4 Hz)
Dreaming	Theta waves (4–7 Hz)
Hypnagogic	Alpha waves (8–13 Hz)
Typical waking	Beta waves (13–30 Hz)
Meditation	Slow alpha/theta
Contemplation	Slow alpha/theta plus beta and delta

states of consciousness. Table 8.1 shows a typical summary of some of this type of research. More recent studies have focused on functional MRI and Positron Emission Tomography (PET).

Whatever the final signatures and fingerprints turn out to be (and there could be dozens or even hundreds of them), it should be understood that these brain states are the correlates not just of general consciousness states (UL), but the UR correlates of items such as the Wilber-Combs Lattice and states such as Daniel P. Brown's trained meditative state-stages. Once these initial research programs elucidate general signatures, more intensive research might, for example, plan on taking a group of mediators from beginning to intermediate to advanced state-stages of meditation and contemplation (ranging from 0 to 20 yrs. or longer), simul-tracking the UR signatures of these UL events.

But the only point I would like to emphasize here is that not only does AQAL make room for, and encourage, such research, it has a non-reductionistic framework and theory for accounting for brain states and mind states and their relationships to each other (and their intersubjective background). As this brain research continues and even accelerates, such meta-theories and frameworks—whether AQAL or others like it—will become increasingly needed to make sense of the plethora of data, because information alone is meaningless.

Is God Real?

Since the question came up, let's briefly go into it. When it comes to spiritual realities, the fact that when you are in a meditative state of oneness, a G-spot might light up (or whatever brain correlate is being tracked), says absolutely *nothing* about the ontological status of the **referent** in that state. Any G-spot activity in the brain is the *correlate* of a meditative state, not its *content*. When I look at an apple, an area in the brain associated with its perception lights up, but we do not therefore assume that the apple exists only in the brain. So why should we assume that God exists only in the brain because the same thing happens?

When a state or stage of consciousness is activated in the UL, there is a corresponding brain state that is activated in the UR. Consciousness (UL) itself often has **signs that indicate referents.** The *ontological status* of those referents is determined by various means, the most common of which is a collective reality check. For example, I see my dog Isaac, which also lights up certain areas in my brain. That is, while that UL-consciousness state is occurring, there is a UR-brain state simultaneously occurring (each event has *correlates* in all 4 quadrants). I might want to convey the fact that my dog is here, so I say, "Come and see my dog Isaac." There are 4 things involved here: signs, signifiers, signifieds, and referent.

The actual words "dog" and "Isaac" are **signs** that have two components, signifiers and signifieds. The **signifiers** are the material words or sounds: "dog" and "Isaac." What comes to mind when you hear or see a word such as "dog" is the **signified.** Isaac the actual dog is the **referent.** If you come and look and you also see Isaac, we generally assume that the referent, Isaac, is real and not just imagined or hallucinated. So in this case, the signifier "Isaac" has a real referent.

Now, what if I say, talking to my friend, "Do you think Sally loves me?" Those signifiers seem simple enough, but they actually involve being able to take a 3rd-person perspective to see the realities involved. So the **referents** of those signs **exist only in a worldspace** of orange or higher. You simply *cannot see* what that sentence means until then, even though you can see the sensorimotor words and material bodies involved. So even though you can hear and see the *signifiers* in that sentence, you cannot get the correct *signified*, nor therefore can you see the actual *referent*. I can see the words, but their meaning is "over my head," and I will simply assume that the referent doesn't exist at all, because I can find no evidence for it whatsoever anywhere that I look.

That is something developmentalists have known all along: there isn't a single pregiven world lying around out there waiting for all and sundry to see. Different phenomenological worlds—*real* worlds—come into being with each new level of consciousness development. Systems theory, for example, which comes into existence around turquoise, simply cannot be seen by orange (or lower) levels of consciousness—global systems are simply "over its head." Those systems exist, they just can't be seen or brought forth until turquoise. So the signifier "globally mutually interacting systems" does not appear real until turquoise, at which point the signifier will call up the correct signified and the actual referent will be seen and understood.

That is the reason that structuralism (and then poststructuralism) was central to the whole "constructivist" revolution in epistemology. There isn't the world of "naive empiricism" just lying around out there waiting to be seen. Naive empiricism itself doesn't exist until orange! Different worlds are brought forth by the structures of consciousness doing the perceiving and co-creating. In AQAL, these "con-structing structures" are anchored in all 4 quadrants (including the Right-Hand or "objective" quadrants), so this never degenerates into the extreme "social construction" of all realities. But a central fact does remain: **the referents of all signifiers exist only at certain developmental stages and states.**

So, take the signifiers "God," "Emptiness," and "*nirvikalpa samadhi.*" Are their referents "real"? Do they exist? And the only possible answer is: *get into the stage or state from which the sentence is being written, and then look for yourself.* If you are not in the same state/ stage as the author of the signifiers, then you will never have the correct signified, and hence the actual referent cannot be seen. It's "over my head."

On the other hand, the virtually unanimous conclusion of those who bring awareness to, for example, the causal state, is that the signifier "Emptiness" has a real referent. The conclusion of those who stably bring awareness to the nondual state is that the signifier "Godhead" has a real referent. And so on. When the G-spot lights up in those cases, you are seeing something just as real as the apple that lights up other parts of the brain.

But without the correct training in states and stages, "Godhead" and "nirvikalpa" and "Buddha-nature" and "Christ-consciousness" and "nirguna Brahman" and "metanoia" will remain all Greek to you, they will have no real referent or meaning for you. In that case, when a meditator lights up the G-spot, you just won't be able to see what they are seeing, and so you will be forced to assume that it's all "just in the brain."

Silly you. In the meantime, brain-state research like this is quickly being slotted into the scientific materialistic view of things, with the unfortunate result that it probably hurts spirituality more than it helps. But it's absolutely crucial research and most certainly needs to go forward.

A quadratic view allows us to acknowledge and include that very important brain research in the UR, but also let's understand the fundamental rule of any reality check: if I want to know if something is real, I *must* get in the same state or stage from which the assertion was issued, and then look. If I don't do that, then please, I shouldn't talk about things that are over my head. . . .*

Zone #5—Cognitive Science and Autopoietic Organisms

We've spent more than 50% of this book talking about interiors, including the scientific studies of the interiors, so we must have covered most of **cognitive science**, right? Actually, almost none of it. To understand why is to understand one of the most fascinating perspectives (and methodologies) available to human beings: the outside view of an inside view

* And conversely, that lets us see why (as we have found out the hard way) doing more brain research for those who are not in the corresponding state or stage convinces them of nothing. . . .

of an objective organism (**3-p × 1-p × 3p**)—or zone-#5 approaches to Right-Hand realities.

Let me briefly introduce this view by reminding people of what Maturana and Varela did with their rather revolutionary *biological phenomenology*, which they also called "*the inside view* of the organism." They made it clear that they did not mean "phenomenology" in the sense of trying to understand what the organism—let's say a frog—was experiencing subjectively. They were not trying to reconstruct the "I-space" of a frog (which would be UL phenomenology). Rather, they were simply trying to reconstruct what was available in the subjective-cognitive world of the frog, but they were still thinking about that in objective terms. It was the "inside view" of the frog approached objectively—hence, an objective account (3-p) of the inside or subjective view (1-p) of the frog, which itself is still approached in objective or scientific terms (3p). Thus, **3-p × 1-p × 3p**. That "1-p" or "1st-person" term in the middle is what their **biological phenomenology** or "the view from within the organism" was all about.

And that was enough to revolutionize biology and biological epistemology. At first it shocked the biological world, which was used to using models such as systems theory to understand the behavior of the frog. But Maturana and Varela pointed out that, when it comes to the frog's actual phenomenology, *systems theory plays no role at all—in fact, it doesn't even exist in the frog's world.*

Which is absolutely true. There is a role for systems theory, but that is part of the outside view of the organism, not its inside view. Rather, a biological organism is an autonomous, coherent, and *self-making* entity (**auto-poiesis** means **self-making**), and this self-making organic entity cognizes and actively brings forth a world, it does not merely "perceive" a world that is already given. In short, the biological organism co-creates the world it perceives. (This was, in a very positive sense, a postmodern biology.)

This approach revolutionized not only biology, but also many of the other scientific approaches to exterior holons. This is the fundamental difference between **classical behaviorism** and **autopoietic behaviorism**. The former looks at the objective organism from without (zone #6), the latter, from within (zone #5).

As for zone-#5 approaches to the individual (in the UR). Cognitive science, which is now the most widely adopted approach to the study of consciousness (and hence, indirectly, spirituality, if the topic is allowed), is the "official" view of modern science of what is real and not real when it comes to consciousness and its contents. Typical theorists in this area include Daniel Dennett, Ray Jackendoff, Patricia Churchland, Paul Churchland, Alwyn Scott (*Stairway to the Mind*), and so on. . . .

In essence, what they—and virtually all cognitive scientists—are doing is utilizing the same perspective-space employed by Maturana and Varela. They are trying to create not neurophysiology but "neurophysio-logical phenomenology"—what the organism and its brain look like from within, but still conceived in essentially objectivistic terms. They are looking at what happens in an it-brain when it perceives it-objects and it-data moving through neuronal it-circuits, but always with an eye on the view from within that brain looking out ($3\text{-}p \times 1\text{-}p \times 3p$).

We needn't say too much more here; the textbooks on cognitive science are pretty straightforward, although their quadrant absolutism can make for truncated reading.* Other important approaches that have increased our understanding of this zone and its contents/referents include **bio-medical psychiatry, evolutionary psychology**, and aspects of **sociobiology**.

The discoveries of cognitive science and related autopoietic approaches are truly important and form part of any integral theory of consciousness and spirituality, because what cognitive science is discovering are some of the UR correlates of various UL occasions, and only when these are taken together can we even begin to understand human consciousness and its referents, whether those referents be a rock, my dog, or God.

Neurophenomenology: Bridging Zones #5 and #1

Francisco Varela (a founding member of Integral Institute) went on to develop what he called *neurophenomenology*, an important type of sim-

---

*If only the Upper-Right quadrant is acknowledged as real, this generates all of the downsides of monological approaches in all their unpleasantness (which we will detail in the next chapter). The most difficult issue this discipline faces is called "the hard problem"—which is the mind/body problem, but now usually stated in terms of the mind/brain problem, a problem that we might state as: once I have erased consciousness from the universe by the very nature of my methodology, which cannot detect consciousness anywhere, then how can my reductionistic approach account for it, which would not recognize the solution anyway, even if I stumbled on it? I'm not sure they word it exactly like that, but you get the drift. The solution to the hard problem requires methodologies that are not recognized or allowed by the problem. (Part of the mind-body problem, for example, can only be solved with the consciousness enacted with *satori*. See *Integral Psychology*, chap. 14.)

ultracking of various data generated by 1st-person and 3rd-person approaches to consciousness. Francisco was a longtime Buddhist meditator, and so he was naturally interested in how to unite interior phenomenology (zone-#1) and autopoietic cognitive science (zone-#5). This combination of zone-#1 phenomenology with zone-#5 cognitive science is one of the first serious attempts to get the UL and the UR together based on the latest in science and the best in phenomenology. My major criticism, within that attempt, is that it leaves out zone-#2 approaches in the UL and zone #4 in the LL, and thus has nothing resembling stages or intersubjectivity, which is a serious lack. But for what it accomplishes, it is a landmark on the long road to a more integral approach.

Another of our favorite authors in this regard is David Chalmers, a member of Integral Institute, who is admirably (and absolutely brilliantly) fighting the widespread attempts to reduce 1st-person consciousness/mind (Upper Left) to 3rd-person brain/body (Upper Right). See in particular *Philosophy of Mind: Classical and Contemporary Readings.*

Zone #7: Social Autopoiesis, or, Gaia Does Not Exist

Maturana and Varela originally developed their "view from within" for individual organisms, like the frog (or what we call *individual* holons). They assumed that social systems (social holons) were a higher level of wholeness than individual organisms, and that they could derive a social system as simply the next level in their hierarchy of autopoiesis. In other words, their developmental holarchy was: individual components are autopoietically brought together into single organisms, which are autopoietically brought together into societies of organisms: cells, organisms, societies. Societies are composed of organisms in the same way that organisms are composed of cells.

Niklas Luhmann, generally regarded as the world's greatest systems theorist, made two very important corrections to that view (both of which are consistent with, indeed predicted by, AQAL theory). Both of these are extremely subtle, difficult issues, but also extremely important, so I will simply mention them, and those interested can follow up with endnote references where these topics are pursued at length.

First, Luhmann pointed out that societies—or social systems—are composed not of organisms, but of *the communication between organ-*

isms. Put simply, the Web-of-Life theorists had everywhere assumed that "all organisms are strands in the Great Web," but Luhmann demonstrated that what is *internal* to the Great Web is not organisms but the communication between them. The Web of Life as normally portrayed simply does not exist—a social holon is not made of organisms in the same way organisms are made of cells. He corrected Maturana and Varela on this simple but crucial point, and sophisticated systems theorists almost everywhere followed suit.

The way we put it is like this. A social (sociocultural) holon is composed of individual holons plus their interactions (one example of which is exchanged communication). The individual holons are **inside** the social holon, their exchanged communication is **internal** to the social holon. This has LL (cultural) and LR (social) dimensions, but I'll use the Lower Left as a simple example:

You and I have a close circle of friends. We know exactly who is inside this circle of friends, and who is outside it. For example, this circle includes James and George, but not Bob. So you, me, James, and George are **inside** this particular "we," and Bob is **outside** of the circle (or outside the boundary of the "we").

But you, me, James, and George are not *parts* of a super-organism called "we," but rather are members of this "we." So this "we" is not made out of us (we are not its **internal** "stuff"). Rather, the "we" is made of our exchanged communication and interactions. So you, me, James, and George are **inside** the "we," our communication is **internal** to it. (Get it?)*

---

*This circle of friends has a LL "we," composed of collective **signifieds**, and a LR "its," composed of exchanged material **signifiers**—gross, subtle, and causal. For AQAL theory, what is *internal* to a social system are not the members of the system but the exchanged *signifiers* between the members. In the LR, *organisms or social members are **inside*** the social system (or inside the boundary of its), their exchanged *signifiers are **internal*** to the system. Correlatively occurring in the LL, *cultural members are inside* the cultural holon or "we," while what is *internal* to the "we" is the nexus-agency of mutually resonating (i.e., intersubjective) or *shared signifieds* in the members. Again, this is essentially similar to Luhmann's point, but sophisticated by breaking "shared communication" into shared signifiers (LR) and shared signifieds (LL), which also lays the foundation for an integral semiotics (see vol. 2 of the Kosmos Trilogy).

Another way we say this, in the LR, is that social systems are composed of *members plus their exchanged artifacts*; the members are inside, the artifacts are internal to, the social system. ("Artifacts"—exchanged material artifacts—means "signifiers." This topic is pursued at length in Excerpts A–G.)

The point is that Gaia simply does not exist—not as an organism. Gaia exists, but as a club. That is, there is a **Gaian collective** of organisms as members, but not as parts or links or strands. And the internal "stuff" of the Gaian collective is *holarchical networks of communication* (i.e., holarchies of exchanged material signifiers in the LR and mutually resonating signifieds in the LL). But both Gaia and the Web of Life, as typically portrayed, just don't exist. (Most people don't even know what James Lovelock meant by "Gaia" when he introduced it as a scientific hypothesis. If you think you do, check out the footnote.)* But as typically portrayed, Gaia and the Web of Life are truly myths of an old paradigm (which ironically calls itself "the new paradigm").

Second, Luhmann then showed that you could still take the autopoietic perspective and apply that to the internal systems of communication, and then you got the "view from within" the social system. Exactly right. That is the zone-#7 approach in the Lower-Right quadrant, in contrast to classical dynamical systems theory (or zone #8), which still viewed members of the system as part of the system. Zone #8 is still an important perspective that needs to be preserved, but some of the things that it thought were true—when it was the only perspective being used—need to be transcended for a larger integration. "Transcend and include" is "negate and preserve," and that which is negated is always a partiality made absolute.

But all of this is easy to remember. Every holon has 4 quadrants, and things like Gaia are the exterior collective (or Lower-Right) dimension of an individual holon, and not a super-individual holon stacked on top of individual holons.

ZONE #8: DYNAMICAL SYSTEMS THEORY AND CHAOS/COMPLEXITY THEORY

A social (LR) holon is composed of its members plus their exchanged artifacts. The networks of exchange can be looked at from without and

---

*Gaia is the network of *prokaryotic cells circling the planet.* Prokaryotic cells are early, primitive, single-celled organisms (contrasted with eukaryotic cells, which are "true cells"). Thus, Gaia, or the collective of prokaryotic cells, as a scientific hypothesis (which I think is true), does NOT include things like all life forms, humans, mammals, reptiles, fish, plants, the biosphere, etc. The evolutionary location of Gaia is correctly entered in the LR on figure 7.1 as the collective dimension of prokaryotic cells (which are listed in the UR). In AQAL theory, because senior holons transcend

from within, as we have seen. The classical systems theory perspective (zone #8) looks at the social holon from without, and arrives at a Web of Life arranged in nested hierarchies. As usual, that view is not wrong but partial, and when it is taken as the only correct view, badly misperceives the nature of social systems and their internal communication networks. Even though systems theory, covering zone #8, is only 1/8th of reality, as it were, it nonetheless claimed to have the Total Picture, a bit of an embarrassment from an integral view. But to its everlasting credit, systems theory was one of the first attempts, and historically the most significant, to introduce a measure of holism into the prevailing atomistic world of the Upper Right, which dominated the world of scientific materialism. Although the list of its pioneers is long, Ludwig von Bertalanffy particularly deserves a special mention; he was a true hero in so many ways.

At their best, the Lower-Right quadrant approaches move toward seeing Spirit in 3rd-person, or the manifestation of Spirit in its material, objective, 3rd-person mode. Gaia, the Web of Life, the Interlocking Order, the *Système de la Nature* (as Enlightenment philosophers dubbed it), the Grand System of mutually interrelated processes—all of these, whether they recognize it or not, often move toward a genuine awe and worship of Spirit in 3rd-person.

It's when left to its own devices that this approach degenerates into subtle reductionism and monological imperialism. To understand why that is so is to understand the core of the postmodern revolution, a revolution tapped into by Maturana and Varela, among so many others, and a revolution with which any integral view categorically must come to terms.

Monological Imperialism and the Myth of the Given

If there is a common thread to the general postmodern current, it is a radical critique of monological consciousness—variously referred to as **the myth of the given, monological empiricism, the philosophy of**

and include junior holons, then the Gaian prokaryotic holons are *internal* to all higher life forms, and not vice versa, as the old-paradigm myths have it —i.e, mammals include Gaia, Gaia does not include mammals. That is, Gaia is in us, we are not in Gaia. But for just that reason, killing Gaia is suicidal to humans—the foundation of a nonreductionistic ecology.

the subject, and **the philosophy of consciousness**, to name a few. As I started to indicate, what "monological" basically means is "not dialogical"—or not intersubjective, not contextual, not constructivist, not understanding the constitutive nature of cultural backgrounds—basically, not recognizing zones #2 and #4.

The myth of the given or monological consciousness is essentially another name for phenomenology and mere empiricism in any of a hundred guises—whether regular empiricism, radical empiricism, interior empiricism, transpersonal empiricism, empirical phenomenology, transcendental phenomenology, radical phenomenology, and so forth. As important as they might be, what all of them have in common is **the myth of the given**, which includes:

- *the belief that reality is simply given to me, or that there is a single pregiven world that consciousness delivers to me more or less as it is*, instead of a world that is con-structured in various ways before it ever reaches my empirical or phenomenal awareness.

- *the belief that the consciousness of an individual will deliver truth.* This is why Habermas calls the myth of the given by the phrase "the philosophy of consciousness"—and that is what he is criticizing because it is blind to intersubjectivity, among other things. As we have been saying throughout this book, consciousness itself simply cannot see zones #2 and #4, and therefore is deficient in and of itself (e.g., "Not through introspection but through history do we come to know ourselves"). You can introspect all you want and you won't see those other truths. So consciousness itself is deficient—whether personal or transpersonal, whether pure or not pure, essential or relative, high or low, big mind or small mind, vipassana, bare attention, centering prayer, contemplative awareness—none of them can see these other truths, and that is why Habermas and the postmodernists extensively criticize "the philosophy of consciousness."

- *a failure to understand that the truth that the subject delivers is constructed in part by intersubjective cultural networks.* This is why the myth of the given is also called "the philosophy of the subject"—what we also need is "the philosophy of the intersubject, or intersubjectivity."

- *the belief that the mirror of nature, or the reflection paradigm, is an adequate methodology.* The recent move in spiritual approaches is to take the reflection paradigm (or phenomenology) and simply try to extend it to cover other realities (such as transpersonal, spiritual, meta-normal, planetary consciousness, complexity thinking, etc.). This is essentially the belief that the reflection paradigm, or monological empiricism and monological phenomenology, will cover transpersonal and spiritual realities. But the subject does not reflect reality, it co-creates it.

All of those, the postmodernists agree, are shot through with the myth of the given. In other words, many approaches, wishing to get spiritual realities acknowledged by the modern world, simply take empirical methodology and try to extend it, make it bigger, push it into areas such as meditation, Gaia, transpersonal consciousness, brain scans with meditation, empirical tests of cognitive capacity with contemplation, chaos and complexity science, holograms and holographic information, the akashic field, and so on. Although they might overcome one problem—such as Newtonian-Cartesian mechanism, for example—by introducing something like "mutually interdependent networks of dynamically related processes"—*not a single one of those approaches addresses the more fundamental problem* that the postmodernists are criticizing, namely, that all of those approaches are still caught in the myth of the given and the ignoring of intersubjectivity. Indeed, those approaches give no indication that they even know what it means.*

One of the general aims of this book is to summarize an integral framework and then point out how it can help spiritual approaches fit into the modern and postmodern world; corollary to that is pointing out both the positives and negatives of various present-day approaches to spiritual realities. Nowhere is the deficiency more glaring, jarring, and obvious—and yet fairly easily remedied—than when it comes to the basic postmodern message and how its truths of contextualism, inter-subjectivity, constructivism, and aperspectivism can be incorporated into various spiritual approaches. But for the most part, it's as if the entire postmodern message simply passed these approaches by, leaving them untouched, bathed in their inadequacies, such as their sometimes explicit premodernism and their implicit modernism, with its expanded empiricism, its monological awareness, and above all, its fabric laced with the myth of the given.

For those interested, I will give an annotated list of representative

---

*If you are so afflicted, a good place to begin might be *The Marriage of Sense and Soul*, chap. 9, "Postmodernism."

examples of spiritual approaches lacking any postmodern currents. Again, this is not so much a criticism as a suggestive guide for how to incorporate postmodern into their premodern and/or modern epistemologies so as to move them toward a more integral embrace. Please see appendix III if you are interested in this annotated review of the works of: C.P. Snow, *The Two Cultures*; Margaret Wheatley, *Leadership and the New Science*; Edgar Morin, *Homeland Earth*; A. H. Almaas, *The Inner Journey Home*; Byron Katie, *Loving What Is*; Fritjof Capra, *The Web of Life*; David R. Hawkins, *Power vs. Force*: *The Hidden Determinants of Human Behavior*; William James, *The Varieties of Religious Experience*; Daniel Goleman, *The Varieties of Meditative Experience*; Francisco Varela, "Neurophenomenology," *Journal of Consciousness Studies*; Ervin Laszlo, *Science and the Akashic Field*; Deepak Chopra, *The Book of Secrets* and *How to Know God*; the film *What the Bleep Do We Know!?*; Michel de Certeau, *Heterologies: Discourse on the Other*; Michael Lerner, *Jewish Renewal*; Rupert Sheldrake, *The Rebirth of Nature*; Michael Murphy, *The Future of the Body*; and Thich Nhat Hanh, *Living Buddha, Living Christ*.

But make no mistake, because the postmodernists are brutal: those approaches, apart from their virtues, are implicitly embracing the myth of the given. This is monological phenomenology at its worst, simply because it believes itself to be so much more than it is, a lie in the face of the postmodern turn of Spirit itself in its continuing flowering.

To me personally, this is simply sad, because all of it can be salvaged with a few simple moves. But I've been watching this field for almost 30 years, and few of its authors have yet gotten the point about intersubjectivity (which basically means, they have not included the Lower-Left quadrant; or more specifically, zone #2 in the UL and zone #4 in the LL). A constructive postmodern approach—taken up as part of an integral approach (integrating premodern, modern, and postmodern)—can leave their important work and research just as it is, but plug their problematic epistemologies into an integral framework that gives them a fuller context. Failing that, the myth of the given, chaining minds to illusions, lives on in these endeavors, whose own self-image claims liberation, and yet the myth of the given creates the children of the lie.

9

The Conveyor Belt

THE LAST TOPIC I would like to discuss is what might be called the **conveyor belt**. It is, I suspect, the single greatest problem facing the world in the interior quadrants, bar none. If you think that is hyperbole, read on.

Further, fixing this problem, if there is a fix, would provide a startling new role for religion in the modern and postmodern world.

NAZIS RULE

Start with a few facts. Depending on which scales you use, somewhere between 50%–70% of the world's population is at the **ethnocentric or lower** levels of development. This means amber or lower in any of the lines. To put it in the bluntest terms possible, this means around 70% of the world's population is Nazis.

In the great developmental unfolding from egocentric to ethnocentric to worldcentric and higher, 70% of the world's population has not yet stably made it to worldcentric, postconventional levels of development. "Nazis" is simply an extreme way to state that fact. But whether those are fundamentalist Southern Baptists in Georgia, Shin Buddhists in Kyoto, al-Qaeda Muslims in Iran, or fundamentalist Marxists in China, they represent the vast majority of the world's population in terms of vertical development.

And please, no politically correct tsk-tsking here. I'm talking about some of my best friends and most of my family (certainly all of the cousins).

A second fact is that this is not something that goes away or can go away. *Everybody is born at square one and must develop through the general waves of development.* Put it this way: Every time somebody somewhere has sex, they are producing a fresh supply of Nazis.

So 70% is now ethnocentric or lower. This would be enough to rattle the average onlooker. But it gets a bit worse. Who owns the ideas and beliefs that are subscribed to by this 70%?

Basically, the world's great religions.

To word it differently, in the grand developmental waves available to humans, the archaic, magic, and mythic waves are predominantly the province of the world's great religious and mythic systems. This in itself is not a bad thing; in fact, it is a necessary and absolutely crucial function of the world's great mythologies. Every human is born at square one and begins his or her unfolding from there, moving from archaic to magic to mythic and possibly higher, and if the world's mythologies were not a repository of these early-level beliefs, every human born would have to reinvent them anew. Part of the great untold saga of the role of the world's great religions is that, in at least some ways, they are the vehicle for these necessary (and unavoidable) stages of human development.

But in today's world—unlike the great epochs in which the magico-mythic systems first developed—these up-to-amber-level beliefs pose certain problems. The first is that there are several levels of consciousness that have developed since those times, particularly modern orange and to some degree postmodern green. This introduces a **vertical component clash** in the AQAL matrix that can be extremely severe, particularly in that the orange and higher levels are postconventional and worldcentric, whereas amber and lower are, as we said, ethnocentric, conventional, and conformist (at best).

This vertical-level clash is the single greatest source of friction, in the interior quadrants, that is now present in the world's psychograph. These great tectonic plates (red, amber, orange) are slamming into each other with a ferocious impact, and the earthquakes that are resulting, and will continue to result, are killing millions of human beings around the planet.

THE PSYCHOGRAPH OF TERRORISM

In doing research for *The Many Faces of Terrorism* (forthcoming), I looked at the last fifty or so major terrorist acts around the world, from the Protestant bombing of abortion clinics in the South to Buddhist sub-way attacks in Tokyo to Sikh separatists in India to Muslim terrorist acts including 9/11.

Astonishingly, they all had the same basic psychograph: **amber beliefs with red self**. Their cognitive framework was amber, mythic-membership, conformist, traditional; and in all cases, that traditional framework was owned by one of the world's great religions, or its religious-mythic system of thought and belief. Their self, or their center of gravity, was red, egocentric, power-driven. Although they espoused amber religious beliefs, absolutistic values, and traditional-conformist morals, their center of gravity was a notch lower, at red, with all of its ferocious power drives and egocentric impulses, ready to break even sacred religious (amber) tradition if it suited their needs.

In short, their talk was amber, their walk was red.

And they all said exactly the same thing about why they did it, why they committed acts judged to be terrorist by some. Although not using these technical terms, they all maintained that *the modern* (**orange**) world will not make room for my sacred (**amber**) beliefs, and therefore I am going to blow up that world every chance I get, in God's name and with His blessings. Those whom I kill have, in every way, brought this on themselves, which is why my acts are not murder, not wrong, and not punishable. In fact, if I am killed in this sacred cause, I will go to heaven. (In some cases, particularly Muslim and Sikh, suicide is viewed as a career promotion.)

The Orange Pressure-Cooker Lid

The way it is now, people are born and begin growing through the great waves of development, archaic to magic (red) to mythic (amber) to ratio-nal (orange) to pluralistic (green) to integral (indigo) and beyond. They do so, around the world, in cultures whose LL-quadrant generally sup-ports some sort of religious belief system. Somewhere in their develop-ment, around amber to orange, as they could be making a shift from a mythic/ethnocentric spirit to worldcentric/rational spirit, they hit a "steel ceiling." Amber myth is owned by premodern religion, and orange reason is owned by science and the modern world. And they can find no way to move from their amber beliefs to orange beliefs when it comes to their religious faith.

Their spiritual line of intelligence is frozen at amber, frozen at the fundamentalist mythic-membership level, and frozen there by an orange world that can find no orange expressions of spiritual intelligence.

This "pressure cooker" lid exists around the world today, wherever ethnocentric fundamentalist beliefs run into worldcentric reason and postconventional morals. This massive **orange pressure-cooker lid clamping down on amber** is perhaps the single greatest problem facing the world today in the interior quadrants.

THE BRUTAL CHOICE FACED BY COLLEGE STUDENTS AROUND THE WORLD

Here is a different aspect of the same problem: a recent poll conducted by UCLA showed that, in America, 79% of college juniors say spirituality is important or very important in their lives, and 3 out of 4 of them pray(!). Yet they cannot discuss their faith with their professors, who are mostly orange to green, and who ridicule it; yet they are no longer really comfortable with the mythic and ethnocentric version of their amber beliefs and the fundamentalist version of religion held by many of their friends. A typical Christian student, for example, is embarrassed to talk about his religion with his professors, and even more embarrassed by his Christian friends.

(Psychographically, this is the same problem faced by the terrorists: amber beliefs find no room in an orange world.)

College students are therefore faced with a brutal choice: continue to believe in the amber-stage of spiritual development, OR renounce their faith.

That is exactly their horrifying option—live with amber and embrace Christ, or move to orange and renounce Christ—and it is virtually the only option given to these college students. * In the development of their spiritual intelligence, they are frozen at an amber stage (e.g., Fowler's stage 3), and have no avenues where they can explore *the orange or higher levels in the development of spiritual intelligence* (particularly the synthetic-conventional level, or stage 4, and the individuative-reflective

---

*If they do choose the former, they often must live in "fundamentalist fraternity" houses, whose occupants remain at the amber/ethnocentric stage of "anybody who doesn't believe in Jesus is damned in hell forever," which is not exactly conducive to the finest of liberal-worldcentric educations. On the other hand, liberal education itself, at least in its present form, represses spiritual intelligence beyond amber, so this is indeed a brutal choice.

level, or stage 5, both of which can start to emerge at this time if nothing represses them, which a typical college education does). They are in effect infantilized in their approach to Spirit.

Their other option is to renounce their faith and move into the orange and higher levels of development devoid of spiritual orientation. Since both of those choices are horrid, most college students, as the study showed, simply pray in the closet.

Terrorists make another choice.

THE LEVEL/LINE FALLACY

Both of those problems have the same solution, if differently implemented: *make available and better known the orange (and higher) levels of the development of spiritual intelligence.*

The Western intellectual tradition, beginning around the Enlightenment, actively *repressed* any higher levels of its own spiritual intelligence. Historically, with the rise of modernity, the mythic God was thoroughly abandoned—the entire "Death of God" movement meant **the death of the mythic God**, a mythic conception for which rational modernity could find little evidence.

And here they particularly made a crippling error: in correctly spotting the immaturity of the notion of a mythic God—or the *mythic level* of the spiritual line—they threw out not just the mythic *level* of spiritual intelligence *but the entire line* of spiritual intelligence. So upset were they with the mythic level, they tossed the baby of the spiritual line with the bathwater of its mythic level of development. They jettisoned the amber God, and instead of finding orange God, and then green God, and turquoise God, and indigo God, they ditched God altogether, they began the repression of the sublime, *the repression of their own higher levels of spiritual intelligence.* The intellectual West has fundamentally never recovered from this cultural disaster.

The Western intellectual tradition—and that now happens to mean the modern (orange) world in general—thus came crashing into the modern age bereft of any higher, post-mythic forms of spiritual intelligence. Each level of consciousness has a version of science, art, spirituality, and morals, among other lines. These are simply four different multiple intelligences: **cognitive, aesthetic, spiritual,** and **moral.** * There

*These are self-consciously differentiated at orange, but as major lines, they are present at virtually all stages of development. Further, these are not quadrants, but what I call **judgments**, and each judgment is an intelligence or line.

is, for example, a red science and red spirituality, an amber science and amber spirituality, an orange science and orange spirituality, and so on. But when modernity confused the mythic level of spiritual intelligence with spiritual intelligence itself, and therefore ridiculed anything that looked spiritual or religious, it created what can only be called a "ludicrous layer cake": *all of science* was identified with the orange level (rationality), and *all of spirituality* was identified with the amber level (mythology). Instead of mythic science and religion, and rational science and religion, there was now only rational science and mythic religion. The former was rational, modern, and all good; the latter was prerational, premodern, and all bad, or at least all ridiculous.

In that catastrophic confusion, we can see an instance of what might be called **the Level/Line Fallacy** (LLF): *the confusing of a level in a line with the line itself.*

Once that confusion occurs, then generally one of two things happen. If the level is despised, the entire line is despised, and thus that multiple intelligence is frozen at the despised level, and any higher development in that line is effectively prevented. This generally results in the repression of that intelligence.

Alternatively, if the level is loved, development in that line is also frozen at that level, but in this case caught not in repression but fixation, with consciousness not attempting to push the despised level away, but compulsively pursuing it and obsessively thinking of it.

In both cases, *the affected multiple intelligence is frozen at the level that the level/line confusion occurs.* In the case of **repression**, the entire line is then denied and suppressed, resulting in its atrophy and dysfunctional manifestations. If this occurs in the spiritual line of development, then in many cases, the repressed spiritual impulses are projected onto others, and then, like the anti-gay-porn crusader who is attacking his own shadow, this person becomes an obsessed, hyper-rational crusader fighting any and all spiritual endeavors, seeing them as complete irrational hogwash (with a pre/post fallacy not far behind). We then have science declaring war on religion.

In the case of **fixation**, the particular level is so glorified that, while development again freezes at the level where the confusion occurs, instead of the multiple intelligence being denied, it is obsessively and ferociously defended against all comers. But the only thing defended is that particular level in the line, which is then identified with the entire line and confused as the only correct type of the particular intelligence allowed. Ironically, in these individuals, as their own higher levels of that multiple intelligence attempt to emerge, they will end up repressing them, repressing their own emergent potentials in that line because they are *fixated to a particular level* in that line. If the line is the spiritual line, then these individuals end up fixated at a lower level of spiritual intelligence (usually mythic), and ironically can project their own higher, emerging spiritual impulses onto others, seeing these higher spiritual impulses as anti-spiritual. They then often end up denying higher levels of both science and religion, and lash out blindly at what amounts to their own higher potentials. We then have mythic religion declaring war on science (and the liberal world in general).

In the modern West, once this Level/Line Fallacy had occurred, intellectuals at leading-edge orange began screening religion and spirituality out of their own allowed awareness. The orange level itself was now crippled in its spiritual line. In other words, *the dominant mode of discourse of the leading-edge social holon was now crippled orange*. And in one fell swoop, this explains an enormous number of historical items.

The Dignity and Disaster of Modernity

It has long been known that modernity involved *the differentiation of the value spheres* (Max Weber). This particularly meant that 3 of the major value spheres—art, morals, and science—were no longer fused, as they had been in the mythic Middle Ages, but were now differentiated and allowed to pursue their own truths. No longer would the truths of science be forced to conform to mythic dogma (e.g., no longer would Galileo be prevented from looking through his telescope). This very positive achievement—which is one of the many extraordinary gains of the Western liberal Enlightenment—is often called **the dignity of modernity.**

And it has long been known that this *differentiation* (which was good) went too far into *dissociation* (which was bad), so that the dignity of modernity became **the disaster of modernity.** Among other things, when the 3 value spheres did not just separate but flew apart, this allowed the hyper-growth of technical-scientific rationality at the expense of the other spheres, and this resulted in what is called the **colonization of the lifeworld** by this technical rationality. You can find variations on that theme in most of the sophisticated critiques of modernity *by kosher Western intellectuals themselves*, from Hegel to Heidegger to Horkheimer to Habermas.

But what has never been made completely clear is why the dissociation actually occurred in the first place. The standard explanations just never seemed to account for all the facts. It now appears very likely that, in addition to the other factors involved and elucidated by these theorists, there was *at the heart of this collapse a profound Level/Line Fallacy.* Once spirituality in toto was thrown overboard, the dominant mode of discourse not only outlawed pre-rational or mythic spirituality, it outlawed rational and post-rational spirituality as well. And precisely because the spiritual line answers the question *"What is it that is of ultimate concern?,"* then this line—and the specific type of intelligence meant to address that question put to us by life—was crippled in the modern West.

In its place, the moral line and the aesthetic line were forced to take up the slack. Modern liberal intellectuals no longer had religion, they only had art and morals.

In other words, when the great modern differentiation of the mythic structure occurred, what *should* have emerged, at the least, were 4 differentiated value spheres, not just 3. As we just saw, in the mythic structure, art, morals, science, and spirituality are as yet undifferentiated; they are functioning at the amber level, but not yet separated into their respective spheres with their own distinct logics (or grammars) and validity claims. But what emerged in modernity, as differentiated, was only "the Big 3"—art and morals and science. Spirituality, due to an LLF, was frozen at the mythic level, and then that mythic level of spirituality was confused with spirituality altogether.

A Brief History of Modernity's LLF

And that happened for one reason in particular: So horrifying was the mythic level of God—and so extensive were the genuine terrors the Church had inflicted on people in the name of that mythic God—that the Enlightenment threw religion over entirely. "Remember the cruelties!," as Voltaire exhorted the Enlightenment, referring to the millions that the Church had tortured and killed, and remember they did. The mythic God was taken to be God altogether. The mythic God was identified with the horrors of the Inquisition and the liquidation of millions (all true), and in a leading-edge cultural convulsion and revulsion—a cultural trauma writ large—religious anything was angrily suppressed. Spiritual intelligence was frozen at amber, a massive Level/Line Fallacy set in place, out went that bathwater, and with it, the baby of ultimate concern.

Freezing the spiritual line at amber mythic-membership is exactly what prevented the spiritual line from moving into the modern liberal Enlightenment, with the other major lines, and being developed at an orange level, so that there would indeed be orange science, orange aesthetics, orange morals, and orange spirituality. Instead, the Big 3 emerged and differentiated, not the Big 4. Spirituality was infantilized, ridiculed, denied, repressed, and kept out of modernity altogether.

Thus, once the Big 3 emerged and differentiated, *the damage had already been done.* The differentiated Big 3 *already* carried within it an inherent instability that virtually guaranteed they would fracture and dissociate. Western intellectual critics couldn't figure out exactly why the Big 3 didn't just differentiate and separate but flew apart and dissociated, resulting in the hyper-growth of rational science at the expense of art and morals. But by the time Western intellectuals began analyzing the problem, the damage had secretly been done. The damage occurred *before the Big 3 showed up.*

This is why, if you start analyzing the Big 3 and try to figure out why the dissociation occurred, you'll never really figure it out (which is why none of the intellectual critics—from Heidegger to Habermas—has spotted the prior problem. Moreover, all of those critics, from Horkheimer and Adorno forward, missed this by a mile because, as moderns, they were already unconsciously suffering this LLF themselves. They honestly believed that spirituality was nothing but a bunch of myths).

With this fundamental LLF in place, what might be called **the grand displacement** began to occur. Because the line of ultimate concern was repressed at amber, and because this is nevertheless a multiple intelligence still active, that inner judgment of ultimate concern *was displaced from religion to science.* In the modern world, it was now science that was implicitly felt to give answers to ultimate questions, and science to which ultimate faith and a pledge of allegiance should occur. Ultimate realities were now felt to be items like mass and energy: mass and energy could never be created nor destroyed, they were eternal, they were ultimately real, they were omnipresent, et cetera. "Mass" and "energy"—ha!—nothing but two of the names of God, but now a God reduced only to Spirit or an absolute in 3rd-person, and even then, hidden and displaced so as to not be contaminated by that nasty religious stuff.

Thus, ultimate concern was displaced to science, a concern that its methods were simply not capable of handling. And *science itself* was always completely honest about its limitations: science *cannot* say whether God exists or does not exist; whether there is an Absolute or not; why we are here, what our ultimate nature is, and so on. Of course science can find no evidence for the Absolute; nor can it find evidence disproving an Absolute. When science is honest, it is thoroughly agnostic and thoroughly quiet on those ultimate questions.

But the human heart is not. And spiritual intelligence, meant to answer or at least address those issues, is not so easily quieted, either. Men and women need an Ultimate because in truth they intuit an Ultimate, and simple honesty requests acknowledging the yearning in your own heart. Yet if the mythic God is dead, and spiritual intelligence frozen at its childhood stage, the only thing left that appears to give answers to those questions of ultimate concern is science. There is a well-known term for what science becomes when it is absolutized: *scientism*. And the liberal Enlightenment, for all its enormous good and all its extraordinary intelligence in other lines, began with science and ended with scientism, and that because of the prior LLF that delivered to the Enlightenment a set of tools bereft of spiritual intelligence.*

When science was absolutized, just there was the hidden instability that led to the dissociation of the value spheres, and then to the colonization of the lifeworld by a scientific rationality that was now carrying the burden of spiritual or ultimate concern—a burden it carried but could never answer or satisfy. When technical rationality colonized the lifeworld, it actually killed (colonized) any spirituality left in the lifeworld, while inherently failing miserably to satisfy the hidden spiritual impulses that were now unconsciously displaced onto it.

This is a prescription for cultural catastrophe. As the Big 3, not the Big 4, emerged from the mythic structure and differentiated into the dignity of modernity, the hidden damage had already occurred. The dignity of modernity could never stabilize *without an orange spiritual intelligence to go alongside of orange cognitive, orange aesthetic, and orange moral intelligence.*

In other words, the fabled dignity of modernity was already sick, sick

---

*Some of the intellectuals of the Enlightenment began as believers in a rational or orange spirituality—Deism being the most famous—but the cultural LLF was so extensive, and scientism already becoming so established, that within a generation the vast majority of intellectuals took it as article of faith (!) that religion in toto was out, and science was in, when it came to matters of ultimate concern—i.e., **scientism** became the spiritual faith of the modern Enlightenment.

before the recognized disaster of modernity occurred, and sick in ways that neither secular humanists nor religious defenders could spot or overcome, the former because they had repressed the spiritual line altogether and wouldn't allow modern orange spirituality to emerge; the latter because they had also frozen the spiritual line at mythic, and, in their own fixated ways, wouldn't allow modern orange spirituality to emerge, either. With the Reformation and Counter-Reformation, the Church dug in its heels, and so did science.

When this massive cultural LLF occurred, and both camps identified spirituality solely with mythic (and thus confused the mythic level of the spiritual line with the spiritual line itself), then that ludicrous layer cake was fully baked: orange, modern, rational, progressive science versus amber, premodern, prerational, reactionary, mythic religion—with science on top, religion on the bottom.

And thus modernity emerged, managed to differentiate the Big 3, congratulated itself on its great dignity (which was partially true), but didn't realize that *within its own self-definition*, there was a damaged psychograph, a structure that was now inherently fated to tilt into dissociation and result in the colonization and domination of the other value spheres by scientific materialism, a worldview now taken on absolute faith by its adherents, and a worldview to which all intellectuals now pledged their allegiance daily.

Almost as soon as that dissociation occurred, there were intellectuals who jumped all over it, attempting to analyze why something was profoundly wrong. But they couldn't spot the problem because they *were* the problem. The damage, we saw, had already occurred, and as they searched through the 3 values spheres of art, morals, and science, they did not and could not notice that part of the problem was the simple absence of a multiple intelligence that should have emerged and differentiated as well. Not being able to spot what wasn't there, they misdiagnosed the fundamental dysfunction of modernity from the beginning. But they did spot the phenomenology of what happened: the Big 3 emerged and differentiated, then dissociated, then art and morals collapsed under the weight of rational science, a science that colonized the other value spheres, and a science that, for some strange reason, had now become the religion of the Enlightenment intellectuals.

Art and morals were no match for this scientism. Nothing less than God could stand up to a steam engine, but *Deus* had already *abscondus*: God had cut and run, or more accurately, was catastrophically repressed. The dominant mode of discourse proclaimed orange spirituality to be taboo, because spirituality per se was now taboo.* With this damage in place, and crippled orange discourse parading for normatively healthy orange, the differentiation of the Big 3 proceeded (c. 1600–1800), and this was mistaken by all as a great dignity, whereas it was a great dignity, for sure, but a great dignity that was already sick, a great dignity harboring the seeds of its own dissociation. And as that dissociation began (c. 1800–1900), Western leading intellectuals were on the scene, wailing and bemoaning the horrible, tragic, and catastrophic fate that had befallen an entire culture.

And about that, they were surely right.

THE DE-REPRESSION OF SPIRITUAL INTELLIGENCE

The cure for this—for the "steel ceiling," for the "pressure-cooker lid" around the world, boiling 70% of the world's population, with explo-

---

*Here we see the real "crime of the Enlightenment," and it had little to do with the standard analyses and critiques offered by (mostly green) liberal intellectuals. It had nothing to do with the despised Newtonian-Cartesian paradigm, which was actually a stunning leap forward in another line of intelligence. (The hatred of Newtonian-Cartesian leap is one of the surest signs of boomeritis; see *Boomeritis* for an in-depth analysis of why.) Neither the Newtonian-Cartesian "paradigm," nor analytic thought, nor patriarchy, nor any of the standard scapegoats had anything to do with the fundamental cause of the eventual dissociation. Those are just green's favorite whipping boys.

Factors in all the quadrants certainly had a hand. Industrialization (LR) can contribute to dissociation, but only if there is no spiritual wisdom at the same level to balance it (which there wasn't). Discoveries about the basic building blocks of the material world (UR) can certainly contribute to dissociation, but only if that quadrant is absolutized (which is exactly what scientism does). Cultural disgust with monarchy, aristocracy, and mythic-membership modes of thought (LL) can contribute to a hyper-idealization of rationality and a repugnance of all things mythic, but that becomes a dissociation of art and morals and science only if there is something in the system that skews science toward scientism (which, with the repression of spiritual intelligence and the grand displacement, there was). All of those factors certainly contributed, but without a prior LLF, they would never have gotten the traction they did, ultimately skewing the system toward a rabid scientism that ate the other spheres alive, leaving in their place a desolation that was pandemic, yet mightily enforced by dominant modes of serious discourse. Among many other things, the "sciences of man," about which Foucault had so much to say, began their career of pronouncing disagreements with them to be illnesses, requiring medical intervention. God was now a disease for which the fledgling science of psychiatry had the cure.

sions of terrorism here and there being only the most obvious symptoms—the cure for this has two aspects, if I may speak for the moment in simple, orienting generalizations.

The LLF needs to be unfrozen on both the repression and fixation sides of the street. On the repressing side, **orange rationality** needs to relax its hatred of amber spirituality and begin to appreciate, or at least acknowledge, spirituality at its own orange level. This is nothing less than the de-repression of its own spiritual intelligence. And let me point out, strongly, that both *atheism* and *agnosticism*, if arrived at via formal operational cognition, are forms of orange spiritual intelligence. Spiritual intelligence is simply the line of intelligence dealing with ultimate concerns and things taken to be absolute; and if a person's considered conclusion is that, for example, you cannot decide whether there is an ultimate reality or not (agnosticism), then that is orange spiritual intelligence. But what orange rationality usually does is one of two things: it claims that science *proves* there is no ultimate reality—which it categorically does not—or imputes absolute reality to finite things like matter and energy, an imputation that is nothing but an implicit spiritual judgment dressed up as science—put bluntly, is nothing but hypocrisy. Both of those are due primarily to the repression of healthy spiritual intelligence, which does not necessarily embrace the existence of an absolute reality, but does deal with its existence openly and honestly, even if it says "I don't know" or "I believe not."

On the fixation side, **amber spirituality** needs to relax its fixation to ethnocentric myth and open itself to higher levels of its own spiritual intelligence—starting with Spirit's expressions in worldcentric reason and postconventional love. We will return to the requirements for this movement later.

All of the above elements—dealing with both repression and fixation—are encapsulated in the notion of the conveyor belt. So let's look more closely at some of its contours.

A Natural Resource as Precious as Oil and Gas

In chapter 4, in discussing the fact that states of consciousness (including spiritual and religious experiences) are interpreted according to the stage one is at, we gave as a simple example the fact that there is a magenta Christ, a red Christ, an amber Christ, an orange Christ, a green Christ, a turquoise Christ, an indigo Christ, and so on.

That's a crucially important point, because, in the modern and post-modern world, every major religion now has at least some advocates of not just amber but orange and green versions of their religious message. But precisely because of that extremely powerful cultural LLF, which exists to this day and which freezes religion at the mythic level, those higher levels are not being emphasized or even officially allowed.

But whether those higher levels are utilized or not, the fact remains that there are first-, second-, and third-tier interpretations of Christ consciousness. And that is an example of the incredibly important fact that religion alone, of all of humanity's endeavors, can serve as a great **conveyor belt** for humanity and its stages of growth. And religion *alone* can do this, for several reasons.

The first is that the world's religions are the repository of the great myths. The early stages of development are archaic and magic and mythic in flavor. And these great myths, laid down 3000 years ago, *could never be created today*, not because humanity has no imagination, but because everybody has a video camera. Just let Moses try to claim he parted the Red Sea today and see how far he gets.

I say that somewhat facetiously, but I am deeply serious. Every infant today begins moving from archaic instincts to magic beliefs to mythic worldviews, and will do so one way or another. Look at Piaget's work and you will see the 5-year-old child today producing all of the major contours of the world's great myths. The mythic-stages of the religious systems speak deeply to these stages of development, and, to repeat, THOSE STAGES ARE NOT GOING AWAY. Everybody is born at square one.

And since humanity today, armed with video cameras, will never get a new supply of fresh, believable myths—of Moses parting the Red Sea, or Jesus born from a biological virgin, or Lao Tzu being 900 years old when he was born, or the Earth resting on a serpent resting on an elephant resting on a turtle, and so on—the world's great mythic-religious systems are a precious human resource, the only ones speaking to those unavoidable stages of human growth. They got their start with the archaic and magic and mythic stages of humanity itself, and hence they are a repository of a precious interior human resource much scarcer than oil and gas—and the world's great religious systems are there to handle those stages in the interior. This is exactly why that 70% is owned by the world's religions.

But the world's great religions are not only that. Precisely because they got their start with the magenta and red and amber stages of humanity itself, they control the *legitimacy* conferred on those beliefs. Because of that, they are the *only* sources of authority that can sanction the orange and higher stages of spiritual intelligence *in their own traditions*. They are the only systems in the world today that can act as a great conveyor belt, helping people move from red to amber to orange to green to turquoise and higher, because they alone can pronounce all of those stages kosher, legitimate, sacred, acceptable—and give them imprimatur within their own lineages.

That is perhaps the most important role for religion in the modern and postmodern world, acting as a sacred conveyor belt for humanity. In today's world, you do not begin, say, medical school by first studying how to apply leeches to your patients, and then how to do phrenology, and then moving to antibiotics and modern techniques of microsurgery. But in divinity school, you do. You start by seriously learning how to apply magic and mythic versions of your religion—to grown men and women!—and then, if you are in anything resembling a progressive school, you will move to deeper and higher meanings, which are orange and green and turquoise and indigo, by whatever names. Already Clement and Origen and Maimonides were doing this with their allegorical method. The religious myths simply *are not empirically real*, and they knew it, and so while honoring the myths, one must move from myth to reason to trans-reason in order to plumb the depths of spiritual realities. That is, one must allow the line of spiritual intelligence to continue its growth from amber into higher levels, and, conversely, forcing the myths to be real is the surest way to remain frozen at that level and slip into a pernicious Level/Line Fallacy. Honoring, cherishing, and celebrating the past myths, definitely; elevating them to absolute reality, definitely not.

But in order for the higher levels in the spiritual line to be recognized and allowed, the spiritual line itself needs to be recognized and honored. Both religion and science are perpetuating this cultural LLF and this epidemic fixation at the mythic level of spiritual development. And both of them need to grow up.

The de-repression of the sublime, **the de-repression of the developmental line of spiritual intelligence,** requires many things, but one of them, which we have been emphasizing, is to possess an orienting Framework that allows and encourages a more spacious view of the role of both science and spirituality in the modern and postmodern world. Trying, as do proponents of intelligent design, to have science prove mythic-level poetry is preposterous. And trying to have science move into scientism and proclaim, not that science can neither prove nor disprove an Ultimate, but that it can itself answer all important ques-tions, is simply pathological orange. An Integral Framework at least attempts to begin to give to Caesar what is Caesar's, to Einstein what is Einstein's, to Picasso what is Picasso's, to Kant what is Kant's, and to Christ what is Christ's.

STAGES OF DEVELOPMENT ARE STATIONS IN LIFE

Human beings, starting at square one, will develop however far they develop, and they have the right to stop wherever they stop. Some indi-viduals will stop at red, some at amber; some will move to orange or higher. Some individuals will develop to a stage, stop for a while, then continue growth; others will stop growing around adolescence and never really grow again. But that is their right; people have the right to stop at whatever stage they stop at.

I try to emphasize this by saying that every **stage** is also a **station** in life. Some people will spend their entire adult lives at red or amber, and *that is their right*. Others will move on. But religion alone, of all endeav-ors, can have a **catechism of the stations in life**: here is a red version of Christ, here is an amber version of Christ, here is an orange version of Christ, here is an indigo version of Christ, and so on.

(American Buddhists often feel that they are above all this because of their non-conceptual orientation. If so, please read chapter 5 again. There is an amber *Lankavatara Sutra*, an orange *Lankavatara Sutra*, a green *Lankavatara Sutra*, a turquoise *Lankavatara Sutra*, an indigo *Lankavatara Sutra*, and so on. Most American Buddhists see only the green *Lankavatara Sutra*. And that is their right, as long as they allow other interpretations, such as turquoise and indigo, the same freedom. The point, then, is very simple: there is a spectrum of spiritual interpreta-tions, and only religion can step into that conveyor-belt function.)

Some people will stop at red, and a magical-red religion will always speak to them, and society most definitely needs some version of red religion. Some people will stop at amber, and a mythic-amber religion will always speak to them, and society most definitely needs some ver-sion of amber religion. Some will stop at orange, and a religion of orange-reason and universal good will is a spirituality that will speak to them, and society deeply needs access to some version of orange religion. Some will stop at green, and some at teal, and some at turquoise. . . .

And religion alone can span that spectrum, acting as a great conveyor belt across the many stages—and stations—of life.

This is an extraordinary role for any institution to play, and, to repeat, spirituality *alone* can do so, because it is the only institution allowed to sanction stages that humanity in its infancy and childhood passed through, now encoded in its mythic-level versions of its spiritual message. This is categorically not the case with medicine, law, physics, biochemistry, architecture, etc., who jettison their childhood versions and adopt only the latest of today's findings. As I said, we do not see physicians today recommending leeches, nor astronomers teaching astrology. But we do find preachers doing so. And that is fine—teaching magic and myth—*as long as the great religions also make available—as kosher—the orange and higher levels and stages of their spirituality*, stages that have kept pace with Spirit's own unfolding into the modern and postmodern and integral ages....

And most particularly, that would mean that religion, and religion alone, can begin to step in and undo the steel ceiling, the pressure-cooker lid, now encircling the earth and choking its interiors to death. Until then, terrorists will keep trying to blow up that lid, and college students will pray in the closet trying to avoid it.

HIGHER STAGES, BUT ALSO HIGHER STATES

The second major role for religion in the modern and postmodern world? Not only make orange and higher **stages** available, but also make contemplative **states** a core of their training.

The nice thing about this role is that states are available at every stage—and therefore every station—in life. Authentic spirituality is available not just at the higher stages of development (or the transpersonal, third-tier stages—which is meaning #1 of the 4 major meanings of spirituality), but aspects or dimensions of spirituality are available as authentic religious experiences (or states) at any of those stages or stations (which is meaning #3). So there is literally something of deep profundity to offer individuals *at every stage or station in life*. Of course, the interpretive depth and inclusive embrace becomes greater at higher stages, but one can take up meditation, contemplation, Pentecostal experiencing, or centering prayer whether one is at red or amber or orange or green, etc., and be plunged into authentic gross, subtle, causal, and nondual religious states. So, if utilized, this truly gives the great religions a broad menu of humanity's great potentials. And no matter what *stage* a practitioner is at, authentic spiritual and contemplative *states* can be offered to a practitioner right at the start. . . .

(Can somebody who takes up meditation at, say, amber, achieve anything like Enlightenment? The answer appears to be yes and no: enlightened states, yes; enlightened stages, yes. Or what we are calling horizontal Enlightenment, yes; vertical Enlightenment, no. But for this issue, please see appendix II.)

Right now, spiritual state-experiences are often disallowed by the dominant mode of discourse of many orthodox religions, and thus are forced elsewhere. For teenagers, this is often the rave scene and drugs. (But frankly, I think the rave scene is healthier than the religions that repress spiritual altered states and force kids to flee in droves to that scene in the first place.)

When spiritual states do surface in religions, they are often pushed into evangelical revivals and Pentecostal ecstatic gatherings, which are usually subtle-state experiences and altered states that are, in fact, of an occasionally deep nature—reaching into Underhill's state of illumination and grace—but they are usually kept segmented into red and sometimes barely amber stages of development. This doesn't get rid of terrorists, but creates them.

The sooner spiritual traditions begin offering both higher stages and higher states, the sooner religion can step into its new role in the modern and postmodern world: the role of the great conveyor belt of humanity at large.

THE EFFECTS OF STATES ON STAGES

There is another reason that religions, in order to act as the great conveyor belt of humanity, should incorporate meditative, contemplative, and nonordinary states (gross, subtle, causal, nondual) into their curricula, and that is not just to stop forcing kids into raves and grown adults into tent revivals, but for the profoundly beneficial effect that states have on stages. As we saw: all things considered equal, *the more quickly you develop through the stages.*

Under no circumstances that we are aware of can you skip stages in any line—*stages cannot be skipped*—but considerable research has demonstrated that the more you experience meditative or contemplative states of consciousness, the faster you develop through the stages of consciousness. No other single practice or technique—not therapy, not breathwork, not transformative workshops, not role-taking, not *hatha yoga*—has been empirically demonstrated to do this. Meditation alone has done so. For example, whereas around 2% of the adult population is at second tier, after four years of meditation, that 2% goes to 38% in the meditation group. This is truly staggering research.

As we saw, the reason meditation does so is simple enough. When you meditate, you are in effect witnessing the mind, thus turning subject into object—which is exactly the core mechanism of development ("the subject of one stage becomes the object of the subject of the next").*

So no matter what general stage you are at when you begin (red, amber, orange, green, etc.), you can directly experience meditative or contemplative or ecstatic or nonordinary states (gross, subtle, causal, nondual), and not only do those states carry profound experiences themselves, they will accelerate your growth and development through the stages.

Combining all of these practices into a spiritual cross-training is **Integral Life Practice**, which we will discuss in the next chapter.

Summary and Conclusion

Here is the overall picture I wanted to convey in this chapter:

Everybody is born at square one. There will always be people at red, and that is fine. There will always be people at amber, and that is fine. There will always be people at orange, and that is fine (and so on). An enlightened society would always make room for that by recognizing that **stages in development** are also **stations in life**. And somebody can stop at any of those stations (of Spirit's own unfolding) and they deserve honor and respect at whatever station they are at.

But the earlier stations—archaic to magic to mythic—involve stages that, nonetheless, are ones that humanity's leading edge passed through in its infancy, childhood, and adolescence. But because religion alone is the repository of the myths created during those times, religion alone is

---

* I have dealt with this at length in *The Eye of Spirit*, so if you are interested, please follow up with that reference. It gives the research on this and discusses it from an integral perspective. The only caveat is that this discussion does not take the W-C Lattice into account, so the exact relation of states and stages is not fully articulated; but you can read between those lines and supply that. The rest of the discussion is still quite germane.

the institution in today's world that gives *legitimacy* to those earlier stages and stations for men and women. Religion alone gives legitimacy to the myths. And religion alone owns that 70% of the world's population at those stages.

All of which is good and beautiful. But precisely because of its ownership of the pre-rational heritage of humanity (and the pre-rational corpus of the great myths), religion alone can help its followers move from the pre-rational, mythic-membership, ethnocentric, absolutistic version of its message to the rational-perspectival, worldcentric, postconventional versions of its own message. *This jump from ethnocentric amber to worldcentric orange is the great leap that religions alone can help humanity make.*

The great religions alone can thus be the conveyor belt that gives *legitimacy* (in both the sociological and religious sense) to the orange (and higher) versions of their essential story and their essential spirituality. This is a difficult jump, as everything from terrorists to closeted college students attests.

The prime contributor to this difficulty is a massive Level/Line Fallacy, which both modern science *and* religion—secular humanists *and* religious advocates—have embraced with stunning rigor, confusing the mythic level of the spiritual line with the entire spiritual line, and then freezing spiritual intelligence at that childhood stage. Both religion and science have fought eagerly to preserve this absolutely ludicrous layer cake, which creates—to abruptly switch metaphors—a pressure-cooker lid around the world, with rational science and the modern world owning everything orange, and religion stuck with all things amber—premodern, prerational, and mythic.

Small wonder that every militant ("terrorist") said exactly the same thing: the modern (orange) world makes no room for my (mythic amber) religious beliefs, and therefore I will blow up the modern world in the name of my God.

This categorically will not stop until the particular religion itself makes room in its own catechism for the orange, worldcentric, modern interpretations of its religious message, and sanctions as kosher those orange interpretations (e.g., Vatican II).

The number of brilliant religious and spiritual writers who have emphasized the orange worldcentric interpretations of, say, Christianity, are enormous. Particularly well known (and recommended) are the works of Bishop John Shelby Spong (e.g., *Rescuing the Bible from Fundamentalism; Why Christianity Must Change or Die; A New Christian-*

ity for a New World: Why Traditional Faith is Dying and How a New Faith Is Being Born); Marcus J. Borg (e.g., The Heart of Christianity); Stephen Carter (e.g., The Culture of Disbelief); F. Forrester Church (God and Other Famous Liberals).

And there is a swelling tide of green/postmodern interpretations of Christianity. A few are John R. Franke and Stanley J. Grenz, Beyond Foundationalism: Shaping Theology in a Postmodern Context; John Milbank, Theology and Social Theory: Beyond Secular Reason; Kevin J. Vanhoozer (ed.), The Cambridge Companion to Postmodern Theology; Brian McLaren, A Generous Orthodoxy; The Bible and Culture Collective, The Postmodern Bible. One would expect many of these adherents to be Gen X and Y, as the green wave continues its swell. What Is Enlightenment? magazine (March–May 2006) reports: "Proving that pomos are gaining tremendous buying power and increasing cultural influence, a study on religious books by Publishers Weekly found that the average age of buyers was a youthful thirty-eight and that the largest group of buyers fell between the ages of twenty-five and thirty-four."

And, of course, one of the real pioneers in moving Christianity into the modern and postmodern world: any of the works of Hans Küng. The works of Raimon Panikkar are also provocative in many profound ways.

But, to return to religions in general, helping individual practitioners to particularly negotiate the amber-to-orange horizon is of primary urgency. This difficulty is best analyzed using quadrants:

In the UL, psychologically, an individual needs to move from ethnocentric beliefs to worldcentric beliefs. This is a difficult transformation from a role-based identity to a person-based identity. This allows the individual to adopt a postconventional, worldcentric moral stance and not just an ethnocentric, us-versus-them mentality. For an individual with a Christian-faith background, the leap comes in realizing that Jesus Christ can be my personal savior, but others may find a different path that also leads to salvation—that the Holy Spirit speaks to men and women in different ways, in different tongues, in different lands, but is fully present nonetheless.

Crucially, in the LL, the individual needs to feel that his or her religion supports a truly universal or catholic Jesus, and not merely an ethnocentric creed. In some cases, this is a hotly contested issue, with, for example, Vatican II opening the door and the last two Popes trying to close it. The dominant mode of discourse of Vatican II allowed healthy orange (worldcentric) Christianity; the last two Popes, for all their embrace of mystical states, and all their outward shows of liberal piety, have toed the line on a dominant mode of discourse that is oppressive amber—an amber that tragically represses their own higher, emergent stages of spiritual intelligence.

How this will be institutionalized (in the LR) will help determine the behavior (UR) that is allowed by a person of faith in the modern and postmodern world. What is particularly required is an institution that embodies the stations of life in its own concrete social (and cultural) system. Will there be a conveyor belt that individuals can safely ride from pre-rational to rational to trans-rational floors, or will religion remain merely the repository of humanity's childhood?

If religion chooses the latter, then all around it, the other disciplines (law, medicine, science, education) will continue to move into the things that adults do, and religion will remain the things that children (and adult children) do—like blow up things. But if religion lives up to its promise as being that endeavor in humanity that allows Spirit to speak through it, and Spirit is indeed evolving in its own manifestation, then religion becomes a conveyor belt for humanity, carrying it from the childhood productions of Spirit to the adolescent productions of Spirit to the adult productions of Spirit . . . and beyond that into the great tomorrow of Spirit's continuing display.

This, surely, is the great role for religion in the modern and postmodern world.

10

Integral Life Practice

AQAL IS A THEORETICAL APPROACH to reality, which we might symbolize as **AQAL-IT**, for AQAL Integral Theoria. But what about the practical approach, the *actual practice* of an integral approach? What about an **AQAL-IP**, for "AQAL Integral Praxis"? Or, we might say, what about an **Integral Life Practice** (ILP), where I could actually exercise, in my life, all the aspects of an Integral view, since those are, in fact, aspects or dimensions of my own being-in-the-world? How could I practice a full me?

A BRIEF HISTORY OF ILP

A modular Integral Life Practice was first proposed in *One Taste*, based on the AQAL framework introduced in *Sex, Ecology, Spirituality* (1995), and then fleshed out with the first Integral Life Practice workshops offered by Integral Institute.* Although grounded in literally hun-

* *Sex, Ecology, Spirituality* introduced the AQAL framework in 1995, which opened up the core methodologies implicit in previous transformative approaches. Based on that, *One Taste* advanced modular integral life practice in all levels, lines, and quadrants. That was refined with the explicit disclosure and formulation of 8 fundamental perspectives and methodologies, in 2000, which led to the notion of training or exercising each of those zones, not just in an academic setting, but in a personal life practice—what is now called AQAL Praxis or Integral Life Practice. In 2003, the staff of Integral Institute began the first Integral Training seminars, which were offered to the public for the first time in 2004.

These seminars and workshops were the results of the combined efforts of a rather extraordinary group of integral pioneers, including Jeff Salzman, Huy Lam, Terry Patten, Diane Hamilton, Bert Parlee, Willow Pearson, Sean Hargens, Cindy Lou

dreds of the major transformative practices, East and West, and fully acknowledging that enormous debt, this approach had several unique features.

Perhaps the most obvious is that it was the first fully integral practice, or one that was based on all 8 zones. When it came to individual practice, Aurobindo was aware of 4 methodologies, his Integral Yoga exercised 3. The major meditative and contemplative traditions, from Theravadan to Cistercian to Hasidic, were aware of 3, exercised 2. Mike Murphy and George Leonard's Integral Transformative Practice was aware of 6, exercised 5. Typical practices of the Human Potential Movement were aware of 3, exercised 2. Nowhere were all 8 perspectives recognized, let alone exercised.

An Integral Life Practice based on all 8 zones particularly opened up practices that, in the Upper-Left quadrant, included the "**3 S's,**" which are so crucial to understanding and facilitating individual growth: shadow, states, and stages. As soon as Integral Institute began offering ILP workshops, it was apparent by the response that the Integral Approach resonated deeply with the passionate desires and inherent dimensions of the participants, and did so in a way that lit up their entire being-in-the-world. Integral Life Practice was born.

COMPONENTS OF AN INTEGRAL LIFE PRACTICE

Integral Life Practice has **4 core modules**, 5 or so auxiliary modules, and dozens of elective modules. Although we have what we consider "gold-star practices" in each module, the whole point of a **modular approach** is that you can select from among dozens of legitimate and time-tested practices in each module. (See fig. 10.1 for a summary of some of the major modules and practices.) The basic rule is simple: pick one practice from each module and exercise them concurrently. This *transformational cross-training* accelerates growth, increases the likelihood of healthy development, and vastly deepens one's capacity for transformational living.

A **module** is simply any aspect of human capacity that can be trained: quadrants, lines, states, types, and so on. ILP recommends **4 core mod-**

Golin, Colin Bigelow, Rollie Stanich, Marco Morelli, Elliott Ingersoll, Jeff Soulen, Barrett Brown, David Johnston, Sofia Diaz, Michael Zimmerman, Brett Thomas, John Forman, Fred Kofman, and Clint Fuhs, among many others. . . .

MODULES

CORE: Body, Mind, Spirit, Shadow — AUXILIARY: Ethics, Sex, Work, Emotions, Relationships

SAMPLE PRACTICES

Body (Physical, Subtle, Causal)	Mind (Framework, View)	Spirit (Meditation, Prayer)	Shadow (Therapie)	Ethics	Sex	Work	Emotions	Relationships
Weightlifting (Physical)	Reading & Study	Zen	Gestalt Therapy	Codes of Conduct	Tantra	Right Livelihood	Transmuting Emotions ★	Integral Relationships ★
Aerobics (Physical)	Belief System	Centering Prayer	Cognitive Therapy	Professional Ethics	Integral Sexual Yoga ★	Professional Training	Emotional Intelligence Training	Integral Parenting ★
F.I.T. ★ (Physical, Subtle)	Integral (AQAL) Framework ★	Big Mind Meditation ★	3-2-1 Process ★	Social & Ecological Activism	Kama Sutra	Money Management	Bhakti Yoga (Devotional Practices)	Communication Skills
Diet: Atkins, Ornish, the Zone (Physical)	Mental Training	Kabbalah	Dreamwork	Self-Discipline	Kundalini Yoga	Work as a Mode of ILP ★	Emotional Mindfulness Practice	Couples Therapy
ILP Diet (Physical) ★	Taking Multiple Perspectives	Compassionate Exchange ★	Interpersonal	Integral Ethics ★	Sexual Transformative Practice	Karma Yoga	Tonglen (Compassionate Exchange Meditation)	Relational Spiritual Practice
T'ai Chi Ch'uan (Subtle)	Any Worldview or Meaning System that Works for You	TM	Psychoanalysis	Sportsmanship		Community Service & Volunteering	Creative Expression & Art	Right Association (Sangha)
Qi Gong (Subtle)		Integral Inquiry ★	Art & Music Therapy	Vows & Oaths		Work as Transformation		Conscious Marriage
Yoga (Physical, Subtle)		The 1-2-3 of God ★						
3-Body Workout (Physical, Subtle, Causal) ★								

★ = Gold Star practices

Figure 10.1. The Integral Life Practice Matrix.

ules, which we consider foundational, and which especially address the 3 S's (in the Upper Left) and the 3 bodies (in the Upper Right).

1. **The Integral Framework Module.** The cognitive or **co-gnosis module** is simply the **AQAL Framework**. Since cognition is primarily the capacity to take perspectives, studying the AQAL Framework helps to open up all 8 perspectives in a conscious, clarifying, luminous fashion. AQAL is not merely an abstract model; as suggested in the Introduction, it is a type of **Integral Operating System** (or **IOS**) that, once it is learned or "downloaded," begins to create a space of multiple perspectives in the psyche. *Since the cognitive line is necessary but not sufficient for all of the other major lines*, the more integral and inclusive your cognitive Framework, the more complete and fulfilling your life can become. This co-gnosis module is necessary but not sufficient for all **stage development.**

2. **The Spiritual or Meditative Module.** "Spiritual," of course, can mean many things; here it particularly refers to meditative or contemplative **states training.** If you look at Figure 3.1 (page 83), you will get an idea of the overall training we have in mind with the meditative module. There are many approaches to meditation and spiritual experiences, of course. ILP uses Big Mind Process coupled with an awareness training (**Integral Inquiry**) that is a concentrated distillation of several major types of meditative training, visionary experiences, and centering prayer.

3. **The 3-2-1 Process,** or the **Shadow Work Module.** Working with one's shadow, or the repressed unconscious, is an absolutely essential component of any transformative life practice. Integral Institute has designed a simple but very effective process of accessing and integrating one's personal shadow material, which helps convert the shadow from 3rd-person symptoms to 2nd-person presence to 1st-person consciousness.

4. **The 3-Body Workout Module.** This is a workout that exercises all 3 bodies—gross, subtle, and causal. Where the first modules particularly address the 3 S's in the Upper Left, this module addresses the 3 bodies in the Upper Right.

Along with these 4 core modules, Integral Institute recommends 5 other modules as being particularly helpful, or auxiliary. These are:

5. **Ethics.**
6. **Sex,** or **Sexual Yoga.**

7. **Work in the World**, or **Karma Yoga.**
8. **Transmuting Emotions.**
9. **Relationships.**

Ethics involves linking behavior in the UR to postconventional moral awareness in the UL. **Sex** (or Sexual Yoga) focuses on the tantric aspects of relationship, especially using UL and LL as a bridge to awakening. **Work in the World** (or Karma Yoga) uses professional work and institutional behavior (LR) as an intrinsic part of one's ILP. **Transmuting Emotions** is advanced work in the UL dealing with transmuting negative emotions into their corresponding wisdoms, which includes **Sexual Yoga. Relationships** focuses on using one's most significant relationships (LL) not only as a means of transformation, but as an expression of integral awareness, with practices spanning parenting, couples, and conscious marriage.

Integral Institute offers seminars, workshops, courses, online material, and home study kits in each of those modules. If you are interested, please see **www.MyILP.com.**

INTEGRAL PROFESSIONAL TRAINING

In addition to the more personally oriented training, Integral Institute offers a wide range of professional seminars and workshops as well, in areas such as Integral Leadership, Integral Psychotherapy, Integral Medicine, and Integral Sustainability, among others. If you are interested in any of these, please visit us at **www.integraltraining.com** (or simply **www.MyILP.com**).

INTEGRAL SPIRITUAL PRACTICE

Integral Institute, in conjunction with Integral Spiritual Center (ISC), has adapted integral practice to work with the world's major spiritual traditions. Here, one can use one's chosen spiritual path and simply "plug it in" to the other components of an Integral Practice, as explained in chapter 5. We welcome any and all faiths and spiritual paths to join us in this endeavor.

If you are interested, please see **www.integralspiritualcenter.org.**

Where Is Spirit Located?

Here's a simple thought experiment. Picture the following men (or make them women if you like), and then tell me which you think are probably the most spiritual?

1. A man in an Armani suit.
2. A man driving a red Ferrari.
3. A man pitching baseball in the major leagues.
4. A professional comedian.
5. A mathematician.
6. A man in a tank top lifting weights.
7. An Olympic swimmer.
8. A college professor.
9. A model.
10. A sexual surrogate.

Which do you think is the most spiritual? Which do you think is the least spiritual?

It's funny, isn't it, the things that we think are not spiritual? Why do we picture most of those people as not being very spiritual? Why do we have such a hard time seeing them as being spiritual? Or conversely, why do we have such a hard time seeing them as being spiritual? Aren't we actually just giving our own prejudices about where we think spirit is or is not to be found? Or worse: aren't we really just announcing how old and fragmented and NOT INTEGRAL our ideas about spirit are? Why is telling jokes not spiritual? Why is something beautiful—a car, a suit—not spiritual? Why is physical excellence not spiritual? Why is sex not spiritual? Why is . . .

It's a new world, it's a new spirituality, it's a new time, it's a new man, it's a new woman. All of the above categories are deeply spiritual. Mostly all that list is, is a list of things we are afraid to allow spirituality to touch. Dead from the neck down, with no humor, no sex, no aesthetic sensibility whatsoever, wasting away, spending one's days and nights ignoring the world and lost in prayer . . . what a strange God, that.

Well, no more. Dead to life, dead to the body, dead to nature, dead to sex, dead to beauty, dead to excellence: that never was a real God, anyway, but merely a desiccated distillation of the things that men and women always had the most difficulty handling, and things from which God became the Great Escape, a distillation and concatenation of every phobic and repressive impulse a human being possessed.

Well, no more. It's a new world, it's a new man, it's a new woman.

The Spirit is integral, and so is the human being.

THE AQAL MATRIX

The AQAL matrix (of "all quadrants, all levels, all lines, all states, all types") can be derived in any number of ways. The most straightforward is simply to acknowledge the existence of the most widely used methodologies in human history. Simply allow the existence of empiricism, and phenomenology, and behaviorism, and contemplation, and hermeneutics, and systems theory . . . and then add up what you have. Give the human beings using those methodologies the decency of supposing that they know what they are doing, and are doing the best they can—instead of assuming that they are complete idiots caught in total error. Each of those disciplines and paradigms has ways to spot bad data and throw it out—they know what they are doing! If you grant them that decency, and allow the results of all of those fundamental and time-tested methodologies, and then put them together in some sort of generally coherent framework, the result is something like the AQAL matrix of possibilities arising in this moment.

Of course, AQAL is not the only way to do so, and it might not be the best way; it is simply the only way I'm aware of. But whatever we decide about AQAL as a meta-theory itself, it should never be forgotten that it is a meta-theory based on the totality of the methodologies mentioned—that is, it is a meta-theoria derived from a meta-praxis. It is the result of a *practice* of inclusion, not a theory about inclusion. A methodology is a practice, an injunction, an exemplar, a paradigm—which brings forth phenomena, experiences, and data (using "data" as William James did, to mean "*experiences in any domain*")—and AQAL is simply a meta-paradigm of simultracking at least 8 methodologies. One of the ways to conceptualize the relationship of all of the resulting experiences and phenomenal worlds is the AQAL matrix. But the practices and their data come first—the actual experiences generated by the injunctions and exemplars—and the theory follows.

The AQAL framework is a vivid reminder that the multidimensional evidence from at least 8 perspectives and methodologies (disclosing 8 zones of your very own being-in-the-world)—that *all of that needs to be taken into account* in understanding any endeavor, and certainly something as important as religion, spirituality, and science in the premodern, modern, and postmodern worlds.

Throw the circle as wide as you can, find a view from 50,000 feet, be inclusive using an integral pluralism and not just a pluralism (which soon fractures, fragments, and falls apart, leaving only the ego to rule), extend your compassionate embrace to the men and women doing the extraordinarily wonderful work in all of those fields and disciplines (covered by the 8 methodologies), reach out and bring their phenomenal worlds into your map of your own world, stretch your mind until it touches infinity and begins to radiate with the brilliance of the overmind, expand the beating of your heart to unleash its inherent desire to love every single thing and person and event in the entire Kosmos, so that you love all the way to infinity and all the way back, smiling when you *actually, finally, amazingly see* the radiant Face of God in the 2nd-Person (or the ultimate Thou as infinite Love, arising then as the ultimate We), even as your own Original Face is God in the 1st-person (or the ultimate I-I as *this moment's* pure nondual Witnessing-Emptiness), knowing too that the entire manifest universe—the Great Holarchy of beings all the way up, all the way down—is God in the 3rd-Person (or the ultimate It as the entire Kosmos): I and Thou and We and It, all brought together in the radiant contours of the simple Suchness of this and every moment, as you feel into the texture of the Kosmos and find your very Self in every warp and woof of a universe now arising as the radiance of the Spirit that can never be denied, *any more than you can deny the awareness of this page*, knowing, too, that Spirit and the awareness of this page are one and the same, and certainly not-two, so that you realize—with the great sages East and West, Lao Tzu to Asanga to Shankara to Paul to Augustine to Parmenides to Plotinus to Descartes to Schelling to Teresa and Lady Tsogyal—the ultimate secret of the spiritual world, namely, that fully enlightened and ever-present Divine awareness is not hard to attain but impossible to avoid.

Why were you looking everywhere, when God is the Looker? Why were you constantly seeking something, when God is the Seeker? When exactly were you planning on finding Spirit, when Spirit is always the Finder? How exactly were you going to force God to show his or her Face, when God's Face is your Original Face—the Witness of this very page—already and right Now? How hard is it to notice that you are already effortlessly aware of this page? Why were you expending so much effort, when ever-present awareness is spontaneously and effort-lessly arising right now, as is the awareness of this book, and the area around it, and your body, and the room you are in—notice them all, and notice that they are all effortlessly arising in your present awareness, they are all effortlessly arising in your timeless Wakefulness, right here, right now—and how much effort do you have to make in order for this present awareness to happen? Where were you planning on seeing God, when God is the ever-present Seer? How much knowledge did you think you had to cram into your head in order to know God, when God is the ever-present Knower? How much of this book—or any book or books— did you think you had to read in order to find Spirit, when the very Reader of this sentence is Spirit? When the very reader of this sentence is God fully revealed? *Feel* the Reader of this sentence, feel the simple feeling of Being, feel the Feeler in you right now, and you are feeling the fully revealed God in his and her radiant glory, a One Taste of the divine Suchness of the entire Kosmos, a not-two-ness of self and Self that leaves you breathlessly enlightened and fully realized in this and every moment. Hear the sounds all around you? Who is not enlightened?

Allow it all. Swallow the Kosmos whole. You *know* that everybody is right. So stop lying about it, and thus move from self to Self. There is room for everything in the Kosmos. Open up and let it all in. Stretch your mind until it breaks open and you need maps no more, and AQAL is a faint memory of a map that helped you find You, and helped I find I-I, and then toss AQAL in the family photo album of that summer when you found God by giving up the search. By giving up the search and resting in the Searcher, and then you needed maps no more. Not for that. The territory alone will suffice, surely, in the radiance of the timeless Now blinding your ego with your Self, overcoming all difficulties in spiritual seeking by giving up seeking itself, nodding your head in recognition that the great game or play is up, the game of Hide and Seek is over, because you were It and You found out.

In the relative world of finite manifestation, an AQAL map is a useful guide to the dimensions of a human being-in-8-worlds, and if we include all of those dimensions and methodologies in our maps of reality, I honestly believe we will see Spirit shining fully in the premodern, modern, and postmodern world, and see a way to bring them all together in a gesture of easy embrace and graceful inclusion, like a full-course meal and not just the appetizer, saturating our being with our Being, and thus Being in the AQAL world with presence and delight, wonder and release, recognition and surrender, humor and lightness, surprise and rightness, justness and relief—it all somehow comes pouring through, drenching us in Being and Consciousness and Duty and Bliss. . . . .

Which finds itself exploding in its own superabundance, unfolding in its own evolutionary plenitude, a riotous development that is loving envelopment, an evolution of Spirit that spins off Kosmic memories of its own yesterday while laying down Kosmic habits as the foundation of its own tomorrow (don't You remember?), so that with a Kosmic conveyor belt—a great and grand and glorious Spiritual elevator—religion has found its place in the modern and postmodern world.

Spirituality—Your own deepest I-I in this We of Mutual Awakening—embraces not only states and experiences, but stages and stations on life's way. And those stages (nothing but zones #2 and #4 of Spirit's own manifestation)—from archaic God to magic God to mythic God to rational God to pluralistic God to integral God and higher—are indeed the stages and stations of a conveyor belt from egocentric to ethnocentric to worldcentric to Kosmocentric, with religion being the only institution in all of humanity's endeavors that can do this.

. . . that can take Your unfoldment and enfold it into the world, that can take my deepest I-I and see My Being realized in My own concrete Becoming, an infinity of Love in the 4-Armed Form, these quadrants of My own occasions. Religion is simply institutionalized spirituality, passing on its good news to the next generation to do with as they see fit, which will then itself be passed on, and thus unto the ends of time. Any society's Religion is the House of its Spirituality, hooked into its evolutionary unfolding, a Kosmic Conveyor from death to immortality, bondage to freedom, suffering to fullness, illusion to awakening, sin to salvation, ignorance to gnosis, all in the good light of time's radiant unfolding.

This conveyor belt of Spirit's own stations: How appropriate, how extraordinary, how obvious—and yet there it is.

If you find this approach interesting and would like to join us, unfolding your own deepest I among the most meaningful We embracing the widest It, we'd love to have you help us with this extraordinary endeavor. (Please see www.integralinstitute.org.)

It's a new day, it's a new dawn, it's a new man, it's a new woman. The new human is integral, and so is the spirituality.

Thank you, from all of us at Integral Institute.

APPENDIXES

APPENDIX I

From the Great Chain of Being to Postmodernism in 3 Easy Steps

OVERVIEW

The traditional Great Chain of Being is usually given as something like: **matter, body, mind, soul,** and **spirit.** In Vedanta Hinduism, for example, these are, respectively, the 5 sheaths or levels of Spirit: *annu-maya-kosha* (the sheath or level made of physical food), the *prana-maya-kosha* (the level made of élan vital), the *mano-maya-kosha* (the level made of mind), the *vijnana-maya-kosha* (the level made of higher mind or soul), and *ananda-maya-kosha* (the level made of transcendental bliss or causal spirit). Vedanta, of course, adds *turiya*, or the transcendental ever-present Self, and *turiyatita*, or the nondual, ever-present, unqualifiable Spirit-as-such, but the simpler 5-level scheme will work for our introductory purposes. We will return to the more "complete" version later.*

This 5-level Great Chain of Being can be represented schematically as in figure I.1 (p. 214). Although we have to be very careful with cross-cultural comparisons, interpretive schemes similar to this Great Chain or "Great Nest of Being" can be found in most of the wisdom traditions of the "premodern" world, as indicated in figures I.2 and I.3, which are diagrams used by Huston Smith to indicate the general similarities (or family resemblances) among these traditions.

With reference to figure I.1, notice that the Great Chain, as conceived by its proponents (from Plotinus to Aurobindo), is indeed more of a Great Nest—or what is often called a *holarchy*—because each senior

---

*Technical points: the *koshas* are levels/structures; *turiya/turiyatita* are states.

213

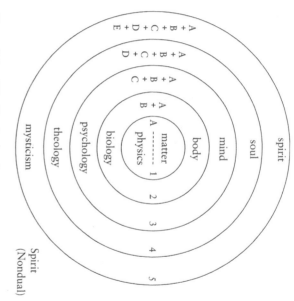

Figure I.1. The Traditional Great Chain of Being.

level goes beyond its junior levels but envelopes them (or "nests" them)—what Plotinus called "a development that is envelopment." Each higher level, however, also radically transcends its juniors and can neither be reduced to its juniors nor explained by them. This is indicated in figure I.1 as (A), (A + B), (A + B + C), and so on, which means that each senior level contains elements or qualities that are emergent and nonreducible.

For example, when body or life (A + B) emerges "out of" matter ("A"), it contains certain qualities (such as sexual reproduction, interior emotions, autopoiesis, élan vital, etc.—all represented by "B") that cannot be accounted for in strictly the material terms of "A." Likewise, when mind (A + B + C) emerges out of life, mind contains emergent characteristics ("C") that cannot be reduced to, nor explained by, life and matter alone. When soul (A + B + C + D) emerges, it transcends mind and life and body. Evolution, then, is this "unfolding" of Spirit from matter to body to mind to soul to Spirit itself, or the realization of the absolute Spirit that was the Goal and Ground of the entire sequence. (This is not necessarily an Omega point of some sort, but an endless unfolding of even higher potentials, which we can imagine today about as well as Neanderthal could imagine us and our world.)

The best introduction to this traditional notion remains E. F. Schu-

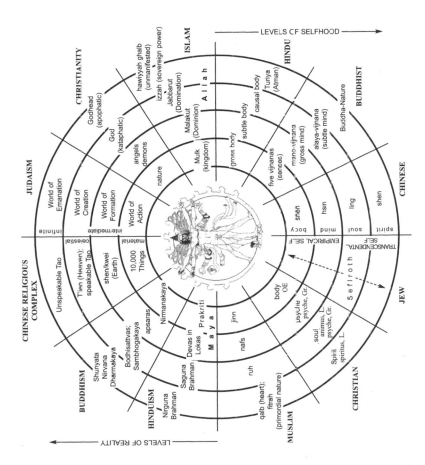

Figure I.2. The Great Chain in Various Wisdom Traditions. Compiled by Huston Smith; graphic layout by Brad Reynolds. Used with permission.

macher's classic *A Guide for the Perplexed,* a title borrowed from Maimonides' great exposition on the same topic. The general idea is that of **a great holarchy of being and knowing,** with the levels of reality in the "outer" world reflected in the levels of self (or levels of "interior" knowing and being), which is particularly suggested by figure I.3.

But, according to the traditions, this entire process of *evolution* or "un-folding" could never occur without a prior process of *involution* or "in-folding." Not only can the higher not be explained in terms of the lower, and not only does the higher not actually emerge "out of" the lower, but the reverse of both of those is true, according to the traditions. That is, the lower dimensions or levels are actually sediments or deposits of the higher dimensions, and they find their meaning because

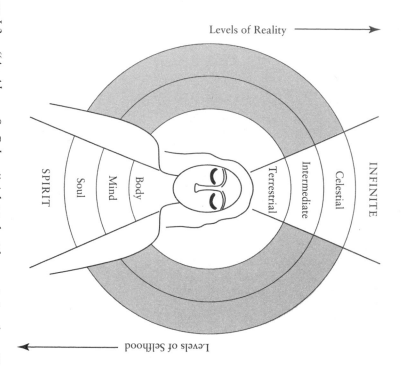

Levels of Reality →

← Levels of Selfhood

SPIRIT
Soul
Mind
Body
Terrestrial
Intermediate
Celestial
INFINITE

Figure I.3. "As Above, So Below." Adapted with permission from Huston Smith, Forgotten Truth: The Common Vision of the World's Religions (San Francisco: HarperSanFrancisco, 1992), p. 62.

of the higher dimensions of which they are a stepped-down or diluted version. This sedimentation process is called **"involution"** or **"emanation."** According to the traditions, before evolution or the unfolding of Spirit can occur, involution or the infolding of Spirit must occur: the higher successively steps down into the lower. Thus, the higher levels appear to emerge "out of" the lower levels during evolution—for example, life appears to emerge out of matter—because, and only because, they were first deposited there by involution. You cannot get the higher out of the lower unless the higher were already there, in potential—sleeping, as it were—waiting to emerge. The "miracle of emergence" is simply Spirit's creative play in the fields of its own manifestation.

Thus, for the traditions, the great cosmic game begins when Spirit throws itself outward, in sport and play (*lila, kenosis*), to create a manifest universe. Spirit "loses" itself, "forgets" itself, takes on a magical facade of manyness (*maya*) in order to have a grand game of hide-and-seek with itself. Spirit first throws itself outward to create soul, which is a stepped-down and diluted reflection of Spirit; soul then steps down into mind, a paler reflection yet of Spirit's radiant glory; mind then steps down into life, and life steps down into matter, which is the densest, lowest, least conscious form of Spirit. We might represent this as: Spirit-as-spirit steps down into Spirit-as-soul, which steps down into Spirit-as-mind, which steps down into Spirit-as-body, which steps down into Spirit-as-matter. These levels in the Great Nest are all *forms of Spirit*, but the forms become less and less conscious, less and less aware of their Source and Suchness, less and less alive to their ever-present Ground, even though they are all nevertheless nothing but Spirit-at-play.

If we can represent the major emergent stages in evolution as (A), (A + B), (A + B + C), and so on—where the addition signs mean that something is emerging or being *added* to manifestation—then we could represent involution as the prior *subtraction* process: Spirit starts out full and complete, with all of manifestation contained as potential in itself, which we can represent in brackets: [A + B + C + D + E]. Spirit first steps down into manifestation—and begins to "lose" itself in manifestation—by shedding its pure spiritual nature and assuming a manifest, finite, limited form—namely, the *soul* [A + B + C + D]. The soul has now forgotten "E," or its radical identity with and as Spirit, and, in the ensuing confusion and angst, the soul flees this terror by stepping down into mind [A + B + C], which has forgotten "D," its soul radiance; and mind flees into life, forgetting "C," or its intelligence; and finally life sheds even its vegetative vitality "B" and appears as inert, insentient, lifeless matter, "A"—at which point something like the Big Bang occurs, whereupon matter blows into concrete existence and it appears that in the entire manifest world, there exists nothing but insentient, dead, lifeless matter.

But this matter is curiously frisky, is it not? It doesn't just seem to lie about, on unemployment insurance, watching TV. This matter astonishingly begins to wind itself up: "order out of chaos" is what complexity physics calls it—or dissipative structures, or self-organization, or dynamic becoming. But the traditionalists were more straightforward about it: "God does not remain petrified and dead; the very stones cry out and raise themselves to Spirit," as Hegel put it.

In other words, according to the traditions, once involution has occurred, then evolution begins or can begin, moving from (A) to (A + B) to (A + B + C), and so on, with each major emergent step being but an unfolding or remembering of the higher dimensions that were secretly infolded or sedimented in the lower during involution. That which was dis-membered, fragmented, and forgotten during involution is re-membered, reunited, made whole, and realized during evolution. Hence, the doctrine of *anamnesis*, or Platonic and Vedantic "remembrance," so common in the traditions: if involution is a forgetting of who you are, evolution is a remembering of who and what you are: *tat tvam asi*; "you are That." *Satori, metanoia, moksha,* and *wu* are some of the classic names for this Self-realization.

1. STEP ONE

As beautiful and brilliant as that interpretive scheme is, it is not without its problems. It is not so much that the scheme itself is wrong, as that the modern and postmodern world has added several profound insights that need to be added or incorporated if we want a more integral or comprehensive view. This is what is meant by "from the Great Chain to postmodernism in 3 easy steps."

The Problem

The Great Nest, involution and evolution, levels of being and knowing: those were some of the profound contributions of the great saints and sages of the premodern world, and can indeed be found in everything from the *Enneads* of Plotinus to the *Lankavatara Sutra* to *The Life Divine* of Aurobindo, all expressions of the great metaphysical systems.

But there is one item we should perhaps keep in mind as we moderns attempt to assess those ideas: the great metaphysical systems were, in the last analysis, interpretive frameworks that the sages gave to their spiritual experiences. These schemes, such as the Great Chain, were *interpretations* of living *experiences*—they were not some sort of fixed, rigid, ontological grids that are true for all eternity. If, in the following, I question the adequacy of some of these **interpretations**, I am not at all questioning the **authenticity of the experiences or realizations** of these great sages. I am simply suggesting that, as evolution itself continues to move forward, new horizons can be used to recontextualize and reframe these experiences in interpretive meshworks that are more adequate in the light of modern and postmodern contributions, so that the net result is something of an integration of the very best of premodern, modern, and postmodern forms of Spirit's own unfolding.

Toward that end, I will suggest 3 central difficulties with the interpretive frameworks of the great metaphysical systems, as well as 3 suggested remedies. In my opinion, we want to keep as much as possible of the great traditional systems while jettisoning their unnecessary metaphysical interpretations, interpretations that not only are *not necessary* to explain the same set of data, but interpretations that *guarantee* that spirituality will not get a fair hearing in the court of modern and postmodern thought.

The first difficulty—what we are calling problem #1—can be seen with this example. If you look at any of the figures representing traditional metaphysics (figs. I.1, I.2, I.3), notice that all of the levels higher than matter are indeed *meta*-physical, which means beyond physics or beyond matter. The **material** level (level 1) includes, for example, the human brain as a complex material entity. This means, according to the metaphysical systems, that the feelings of a worm (which are level 2) are on a higher level of reality than the human brain (which is level 1).

Something is clearly not quite right with that scheme. Part of the problem is that the relation of human consciousness to human neurophysiology is something that is *not obvious* (and not even available) to introspective phenomenology (i.e., to meditation or contemplation), which means that items such as dopamine, serotonin, synaptic pathways, the Krebs cycle, hypothalamic regulation, and so on, were not generally available to the ancients. Again, this does not mean that their spiritual realization was flawed or inadequate, but simply that they did not have the advantage of some of the finite facts that modern science has discovered. Were Plotinus alive today, you can bet that several chapters of the *Enneads* would be devoted to brain physiology and its relation to spirit. Were Shankara alive today, his commentaries on the *Brahma Sutras* would no doubt have extensive discussions on the relation of the *nadis* to neurotransmitters.

Suggested Solution

What might Plotinus or Shankara have concluded about the relation of spiritual realities to material realities such as the brain? I believe they would have agreed to the following; but in any event, here is suggestion #1:

In the manifest world, what we call "matter" is not the lowest rung in the great spectrum of existence, but the *exterior form* of *every* rung in the great spectrum. Matter is not lower, with consciousness higher, but matter and consciousness are the exterior and interior of every occasion.

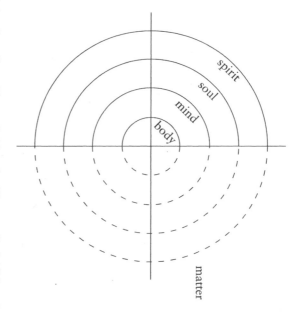

Figure I.4. Step One: Matter Is Not the "Bottom" of All Levels but the "Exterior" of All Levels.

This can be schematically represented as shown in figure 1.4, and in more detail in figure I.5. The basic move here is to take what appears as "matter" off the bottom rung of existence (with all the other levels being higher and "meta"-physical) and instead make it the exterior form of all of the other levels. So let's take figure I.1, where matter is on the bottom level, and convert it into figure I.4, where matter is the exterior form of all of the levels. (I will give examples of these correlations shortly.)

The traditions always understood that the levels "higher" than matter were "invisible" to the ordinary senses, and the same is true with our reformulation: namely, all the interior dimensions (feelings, compassion, awareness, consciousness, mutual understanding, etc.) are invisible to the exterior senses; but we can reach this understanding without unnecessary "metaphysical" interpretations. (I know, what about reincarnation? Hang on a minute. . . .)

For the moment, we are confining our attention to the 2 upper quadrants. In the Upper-Right quadrant, we can see the evolution of exterior

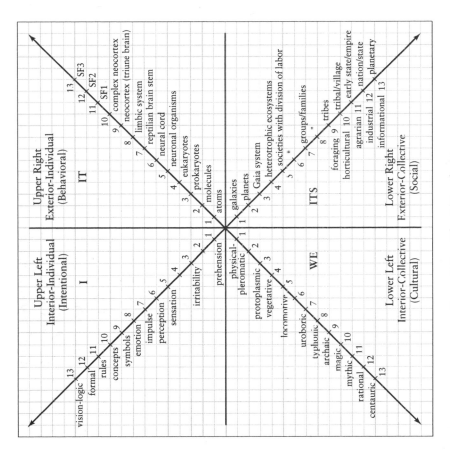

Figure I.5. The 4 Quadrants.

or "material" or "physical" forms, as disclosed by modern science. These exterior forms include, in order of increasing evolutionary complexity, items such as: atoms, molecules, early or prokaryotic cells, true or eukaryotic cells, organisms with a neuronal net, organisms with a neural cord (e.g., shrimp), a reptilian brain stem (e.g., lizard), a limbic system (e.g., horse), a neocortex or triune brain (e.g., humans, with several higher "structure-functions" also listed).

Those are all "exterior" or "material" forms, in that you can see them in the exterior, sensorimotor world. But each of those material forms of *increasing complexity* has, as an *interior correlate,* a level of *increasing consciousness.* Thus: atoms, whose exterior forms are physical entities such as neutrons, protons, and electrons, have an interior of prehension or proto-feelings (proto-awareness); neuronal organisms possess interior sensations; organisms with neural cords have perception; the emergence of animals with a reptilian brain stem sees the emergence of interior impulses and instincts; an exterior limbic system emerges with interior emotions; a triune brain is the exterior or material form of an interior consciousness that can contain, among many other things, formal operational cognition, postconventional morality, vision-logic, linguistic capacities, and so on. (You can see some of these correlations between the Upper Right and the Upper Left in fig. I.5.)

In other words, matter is not on the bottom rung of that evolutionary spiral, but is rather the *exterior* form of an evolution whose *interiors* contain correlative levels of feelings, awareness, consciousness, and so forth. AQAL meta-theory handles this by saying that every mind has a body, or every state of consciousness has a corresponding signature state of matter-energy, or every interior prehension has an exterior form—in short, every occasion in the Upper-Left quadrant has a correlate in the Upper-Right quadrant, and vice versa. It is not merely that higher levels (of life and mind and soul) imprint matter or leave footprints in matter (which itself remains on the lowest level), but that what we call matter is directly the exterior form of each of those interior levels (as suggested in figs. I.4 and I.5).

Thus, what the premodern sages took to be META-physical realities are in many cases INTRA-physical realities: they are not above matter, nor beyond nature, nor meta-physical, nor super-natural: they are not above nature but within nature, not beyond matter but interior to it.

There is simply no way a premodern saint, in deep meditation on the nature of the soul, would or could know that his or her brain-wave patterns were settling into theta-alpha states; no way to know that serotonin was increasing, neural lactic acid was decreasing, cellular oxygen requirements were significantly diminishing, and hemispheric lateralization was occurring. All of the interior revelations of the soul therefore seemed and felt as if they were not physical, not material, not connected to nature at all, not a part of the fabric of material manifestation: they seemed meta-physical in every way.

As we will see, there are some aspects of the higher dimensions that might indeed be truly trans-physical; but the first thing we should note is that a great deal of what premodernity took to be meta-physical is in fact intra-physical, not above nature but within nature. This is the first step in moving from metaphysics to integral post-metaphysics.

2. STEP TWO

The Problem

Step #1 involves adding, to the profound wisdom of the *premodern* traditions, the invaluable contributions of *modern* science. Step #2 involves the further addition of the important contributions of Spirit's *postmodern* turn. These contributions are summarized in the lower two quadrants of figure I.5. The upper quadrants represent an **individual** being; the lower quadrants represent a group, collective, or **system** of individual beings. The Left-Hand quadrants represent the **interiors** of an individual or group; and the Right-Hand quadrants represent the **exteriors** of an individual or group. Thus, the 4 quadrants are the inside and outside of the individual and the collective.

The important point with reference to postmodernity is simply this: just as the metaphysical interpretations that the ancients gave their authentic spiritual experiences could not take advantage of modern scientific discoveries, so they could not take advantage of the profound disclosures of postmodernism, ethnomethodology, cultural contextualism, the sociology of knowledge, and so on. On all of those, taken together, deliver a devastating indictment: much of what the ancient sages took as metaphysical absolutes are actually culturally molded and conditioned. This fact alone has allowed postmodernity to dismiss the great traditions as so much confused nonsense, and that is problem #2.

Suggested Solution

The unavoidable existence of cultural contexts does not mean that there are no cross-cultural truths or universals. It simply means that identifying them has to be done with much more care than metaphysics imagined; and that much of this identifying has to be done with research methodology, not speculative metaphysics.

The postmodern contribution can be included in an integral approach very simply: every individual is nestled in systems of *cultural* and *social* networks, networks that have a profound influence on the knowing and being of individuals themselves. These networks are the Lower-Left (cultural) and Lower-Right (social) quadrants in figure I.5. The LR quadrant represents **social systems**—the *collective systems* or *collective exteriors* of individual organisms, exteriors that can be seen in the exterior or sensorimotor world (recall that all Right-Hand quadrants can be seen "out there" because they are "material" or "exterior". These exterior systems include items such as ecosystems, geopolitical systems, modes of techno-economic production (foraging, horticultural, informational, etc.), and all of the visible, exterior, concrete aspects of collectives or systems. Note again that, for the metaphysical traditions, all of these "material systems" would be on the lowest level of existence, whereas, for integral post-metaphysics, they are simply the collective exterior dimensions of the "higher" (now *interior*) levels. As we saw, super-natural is intra-natural.

The LL or cultural quadrant represents all the *interiors of groups or collectives*, interiors that (like all Left-Hand quadrants) cannot be seen "out there," interiors such as group values, identities, worldviews, cultural beliefs, background contexts, and so on. This quadrant is especially the focus of postmodernism. *Systems theory focuses on the Lower-Right quadrant, and postmodern poststructuralism focuses on the Lower-Left quadrant*—representing the exteriors and interiors of the collective.

Systems theory in its many forms emphasizes the fact that every individual organism is inseparably interconnected with its environment in dynamic webs of relationships and ecosystems, *all of which can be seen "out there"*—which again shows that "matter" is not the lowest level of being but simply the exterior form of all interior levels of being (in this case, the *exterior* form of the collective or *communal system*).

Of course, nothing in systems theory or ecology deals with interior states of beauty, *satori, samadhi*, mutual understanding, values, worldviews, and so forth, because all of those are indeed interior (and therefore inaccessible with ecology or systems theory). Attempting to reduce all realities to one quadrant, as systems theory often does, is known as *quadrant absolutism*, and is something an integral methodological pluralism attempts to avoid.

Postmodernism, on the other hand, is known for focusing on those interior or cultural aspects of an individual's being-in-the-world, where it emphasizes that much of what any society takes to be "given," "true," and "absolute" is in fact *culturally molded, conditioned, and often relative*. That postmodernism itself is often caught in its own quadrant absolutism (where it tries to reduce everything to cultural constructions in the LL) should not detract from the important truths that it has contributed—all of which we summarize by saying that every occasion has a Lower-Left quadrant or dimension.

The 4 quadrants, then, represent 4 inseparable dimensions of any individual's being-in-the-world. These dimensions are so fundamental that every major natural language contains them as 1st-person, 2nd-person, and 3rd-person pronouns, which can be summarized as I, you/we, it, and its. The **UL** is "I," or the interior feelings or awareness of any individual sentient being (atoms to ants to apes). The **UR** is "it," or the exterior form of a sentient being (i.e., its matter and energy—which includes its gross exterior forms—atoms to brains—and also, as we will soon see, subtle energy). The **LR** is the exterior form of a group, collective, or system of sentient beings or individuals. And the **LL** is the interior or collective consciousness, collective values, intersubjective backgrounds, cultural contexts, and so on. Again: the interior and the exterior of the individual and the collective.

I have included one more diagram, which is the 4 quadrants narrowed to some of their forms as they appear in humans (see fig. I.6).

I am not going to make a long drawn-out argument for this, but will simply state my own opinion in the strongest way: any premodern spirituality that does not come to terms with both modernity and postmodernity has no chance of survival in tomorrow's world. One way to effect this integration is by using AQAL ("all quadrants, all levels"), which combines the enduring contributions of premodern, modern, and postmodern. The "**all levels**" part refers to the great spectrum of being and knowing first interpreted so brilliantly by the great premodern sages—matter to body to mind to soul to spirit (we will return to these levels in a moment). The "**all quadrants**" part refers to the refinements brought by modernity (namely, matter is not on the bottom rung but on the exterior of the rungs) and by postmodernity (namely, every individual is set in cultural and social contexts).

Using AQAL allows the great and enduring truths of the traditions to be honored and included, but set in an interpretive framework that situates and contextualizes them much more adequately so that their truths can be seen and heard. Anybody looking at the quadrants can see that modern science focuses on the UR, systems theory on the LR, and postmodernity on the LL—but nobody is really working the UL—except phenomenology, introspection, and meditation—which is where the traditions excelled! In fact, virtually the entire Great Chain fits in the Upper-Left quadrant! That is their great strength. In other words, an understanding of this quadrant and ways to practice it and awaken to its highest dimensions is their great strength and enduring contribution, as useful and needed today as a thousand years ago.

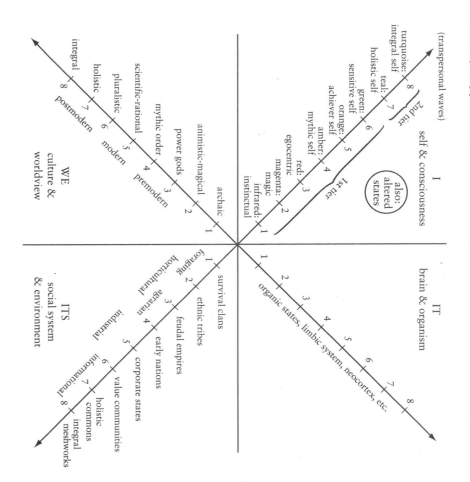

Figure I.6. *Some Aspects of the 4 Quadrants as They Appear in Humans.*

But because the great traditions were ignorant of the other 3 quadrants, then modernity (esp. UR) and postmodernity (esp. LL) completely crucified the traditions for lacking those truths. But modernity and postmodernity threw the baby out with the bathwater, to put it mildly, and ended up with their own severe lacunae. Using AQAL, on the other hand, allows us to acknowledge and incorporate the best of the premodern, modern, and postmodern contributions.

Adopting something like an AQAL framework is the second major step in moving from metaphysics to integral post-metaphysics.

3. STEP THREE

The Problem

Here we begin to address the role and nature of energy—gross energy, subtle energy, and causal energy. I have already suggested that mass and energy are aspects of the UR-dimension of every individual being—that is, they represent some of the *exterior forms* of every individual (and every system, as we will see).

The problem here might be stated as follows. Given (1) the premodern lack of clarity about the role of matter, and (2) the fact that the ancients therefore pictured subtle energies as fundamentally *meta*-physical or super-natural; but given (3) the modern understanding of matter as not bottom but exterior, then (4) how can we reinterpret in a more adequate fashion the relation of subtle energies to gross material forms?

Put simply, because matter is not the bottom of all levels but the exterior of all levels, where does subtle energy fit into this scheme? The premodern traditions actually had a type of spectrum of subtle energy, stretching from the densest to the very subtlest (or causal), each of them being higher and "more beyond" matter. But if matter itself is reinterpreted, how can subtle energy likewise be reinterpreted to keep pace with modern and postmodern revelations of Spirit's own unfolding?

Suggested Solution

The suggested solution in this case comes in the form of three hypotheses, two of which we have seen already, and the third of which deals directly with this issue.

1. *Increasing evolution brings increasing complexity of gross form.* In the Upper Right, for example, we find quarks to protons to atoms to molecules to cells to complex organisms. This increase in complexity of form (via such processes as differentiation and integration) has long been noted by evolutionary biologists. Laszlo: "Thus, while a new level of organization means a simplification of system function, and of the corresponding system structure, it also means the initiation of a process of progressive structural and functional complexification." I think this "complexification" is fairly obvious and needn't detain us.

2. *Increasing complexity of form (in the UR) is correlated with increasing interior consciousness (in the UL).* This was Teilhard de Chardin's "law of complexity and consciousness"—namely, the more of the

former, the more of the latter. As we might put it more precisely, the greater the degree of exterior complexity of material form, the greater the degree of interior consciousness that can be enacted within that form (i.e., correlation of UR and UL).

3. Further—and this is the connecting hypothesis—*increasing complexity of gross form is correlated with increasing subtlety of energies.* As evolution proceeds to more and more complex gross forms, the increasing degree of gross complexity is accompanied by subtler and subtler corresponding (or signature) energy patterns. Since we are at this point focusing on individual beings, we have this: increasing evolution brings increasing complexity of gross form (in the UR), which is correlated with an *increasing degree of corresponding energies* (in the UL), and, in the UR itself, a *subtilization of corresponding energies.* Thus, instead of interpreting higher levels as being essentially divorced from gross matter or gross form, the complexification of gross form is the vehicle of manifestation for both subtler energies and greater consciousness.

If those connecting links hold, that would be the third major step in the move from premodern metaphysics to integral post-metaphysics, a move that, I believe, retains the enduring truths of the great metaphysical traditions but without what appear to be their outmoded interpreta-

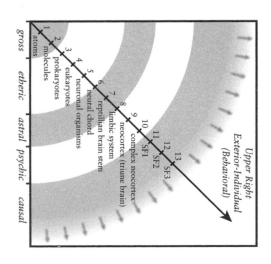

Figure I.7.   *Complexification of Gross Form Is Accompanied by Subtler Energies.*

tive frameworks. The entire discussion of this issue can be found in Excerpt G (www.kenwilber.com). It is a long academic treatment, which takes the major premodern versions of all the types of subtle energy—such as astral, etheric, biofields, psychic, and causal—and carefully correlates them with the level of complexity of gross form in the UR.* One reviewer called it "the first believable and workable synthesis of the major schools of subtle energy." Figure I.7 is one of the many diagrams that gives the basic idea.

Those correlations—and of course the existence of subtle energies themselves—are presented as hypotheses. But the point is that, whether or not they turn out to be valid, subtle energies *can* be fully situated in the UR quadrant—gross matter-form, subtle matter-form, causal matter-form.

Thus, in either event, this allows us to complete the essential steps for a move from metaphysics to integral post-metaphysics, at least in very general outline, which I hope is enough to indicate some of the essential notions involved. . . .

---

*Excerpt G also directly addresses the issue of reincarnation and how it fits with these hypotheses.

APPENDIX II

Integral Post-Metaphysics

What Is Post-Metaphysics?

What is "post-metaphysics"? Let's start by asking: what is metaphysics? Metaphysics is generally taken to be the branch of philosophy that deals with issues of ontology (what is being or reality?) and epistemology (how do we know it?). The term was first prominently used by Aristotle's students for a book they called *Metaphysics* simply because it was written after his book on *Physics*. That's as good a reason as any, I suppose.

If metaphysics began with Aristotle, it ended with Kant. Or, at any rate, took a turn that has defined the way sophisticated philosophers think about reality ever since. Kant's *critical philosophy* replaced ontological objects with structures of the subject. In essence, this means that we do not perceive empirical objects in a completely realistic, pregiven fashion; but rather, structures of the knowing subject impart various characteristics to the known object that then appear to belong to the object—but really don't; they are, rather, co-creations of the knowing subject. Various *a priori* categories of the knowing subject help to fashion or construct reality as we know it. Reality is not a perception, but a conception; at least in part. Ontology per se just does not exist. Metaphysics is then a broad name for the type of thinking that can't figure this out. Or, metaphysics is thinking that falls prey to the myth of the given.

What this means for spirituality in general is that metaphysics needs to be jettisoned, or at the very least, completely rethought. All of the traditional categories of metaphysics—including God, immortality, the soul, mind, body, and knowing—simply cannot stand up to the scrutiny of critical thinking, not in their fundamental, pre-critical, ontological forms. In the modern and postmodern world, they are simply obsolete notions that are as embarrassing to religion as, say, phlogiston, St. Vitus's dance, and phrenology are to medicine.

Take, for example, the Great Chain of Being. The criticisms that have been leveled at the Great Chain by green-meme theorists are, frankly, cheap and unsophisticated, and don't get at the major issues anyway. We start instead with the simple facts as outlined by Arthur Lovejoy's classic study on the subject, *The Great Chain of Being*.

To begin with, the various Great Chain theorists maintained 3 essential points: (1) all phenomena—all things and events, people, animals, minerals, plants—all are manifestations of the superabundance and plenitude of Spirit, so that Spirit is woven intrinsically into each and all, and thus even the entire material and natural world is, as Plato put it, "a visible, sensible God" (**the plenitude of Spirit**); (2) therefore, there are "no gaps" in nature, no missing links, no unbridgeable dualisms, for each and every thing is interwoven with each and every other (**the continuum of being**); and (3) the continuum of being nonetheless shows gradation, for various *emergents* appear in some dimensions that do not appear in others; e.g., wolves can run, rocks can't, so there are "gaps" in the special sense of emergents (**the hierarchy of being**).

Now whatever we moderns or postmoderns might think of the Great Chain as a theory, it nonetheless "*has been the official philosophy of the larger part of civilized humankind through most of its history*"; and further, it was the worldview that "the greater number of the subtler speculative minds and of the great religious teachers [both East and West], in their various fashions, have been engaged in."

The Great Chain of Being itself was said generally to consist of anywhere from 3 or 4 levels (e.g., body, mind, soul, and spirit) to upward of a dozen or more levels. These levels were levels of being (ontology) as well as levels of knowing (epistemology). They were said to be eternally or timelessly given (or "pregiven"), or existing in a merely objective or ontological fashion, such as a Platonic archetype, a collective memory or *vasana* (Asanga, Vasubandhu), a Hegelian Idea, or a Husserlian *eidos*, to name a prominent few. But Lovejoy is absolutely right: the vast majority of humankind's greatest philosophers and spiritual teachers have subscribed to some version of the Great Holarchy of Being and Knowing. Generally speaking, therefore, before you go tossing it into the garbage pail, you'd better have something at least as good to replace it with.

Metaphysics, as a general rule, simply assumed that these levels of reality existed, and then went about using them to explain the world, God, the soul, liberation (nirvana, metanoia, redemption, salvation), and suffering (sin, illusion, *maya*, fallenness, *samsara*). But with the critical turn in post/modern philosophy, these structures themselves required explaining (and defending). And the simplest conclusion to that rather complicated story is, they cannot be defended. They simply do not pass muster with either modern or postmodern thought or critical methodologies. This in itself does not mean they need to be jettisoned (modernity and postmodernity might be wrong in this instance). But the claim of Integral Post-Metaphysics is that you can indeed account for all the really necessary ingredients of metaphysics or a spiritual philosophy without them. These metaphysical assumptions are, quite simply, unnecessary and cumbersome baggage that hurts spirituality more than helps. Spirituality, to survive in the present and future world, is and must be post-metaphysical.

Keep in mind one point that I think is central in all of this. Theories such as the Great Holarchy of Being and Knowing—and virtually anything that could be called "metaphysics"—were simply ways that various philosophers and sages used to interpret their experience. Plotinus was not out walking one day and happened to stumble onto a building with 10 floors in it, with name tags on each floor that said things like "physical," "emotional," "logical mind," "higher mind," "*nous*," and "the One." His idea that reality consisted of 10 major levels of being and knowing was simply the best way that he knew to interpret certain insights and experiences that he had (particularly various mystical experiences of *unio mystica*). But there wasn't a pre-existing building out there labeled "The Great Chain" that had 10 discrete structures or floors in it, and that anybody could see if they went to the same physical place that Plotinus did in his walk through the woods. The Great Holarchy—and metaphysics in general—is simply a superb way to interpret reality if you are trying to account for God, the soul, mystical oneness, and the manifestation of a material world in a way that seems to be an illusion compared to the reality experienced in a state of *unio mystica*.

It is still a superb way to interpret reality. But many aspects of it are deeply, desperately, achingly in need of updating and revising. The first and foremost is: the 10 or so levels of reality are not pre-existing structures lying around out there waiting for all and sundry to stumble on them, like apples and rocks and paper clips. Even IF we allow that there is something like 10 levels of reality, those levels must be understood, not as independently existing structures, but in part as *con-structures of the knowing subject*—that is, **as structures of human consciousness** (hence, the constructivism that is an intrinsic part of Spirit's postmodern turn).

Second, the verification methods for the existence of these structures of consciousness can no longer involve merely asserting their existence because tradition says so; nor basing their existence merely on introspection or meditation (or other allegedly culture-transcending claims and assertions). They will, at the least, involve some version of both *modernity's* demand **for objective evidence** and *postmodernity's* demand **for intersubjective grounding**—without which you are presenting, in the first instance, merely *a given myth* (or given mythology; myths are truth claims without adequate evidence—which are the types of claims modernity fought valiantly to overcome, because they are all-too-often empirical falsehoods housing imperialistic power) or, in the second instance, *the myth of the given* (claims that pretend to be free from culture, which are the types of claims postmodernity fought valiantly to overcome, because they are all-too-often modes of false consciousness housing marginalization and oppression).

Third, these structures of consciousness cannot be conceived as ones that are given eternally or timelessly—they are not archetypes, they are not eternal ideas in the mind of God, they are not collective forms outside of history, they are not atemporal eidetic images, and so on. For the most part, these post-metaphysical levels of being and knowing would have to be conceived **as forms that have developed in time, evolution, and history.** This is not to say that spiritual philosophy can do completely without any *a priori* forms (no philosophy can); but the fewer, the better. And the *a priori* forms that are postulated had better be defensible with at least some reference to modern and postmodern forms of justification (and validity claims). Simply asserting that they exist will categorically not do. And claiming that you know God personally won't help, either.

In this appendix, I would like to do three things. First, give an explanation for the existence of levels or structures of consciousness that does not rely on metaphysical thinking. Next, give two samples of post-metaphysical thinking; the first involves the "address" of a holon in the Kosmos (which means, what do you have to specify in order to actually locate anything in the universe?), and the second involves a new way to speak of spiritual realities, a way that we might indeed call post-metaphysical.

THE SLIDING SCALE OF ENLIGHTENMENT

In chapter 4, we introduced the idea of "the sliding scale of Enlightenment"—namely, if evolution occurs in the world of form, and if Enlightenment involves a sense of being one with the world of evolving form, then how can you define Enlightenment in a way that fully acknowledges the evolving world, yet doesn't rob Enlightenment of its timeless nature? This is an unbelievably challenging issue. . . .

I will repeat the first paragraphs of "The Sliding Scale of Enlightenment" from chapter 4 in order to bring us up to speed. If we can make any sort of headway here, I believe we will have gone a long way toward the creation of an authentic post-metaphysics. So let's get started and see how well we do. First, the repeated paragraphs.

The problem can be stated in several different ways.

- If evolution occurs, how can Enlightenment have any meaning? Enlightenment is supposed to mean something like being one with *everything*, but if *everything is evolving*, and I get enlightened today, then won't my Enlightenment be partial when tomorrow arrives? Do I become unenlightened with the sun's dawn?

- A typical response is to say that Enlightenment is being one with that which is *Timeless* and *Eternal* and *Unborn*, so I can be one with the Timeless and that shouldn't be affected by the world of time (and evolving form), and so that takes care of the problem. But all that does is create a massive duality in Spirit—the timeless and eternal versus the temporal and evolving—and so what I am really saying is that Enlightenment is being one with half of Spirit.

- We saw that a "nondual mysticism" was a "union with *everything* in the gross, subtle, and causal realms." But you can have a nondual state experience at virtually any stage, including magic and mythic, and, e.g., the mythic world does NOT contain phenomena from the higher stages. So you can have a realization of nondual ever-present awareness that is a pure UNITY experience right now, but that experience leaves out a great deal of the universe. Thus *satori* can actually be unity with a fragmented world. Generally speaking, this is not good.

All of the above are variations on the same difficulty, but to make matters worse, that's just the beginning of the problem (call it part A), which can be summarized as follows. The universe—or the manifest universe, anyway—is evolving.* Even if Spirit is defined as the union of Emptiness and Form (where *Emptiness* is timeless, unborn, unmanifest, and not evolving, and *Form* is manifest, temporal, and evolving), the "temporal" or "world-of-Form" part puts a stress on the meaning of Enlightenment that is not easily remedied. The manifest world of Form is evolving and becoming more complex—it is becoming Fuller and Fuller over time. . . . And therefore whatever Enlightenment I may attain today is not going to be as FULL as an Enlightenment I might attain a decade, a century, a millennium from now. If I maintain otherwise, I revert to Enlightenment being defined only as a realization of the timeless and unborn, and then I must deny that Spirit is also the world of manifest Form, and thus I have a very dualistic Spirit.

Several theorists, such as David Deida, have made a wonderful distinction that helps us phrase this part of the problem. Emptiness is **Freedom** and Form is **Fullness.** Enlightenment is a union of both Emptiness and Form, or a union of Freedom and Fullness. To realize infinite Emptiness is to be **free** from all finite things, free from all pain, all suffering, all limitation, all qualities—the *via negativa* that soars to a transcendental freedom from the known, a *nirvikalpa samadhi* beyond desire and death, beyond pain and time, longing and remorse, fear and hope, a timeless Dharmakaya of the Unborn, the great Ayin or Abyss that is free from all finite qualities whatsoever (including that one). On the other side of the street, if to be one with Emptiness is the ultimate Freedom, to be one with the world of Form is the ultimate Fullness—one with the entire manifest realm, one with the Rupakaya (Form Body) in all its glory, finding that eternity is in love with the productions of time. Thus, En-

---

*To say that the manifest universe is evolving is not necessarily to endorse all of the neo-Darwinian view of evolution. I did my graduate work in the biochemistry and biophysics of the visual process ("The photoisomerization of rhodopsin isolated from bovine rod outer segments"), and what we don't understand about the mechanisms of evolution could fill the Library of Congress several times over. I'm no fan of Intelligent Design, either, which is just Creation Science in drag. But you don't need an intelligent designer to realize that evolution seems to involve some sort of "creative allure," or what Whitehead called "the creative advance into novelty." That drive—Eros by any other name—seems a perfectly realistic conclusion, given the facts of evolution as we understand them. Let's just say there is plenty of room for a Kosmos of Eros. But the whole point of a post-metaphysics is that it is the strict application of Occam's razor, refusing to postulate more entities when fewer will do the trick. It's just that Eros is one of those things that just doesn't seem to go away. . . .

lightenment as the union of Emptiness and Form is also Enlightenment as the union of Freedom and Fullness.

I believe that is very true. Part A of the problem is that Form is evolving, or Fullness is evolving—and thus becoming Fuller and Fuller and Fuller, if you will, and hence your Enlightenment today is less and less and less than tomorrow's. And you can't explain that away as not really counting unless you violate nonduality in a fundamental way (by implying that only half of the equation really counts). This was not a problem for the great wisdom traditions, because *they didn't know* that the world of Form was evolving, and so this problem never entered their radar screens. The world of Form held still for them, but today we know that it actually unfolds, it actually evolves. . . . So the union of Emptiness and Form is somehow the union of the Unborn and evolution, and evolution robs Enlightenment of its completion at any given point, because although tomorrow might not be Freer, it will always be Fuller.

It might seem that we could handle this part of the problem by simply saying, at any given time in evolution, Enlightenment is simply being one with Emptiness and the world of Form *at that time.* To be one with everything simply means to be one with everything at that particular time. Thus, for example, a tundra shaman could have a nondual unity experience and be one with Emptiness and one with the world of all Form at that time in history. There was nothing else to be one with, so that covers everything at that time, which is everything there is to worry about. There was nothing Fuller at that time, so there was no higher unity than that. Subsequent eras might be Fuller, and then to be one with everything would involve that. You can't compare the "Unity" of one time with the "Unity" of a later time because they are apples and oranges, even though both are true "Unity" experiences.

And it does solve that problem, until you bring in the stages discovered by Western researchers. Which brings us to part B of the problem. If part A can be handled by the foregoing paragraph, part B cannot, and it is a problem that starts to become apparent even using the metaphysical maps of the wisdom traditions themselves. Because if you use that paragraph, it works—and completely destroys the Great Chain. Once you start seriously confronting part B, it simply but rather completely unravels the entire metaphysical interpretations of spiritual realities— not the spiritual realities themselves, but their interpretations as *metaphysics* (and brings us, I believe, inexorably to "post-metaphysics" as the only way to defend spiritual realities in an unobjectionable fashion in the post/modern world, using the term *post/modern* to mean items that both modernity and postmodernity accept).

As we saw, the metaphysical systems of the great wisdom traditions typically involve something like the Great Chain of Being—the notion that there are, indeed, **levels of being and knowing**—such as the levels of Plotinus (which became the default levels of Neoplatonism throughout the West, from Dionysius to Eckhart), the **Sefirot** of Kabbalah, and the **8 vijñanas** (8 consciousnesses) of Mahayana and Vajrayana Buddhism.

Now the traditions believed that the Great Chain was given all at once, and thus it exists in its entirety right now, even if parts of it aren't realized or awakened to. And that understanding is what comes unraveled when it is realized that the Great Chain actually unfolded over vast stretches of astronomical and geological time. The lower 4 or 5 levels of the Great Chain are usually given as matter, sensation, perception, impulse, emotion, symbols, concepts . . . (as found, e.g., in the *skandhas*). But those levels *actually evolved over 14 billion years of evolution*: matter arose with the Big Bang, sensation with the first life forms, impulse with the first reptiles, emotion with the first mammals, symbols with the first primates, concepts with the first humans. . . .

The amazing thing is how accurate those levels turned out to be, as well as their chronological order; it's just that they unfolded over billions of years. So, as Arthur Lovejoy pointed out, the easiest way to try to salvage the Great Chain of the wisdom traditions when confronted with this 14-billion-year-old history is to simply say, fine, the levels in the Great Chain aren't given all at once; rather, they are actually ones that unfolded over long stretches of time. But if that's so, and Enlightenment is the union of Emptiness and all Form, then the only way to get enlightened is to wait until all of time has unfolded.

That's part B of the problem. The very nature of Enlightenment—and spiritual realities across the board—change dramatically once you are forced to account for the Fuller and Fuller side of the evolutionary street. You can still realize Emptiness and attain absolute Freedom, but on the Fuller side of the street, there are fatal flaws hidden in the realization and in the entire metaphysical systems built around not recognizing that problem (around not recognizing that evolution robs Enlightenment of any stable meaning). Modernity and postmodernity recognized the problem but jettisoned the spiritual realities, when all they should have ditched was the metaphysical interpretations of the realities.

If we do so jettison the metaphysical interpretations, the first thing that has to happen is converting the **levels of knowing and being** (whether the 10 Sefirot, the 8 *vijnanas*, or the 7 *chakras*) from preexisting, ontological levels or planes of reality into levels that have themselves evolved. Charles Peirce spoke of natural laws as being more like *natural habits*, and I agree: we call them **Kosmic habits** or **Kosmic memories**, and that is how the levels of reality (of being and knowing) can be reinterpreted. When they first emerged, the form they took was relatively open and creative, but once a particular response occurred time and time again, it settled into a Kosmic habit harder and harder to shake.

Thus, using the levels of value structures as an example, about 50,000 years ago, the **magenta** value structure (magical-animistic) was about the highest that humanity had evolved at that time. But certain highly evolved individuals began to push into new and creative modes of being and knowing, and they began making responses from a higher level of complexity and consciousness. As more and more individuals shared those responses, the **red** value structure (egocentric, power) began to be laid down as a Kosmic habit. The more it was laid down, the more of a fixed habit it became. Around 10,000 BCE, as the red value structure dominated humanity's responses, a few heroic individuals began pushing into a response that involved more consciousness, more awareness, more complexity—and the **amber** value structure (absolutistic, ethnocentric) began to be laid down for the first time.

In terms of worldviews, this move from red magic to amber mythic involved the creation of extensive systems of mythology that, whatever else they did, allowed the creation of much more complex social systems. Magic could only unify, or socially unite, humans based on bloodlineage and kinship ties. Unless you were related to me by blood, there was no way we could create a "we," and thus, at magic, tribes could not be united with each other socially or culturally. But one of the functions of myth is that, in claiming to be descended from a God not of blood and genetics but of values and beliefs, *mythology could unite vast numbers of humans and nonkinship tribes if they all adopted belief in the same mythic God*: everybody can believe in that God, even if they are not blood-related. Thus the 12 tribes of Israel could be united under Yahweh, and the Prophets (or one variety of them) brought amber law and true belief to the red pagan cultures around them, uniting and creating one people under one mythic God.

At this point in evolution—around 6000 years ago—here is what would be available (to put it very simplistically): As for levels of consciousness (levels of knowing and being, which the Great Chain theorists mistook to be fixed and given), humans had evolved from **archaic** ape to **magenta** magic to **red** power to **amber** mythic-membership. All 4 of those levels of consciousness in numerous lines would now be available to humans. Everybody is born at square one and has to develop through these now "fixed" levels, fixed only because they have settled into Kosmic habits of a Peircean nature; and all that would be required to account for the *creation* of ever-higher levels of being and knowing is an autopoietic, dissipative-structure tendency in the universe—"Eros" in a more poetic version. Not much more "metaphysics" is required than Whitehead's "creative advance into novelty." Yet this minimalist metaphysics can generate a Great Chain and all of its essential accoutrements without having to postulate pre-existing independent ontological structures of any variety.*

At the same time, a few creative and heroic souls would be pushing into **orange** and a bit beyond. But none of these levels are Platonic givens; they are not pre-existing ontological structures in some eternally fixed Great Chain; they evolved and were laid down by factors in all 4 quadrants as they developed (or tetra-evolved) over time and became Kosmic habits of humanity, habits available to all future humans—in fact, handed to all future humans as deeply set habits that, for all practical purposes, are then fixed (as Kosmic habits, not Platonic archetypes), and thus levels that, to a Great Chain theorist writing some 2000 years ago, would *appear* eternally given (but had actually evolved). No metaphysical baggage—no archetypes, no ontological planes of reality, no independent levels of being that are lying around waiting to be seen by humans—none of that is needed in order to get the same results and explain the existence of these "fixed" levels. Moreover, these levels are then *independent of any particular* human that is born, and thus they cannot be reduced to psychology. Everything that is required can be derived post-metaphysically.

At that same period (6000 years ago), human beings also had waking, dreaming, and deep sleep states of consciousness, which could be peak-experienced in various forms of mysticism—nature, deity, formless, and nondual. Although those states are ever-present, humanity as a whole seemed to learn to master them in roughly the same order as meditators do today: moving from exterior gross immersion (paganism) to deity mysticism (ascending and transcendental) to formless Abyss (the great

---

*For a more precise account, see the discussions of "involutionary givens" in Excerpts A–G.

Axial Age) to ever-present Nondual. Unlike structures of consciousness, however, there is much fluidity in the sequence of trained states of consciousness, and individuals can peak-experience any of these states to various degrees. But during the great mythic (amber) eras around the world, humanity as a whole was exploring the heavenly realms of the subtle-dream world: humanity not only moved from red power tribes to amber mythic-membership societies *structurally*, their most evolved religious figures moved from *states* of nature pagan mysticism to interior deity mysticism and prophetic vision, the confrontation with a luminosity and creative source not of this world (although even higher states were sometimes available).

So let's pause here and recall the original question: how can we define Enlightenment in a way that has any meaning during that time? Would it even exist during that period, when humanity structurally was deeply ethnocentric (amber)? If so, what would Enlightenment consist of? And if we find a definition of Enlightenment that works for that period, can it believably be applied to today?

Recall that the generic definition of Enlightenment is the full realization of, or being one with, Emptiness and all Form. Many lesser spiritual experiences and realizations are possible, but we are taking "Enlightenment"—with a capital "E"—as a type of end limit of the fullest and highest spiritual realization possible (which is why I have almost always capitalized it throughout this book).

So how can we define Enlightenment with this in mind? The answer we have suggested throughout this book is: **Enlightenment is the realization of oneness with all states and all structures that are in existence at any given time.**

Stabilization in causal Emptiness provides the Freedom at any given time; but the world of Form evolves, not according to a predetermined plan, but as an evolutionarily creative process. If one wishes, this process can certainly be seen as Spirit's creative sport and play (which I believe is true, and removes us from scientific materialism of various forms),*

---

* And also removes us from being advocates of Intelligent Design. Proponents of ID have one truth on their side: scientific materialism cannot explain all of evolution (it can explain pretty much everything except major holistic transformational leaps). With that, I quite agree. But all that is required to get and keep evolution moving forward is a minimalist Eros (as an involutionary given). This force of creative advance into novelty is one form of Spirit-in-action, and that Eros is all that is then required for evolutionary theory to work just fine. That's why evolution shows so many fits and starts; it's a creative artwork, not an intelligent engineering product

but the "levels in the Great Chain" simply no longer preexist or are given in anything like their fixed forms. As the world of Form evolves, what is required to be one with that world is for individuals to evolve and develop in their own cases up to *the highest levels then in existence*. Higher than that, there isn't, ontologically speaking.

And thus Spirit's Rupakaya or the World of Form is no longer conceived as a pre-existing Great Chain, but as the Totality of Form at any given time. And being one with that Totality is the Fullness side of the street.

But an individual can realize a complete oneness only by moving through not just all of the available structures, but also the available states. Thus, an enlightened person is somebody who has developed to the highest available structures in the Kosmos at that time, and navigated through the available states (i.e., brought Wakefulness through the states, generally from gross to subtle to causal to nondual).*

As indicated in chap. 4, we early researchers tended to confuse higher states with higher structures, and then stack the higher states on top of the conventional structures. I did so in *Up from Eden*, where the structures are called "average mode" and the states are called "most advanced mode." *Up from Eden* traces those two "lines," when actually what it is tracing—quite accurately—is (1) the average center of gravity of the vertical **structure-stages** that were emerging at any give epoch (the "average mode"—archaic to magic to mythic to rational to integral-aperspectival) and (2) the progression in trained states that was also emerging during those eras—where Wakefulness penetrated gross to subtle to causal to nondual ("most advanced mode"), which are **state-stages** that *Eden* also calls the path of shamans/yogis (gross to subtle), the path of saints (subtle to causal), and the path of sages (causal to nondual). What this really amounts to is a W-C Lattice for phylogenetic development, with structures up the vertical scale and states across the horizontal scale. *Up*

(because if so, that Engineer is an idiot). The proponents of ID parlay their one little truth into the demand that the Jehovah of Genesis be that Eros, and there is not the slightest evidence for that anywhere in heaven or on earth.

*The states aspect of this definition can be fine-tuned in many different ways. As previously indicated, although the major states are ever-present, and although from the very earliest phylogenetic stages, human beings had access to waking, dreaming, deep sleep, and nondual states, humanity on the whole seemed to learn to master them in roughly the same order as mediators do today: moving from exterior gross immersion (paganism) to deity mysticism (ascending and transcendental) to formless Abyss (the great Axial Age) to ever-present Nondual. Unlike structures of consciousness, however, there is much fluidity in the sequence of trained states of consciousness, and individuals can peak-experience any of these states to various degrees. But there is definitely a historical progression in the deepest states through which Wakefulness or Witnessing had generally pushed at any given time.

The general contours of this definition of Enlightenment work very well in explaining the "sliding scale" of evolutionary Enlightenment: the Emptiness stays the same—Timeless, Unborn, Unmanifest, Undying—but the Form continues to evolve, and Enlightenment is being one with both of them—both Emptiness and Form—a oneness that, on the Form side of Fuller and Fuller and Fuller, includes levels in the Kosmos that are being laid down now, not as Platonic archetypes, but as evolving Forms, Forms that, once they are laid down, appear indeed as if they were eternally given as pre-existing ontological structures but are actually Kosmic habits.

So, to return to the mythic (amber) era in our simplistic example, in order to be completely one with the World of Form (the Fuller side of the street), what exactly would an individual have to be one with—what does "one with the Totality of Form" involve at that (amber) time? In the world of Form, there are now in existence 4 levels of being and knowing that are given and "fixed"—not as archetypes but as Kosmic habits (magenta, red, amber, and beginning orange). These levels are now **actual structures** in the Kosmos, and thus in order for a person to

---

from Eden is still very valid and accurate if you take that into account.

Thus, although all 4 or 5 major states were available to any individual at any of the great eras that were defined by the widespread emergence of a higher stage (archaic to magic to mythic to rational to integral-aperspectival), humanity on the whole tended to move through Wakeful access to the great states in the same general progression as meditators do today, and this constitutes the second progression that *Up from Eden* traces. The general correlations of those two (average-mode *stage* and most-advanced *state*) are exactly as *Eden* suggests: magic/gross, mythic/subtle, rational/causal, integral/nondual. The point about states is that they constitute a looser scale than stages because they can be peak-experienced, but in general the most evolved religious figures moved from *states* of nature pagan mysticism and subtle energies (path of shamans/yogis) to interior deity mysticism and prophetic vision, the confrontation with a luminosity and creative source not of this world (the path of saints) to causal emptiness and unmanifest absorption (the path of sages) to nondual union of emptiness and all form (the path of siddhas and tantra).

So our definition of Enlightenment can be fine-tuned on the states side to indicate this general progression in realistic access to states that was available at any of the major stages/epochs. A "total oneness" is then exactly the highest stage and state expectable at any given time in history, which is exactly as *Eden* discovered: magic/gross, mythic/subtle, rational/causal, integral/nondual. In the text I am focusing on the stage progression, but this state progression is also an important variable, and fits precisely with our sliding scale and definition of Enlightenment. Discovering the correlations between the general epochs of stages and the progression of states penetrated by Wakefulness is still one of *Eden*'s best contributions, I think.

be one with all Form, they would have to be one with those Forms—they would have to have *transcended and included all 4 of those levels in their own development*: they would have to have moved from archaic to magical-animistic to red power to amber-mythic structures (converting those *subjects into objects* that are then *transcended and included* in awareness). Doing so, they would indeed have transcended and included the entire world of Form in their own being—**there are no higher levels anywhere** waiting to drop down from Platonic heaven, **so a perfect oneness could in fact be achieved**, at least in this variable.

How about the states variable? If an individual has taken Wakefulness from the gross into the subtle, causal, and nondual states, so that those states are mastered to some degree (converting subjects to objects that are then included in awareness or consciousness), then they would be able to realize a oneness with all of those general states as well. Once one had done both (had transcended and included all states and stages in existence at that time), then in the entire Kosmos, there would be no higher states or stages available—this person would quite literally, in any meaningful sense, have realized a oneness with the entire Kosmos, with both Emptiness and Form in all of its levels, with both Dharmakaya (or Timeless Spirit) and Rupakaya (or Temporal Spirit). This person, some 6000 years ago, would be as deeply Enlightened as Enlightened could be. (Or, as we also put it, this person would be both horizontally and vertically Enlightened at that time in history.)*

And notice that this individual would be deeply ethnocentric. He or she would have no choice; there are no worldcentric (or postconventional) structures anywhere in the Kosmos that have yet evolved. No matter how deeply realized (and fully mastering all available states and stages), this person would of necessity believe salvation exists only for one chosen people, or one class, or one sex, or one path.

Somewhere around the 1st millennium BCE, the next major level of consciousness, orange, began to emerge as a creative response to problems that could not be solved by amber. (This new evolutionary emergent can be viewed, as evolution in general can, as the creativity of Spirit-in-action expressing itself through its own AQAL manifestation. Or you can embrace the silliness of random mutation and natural selection; in this case, it doesn't really matter. The point is that new things emerge, and they are selected and carried forward by whatever mecha-

*For a fine-tuned version based on actually accessible states, see previous footnote, pages 242–243.

nism you are comfortable believing. I simply refer to them, as noted, as Kosmic habits, and as for their exact nature, we can debate that all day. But wherever these new things come from, they are there.)

While orange was being laid down as a Kosmic habit, or the sedimentation of creatively emergent choices of humanity in the face of new challenges, humanity as a whole was also pushing its mastery of states from subtle-dream into causal-formless (see, e.g., *Up from Eden*). The combination of worldcentric structures and causal-state access caused a worldwide explosion of growth in consciousness, known in general as the great Axial Age. Around the world at that time (c. 6th century BCE), you find individuals not only advocating worldcentric or universal morality for the first time, but also sages who begin to speak of an infinite causal Abyss or nirvana entirely Free of the woes of this samsaric world, or you find a claim that the individual soul and God are one in Godhead ("I and the Father are One"). All of these were startlingly new realizations, as humanity continued its creative evolution.

Cut to today, where 3 or 4 new, major, universal structures have been laid down since the Axial Age (roughly, orange, green, teal, and turquoise). In today's (Western) culture, about 40% of the population is at amber, about 50% at orange, 20% at green, and 2% at turquoise. * Are there any higher levels available today? Not states, but structures/levels? The answer appears to be yes, there seem to be at least 3 or 4 structures/stages/levels higher than turquoise. These, too, are not pre-existing ontological or metaphysical structures already existing somewhere, but are the first very tentative structures being laid down by highly evolved souls pushing into new territory—and co-creating them as they do (i.e., tetra-creating them).

These higher post-turquoise structures began to be laid down when the first pioneers pushed into this new and as-yet-unformed territory, some as early as a thousand years ago or so, co-creating the territory as they explored it. But to date, the sum total of humans who have stably moved into these higher structures is only a few thousand individuals, if that, or well less than 1/100th of 1% of humanity. In figure 2.4 (opposite page 68), I have listed some of these higher levels in the cognitive line, based on Aurobindo: above vision-logic or the higher mind, we have the illumined mind, the intuitive mind, the overmind, and the supermind, with higher ones in the making, no doubt. In the self line, Susann Cook-Greuter has investigated the first 2 of these higher levels, which in figure

---

*This is a composite result of several sources, including Kegan, SD, Paul Ray, Loevinger, and Wilber. It doesn't add up to 100%, because there are overlaps.

2.4 are called "ego-aware" and "transpersonal." These are permanent structural competences, not states.

If you think of these structures/levels as Kosmic habits, then the older the level, the more deeply it has become etched into the Kosmos. I use the analogy of the Grand Canyon: it is so old that it is cut several kilometers deep. That would be like the red level, which began around 50,000 years ago and is cut very deep into the Kosmos. Amber, which began around 10,000 years ago, would be a Kosmic canyon maybe 500 meters deep. Orange, which began around the Axial period but really flowered with the Western Enlightenment—a mere 300 years ago—is perhaps 100 meters deep. Green, which, as a significant percentage of the population, began in the 1960s, is only around 10 meters deep. Teal and turquoise are really just being laid down, and are maybe 1 meter deep. Structures higher than turquoise are like people dragging sticks across the ground, starting to cut Kosmic habits into the universe, which will begin, as they all did, as small trickles, then small streams, then raging rivers cutting canyons into the Kosmos, canyons that are then actual structures in the Kosmos (and hence appear as ontologically pre-existing). But today, structures higher than turquoise are indeed like people dragging sticks across the ground. Indigo is maybe 3 or 4 centimeters deep, and ultraviolet is little more than a faint scratch on the surface of one's Original Face. . . .

As more and more people push into the post-turquoise levels of development, those levels/structures will be created or enacted and laid down; those structures that tetra-mesh with AQAL reality at that altitude will be selected and carried forward, and then increasingly sedimented as sturdy Kosmic habits, which will then be, in effect, given structures of consciousness whose deep structures are no longer negotiable by individuals.

We can, in other words, generate all of the essentials of the great metaphysical systems but with virtually none of their metaphysical baggage.

So, in today's world, what would constitute Enlightenment? What are the highest states and stages available in the Kosmos? At the very least, it would mean indigo altitude in the cognitive and self lines, as well as a mastery of the 4 or so major states (which includes access to gross, subtle, causal, and nondual). All sorts of other possible realizations exist, some of them very profound. But "total realization" or "full Enlightenment" would include being one with the major stages ("horizontal Enlightenment") and one with the major states ("vertical Enlightenment") that exist at any given time, and today that means: at least indigo altitude and nondual states.

(And once you are there, then what? Once you have identified with all states and all stages, then you stand at the leading edge, identified with Eros itself, pushing into new and higher territory, and tetra-creating it as you go along. . . .)

Notice that somebody today who is at mythic-membership amber, even though they might have fully mastered gross, subtle, causal, and nondual states (including *Anu* and *Ati Yoga*), *would not and could not be fully Enlightened*. Horizontally, yes; vertically, no. The world has moved on; Spirit has unfolded more of its own being; there are more structure-stages you must be one with in today's world in order to be one with the Kosmos. . . .

In other words, the same structure that 6000 years ago could be said to be fully Enlightened, is no longer so today. Somebody at mythic-membership today is no longer one with the Totality of all Form, because there are, "over the head" of amber, the orange and green and teal and turquoise structures. Those are now real, "ontological," *actually existing structures* in the Kosmos, as real as if they were Platonic eternal givens (except they aren't), and if a person has not transcended and included those levels in their own development, then there are major levels of reality that they (the amber individuals) are not one with. Even if they master nondual states of a perfect nondual union of Emptiness and Form, even if they master *Ati Yoga* and *thögal* visions and the 5 ranks of Tozan, even if they master centering prayer and the deepest contemplative states, even if they rest constantly in Ayin, they are not fully Enlightened: there are aspects of Form that never enter this person's world, and thus—exactly as we were meant to explain—this person's *satori* is oneness with a partial world.

And yet, in the mythic/amber era, the same realization was indeed oneness with the entire Kosmos, and thus counted as full Enlightenment. Thus this definition of Enlightenment fits all the requirements that we started with: it can explain Enlightenment today as well as yesterday; it allows for a timeless component; but also includes a temporal, evolving, historical component.

We started with a handful of extremely subtle problems generated by evolution in the world of Form. We found that only a post-metaphysical approach could handle them (because postulating fixed, eternal, independently existing archetypes, Platonic or otherwise, not only cannot pass muster with modern and postmodern epistemologies, it actually self-deconstructs when attempting to explain anything in the world of evolving Form). We saw, further, that there is a definition of Enlightenment that is meaningfully sliding, and thus can honor the timeless, unchanging, ever-present Emptiness of the great Unborn (Godhead, Dharmakaya, Ayin), as well as the temporal evolution of the ever Fuller and Fuller world of Form (or Rupakaya). A person's realization today is not Freer than Buddha's (Emptiness is Emptiness), but it is Fuller than Buddha's (and will be even Fuller down the road)—and yet both the Buddhas of 2000 years ago and the Buddhas of today are *equally* enlightened by any *meaningful* definition of Enlightenment.

(But, by the same token, a 1000-year-old path can *today*, by itself, no longer be the carrier of a full Enlightenment.)

Thus, with all of these items in mind, we defined Enlightenment as **the realization of oneness with all the major states and major structures that are in existence at any given time in history.**

And none of that requires any metaphysical baggage. It is not generated with metaphysical thinking but with an Integral Methodological Pluralism that honors and incorporates the enduring aspects of premodern, modern, and postmodern methodologies. It does not require metaphysical validity claims, which are claims based on a combination of *shruti* and *smriti*—that is, based on the mere assertions of a tradition or the recollections of mindfulness introspection, neither of which are integral enough to cover the demands of modernity and postmodernity.

Put differently, all of the *ontologically pre-existing levels* of being and knowing—from the 8 *vijnanas* of Yogachara to the Sefirot of Kabbalah—which both modernity and postmodernity absolutely savaged, are simply no longer needed, because we can generate the essentials of every one of those levels but in a completely post-metaphysical way. Kant, in an argument accepted by both modernity and postmodernity in a variety of forms, demolished their ontological referents—and rightly so—and placed a demand for the proof of the existence of a worldspace on the epistemological grounding of that space, a demand with which an AQAL post-metaphysics fully complies. This "post-Kantian post-metaphysics"—or something like it—is the only avenue open to a spiritual philosophy in the modern and postmodern world.

WHAT IS THE ADDRESS OF AN OBJECT IN THE KOSMOS?

To show just how far away from metaphysics today's spiritual thinking must move, take the following thought experiment. Let's take four referents, indicated by the signifiers *dog*, *Santa Claus*, *the square root of a negative one*, and *Emptiness*.

Where do the referents of those signifiers exist? Or, if they exist, where can they be found? Does Santa Claus exist; if so, where? Does the square root of a negative one exist; if so, where can it be found? And so on. . . .

In chapter 2, we briefly mentioned the idea that: **Kosmic address = altitude + perspective.** What I would like to do is unpack that idea a little bit more, to show both what post-metaphysical thinking is like, and how spiritual realities—or any realities, for that matter—need to be conceptualized in a post/modern world (using the word "post/modern" to mean items that both modernity and postmodernity accept).

Let's start with the standard 4-quadrant figure, which we have seen several times in this book and which, for convenience, is repeated here as figure II.1.

For the moment, let's assume that diagram is accurate. It looks like a fairly simple representation of some commonly accepted realities—things like atoms, molecules, symbols, concepts, ecological systems, and so on. But remember that things like, for example, holarchical planetary systems can only be seen and grasped starting at around turquoise. So if we are looking for the "location" of something like global ecosystems, the first rule is simple: ecosystems exist only in a worldspace of turquoise or higher.

Ah, we say, but surely ecosystems existed in the real world 100,000 years ago, even if humans were only at, say, magenta, and could not see or conceive them. But that is exactly what you are NOT allowed to do according to many modern and all postmodern epistemologies. You cannot postulate a single, pregiven, ahistorical world that is "simply there" and to which representational methods give various degrees of access. If that were so, then what we think of today as "ecosystems" will probably be understood, a thousand years from now, to be energy sinks of dark matter controlling access to an 11th-dimensional world of hyperspace. . . . Well, you get the point. If we claim that our epistemologies are basically representational maps (or mirrors of nature), then just as we of today will invalidate what was taken as knowledge 1000 years ago, so tomorrow will invalidate our knowledge of today. *So nobody ever has any truth*, just various degrees of falsehood. This is the myth of the given; this is everything postmodernity savaged; and this is not something we can believably call upon.

But the simple point is this: whatever ecosystems are, they were NOT

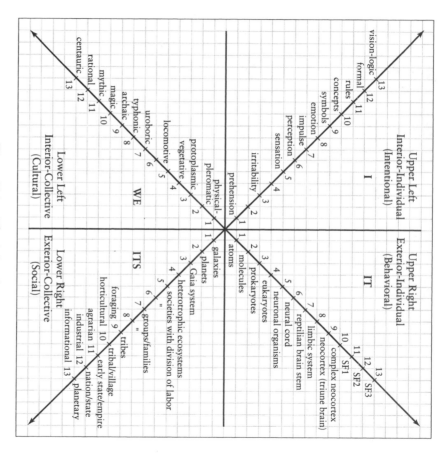

Figure II.1. The 4 Quadrants.

seen or understood 100,000 years ago. (As Clare Graves used to point out, tribal consciousness "has a name for every bend in the river but no name for the river.") Ecosystems enter consciousness only at turquoise or higher. And since "enter consciousness" and "exist" are essentially identical in the post/modern world, then we can safely say that whatever ecosystems are, they can only be *found* in a turquoise world.*

*This is not subjective idealism, nor does this stop us from saying that ecosystems had some sort of existence in magenta and earlier times. Just as the rejection of the myth of the given still allows for what are called "intrinsic features" of sensory experience, we can say that if ecosystems did not ex-ist or stand forth in the magenta worldspace, they nonetheless "subsisted" in it, or were present as intrinsic features

So, in the equation, **address = altitude + perspective**, that is exactly what the "altitude" part of a Kosmic address means. Referents (or "real objects") ex-ist (or can be found) only in specific worldspaces that are, among other things, developmentally ordered, or have a particular "altitude." For the rest of this appendix, I will simply use 10 major post-metaphysical levels of being and knowing, which are simply the first 10 levels given in figures 2.4 and 2.5, which I will repeat here for ease of reference:

1. **infrared**—archaic, sensorimotor.
2. **magenta**—magical-animistic.
3. **red**—egocentric, power, magic-mythic.
4. **amber**—mythic, ethnocentric, traditional.
5. **orange**—rational, worldcentric, pragmatic, modern.
6. **green**—pluralistic, multicultural, postmodern.
7. **teal**—beginning integral, low vision-logic, systemic.
8. **turquoise**—global mind, high vision-logic, higher mind.
9. **indigo**—para-mind, trans-global, illumined mind.
10. **violet**—meta-mind and overmind.

I will also refer to these levels by number, realizing that those numbers are rather arbitrary. And again, for argument's sake, let's simply assume those levels are there as post-metaphysical structures of consciousness validated by methodologies such as those in zone #2.

So, to return to the idea of a Kosmic address. Eco-systems **exist** only in turquoise or higher worldspaces. And here, **"exist"** means **"ex-ist"**:

of the Kosmos not cognized by magenta. But the point that still removes this from the myth of the given is that the *intrinsic features themselves* are not pregiven but are simply the co-products of the highest level of consciousness making the claim. In other words, intrinsic features themselves are, in part, interpretive and con-structed. Those intrinsic features are then retro-read into earlier times—which is fine, they are just not intrinsic features of a pregiven world, but intrinsic features of a turquoise worldspace (which will, of course, be largely rejected—or more accurately, tran-scended and included—by indigo, whose own intrinsic features will be rejected by violet, and so on). In other words, these are not intrinsically intrinsic features, but interpretively intrinsic features. The point is that whatever is actually "intrinsic" to the Kosmos changes with each new worldspace; and thus both what ex-ists and what sub-sists are con-structions of consciousness (but not only consciousness, of course, because each occasion is tetra-structured). In this example, we are simply pointing out that ecosystems do not ex-ist in the magenta worldspace and cannot be found anywhere in its phenomenology.

to stand out, to be known, to be disclosed, to be tetra-enacted—anything except being part of a pregiven world lying around out there waiting to be perceived. Part of an object's Kosmic address is the fact that objects come into being, or are enacted, only at various developmental levels of complexity and consciousness. Whether they exist in some other way CANNOT BE KNOWN in any event, and assuming that they do exist entirely independently of a knowing mind is nothing but the myth of the given and the representational paradigm—that is, is just another type of metaphysical thinking and thus not adequately grounded. At any event, post-metaphysical thinking does not rely on the existence of a pregiven world and the myth of that givenness.*

Let's go back to figure II.1, and ask again, *where do the objects represented in that diagram exist?* Answer: most of them exist in a turquoise or higher worldspace. Everything from ecosystems to atoms simply *cannot be found* at infrared, magenta, red, or amber. They started to be disclosed, or exist, only from orange to turquoise, and thus, on the whole, the **referents** (or real and existing objects) that are represented by the **signifiers** in figure II.1 (such as "ecosystems" and "structure-functions SF1, SF2") exist only at an **altitude** of turquoise or higher.

That's the altitude part of a Kosmic address; what's the perspective part? It's simply the quadrant in which the referent ex-ists. Metaphysical thinking assumes a perspective-free universe, and then makes assertions about things that exist as if they were free of perspectives and free of contexts in general, which is not only the myth of the given, but a desperately egocentric version of the myth of the given. All real objects are first and foremost perspectives. NOT "are seen from perspectives," but "ARE perspectives." Again, assuming there is something pre-existing in an ahistorical world and waiting to be seen is just metaphysics (and the myth of the given). All occasions possess 4 dimensions/perspectives/quadrants. These are 4 dimensions of what they are, and not something apart from that—because there is no "apart from" how a thing appears; there is simply how it appears, and it ALWAYS ALREADY appears as a perspective.

So, at the least, we need to specify the quadrant that is being enacted when the referent is being indicated.† An ecosystem, for example, is an "its," or a Lower-Right entity/occasion. So where does an ecosystem

Ecosystem = turquoise + Lower Right

Now this Kosmic address is just the general street address, if you will. It simply gets you in the general ballpark—or at most, in the general building on a street—but nothing more. It doesn't tell you about its occupants, or its actual contours, or its specific elements, and so on. **But this general Kosmic address is a stark and demanding reminder that "things" do not exist in a pregiven world just lying around out there.** Among many other things, they come into existence at various levels of developmental complexity and consciousness, and they are always already disclosed as particular perspectives, including (but not limited to) subjective I, objective it, intersubjective you/we, and interobjective its.

(A more complete Kosmic address would include the full AQAL aspects of any occasion, but the point is that, at the very minimum, you need quadrants and levels, or perspectives and altitude.)

So far, so good—but wait! We're really just getting started. In a post-metaphysical world, where there are no absolute foundations and all things are perspectives before they are anything else, we must take the next and even more crucial step. We just gave the Kosmic address of the referent, or the perceived phenomenon (in this case, the eco-system). But what about the address of the perceiver? We gave the address of the object; what about the address of the subject? Remember, in a post-metaphysical world, they cannot be radically separated. **So the Kosmic address of both the perceiver and the perceived must be indicated in order to situate the existence of anything in the universe.**

Now things start to get really interesting, because, exactly as in Einstein's special theory of relativity, things become absolutely relative to each other. Not merely relative, but absolutely relative. (As everybody knows, Einstein's theory is badly misnamed; he thought about calling it things like absolute theory and invariance theory. The idea is that there is no fixed point anywhere in the universe that can be considered center; each thing can be located only relative to each other; this still creates absolutes and universals, but in a sliding system of reference to each other and to the system as a whole at any given time, with time itself being set by the invariant speed of light.)

Here we need the idea of quadrants and quadrivium. A **quadrant** is a *subject's* perspective; a **quadrivium** is the perspective the *object* is being looked at from. Only individual holons have or *possess* 4 quadrants; but anything can be looked at *through* or *from* those 4 quadrants (which are then quadrivia).

Thus, for example, as an individual holon, I possess at least 4 quadrant-perspectives: my being *contains* an I-perspective, a we-perspective, an it-perspective, and an its-perspective. But a Pepsi bottle does not possess 4 quadrants, because it is not a sentient being. However, it can be looked at *from* any of my 4 quadrants/perspectives. I can look at the bottle from an I-perspective and tell you what I personally think or feel about the Pepsi bottle. You and I can discuss the bottle and form a we-perspective. And I can look at the bottle in a scientific fashion (it and its), and discuss perhaps its molecular structure.

Thus, I possess 4 quadrants; the bottle can be looked at through the 4 quadrants (which then constitute a quadrivia). Or in general: the perceiving subject has quadrants, which must be specified as part of its Kosmic address; and the perceived object, referent, or phenomenon has a quadrivium, which must be specified as part of its Kosmic address.

Another way to say it—more loosely—is that because an object is being looked at through or from a particular quadrant, then the *subject* is looking at the object *through* a quadrant, and the *object* itself exists "in" a quadrant. In both cases, the quadrant of the perceiver and the quadrant (quadrivium) of the perceived must be specified for the Kosmic address of the referent to be known.*

And that makes everything **absolutely relative** to everything else. There is no ground, there is no metaphysics, there is no myth of the given; all that is solid melts into air, all that is foundational evaporates—and yet we can still generate all of the essentials of the great metaphysical systems but without their thoroughly discredited metaphysical baggage, which they don't need anyway. . . .

So, let's run through it. Here are our summary points on how to locate anything in a post-metaphysical universe:

1. Since there is no fixed center of the universe, or even foundational level (it's turtles all the way down), then the location of any phenomenon or thing or event or process or holon can only be specified in relation to a set of each other.

---

*With this information, we can now see that "8 zones" and "8 perspectives/methodologies" are just a more complex version of quadrants and quadrivia. That is, the 8 zones are "8 quadrants," or 8 actual dimensions-perspectives of an individual holon, and the 8 perspectives/methodologies are 8 fundamental ways that anything can be viewed via those dimensions (and the methodologies that can be used within them).

What is Latin for 8 quadrivia—an octavia? This is starting to sound like a list of Roman emperors. But it should also be obvious that I am not using Latin correctly here. I believe the plural of *quadrivium* is *quadrivii*.

2. Further, there is no pregiven world, existing independently and apart from all perception of it. Nor are all things merely perceptions. Rather, there is the sum total of the mutually disclosing things and events that disclose themselves relative to each other (i.e., relative to each other's perspective). In reality, this means that each thing *is* a perspective before it is anything else. And this means that in the manifest world, there are no perceptions, only perspectives. Put bluntly, perception, prehension, awareness, consciousness, etc., are all 3rd-person, monological abstractions with no reality whatsoever. As far as we know or can know, the manifest world is made of sentient beings with perspectives, not things with properties, nor subjects with perception, nor vacuum potentials, nor *dharmas*, nor strings, nor holograms, nor biofields, etc. Those are all perspectives relative to some sentient being.

3. Therefore, in order to specify the "location" of any occasion—in order to specify where it can be found—we have to specify the location of both the perceiver and the perceived, relative to each other. This location has at least two components: a vertical, developmental, and evolutionary component (**altitude**), and the perspective in which (**quadrivium**) or through which (**quadrium**) the occasion is being accessed. We can specify other components to help us locate a phenomenon, but those two (levels and quadrants) are the minimum. *So we need the altitude and the perspective of both the perceiver and perceived.* We can represent this simplistically as follows:

Kosmic address = altitude + perspective

And we need to specify these for both the perceiver/subject and the perceived/object:

Kosmic address = (altitude + perspective)$_s$ × (altitude + perspective)$_o$

Because the perspective of the subject is a quadrant (or the perspective through which something is seen), and the perspective of the object is a quadrivium (or the perspective a thing is being looked at from), then we can also write that as follows:

Kosmic address = (altitude + quadrant) × (altitude + quadrivium)

Of course, we can also specify any of the other components of an occasion's location in the AQAL matrix. We can specify the quadrant, level, line, state, or type *through which* I am looking at the world when I claim to perceive the object. And we can specify the quadrivium, level, line, state, or type "*in which*" the object exists (or is claimed to exist). But the altitude (**level**) and the quadrants (**perspectives**) are the minimum in order to orient us in a Kosmos with both depth and span.

Thus, as we said, the seemingly innocent and obvious map given in figure II.1 is not so innocent after all. It certainly is not a map of a pregiven world, because, among other things, not everyone can see its objects. Implicit in its representations and signifiers are the following items:

If I am at a developmental altitude of turquoise or higher, and I utilize the cognitive line of intelligence, and I take the sum total of general conclusions from the various human disciplines that have also reached at least turquoise, then I can lay them all out on a 3rd-person grid that looks something like figure II.1.

Likewise, the realities depicted in figure II.1 are not realities that are existing in some pregiven world awaiting perception by any sentient being who stumbles on it. The realities depicted in figure II.1 can only be found in a turquoise (or higher) worldspace. Ecosystems do not ex-ist in the red world or the amber world or the orange world. Vision-logic does not ex-ist in the red world or the blue world or the orange world. Atoms do not ex-ist in the red world or the amber world. The vacuum potential does not ex-ist in the red world or the amber world or the orange world or the green world. No, for the most part, the realities depicted on figure II.1 ex-ist only in the turquoise world (or, in a turquoise worldspace). Figure II.1 is not a map of "the real world," because there is no "the real world"—there is no pregiven world awaiting perception, only mutually disclosing perspectives awaiting enactment.

Likewise, the realities depicted in figure II.1 cannot be seen by any subject. They can only be seen by a subject at a turquoise level of developmental altitude in the cognitive line. Systems holarchies do not ex-ist for, and cannot be seen by, red subjects or amber subjects or orange subjects or green subjects. They can be enacted only by turquoise (or higher) subjects.

Thus, the **referents** (or real objects) of the **signifiers** in figure II.1 ex-ist in a turquoise worldspace in a 3rd-person dimension/perspective. And they can be seen (brought forth or enacted) only by subjects at a turquoise altitude in a 3rd-person perspective—which is to say, only subjects with that Kosmic address will be able to bring forth the correct **signifieds** that correspond with the signifiers in figure II.1, and thus will be able to see and understand the real **referents** of those **signifiers.** (That is, will be able to enter into communities of knowing who work together to decide on the contours of reality enacted at those Kosmic addresses, and whether something does or does not, in fact, exist at those addresses).

Without signifying the Kosmic address of both the perceiver and the perceived, any statements about the world or about reality are simply, categorically, absolutely meaningless. The **myth of the given** is simply the briefest way to indicate that, but we can see now that the myth of the given was only the tip of the iceberg: there is no given world, *not only* because intersubjectivity is a constitutive part of objective and subjective realities, *but also* because even specifying intersubjectivity is not nearly enough to get over that myth in all its dimensions: you need to specify the Kosmic locations of both the perceiver and the perceived in order to be engaged in anything except metaphysics. Because, we can now see, metaphysics from an AQAL perspective means anything that does not (or cannot) generally specify the quadrant, level, line, state, and type of an occasion. If a writer does not consciously specify those components—that is, if some version of a Kosmic address is not specified—it is virtually always because that writer is unconsciously assuming that those components are pregiven and thus don't need to be specified. They don't specify them because they don't know they are there, and variable.

For example, most writers will give maps of reality something like the great systems holarchies outlined in chapter 7, or the Web of Life, or a series of assertions about quantum vacuum potentials, or the Sefirot, or the *vijnanas*, etc., and have no idea that those realities exist, if they exist at all, only in particular worldspaces with particular perspectives. So they present their maps of reality as if there is a pregiven reality and they have the **correct** representation of it. That is horrid metaphysics according to even the postmodern definition of metaphysics! But I am going a step further and claiming that even the postmodernists who claim to overcome metaphysics are actually caught in subtler versions of it, because metaphysics is anything that does not self-consciously disclose all of the AQAL components of any occasion. When a writer does not disclose those components, it is almost always because he or she doesn't know they are there; and not knowing they are there, cannot stop those realities from unconsciously slipping into extensive versions of the myth of the given. When Laszlo, for example, does not disclose that quantum potentials ex-ist only at turquoise, it's because he assumes they are given for all. Thus, altitude becomes an implicit part of the myth of the given for Laszlo: he doesn't think you have to specify altitude because he doesn't know that different referents exist in different worldspaces, and hence he is simply caught in another version of the myth of the given, or metaphysics.

The corollary meaning of metaphysics, of course, is "assertions without evidence." And that is correct. All of those approaches that do not specify the Kosmic address of the referents of the signifiers of their assertions are caught in meaningless assertions and abstractions.

And that brings us to what is surely the most interesting demand of any integral post-metaphysics: **The meaning of a statement is the means of its enactment.** Once we understand that, I believe we will find that there is an entirely new way to discuss spiritual realities, and one that has, intrinsic to it, ways and means to prove the existence of those spiritual realities.

Where Is Santa Claus?

Let me introduce this section by referring again to our simple 10-level altitude map (which is a general map of certain aspects of the Kosmos as they appear to a violet worldspace in 3rd-person perspective). And let's remember that in order to make any meaningful assertions about anything, you have to generally be able to specify the Kosmic address (altitude + perspective) of both the perceiver and the perceived. **Because otherwise, you are implicitly assuming those are simply given,** and thus you are caught in metaphysics, or assertions without meaning.

So let's begin this section by giving a quick list of a few types of phenomena found in the 10 worldspaces of our simple map, according to those who adequately follow the paradigms and injunctions that enact those worldspaces as determined by various knowledge communities in those worldspaces. The following list is meant to be extremely schematic and generalized, just to make a few points, and not meant to be accurate in all details. I'll give 8 of the 10 levels to show what is involved:

magenta—magical-animistic.

Demons, dragons, wizards, rage, lust, rocks, rivers, trees, curses, voodoo, ancestors, clans, huts, villages, horses, spearheads.

red—egocentric, power, magic-mythic.

Warlords, tribes, 5 elements (earth, air, wind, fire, ether), anger, envy, power, titans, domination, oppression, slavery, genocide, spirit as gods and goddesses of elemental powers.

amber—mythic, ethnocentric, traditional.

Cathedrals, the righteous man, chivalry, salvation, charity, 2nd-person perspective, spirit as omniscient, omnipotent, omni-present Great Other.

orange—rational, worldcentric, pragmatic, modern.

Atoms, electrons, protons, periodic table of the 100+ elements, skyscrapers, rockets, worldcentric compassion, universal moral ideals, television, radio, 3rd-person perspective, square root of a negative one, airplanes, automobiles, spirit as Great Designer and/or Ground of Being.

green—pluralistic, multicultural, postmodern.

Pluralistic systems, the Internet and World Wide Web, 4th-person perspective, values commons, imaginary numbers, hypercars, spirit as deep ecology and human harmony

turquoise—global mind, high vision-logic, higher mind.

Gaian collective, strings, differential/integral calculus, nth-dimensional hyperspace, 5th-person perspective, quantum potential energy sources, spirit as planetary holarchy.

indigo—para-mind, trans-global, illumined mind.

Luminous clarity and compassion of 6th-person perspective, trans-planetary social ideals, mega-tribes, truth/goodness/beauty self-seen in global gestalts, spirit as infinite Light/Love.

violet—meta-mind and overmind.

Overmind brilliant clarity, infinite love and compassion of 7th-person perspectives and beyond, including all sentient beings from their perspectives, trans-dimensional social ideals, spirit as radical interiority and infinite holarchy.

As we have seen, we can't say one of those is right and others wrong; besides, various elements of ALL of those levels are carried forward. As with the holarchy of atoms to molecules to cells to organisms, we wouldn't say, "I want to keep organisms and get rid of atoms and molecules and cells." Likewise, even though we would want to have our worldview informed by as high an altitude as possible, it is not a simple matter of hanging onto violet and jettisoning everything else. There is a real sense in saying that there are, at violet, 10 actual levels of being and knowing as Kosmic habits—and therefore as stages in human development and levels in the compound being of individuals. (Although there are ways to determine which elements on any level are enduring and which are transitional, illusory, or misinformed, the point is that we would still have to specify in which level/worldspace those specific elements are said to exist.)

The point is that by doing a type of "mega-phenomenology" of all the phenomena known to be arising in the major levels and worldspaces (of which our short list above is a very crude example), we create a type of super dictionary (or *GigaGlossary*) of the location of the **referents** of most of the major **signifiers** capable of being uttered by humans (up to this time in evolution) and capable of being understood by humans who possess the adequate corresponding consciousness to bring forth the corresponding **signified**.

Thus, using our simple list as an example GigaGloss, we can answer some otherwise outlandishly impossible questions very easily. Here are a few examples:

The square root of a negative one is a *signifier* whose *referent* exists in the orange worldspace and can be accurately cognized or seen by trained mathematicians who call to mind the correct *signifieds* via various mathematical injunctions at that altitude and in 3rd-person perspective.

A **global ecosystem** is a *signifier* whose *referent* is a very complex multidimensional holarchy existing in a turquoise worldspace; this actual referent can be directly cognized and seen by subjects at a turquoise altitude, in 3rd-person perspective, who study ecological sciences.

Santa Claus is a *signifier* whose *referent* exists in a magenta worldspace and can be seen or cognized by subjects at magenta altitude (provided, of course, that their LL-quadrant loads their intersubjective background with the necessary surface structures; this is true for all of these examples, so I will only occasionally mention it).

As for "pure physical objects" (or "sensorimotor objects"), they don't exist. The "physical world" is not a perception but an interpretation (or, we might say, the physical world is not a perception but a conceptual perception or "conperception," which of course also involves perspectives). There is no pregiven world, but simply a series of worlds that come into being (or co-emerge, or are tetra-enacted) with different orders of consciousness. Thus:

A dog as a vital animal spirit exists in a magenta worldspace. A dog as a biological organism exists in an amber worldspace. A dog as a biological organism that is the product of evolution exists in an orange worldspace. A dog as a molecular biological system that is an expression of DNA/RNA sequencing operating through evolving planetary ecosystems exists in a turquoise worldspace. *There simply is no such thing as "the dog"* that is the one, true, pregiven dog to which our conceptions give varying representations, but rather *different dogs* that come into being or are enacted with our evolving concepts and consciousness.

Matter is not the bottom level of the spectrum of being, but the *exterior of every level* of the spectrum, and so with each new rung, there is new matter, and the entire world changes, again.

The point is that different worldspaces contain different phenomena.

It is not a matter of saying which worldspace is the "real" worldspace, because any age will always feel that its view is the real view. But there is no "real" or "pregiven" world, only these various worldspaces that creatively evolve and unfold in novel ways, then settle into Kosmic habits that then must be negotiated by all subsequent humans as stages in their own unfolding and levels in their own compound individuality. Each worldspace contains billions of phenomena that arise as its contents, and that define each other relative to the totality of each other, a relational totality that includes altitudes and perspectives.

Human beings can create languages—systems of signs and symbols— that represent various realities. For the most part, the *referent* of these *signifiers* exist in one or more of these worldspaces, and subjects can perceive these referents if they possess the corresponding developmental *signified*. But in order for any philosophical assertions to have actual meaning, the Kosmic address of the referent needs to be indicated—what level of worldspace it exists at, and what perspective it is being viewed through. Failing to do so implies that a speaker does not realize that there are different worldspaces, but is simply assuming that his or her worldspace is the one and only pregiven world, which lands the individual in the myth of the given and various sorts of (meaningless) metaphysics.

We will see where this mega-phenomenology and GigaGlossary leads us, but first, one final piece of information, and then we can draw our conclusions.

WHAT GOD IS LIKE, WHAT GOD IS NOT, AND WHAT GOD IS

Generally speaking, there are three ways we can talk about something in 3rd-person perspective. We can say what the thing **is like** (metaphoric, analogic, kataphatic); what it **is not** (negativa, apophatic); and what **it is** (asseric, ontic).

I think those are obvious enough. Let me simply add that we can represent these modes of speech with the symbols (*), (−), and (+), respectively. Thus, if I am speaking of Spirit metaphorically, I might write: Spirit(*) is a radiant citadel in the dark night of angelic flight. Or if speaking of Spirit apophatically, I might write: Spirit(–) is not lightness, is not darkness, is not this, is not that. And if speaking of Spirit ontically, I might write: Spirit(+) is infinite love.

But let's immediately note that when it comes to spiritual realities, the first two modes have never been challenged by critics. You can speak poetically or negatively about spirit all you want. But when you make positive, ontological claims, the critics roar. But with an AQAL post-metaphysics, questions of spiritual realities are put on the same footing as any other referents. The problem, as a problem, simply does not exist.

Recall our previous point about the necessity to specify the Kosmic address of any entity we are speaking about—or, more accurately, the Kosmic address of both the perceiver and the perceived. Because now the point becomes very clear. In reference to our simple GigaGloss, in order to say what anything is (spiritual or otherwise), or whenever we want to use the ontic mode of speech (+), *we must be able to put its Kosmic address in the parentheses* in order to be able to make any assertions about it at all. Otherwise we are caught in rubbish; we are making ontological assertions about objects whose actual locations we cannot demonstrate or even find. It is, in the worst sense, arid metaphysics and nonsensical assertions.

We can use levels for the Kosmic address in order to give some simple examples. Thus:

- Santa Claus(2) is an experience that many children have.
- Our global ecosystems(8) are being slowly destroyed by toxic waste dumps.
- Infinite strings(8) are now thought to be nth-dimensional foundations of all material existents.
- When Susan turned 15, she had her first experience of overwhelming universal love(6), a love that seemed to permeate her every cell and announce its presence intimately.
- The oppression of racial minorities is an experience that runs deeply in the ethnocentric strands(4) of our own society.
- Spirit as infinite love(9) is an experience I have stably had in meditation now for about 3 years.
- I love(2) my dog Isaac, even though I know he's a little shit and a total materialistic machine(5), although yesterday I had this incredibly powerful experience of him as part of a planetary consciousness(8).

In those examples, we are using altitude as a simplistic Kosmic address just to show what is involved. We could also use the phenomena that appear in specific states of consciousness, and indicate their address using, for example (S/g) for gross state, (S/s) for subtle state, (S/c) for causal state, and (S/nd) for nondual state. Then, using just states instead of just levels for a simplistic address, we might say: Spirit as emptiness(S/c) is a reality for most long-term meditators. Or: Meister Eckhart gave pointing-out instructions for ever-present Spirit(S/nd).

Is this becoming clear, I hope? Let me give a further example by enlarging the address by adding perspective to level—the minimum you need for an address, anyway, but again in an incredibly simplistic way just to indicate what's involved. Let's let 1st-, 2nd-, and 3rd-person perspective be indicated by "1-p," "2-p," and "3-p," respectively; let's indicate states as above with "S/", and add "L/" for level (e.g., L/3, L/7). Then we might say, to revisit a few of the previous examples:

- Our global ecosystems(3-p, L/8) are being slowly destroyed by toxic waste dumps. When I think of that, my Gaia consciousness(1-p, L/8) is deeply hurt.*

---

*This is a good example of locating pretty much anything. Gaia is a social holon (not an individual holon) that ex-ists at L/8 and higher. A person may not understand that objectively Gaia is not a planetary organism but a planetary collective (i.e., the global ecosystem), and yet still they can have a subjective experience of global oneness that they label "Gaia." The objective Gaian system as collective is (3-p, L/8), whereas the subjective idea of Gaia as individual is (1-p, L/8). Both of them exist and can be located; the falsehood is the mistaken belief that the latter reality correctly represents the former reality.

That is, the falsehood for such a person—and you can definitely have falsehoods, illusions, mistaken notions, etc.—is the belief that the latter (the signifier "Gaia as planetary organism") has an actual objective referent in the Right-Hand world, whereas its referent exists only in subjective or LH space. In the Right Hand, Gaia is a system, not an individual, and the evidence to date indicates that those who think otherwise are caught in a falsehood. (This is what we call a referential falsehood, in that the referent of the signifier, although it exists somewhere, does not exist where the person believes it does. In other words, they got the wrong address for the referent. There are also phenomenal falsehoods, where an individual imagines that the phenomenon he sees is true for everybody. The 3 strands are meant to correct phenomenal falsehoods. There are other important types of falsehoods—no need to pursue them here—but notice that the falsehoods themselves exist in a worldspace—as all things, real or imaginary, do. It's just that the falsely held impressions explicitly or implicitly claim to have referents or relations with items whose Kosmic addresses are incorrect, among other possible problems.)

- Infinite strings(3-p, $L/8$) are now thought to be n^{th}-dimensional foundations of all material existents.

- When Susan turned 15, she had her first experience of overwhelming universal love(1-p, $L/6$), a love that seemed to permeate her every cell and announce its presence intimately. So intense was this awareness, it triggered a realization of oneness with everything(1-p, S/nd).

Take another previous example: "Spirit as infinite love$^{(9)}$ is an experience I have stably had in meditation now for about 3 years." But notice that I can experience "infinite love" in at least 3 perspectives: as a 3rd-person Force that I feel permeates the entire universe; as a 2nd-person Thou with whom I am in communion; as a 1st-person omnipresent Presence with which I identify. Specifying those addresses, or being able to specify them, is the first step toward subjecting them to things like the 3 strands of good knowing in order to determine their actuality.* For example, "I bow before the living Spirit as infinite Love(2-p, $L/9$)," or "Love is a universal and infinite force of self-organizing self-transcendence(3-p, $L/9$) operating on evolution," or "Infinite Love is the Self of the Kosmos that I am(1-p, $L/9$)"—and so on.

The point is that any ontic or asserric mode ($+$) must be able to specify the Kosmic address of the referent of the signifiers, and this is true whether the referents are material, emotional, mental, spiritual, it doesn't matter. Spiritual realities are on exactly the same footing as electrons, Gaia, rocks, and the square root of a negative one.†

*See previous footnote, page 263.

†The Kosmic address of any particular holon is given most fully, of course, by its full AQAL parameters, to the extent they have been determined; the more parameters, the more precise the address. I have suggested that a minimal address is given by quadrant/perspective and altitude/level, but one can include more parameters, if known. Note that quadrant can be represented by either a perspective, such as 3-p, or more precisely, the # of the quadrant itself, i.e., $Q/1$ (UL), $Q/2$ (LL), $Q/3$ (UR), $Q/4$ (LR), since quadrants are more foundational, although either of those representations is fine.

Levels can be indicated with numbers, but since those change depending on how many levels are being used, the fall-back standard representation is to use colors for altitude, with the major levels symbolized as ir, m, r, a, o, g, te, t, i, v, uv (thus, L/m for magenta, L/o for orange, L/i for indigo, and so on).

Lines can be indicated with "$l/$," and the names of the major lines in the UL with: cognitive: ç, moral: m, interpersonal: ip, psychosexual: ps, aesthetic/artistic: a, kinesthetic: k, proximate-self: s, values: v, musical: mu, logico-mathematical: lm, intrapersonal: in. Types can be indicated with "$t/$"; some of those in the UL might

The problem for many spiritual realities (e.g., patriarchal Jehovah) is not that they don't exist, but that they exist on some of the lower levels of being and knowing, and hence are realities called into question by higher levels, which is entirely understandable. But spiritual realities per se do not exist merely on the lower levels; they are aspects of *every* level

---

include: masculine: m, feminine: f, enneagram: E plus # (e.g., E5, E7), and so on. (Lines, types, and states in the other quadrants can also, of course, be represented, using convenient symbols of choice.)

The more of the five elements used, the more complete the Kosmic address (Q/, L/, l/, S/, t/). When more than one of those elements are used, we follow that order (which we didn't in the text when using only altitude and quadrants, since their explanations were introduced in a different sequence, but nonetheless this is the correct order).

For a particular knowing subject (i.e., a holon with quadrants), this might be: researcher John Doe is coming from a 3rd-person perspective (i.e., using Q/3-perspective or it-perspective), altitude Level 5 or orange (L/5 or L/o), line/cognitive (l/c), State/gross (S/g), type/masculine (t/m), all of which is (Q/3, L/5, l/c, S/g, t/m). John Doe might be researching (via quadrivia) an object in the LR that possesses a solid state (S/s), clade line *homo erectus* (symbol: he; thus: l/he), female type (t/f), as it is a member of the global ecosystem, colloquially known as Gaia (whose full contours don't emerge until altitude 8). This might be indicated with the sentence: John Doe (Q/3, L/5, l/c, S/g, t/m) is focusing his attention on female homo erectus in its interaction with Gaia (Q/4, L/8, l/he, S/s, t/f). Generically, the Kosmic address of this interaction is:

Subject(Q/3, L/5, l/c, S/g, t/m) × Object(Q/4, L/8, l/he, S/s, t/f)

One of the ways this can be drastically simplified to just perspectives is: 1p × 3-p × 3p, or my 1st person (John Doe) is taking a 3rd-person view of a 3rd person (plural) system, which is the very simplified integral-math version used in this text; but you can see how sophisticated the representations can become. You can also probably start to see the problems for John: he is taking an it-view of an its-system, but the system exists at altitude 8 and John is flying at altitude 5. Among other things, he will therefore see the object in terms merely of instrumental rationality using the cognitive line (instead of cross-paradigmatic cognition, which sees yet higher levels of complexity); it's not that everything he sees will be distorted, but the interaction's crucial depth will be. In biological genetics, exactly this problem prevented the discovery of the actual unit of natural selection, which happens to be a holon at any level of complexity (see the discussion in SES on different units of natural selection at various levels of complexity). As for what these types of problems of inadequate altitude in researchers have done to the fields of psychology and spirituality, please, don't get me started.

Finally, the Kosmic address of that interaction (which I will keep in bold) is not merely the "view from nowhere." If that interaction (John Doe studying Gaia) is

of consciousness that we are aware of. The problem is not that spiritual realities don't exist or are hard to prove; it's that their earlier forms exist on lower levels and hence are not as real as some of the later levels, but those higher levels themselves have their own spiritual realities, as categorically disclosed by the GigaGloss. *The problem of the proof of God's existence simply evaporates.* The existence of Spirit is no harder to prove than the existence of rocks, electrons, negative ones, or Gaia. Simply look it up in the GigaGloss.

And one of the first things you find in the GigaGloss is that, to put it crudely, there are levels of God. That is, levels of the answers that spiritual intelligence delivers to the question, "What is of ultimate concern, or ultimate reality, or ultimate ground?" There is a magic Ground, a mythic Ground, a rational Ground, a pluralistic Ground, a second-tier Ground, a third-tier Ground, and so on. As well as a gross, subtle, causal, and nondual version of each of those. **But all of those signifiers have real referents in the only place that referents of any sort exist anyway: in a state or structure of consciousness.** All referents exist, if they exist at all, in a worldspace, whose address is given minimally by quadrant (perspective engaged) and altitude/level (structure of consciousness enacted).

If the problem of proving God's existence evaporates, it is replaced by the problem of specifying the level or state (or Kosmic address) of the spiritual realities in question, and that implies—as it does for all Kosmic addresses—that one must be able to specify the injunctions that bring forth or enact the particular worldspaces. Which brings us to our last point: the meaning of an assertion is the means of its enactment.

being presented and discussed, say, in a cognitive 3rd-person stance by a male (let's be generous and say that I am) at an ultraviolet altitude in line/cognitive, then the Kosmic address of that occasion is:

$$\text{Subject}'(Q/3, L/10, I/c, S/ind, t/m) \times \textbf{(Subject}'(Q/3, L/5, I/c, S/g, t/m) \times \textbf{Object}'(Q/4, L/8, I/he, S/s, t/f)$$

This might be simplified to just perspectives as **1p × 3-p × 3p(1p × 3-p × 3p)**, or my 1st person is taking a 3rd-person point of view of his 1st person taking an objective (3-p) view of that 3rd person system. The point is that there is no absolute "view from nowhere," but that in the manifest realm, all perceptions are *always also* perspectives, the endless reflections of a Kosmos in a hall of mirrors that it created in order to see itself.

The Meaning Is the Injunction

As I have explained in detail elsewhere,* all "good knowledge" consists of at least 3 major strands:

1. **An injunction** (paradigm, exemplar, experiment, enaction), which is always of the form "If you want to know this, do this."
2. **An experience** (datum, tuition, prehension, awareness), which is an illumination of the phenomena brought forth or enacted by the injunction.
3. **A communal confirmation/rejection,** which is a checking with others who have completed the first 2 strands.

All of that is consistent with what we have just seen. If you want to make a positive assertion about an entity, particularly if that assertion claims or implies its existence, you must be able to specify the Kosmic address of the entity (i.e., the Kosmic address of the referent of the signifier)—which refers to the Kosmic address of the perceived—and you **must** also be able to specify the Kosmic address of the perceiver, and that implies being able to specify what **injunctions** (paradigms, exemplars, enactions) **a perceiving subject must perform** in order to be at a Kosmic address that CAN perceive the object.

Thus, we cannot make any ontic or assertic statement—whether scientific, spiritual, ecological, medical, etc.—without being able to specify the Kosmic address of the object and the Kosmic address of the subject, which also means, the **injunctions** that the subject must perform in order to enact and access the worldspace of the object.

We can symbolize this injunctive mode of speech with an (!). Thus, for example, we might say: One form of Spirit(!) is that which is perceived in a formless state of consciousness. The injunctive mode is simply announcing the actual injunctions or actions needed to be taken in order to see the object or phenomenon in question.

And so we come to: The meaning of an assertic or ontic statement is the means or injunctions of its enactment. Thus, for example, if I want to know if it is raining outside, then I must walk over to the window, pull back the drapes, and look. If I want to know what Susan felt like when she had her first experience of universal love, I must as a perceiving subject develop to at least an orange altitude in both the cognitive line

---

*See, e.g., *Eye to Eye* and *The Marriage of Sense and Soul.*

and the moral line. If I want to know why the Schroedinger wave equation collapses when a photon hits a neutron, then I must develop to at least a turquoise level in the cognitive line, then study quantum physics and mathematics for a decade or two, and then look.

Similarly, if I want to know if there is a referent to the signifier Ayin or Godhead, then one among the necessary routes is to take up a concentrative form of meditation and learn to be able to keep my mind focused unwaveringly on an object for at least 30 minutes. (The longest the average adult can focus on an object in an unbroken fashion is for less than one minute.) Once I can do that, which usually takes daily practice for about 3 years, then I need to look in an unbroken fashion at the nature of phenomenal reality as it arises moment to moment and see if there is, as directly seen or cognized in my own consciousness, anything that appears to be an empty ground to all of them. And then I need to compare this reality with my ordinary state of consciousness and decide which seems more real. Although exact numbers are hard to come by, a clear majority of those who complete this experiment report that the signifier Ayin or Emptiness has a real referent as disclosed by injunctive paradigm. That is, those who are qualified to make the judgment agree that it can be said that, among other things, Spirit(!) is a vast infinite Abyss or Emptiness(1-p, S/c), out of which all things arise.

We saw that if we cannot specify the Kosmic address of the perceiver and perceived, we have assertions without evidence, or metaphysics. And we can now see that this also means that *we must be able to specify the injunctions necessary for the subject to be able to enact the Kosmic address of the object.* The meaning of any assertion is therefore, among other things, the injunctions or means or exemplars for enacting the worldspace in which the referent exists or is said to exist (and where its existence can, in fact, be confirmed or refuted by a community of the adequate). Hence, in shorthand, **the meaning of a statement is the injunction of its enactment.** No injunction, no enactment, no meaning. That is, mere metaphysics.

This can all be put very simply. **Any language other than injunctive is metaphysics.** That applies to any domain of thought. But in spiritual thought, that means that *any Spirit*(+) language must be replaceable with Spirit(!) language in order to have any referential or actual meaning, and that means that *the injunctions necessary to bring forth the phenomena with the Kosmic address claimed for the referent must be able to be specified.*

Thus, if "ka" means Kosmic address, then we can say that, in order to escape metaphysics, all Spirit$^{(+)}$ language must be replaceable with Spirit$^{(!)}$ and Spirit$^{(ka)}$ language, with the Spirit$^{(!)}$ language simply being the instructional and injunctive language (e.g., exemplars, injunctions, paradigms) necessary for the subject to enact the Kosmic address of the spiritual object or referent or datum, given by the Spirit$^{(ka)}$ language (such as Ayin$^{(1\text{-}p,\ S/c)}$, Big Mind$^{(1\text{-}p,\ S/nd)}$, or Gaia$^{(1\text{-}p,\ L/8)}$), itself determined by various types of GigaGlossaries grounded in Integral Methodological Pluralism.

Anything other than Spirit$^{(!)}$ and Spirit$^{(ka)}$ sentences are metaphysical power plays. They might be poetry, which is great; or metaphorical, which is very nice; or negative, which is fine. But they are not positive realities without specifying the injunctions that will enact the worldspaces in which they ex-ist or are said to ex-ist.* No injunction, no meaning, no reality. Just metaphysical gibberish in an age that is no longer capable of being impressed by such. . . .

A Simple Summary

All of the foregoing is, as I have often mentioned (starting with "A Note to the Reader"), done in the most general of orientating generalizations. What I am trying to convey is a set of possibilities—possibilities about how to move out of metaphysics (which is dead anyway: it is not God that is dead, but the metaphysical God) and into Integral Post-Metaphysics—or simply from Metaphysics to Integralism. As with any gestalt, the parts can't be grasped until the whole is grasped, but the whole can't be grasped until the parts are, so I have rushed breathlessly through a dozen parts of Integral Post-Metaphysics in the hope of getting enough of them across that the gestalt of a post-metaphysics might start to form in one's awareness, at least, again, as a set of possibilities.

---

*The virtue of positivism, among its reductionistic furies, is that when it concluded that "the meaning of a statement is the means of its verification," they were at least hitting on the fact that part of any reality is the means of its enactment. A megaphenomenology is a mega-positivism in that one very specific sense. This is why "positive proof" is not a problem for a GigaGlossary.

Positivism got into trouble when it tried to reduce all worldspaces to 3rd-person, Upper-Right, L/5 and higher entities (and numbers representing them)—or $3p \times 3\text{-}p \times 3p$ at L/5 and higher. The positivistic reduction, which itself exists in the UL, L/5 and higher, is a referential falsehood (see footnote on page 263).

So in this summary, what I will do, in keeping with this theme of aggressive simplification, is present a summary that is even simpler than what I have presented thus far. This will either help or totally confuse. Let's see . . .

If you look at Huston's Smith's diagram "As Above, So Below," in figure I.3 (page 216), you will see that up the left of the diagram are "Levels of Reality," and down the right are "Levels of Selfhood." In one form or another, this is the grand metaphysical scheme of the world's great wisdom traditions. It conveys a series of profound and enduring truths; that reality is multidimensional, or organically structured into holarchies of being ("levels of reality") and holarchies of knowing ("levels of selfhood"); that what is known is dependent upon the level of reality being known or accessed, as well as the level of self doing the knowing; and that there are levels of being and knowing beyond the ordinary, empirical, terrestrial, physical plane of existence (these levels were, of course, thought to be literally meta-physical or trans-physical).

As widespread as those conclusions were, they were, nonetheless, simply interpretations given to experiences. The experiences were authentic; the interpretations are outmoded.

In particular, the idea that there are levels of being and knowing beyond the physical (i.e., literally meta-physical) is badly in need of reconstruction. This is not to say that there are no trans-physical realities whatsoever; only that most of the items taken to be trans- or meta-physical by the ancients (e.g., feelings, thoughts, ideas) actually have, at the very least, physical correlates. When modernity discovered this fact, it rejected the great wisdom traditions almost in their entirety. Of course, modernity has its own hidden metaphysics (as does postmodernity), but when the great, amber, mythic-metaphysical systems came down, spirituality received a hit from which it has never recovered. What is required is to reconstruct the enduring truths of the great wisdom traditions but without their metaphysics.

For the traditions, as schematically summarized in Huston's diagram, there were levels of reality, conceived often as actual realms or trans-physical locations (heavens, *lokas, dhatus*), and the number and types of objects in those levels constituted **ontology.** The knowledge of those independently existing objects constituted **epistemology.** Because there were levels of reality, there were corresponding levels of knowing (or levels of selfhood). As indicated in figure I.3, the **body** could know or perceive the objects in the physical or *terrestrial realm;* the **mind** could see the objects in the *intermediate realm*; the **soul** could see objects in the *celestial realm*; and the **spirit** could see objects in the *infinite realm*.

The problem is that those realms or levels of metaphysical reality (higher than body) simply could not be found by modernity (or postmodernity), and thus the entire edifice of the great wisdom traditions was abandoned. And understandably so: there simply are no independently existing structures or levels of reality lying around waiting for all and sundry to see. And so modernity took the levels of reality (ontology) and collapsed them into *just* the levels of knowing or selfhood: items that premodernity thought were levels of metaphysical reality (like the realms of the hungry ghosts, *asuras*, titans, *pretas*, and demigods) were said to be just psychological emotions or archetypes. And then modernity took the levels of selfhood (body, mind, soul, spirit) and reduced them to their lowest level—that of the body, or merely physical realities. At that point, what was left of the great spiritual traditions could be put in a thimble, and a materialistic thimble at that.

Modernity (and postmodernity) had persuasive reasons for their anti-metaphysical crusades (reasons that need to be acknowledged), but in the process, so many babies were tossed with so much bathwater that the end result was a pandemic nihilism and aperspectival madness that came to define the post/modern West. What we want to do is back up a step or two, turn anti-metaphysics into post-metaphysics, and attempt to come to terms with the enduring truths in the premodern *and* modern *and* postmodern turns, starting by reconstructing the great wisdom traditions and their essential notions.

One of the first reconstructions relates directly to the idea of "levels of reality." Namely, they don't exist. Not like so many of the traditions thought, as ontological levels of pre-existing being. Rather, those "objective" levels are co-created or con-structed by the knowing subject. Critical (Kantian) philosophy replaced metaphysics (or ontological objects) with epistemology (or structures in the subject), and this general move is unavoidable in the post/modern world.

Thus, the levels of reality are actually constructions of the levels of selfhood (and knowing).* In figure 1.3, all of the levels "over" her are actually (in many important ways) levels of selfhood "within" her. There

---

*Actually, tetra-structions. I hope it is obvious that whenever I say "con-structions" of consciousness, I mean tetra-structions of the Kosmos. "Con-structions of con-sciousness" is simply the LH components—particularly the LL—that are aspects of that tetra-struction and tetra-evolution of any occasion.

is no celestial realm, no intermediate realm, etc.—not as levels up there, or out there, or over there. Rather, those levels of reality are somehow intimately tied to levels of self (or levels of consciousness, levels of knowing).

We add two more important qualifiers: those levels of selfhood (red, amber, green, turquoise, indigo, etc.) are not pre-existing levels, but rather ones that have evolved. But because they have evolved for the species, they are not merely levels of psychology (or levels of selfhood in that sense), because once a level has evolved, it is a very real structure existing in the universe. (Instead of arguing endlessly about the details of their status, which simply detracts from the fact that they are there, we simply call these structures examples of **Kosmic habits** or **Kosmic memories**.)

Once a structure has evolved, *it exists independently of any particular human*, and becomes something that all humans must confront (i.e., develop through). At that point, it takes on all the "ontological" status required by any spiritual philosophy. So these "levels of selfhood" are not merely "within" her, either—it makes no sense whatsoever to locate them as that. They are, rather, tetra-enacted structures of the Kosmos, so that both "up there" and "in here" become outmoded and cumbersome metaphors (and certainly nothing to embrace as metaphysics).

That leaves little of the metaphysical framework of figure I.3. There are no levels of reality up there and no levels of selfhood in here. Yet we can still generate all of the actual experiences and phenomena of the concentric spheres and spiritual realities represented in figure I.3, and we can do so without an independent ontology and epistemology, and without reducing them to psychology, either.

In the metaphysical traditions, an object (or that which is known) existed in or on a plane or level of reality, so that the referent of a spiritual statement was a reality existing in one of those planes or realms. The subject or knower existed on a corresponding level of selfhood and then simply perceived the pre-existing object. But in post-metaphysics, objects exist in worldspaces that are enacted in part by the knowing subject, and both subject and object of any variety are defined by evolutionary or developmental *altitude* (not levels of pre-existing *ontology*) and the *perspective* doing the enacting (not a *perception* of epistemology)).

Nor are these structures merely subjective, because once evolved, they are trans-individual or collective Kosmic habits, which push against any human psychology and guide its growth. Both "up there" and "in here" disappear into tetra-enacted structures of the Kosmos. Once that is in place, the Kosmic address (altitude + perspective) of any referent for any signifier uttered by any human can potentially be specified. Because all referents exist in a worldspace, and because all worldspaces are enacted (or, all phenomena are brought forth by injunctions/paradigms), then the location of a referent is intimately tied to the injunctions necessary to bring forth that worldspace in the subject and object. (Accordingly, the meaning of any positive assertion is the injunction or injunctions involved in bringing forth, enacting, or disclosing the worldspace in which the referent exists or is said to exist. No injunctions, no meaning, no reality.)

At that point, figure I.3 has indeed progressed into figures I.4 and I.5, and we have gone "from the great chain to postmodernism in 3 easy steps." Metaphysics is replaced by critical philosophy; ontology is replaced by worldspace; epistemology is replaced by injunctions. Of course, most of the detailed work remains to be done. But one thing is obvious: without doing so, the premodern traditions are dead in any sophisticated circles in the modern and postmodern world.

The Beginning of the Post-Metaphysical (or Integral) Age

Problems like the proof of God's existence are problems faced by metaphysics, but they are not problems faced by post-metaphysics. It's not that those problems are solved, but that they simply don't arise in the first place. Instead, any genuine post-metaphysics faces issues of Integral Methodological Pluralism and how best to proceed with that in order to create, among other things, various sorts of GigaGlossaries that replace problems of proof with problems of specifying Kosmic addresses and injunctions for enacting them. But those are merely extremely difficult issues; the issues faced by metaphysics are extremely impossible issues.

Given what an AQAL post-metaphysics discloses, it becomes apparent how well-meaning but still meaningless virtually everything being written about spirituality is. Spiritual treatises are mostly an endless series of ontic assertions about spiritual realities—and assertions with no injunctions, no enactions, no altitude, no perspectives, no Kosmic address of either the perceiver or the perceived. They are, in every sense, meaningless metaphysics, not only plagued with extensively elaborate myths of the given, but riddled with staggering numbers of ontic and assertic claims devoid of justification.

And yet, as I have also been very much trying to convey, all of this is fairly easily remedied. Many of the spiritual realities referred to by these writers do in fact have all the requisites for converting them from meaningless metaphysics to meaningful post-metaphysics. They can be refitted in an AQAL matrix, specifying their Kosmic addresses and injunctions. At Integral Institute, we are working on extensive "refitting jobs" for many of these. But until these types of integral updates occur, religion and spirituality will remain metaphysics dismissed by intelligent men and women, or reduced to their mythic-level manifestations, where they are embraced by, frankly, less intelligent men and women. The bright promise of spirituality as the core intelligence of ultimate concern is arrested at its mythic childhood level, or when it manages to make it to teal or turquoise, does so as nothing but metaphysical assertions with no addresses and no injunctions (and therefore no meaning whatsoever), or anchors itself in states of consciousness that have profound reality but are severed from the rest of the Kosmos (of quadrants, levels, lines, and types), and thus ends up fragmenting and splintering its own practitioners. Everywhere the bright promise of spiritual intelligence is crippled, cropped, and crucified, run into blind alleys of horrifying neglect, mugged in rational parking lots, suffocated with clouds of materialism, regressed to new-age infantilism, housed in mythic and metaphysical nonsense, this bright promise of my own ultimate concern.

When will it stop? When will your own deepest tomorrow begin?

It's a new time, it's a new day, it's a new dawn, it's a new man, it's a new woman. If you want to stand at the leading edge, identified with Eros itself, and push into new territories of your own deepest and highest possibilities, changing the world as you do, please join us at www.integralinstitute.org.

APPENDIX III

The Myth of the Given Lives On . . . .

Here, in no particular order, are some approaches (pre-modern and modern) that could benefit from a constructive post-modern turn. These are approaches that have some truly wonderful contributions to make, but they are clearly devoid of any extensive understanding or incorporation of the postmodern revolution that replaced perception with perspective, the myth of the given with intersubjectivity, and the representational paradigm with the constructivist/genealogical paradigm. The following approaches are simply representative examples of those that are embedded in the myth of the given and the illusions it generates. And the tragedy, as I will repeat several times, is that this is so easily remedied.

Let me preface this with an example of why I think this is so important, particularly for any variety of spiritual studies.

The Two Cultures

The intellectuals and knowledge workers in the West are still divided into what C. P. Snow, some five decades ago, called *The Two Cultures*—namely, the sciences and the humanities. (Notice immediately that the two cultures are the Left-Hand world of the humanities and the Right-Hand world of the natural sciences.) The fact that they won't speak to each other is bad enough, but spiritual studies have today been rejected by both. Even what might be considered extremely sophisticated, rational, non-mythic, experiential, elaborate systems of spiritual thinking and practice—for example, Buddhist phenomenology, Vedanta philosophy,

Kabbalistic hermeneutics—are simply not taken seriously by the main streams of higher education and learning.

It is common to say that the reason that something as profound as Buddhist phenomenology has been rejected by the intelligentsia is that a materialistic type of science or scientism—which completely rejects introspection, awareness, interiority, etc.—has caused this "taboo of subjectivity," as B. Alan Wallace put it in his wonderful book by that title. The idea is that scientific materialism is so powerful and dominant in higher thinking that it has all but demolished the chances of sophisticated spiritual studies being taken seriously anywhere. The humanities therefore won't go near spiritual studies, either. Nasty materialistic science (and especially, gulp, Newtonian-Cartesian science) killed nice spiritual studies.

But that's not the reason; it's not really even close. Science did not kill spirituality; the humanities themselves aggressively rejected introspection, consciousness, and subjectivity. The problem is that the humanities rejected introspection, interiority, and subjectivity, and rejected them with an aggression and thoroughness that didn't even give scientific materialism a chance to get its hands on them. (Oh, it would reject them, too, it just never had a chance.) The fact is that both of the Two Cultures told spirituality (and interiority and subjectivity) to get lost. During a period stretching roughly over the last half of the 20th century (1950–2000), not just science but also the humanities rejected interiority. If we can understand why that happened, we will be right at the very heart of the problem of spirituality in the modern and postmodern world.

No surprise that science rejected spirituality, but why on earth did the humanities themselves aggressively reject spirituality, introspection, consciousness, and subjectivity? Dilthey summed it up: "Not through introspection but only through history do we come to know ourselves." The subject of awareness generally imagines that it can simply introspect its own awareness and come to know and understand itself, and yet the newly forming geist sciences (from genealogy to linguistics) were making it quite clear that this was not the case at all. Subjectivity, they concluded, is completely ignorant of the fact that virtually everything that shows up in its awareness is the product of vast intersubjective networks that cannot themselves be seen. These networks, in part the products of history, as Dilthey's statement indicates, are vast cultural backgrounds that actually create the spaces in which subjectivity and consciousness can even operate, and subjectivity remains blissfully ignorant of these formative networks, as it introspects its time away, imagining that it knows itself. As such, it is caught in an elaborate network of lies and self-deceptions,

Here's a simple example, using Spiral Dynamics. Spiral Dynamics is itself an unremarkable remnant of the early, pioneering developmental structuralists, and works well in this regard, because it was exactly these kinds of discoveries that, at the turn of the 20th century, began to usher in the postmodern revolution, which flowered in the period we are discussing (1950–2000).

Once you learn any developmental scheme, such as SD, a peculiar fact starts to become apparent. You can be listening to somebody who is coming from, say, the **multiplistic level** (orange altitude), and it is obvious that this person is not thinking of these ideas himself; almost everything he says is completely predictable. He never studied Clare Graves or any other developmentalist, and yet there it is, predictable value after predictable value. He has no idea that he is the mouthpiece of this structure, a structure he doesn't even know is there. It almost seems as if it is not he who is speaking, but **the orange structure itself that is speaking through him**—this vast intersubjective network is speaking through him.

Worse, he can introspect all he wants, and yet he still won't realize this. He is simply a mouthpiece for a structure that is speaking through him. He thinks he is original; he thinks he controls the contents of his thoughts; he thinks he can introspect and understand himself; he thinks he has free will—and yet he's just a mouthpiece. He is not speaking, he is being spoken.

The same is true for dozens of other aspects of subjectivity and awareness: they are the products of impersonal structures and intersubjective networks, and worse, structures and networks that cannot themselves be seen by subjectivity or awareness (not directly, anyway). By midcentury, an enormous understanding of these impersonal structures and intersubjective networks had been gained, particularly in linguistics, grammar, syntax, structures of consciousness, and developmental *a priori* structures. And they all pointed to one thing: the subject of awareness is the product of intersubjective networks about which it suspects little, knows less.

Thus the stage was set for the Great Left-Hand War between modernism and postmodernism in the humanities. Here is what had happened. We have the Two Cultures: the Left-Hand culture of the humanities and the Right-Hand culture of the natural sciences. The perpetual battle in the RH world is and always has been between some form of atomism and some form of systems thinking; and the atomists usually win, although never decisively. But both of them are, and have been, physicalistic or materialistic. Ever since Democritus, there have been incredibly intelligent men and women who think that frisky dirt alone is real. Whether that dirt is systems dirt or Newtonian dirt had absolutely nothing to do with anything that is significant in this story.

The real action was shaping up in the interior or Left-Hand culture, because it had already begun to divide into the two dominant camps that would come to define the humanities in the second half of the 20th century. The winner of this Great LH War would control the second culture, that of the humanities, for the foreseeable future.

THE GREAT LH WAR: THE SUBJECTIVISTS VERSUS THE INTERSUBJECTIVISTS

The first camp was the Subjectivists; the second camp, the Intersubjectivists. The **Subjectivists** included all those approaches to the humanities that did indeed rely on introspection, subjectivity, consciousness, awareness, and interiority. The most famous, and certainly the most central in the coming war, was *phenomenology*, and the most brilliant advocate of that was Edmund Husserl.

The second camp was the **Intersubjectivists.** Whatever their differences, they were united in an understanding that by the time consciousness delivers an object to awareness, said consciousness has been molded, shaped, created, and constructed by a vast network of impersonal systems and structures, foremost among which are linguistic systems, cultural backgrounds, and structures of consciousness. None of these can be seen by consciousness itself; none of these can be seen by subjectivity; and thus *subjectivity is exactly what has to be called into question*—and, in the final analysis, deconstructed. The phenomena that awareness delivers are not what they claim they are, but rather are the results or products of subterranean constructions of vast intersubjective drivers. Thus, it is not by subjective introspection, but by understanding these intersubjective structures, that we come to know ourselves.

We saw that an individual can introspect all day long and he will never see anything that says, "This is the orange structure," or "This is the green structure, or turquoise structure," and so on. The phenomena that show up in his awareness are already created by structures that he cannot see and does not even expect; yet the phenomena present themselves as if they are real in and of themselves—as if they are actually your thoughts, your desires, your values—when clearly they are not, and thus *the very objects of your own present awareness are deeply deceptive*. Phenomenology, relying on introspection, does not know this, and thus phenomenology, taken in and by itself, is the study of those lies mistaken as truths.

The Intersubjectivists were united on those basic points. There were several subcamps, but the most important included *semiotics* (Ferdinand de Saussure), the study of *cultural backgrounds* (Martin Heidegger), the early *structuralists* (Roman Jakobson, Claude Lévi-Strauss), *developmental structuralists* (James Mark Baldwin), and the titular godfather of the lies that consciousness delivers, and the necessity of *genealogy* to spot them, Friederich Nietzsche.

In other words, in the Great War of the interior or Left-Hand cultures, the Subjectivists were the humanities who relied on the *inside of* interior holons—zone #1 for the individual and zone #3 for the collective—and the Intersubjectivists were those who relied on the *outside of* interior holons—zone #2 for the individual and zone #4 for the collective. (See figs. 1.2, 1.3, and 1.4.)

Of pivotal interest in this great and coming war was a young, brilliant, alienated French intellectual, Michel Foucault. By the middle of the century, it was clear that whichever way somebody like Foucault went, so would go the world of the Left-Hand culture.

Foucault does not go after science or scientific materialism; to anybody in the know, that's just not interesting, because scientific materialism is simply doing what it always does; and besides, science per se is fine. Foucault does not go after science; he goes after Husserl.

It is Husserl who infuriates Foucault; as does Jean-Paul Sartre, because both of them are champions of introspection, of the belief that consciousness does not inherently lie, that consciousness delivers truth to my awareness. Phenomenology, existentialism, humanism (all the major Subjectivist camps)—these are the things that Foucault goes after, with a vengeance. He particularly tears into humanities dressed up like sciences, as if their lies could be combined with reductionism and have anything other than a disastrous result.

It is not beside the point that Foucault is gay, before a time when being gay was anything other than deeply alienating and socially condemned. Because, the Intersubjectivists would increasingly come to believe, numerous forms of social oppression are actually hiding out in these vast systems of intersubjective structures, and if you can't even see these structures, how can you work to overcome them? Being gay, every alarm bell went off when Foucault would read accounts of phenomenology, which purported to give "the true essences" and "unchanging meaning" of a thing, simply by turning it around in your mind. But what if the damage had already occurred before the phenomena ever made it to consciousness? Foucault's homosexuality was claimed to be a sickness, and about this alleged sickness, not only did phenomenology and existentialism have no objections, it had no tools to even spot that this was oppression. In terms of his that would soon become famous and influential worldwide, Foucault found that his own discourse was being marginalized—and the results were one form of brutality or another, parading as "the way things are." (The list of the types of marginalizing forces controlling dominant modes of discourse grew enormously: androcentrism, speciesism, sexism, racism, ageism—as soon became obvious, if the subjective is intersubjective, then the personal is the political.)

As the Great LH War progressed, it was becoming clear that phenomenology, existentialism, and humanism could not even handle fundamental items like language and linguistic meaning. Foucault would often comment on this. "So the problem of language appeared and it was clear that phenomenology was no match for structural analysis in accounting for the effects of meaning that could be produced by a structure of the linguistic type. And quite naturally, with the phenomenological spouse finding herself disqualified by her inability to address language, structuralism became the new bride."

Foucault is referring to the fact that a word has meaning only because of its context (e.g., "bark," "bark of a dog" and "bark of a tree"—the word "bark" has meaning only because of the other words around it); and those words have meaning only because of other words, and eventually the entire network or system of signs must be studied in order to understand the meaning of any given sign or object or phenomenon in my awareness. The Subjectivists studied the individual phenomena that arose and tried to derive meaning that way; the Intersubjectivists studied the vast *systems* and *networks* of phenomena wherein, it soon became clear, the actual meaning could be found. It was obvious, as Foucault says, that phenomenology was simply no match for structuralism. The subject is not creating meaning (any more than somebody at orange is really thinking up his own values), but rather vast systems and intersubjective networks create meaning. The subject was kaput.

Hence, catch phrases such as "**the death of the subject**" and "**What comes after the subject?**" began to summarize some of the essential differences of the two camps. The Subjectivists were in every way **modernists;** they believed in introspection, in empiricism, in subjectivity—everything that would come to be known, derisively, by phrases such as the myth of the given, the philosophy of consciousness, the philosophy of the subject, the reflection paradigm, and the monological mirror of nature.

The Intersubjectivists were becoming the **postmodernists,** first in the hands of structuralism, semiotics, and linguistics; and then post-structuralism, neo-structuralism, deconstruction, grammatology, genealogy.

But one thing was clear: however you looked at it, the fact remained that vast networks of intersubjective systems—from linguistic structures to Graves values systems—are governing one's awareness and consciousness. You can introspect and meditate all you want, and you won't see them—and they won't go away. We even know now that you can have profound and repeated *satoris*—and still be at red, or amber, or orange, or green—and *these structures will keep speaking through you,* and you will keep dancing to the strings they are pulling. And you will keep thinking you are free. . . .

The Winner of the Great LH War

Paris, May 1968, the war reached a decisive turning point: the Subjectivists took a massive beating, and would never fundamentally recover (unless and until the Integral Age rehabilitated and incorporated their incredibly important partial truths). Gone from any serious discourse in academia were humanism, existentialism, phenomenology, subjectivity, consciousness. Into academia, triumphantly, came the Intersubjectivists—post-structuralism, postmodernism, semiology, grammatology, archaeology, genealogy.

By 1979, Derrida was the most-often-quoted writer in all of the humanities in American universities. The Great War was over, the Intersubjectivists were triumphant, and it was the Intersubjectivists who categorically, thoroughly, and absolutely rejected any spirituality, introspective meditation, contemplative consciousness, subjectivity and interiority.* The simplest reason is that all of those are caught in the myth of the given.

---

*Except as linguistic games, Wittgensteinian or otherwise, which themselves lack any real depth or interiority. In postmodernity, including postmodern academia, you are allowed to play all the spiritual games you want, as long as they aren't spiritual. Postmodernism is awash in superficialities and performative contradictions of that

BOTH MODERNISM AND POSTMODERNISM REJECTED SPIRITUALITY

We have seen that of Snow's Two Cultures, one of them is the Left-Hand culture of the humanities, the other is the Right-Hand culture of the natural sciences.

We also saw that it's not just that these two cultures are at war with each other. Both of them have their own internal wars. The major war in the Right-Hand world of science has always been between the atomists and the systems approaches. In the Left-Hand world, the great and absolutely pivotal war of the last century was between the modern Subjectivists (zones #1 and #3) and the postmodern Intersubjectivists (zones #2 and #4).

(You would think that the idea would be to integrate all 4 major camps, which indeed it is, a fact that did not really start to come to light until the closing decades of the 20th century and the dawn of the Integral Age. But for that to happen, the truths of all 4 of these approaches must first be appreciated and incorporated, and, so far, we are a long way from that on all sides, as witness the books discussed in the next section of this appendix.)

Here is the point. The books in this appendix are representative of incredibly sophisticated spiritual approaches, and yet none of them have yet come to terms with the important truths of the postmodern Intersubjectivists. And this, more than anything, is what has crippled meditation, contemplation, and spiritual studies in the humanities. It is not science or scientific materialism that has done this, because that was never the issue to begin with. The Great War was within the humanities, and here the spiritual writers and virtually all of the **"new paradigm"** writers completely misdiagnosed the situation, with disastrous consequences.

From Capra to Chopra, the spiritualists felt that if they could show that *mysticism had modern scientific support*, this would help get a spiritual worldview accepted in the humanities. This was EXACTLY THE WRONG MOVE in every way. The enemy was never science, which won't listen anyway. The enemy was the Intersubjectivists. And by showing, or trying to show, that spirituality could be grounded in quantum physics, or dynamical systems theory, or chaos theory, or autopoiesis, they played right into the hands of the Intersubjectivists.

variety, but that isn't serious spirituality, although there are openings there, as elsewhere.

The reason is that the postmodern Intersubjectivists were attacking the entire sweep of modernity, which certainly included modern science, but also the modern approaches to the interior domains—they were attacking, we have seen, things like phenomenology, monological methodology, and the myth of the given. And modern science—from quantum physics to systems theory—is likewise a victim to those same problems, starting with the myth of the given. Trying to show that meditation, Buddhism, spirituality, and the new paradigm were all grounded in the "new sciences," is EXACTLY what the Intersubjectivists suspected all along—namely, that contemplative spirituality is merely a monological approach caught in the myth of the given. Which indeed it is. But by having somebody actually spell it out, by seeing endless claims like *The Tao of Physics*, the Intersubjectivists were even more easily able to thoroughly reject monological Taoism along with the monological physics. Which they did.

What had happened, after the Great LH War, is that the two cultures had shifted. There are still the sciences and the humanities, but for the winner on the humanities side of the street—namely, the postmodern Intersubjectivists—all of the modern humanities (phenomenology, existentialism, and introspection) are viewed as being all of a piece with the modern sciences (from systems theory to chaos and complexity theory), because what all of them do indeed have in common is **the myth of the given, the philosophy of the subject, and a deeply monological methodology.** In those very specific areas, the Subjectivists and the scientific materialists were all of a methodological piece.

Which is indeed the case. And because the Subjectivists (from spiritual studies to Buddhism to new paradigm to meditation to contemplative studies) are all approaches that have failed miserably to come to terms with the Intersubjectivists, and because the Intersubjectivists rule the second culture of the humanities, then all of spiritual studies have been dismissed from any serious academic study. Rejected by modern science because they are interior, and rejected by postmodern humanities because in many ways they share a monological methodology with science, spiritual studies are more or less dead in Western academic culture.*

The following books are those that inadvertently have helped with this death, by giving no indication that they understand or are even aware of this Great War that has been fought, and won, by the Intersubjectivists. These books think that the big battle was between, say, William James and scientific materialism, when, in fact, *both of those were*

---

* As anything other than linguistic games or archaeology specimens.

on the same side in this war. The fact that these books can't even tell you why that is the case shows just how desperately ignorant the "new paradigm" and "new mysticism" books are, bless them.

A Few Books, at Random

Leadership and the New Science: Discovering Order in a Chaotic World, by Margaret Wheatley. Application of (monological) complexity systems theory to business. Chaos and complexity systems theory is "the new science"—it's fairly new, for sure, but it's still monological to the core. Extending monological systems is still monological, just a lot more of it. This is what is so easily missed: using systems theory, because it seems inclusive or holistic, only gets half the necessary story, at best—it expands our models to cover all of the Right-Hand world, but does not expand the models to incorporate insights from the Left-Hand world. This is why relying on systems theory is subtle reductionism—a fact that confuses systems theorists to no end.

The same mistake is being made when organizations such as the Shambhala Institute take this expanded systems approach and equate it with the Dharmakaya (or nondual Spirit), just because it is expanded—but so is the myth of the given expanded in this approach. And teaching expanded myths is not generally thought to constitute Enlightenment.

Homeland Earth: A Manifesto for the New Millennium, by Edgar Morin. Morin is a wonderful writer in so many ways, but misses the essential integral message; he attempts a teal/turquoise "unitas multiplex" in methodology, but he is basically a modernist attempting green inclusivity. *La Méthode*, his opus, was developed before the postmodern revolution and is essentially an extension of monological scientific methodology in a meta fashion into new, more inclusive (and still monological) areas. In other words, a genuine understanding of intersubjectivity is missing almost entirely in his work. He also fails to grasp the injunctive nature of 1st-, 2nd-, and 3rd-person knowledge, and so his "integral" thought is really just a $3\text{-}p \times 1\text{-}p \times 3p$, at most. (For just that reason, Morin is a favorite of 415-paradigm theorists.) Thus, he will expansively and passionately maintain that you need to include things like art and morals and science, or the good, the true, and the beautiful—which is absolutely wonderful—but then utterly miss the nature of the injunctions necessary to bring forth those domains, without which you have a horrifically imperialistic, subtle reductionism. Another way of noting this is that he is basically a **3-p(1-p + 2-p + 3-p)**—that is, he includes items like art and morals, but only in a 3 – p or meta-monological embrace, not incorporating *their own actual injunctions* into his unitas. This is indeed imperialistic subtle reductionism.

The Inner Journey Home: The Soul's Realization of the Unity of Reality, by A. H. Almaas (pen name of A. Hameed Ali). Hameed is the finest metapsychologist writing today. I'm a big fan and love his work. But it could be improved so easily by a finer awareness of postmodern currents. The remnants of his reliance on archetypes, metaphysics, essence, aspects, and Husserlian phenomenology—all of which are monological and laced with the myth of the given, even if a transpersonal given—can easily be jettisoned without affecting his work in the least.

Loving What Is: Four Questions That Can Change Your Life, by Byron Katie. I include this book because it is a good example of a wonderful new set of techniques for spiritual intelligence and glimpsing causal emptiness, but in not understanding (and therefore implicitly accepting) the myth of the given, "the Work," allows postmodernists to completely dismiss it, which is a shame—they could use a little of her work, not to mention Hameed's and the rest of the authors critiqued here.

The Web of Life: A New Scientific Understanding of Living Systems, by Fritjof Capra. Capra believes that the world's basic problem is that it doesn't understand dynamical systems and complexity theory. (If only Saddam Hussein could have learned dynamical complexity theory, instead of spending so much of his time studying the Newtonian-Cartesian paradigm, how different the world could have been.) But the world's major interior problem is that 70% of its population is ethnocentric or lower, and isn't even up to the level where it *could* embrace the Newtonian-Cartesian paradigm. And then by the time that about 10% of the world's population makes it to green, where it can begin to understand complexity theory, Capra would like that 10% to embrace monological systems theory, entirely devoid of the interior quadrants (on their own terms), and especially devoid of zones #2 and #4, which cannot be seen with his scientific methodologies. This is classic flatland subtle reductionism, extending the myth of the given into more territories, thus extending falsehoods into new and larger areas.

Power vs. Force: The Hidden Determinants of Human Behavior, by David R. Hawkins. Terrifically interesting ideas, but caught in subtle reductionism and the myth of the given. All the "hidden determinants" he mentions in the subtitle are monological instead of tetra-logical.

The Varieties of Religious Experience, by William James. I mention this as an example of the typically good news / bad news nature of the books in this appendix: the good news is that it extends research and inquiry into transpersonal, religious, and spiritual experiences, which previously were largely dismissed by academia; the bad news is that the methodology by which it does so is monological empiricism (and monological phenomenology)—it extends the crippled philosophy of consciousness into new and expanded areas.

James was a genius and a pioneer in so many ways, and the fact that he took states of consciousness as seriously as he did was extraordinary; but monological is monological, and in that instance he merely extended the imperialism of the philosophy of the subject. Fortunately, James's sheer genius pushes him beyond his own self-imposed limitations. His empiricism is always open to hermeneutics, the representational paradigm is supplemented with Peircean pragmatics, and—above all—his is a soul in which Truth and Goodness and Beauty are still a holy and unbreakable trinity.

But radical empiricism is still empiricism. That is, radical empiricism is radical monologicalism. Stages in zone #2 and the constitutive nature of zone #4 are alien to him. Had he availed himself of more of the work of his contemporary James Mark Baldwin, how different it all might have been. This imperialistic empiricism is the worm in the core of this otherwise extraordinary work.

It's interesting to note that, in fact, Charles Peirce himself criticized James for exactly this central problem. James and Peirce were lifelong friends, despite their little tiff over James's appropriation of the term "pragmatism" from Peirce, who coined it. (Peirce subsequently changed the name of his philosophy to "pragmaticism," which was "a term," he said, "so ugly as to discourage theft.") Despite their friendship, Peirce felt James's approach of "pure empiricism" was deeply flawed. Peirce—who, as noted, is generally regarded as America's greatest philosophical genius—nailed James with a simple sentence: *Perception is semiotic.*

In other words, perception is always already an interpretation. At least in part. Failing to see this is the common mistake of naive phenomenology and naive empiricism in all their forms. Understanding this also let Peirce point out two further problems, which people simply will not understand if they don't get the first problem with monological empiricism itself. Namely, it let Peirce say of James, "Of course, he is materialistic to the core." And further: "He inclines toward Cartesian dualism." Whenever I mention this to fans of James, they usually express shock, which tells me that they haven't gotten the postmodern revolution, because otherwise it makes perfect sense. But for those who fail to understand this, James is even seen as somebody who overcame materialism and dualism, whereas he merely embodied their subtler monological forms. Peirce went on to humorously say of James's implicit materialism that this is so "in a methodological sense, but not religiously, since he does not deny a separable soul nor a future life; for materialism is that form of philosophy which leaves the universe as incomprehensible as it finds it." What Peirce means is, what monological delivers is incomprehensible; perception itself is actually semiotic.

We can also see, further, why James—as well as virtually all meditation and phenomenology—is, as often noted, modernist in essence, and why Peirce was a great postmodernist about a century ahead of his time (who else could see natural laws as natural habits, without falling into magenta magic?). Peirce maintained that all perception is already an interpretation, and interpretation is triadic in structure: it demands a sign, an object (referent), and an interpretant. You can see the similarity with Ferdinand de Saussure, who maintained that the sign is composed of a signifier and signified in a system of interpreted differences. Peirce coined the term "semiotics"; Saussure called what he was doing "semiology." AQAL has drawn on both of them: there is a sign (signifier plus signified), referent, semantic, syntax, and pragmatics.*

The point with regard to James is that he classically did not understand semiotics (or the Lower-Left quadrant and its intrinsically constitutive nature). Peirce did; hence the powerfully accurate critique of

---

*To give a quadratic view: the sign is composed of UR-signifier and UL-signified (and yes, à la postmodernism, there are often huge gaps between them, resulting in deferral of meaning). Integral Theory defines a sign as "any aspect of reality that signifies another, to another." Signs exist in systems of semantics (LL) and syntax (LR), held together by pragmatics (whose telos is to integrate the 4 quadrants of any semiotic occasion: and all occasions are semiotic, although only higher animals have linguistic forms of semiotics: the 4 quadrants go all the way down, taking semiotics with them). Whitehead, incidentally, follows James in this regard, which is why Whitehead is indeed monological in essence (which AQAL attempts to amend by speaking of "quadratic prehension").

James, which today's advocates of bare attention, pure awareness, and pure experience would do well to heed.*

One last word. I showed this critique to a well-known Eastern teacher; the first thing he is said is, "The rejection of the philosophy of consciousness is the typical Western denial of consciousness and Spirit and interiority. It's just more scientific materialism." This, of course, and very sadly, misses the point. I am not denying pure Emptiness or unqualifiable Consciousness as such, but that is something that belongs only to the purely unmanifest, whereas the world of manifestation is the world of perspectives, and hence semiotics. In other words, "the philosophy of consciousness" is a critique not of absolute-unqualifiable consciousness or *shunyata* or *nirguna*, but, *in the manifest realm*, a critique of the UL divorced from the LL. If you think of a diagram of the 4 quadrants, the nondual or ultimate reality is the paper on which the diagram is written; the "philosophy of consciousness," or the "philosophy of the subject" refers to the UL quadrant; the *criticism* is that the UL cannot be considered apart form the LL. It is true that many Western thinkers deny the nondual paper; but Eastern thinkers deny (or are ignorant of) the LL-quadrant in the manifest realm and hence are caught in the myth of the given and the philosophy of the subject—and both of them are wrong. As long as Eastern teachers fail to get this elemental point, they will fail to get a fair hearing in the modern and postmodern world.

The Varieties of Meditative Experience, by Daniel Goleman. This is a superb book in so many ways. The title is deliberately modeled on Wil-

---

*Another way to put it is that there is Absolute Subjectivity (*Brahman-atman*), which is actually Nonduality or pure perception (which is also unqualifiable *shunyata* and formless, unmanifest *nirvana*), and then there is the manifest realm of relative subject and object (which is a realm not of pure perception but perspectives). In the manifest realm, the relative subject is actually embedded in chains of intersubjectivity (as is the object enmeshed in interobjectivity)—and failing to see this is referred to as the myth of the given, the philosophy of the (mere) subject, and the philosophy of consciousness. So where the West tends to deny Absolute Subjectivity or Consciousness as Such—or, more accurately, pure Emptiness (the paper on which the 4 quadrants are drawn)—the East is caught in the myth of the given and the philosophy of the subject. The East gets the Absolute right, but the manifest realm it badly mangles. As we have said throughout the text, the Nondual might indeed be the union of Emptiness and Form, but the world of Form is AQAL, and failing to see this is to fail to have an adequate Framework or View.

liam James's extraordinary work. But what is hard for many people to understand is that meditation is monological awareness, trained and extended. If nondual reality is the union of Emptiness and Form, meditation gets the Emptiness right but not the Form. It gets Emptiness right because there are no parts to get wrong; but it misses the nature of Form, at least in part, because meditative awareness (or the philosophy of consciousness) simply cannot see zones #2 and #4. So meditation can help you get freely Free but not fully Full. It realizes Freedom/Emptiness, but not Fullness/Form (it doesn't get tetra-Full). This is why meditative/contemplative practices both East and West include neither structural-stages nor the LL perspective, which cripples their inclusivity and leaves them open to virulent attacks by postmodernists, alas. (As we saw, it is Husserl that Foucault goes after. . . .)

Another way to put this is that meditation is the philosophy of consciousness extended from personal into transpersonal realms, carrying its inadequacies and illusions with it. Meditation is still hobbled by the myth of the given because it is still monological; it still assumes that what I see in meditation or contemplative prayer is actually real, instead of partially con-structed via cultural backgrounds (syntactic and semantic). How many Christian contemplatives, when they are meditating and see "interior deities," see them with 10,000 arms (a common form of Avalokiteshvara in the East)? The point is that even higher, transpersonal, spiritual realities are partially molded and constructed by vast networks of always implicit cultural backgrounds. Meditative and contemplative realities are never simply given,* but rather, are constructed or "tetra-structed" (in this case, especially by zone #4), something that *meditation will never tell you and can never tell you.* As we have seen, zones #2 and #4 cannot be seen by introspecting the mind. Meditation is the extension of the myth of the given into higher realities, thus ensuring that you never escape its deep illusions, even in Enlightenment (unless you use something like an integral framework to foreground these networks and make them the object of meditation . . .).

---

*See the discussion of Daniel P. Brown in chap. 3. Meditators think that they actually ARE SEEING *dharmas*, but they aren't. As the study makes so obvious, what different meditators with different cultural backgrounds and frameworks see are co-constructions of the interpretations they use. Awareness and meditation per se are simply perpetuating the myth of the given and the illusions it generates. Monological meditation and contemplation share that with monological science, which is why the Postmodernists lump all of them together in this one decisive regard.

Again, meditation is not wrong but partial, and unless its partialness is addressed, it simply houses these implicit lies, assuring that liberation is never really full, and even *satori* conceals and perpetuates the myth of the given. . . .

"Neurophenomenology," *Journal of Consciousness Studies*, by Francisco Varela. As one might expect, Francisco Varela, in his otherwise profound neurophenomenology, includes the *shared hermeneutics phenomenology* of zone #3 (precisely because he includes phenomenology, or zone #1); but he is unfortunately blind to zone #2 and its correlative aspects in zone #4—and thus the overall nature of intersubjectivity and its deep significance is absent in neurophenomenology.

Francisco, before his untimely death, helped found the Mind and Life Institute, associated with the Dalai Lama, an organization otherwise wonderfully dedicated to expanding phenomenology from prepersonal to personal to transpersonal forms in the UL (using meditation), while using brain monitoring to simul-track those changes in the UR. But a lack of post/structural intersubjectivity has allowed this to be severely criticized (and dismissed) by postmodernists. This has also hindered Buddhist phenomenology from having any significant impact in academia. Buddhist epistemology (including Zen, *vipassana*, and Vajrayana) is steeped in the myth of the given, and because none of that has been effectively addressed, Buddhist epistemology has more or less died in the West, which is a great shame, I would even say something of a cultural catastrophe. It's not entirely too late for an integral Framework to help, but we shall see. . . .

Science and the Akashic Field: An Integral Theory of Everything, by Ervin Laszlo. Intersubjectivity is not only ignored by Ervin Laszlo but, on the rare occasions it isn't, it is badly misinterpreted and caught in a widely extended and imperialistic subtle reductionism (possibly the worst subtle reductionism I have seen, given his braggadocio about its inclusiveness). As we saw in appendix II, you can't simply give a 3rd-person description of your allegedly integral reality without giving the 1st-person injunctions that will transform consciousness to the levels from which that reality can be seen. Giving merely a series of 3rd-person assertions is, again, subtle reductionism and monological imperialism.

This is why to enter Laszlo's world is to enter a world of monological everything, extended brusquely and breathlessly into every nook and cranny of the Kosmos. What truly does leave you breathless is the intense nature of the subtle reductionism and the aggressive methodological imperialism, all of which Laszlo calls "an integral theory of everything." This is just embarrassing.

Laszlo is indeed a classic $3\text{-p} \times 3\text{-p} \times 3\text{p}$, alternating, when it comes to interiors, with a $3\text{-p} \times 1\text{-p} \times 3\text{p}$. That is, he never gets to the interiors *as* interiors; never hermeneutics but always a cognitive-science type of approach: he will assert that consciousness is foundational and is the inside of all matter, but he simply *asserts* all of that with objectivistic fervor, and never actually explores the interiors on their own terms nor gives any understanding that he even sees methodologies #1 through #4, and on the rare occasion that he does, he again simply asserts they are there, but never gives the injunctions for enacting them. He is essentially a zone-#8 theorist and has been most of his life.

Many years ago, I edited an imprint series—The New Science Library—at Shambhala Publications (I asked Francisco Varela and Jeremy Hayward to be my co-editors, and they agreed). I accepted one of Laszlo's books for it—*Evolution: The Grand Synthesis*—although Francisco Varela strenuously objected to publishing it (his concern, sharply stated, was that "Laszlo is a lightweight"). I felt the book was a wonderful overview of evolution and deserved publication on that account, and so we ended up doing so, although it was already imperialistically subsuming virtually every other methodology under its subtle scientism. (We let it go at the time because it was a scientific imprint series, but still . . .).

During that time, I also edited *The Holographic Paradigm*; ironically, I was the only dissenting voice in the anthology where everybody hailed it as "the new paradigm." At the time—this was almost 30 years ago—I felt that "the holographic paradigm" would become the foundation of a certain type of widespread boomeritis worldview, which indeed it did. (See *What the Bleep!?*, below.) Each year, some new discovery in physics was hailed as proof that *your very own consciousness* is needed to collapse the quantum wave packet and bring an object into existence, and thus *the philosophy of the subject* was imperialistically pushed to the very foundations of the universe (hence, boomeritis). Fred Alan Wolf, by far the zaniest popularizer of this misunderstood physics, says that your looking at an ashtray actually "qwaffs" the ashtray into existence. (I wonder, if you and I are both looking at the ashtray, is it your consciousness or mine that brings it into existence?) In any event, this is NOT the same thing as the postmodern claim that intersubjectivity is constitutive of a referent's reality, but actually just the opposite: your own ego creates reality.

As of a decade ago, the *quantum vacuum* had become the leading contender here. This was coupled with the necessity to call anything "the new paradigm," even though that word was being used in almost the exact opposite way that Thomas Kuhn had proposed, as Kuhn himself strenuously pointed out, to no avail. Kuhn's actual point is quite similar to the one we advanced in appendix II, namely, that all real knowledge is grounded in injunctions or exemplars, and if you have no injunction, you have no data and no meaning, period.

This also points out why Habermas refers to systems theory as being *egocentric* (his term), which totally confuses systems theorists. But Habermas's point is simple and true enough: the philosophy of the subject has no intersubjectivity to correct its narcissism, theoretical or otherwise, and hence the subject imperialistically reigns (e.g., systems theory claims that it includes everything, and it accepts no other that could extend the monological philosophy of the subject into transpersonal realms, or into quantum realms, or into interior realms—you are simply on an imperialistic (egocentric) crusade. And when this is the case, the theoretical narcissism often calls forth personal narcissism—hence, the boomeritis often not far around the corner.

And thus, as for "the theory of everything," that Laszlo proposes—and excuse my jadedness here—you know it will have something to do with "holograms" and the "quantum vacuum," and it will have to be called "the new paradigm." And given the popularity of the Integral Approach, you know it will contain the word "integral," too. Well, here it is, and he manages to get all four buzz words into a few sentences: "The hypothesis we can now advance may be daring, but it is logical. *The quantum vacuum generates the holographic field that is the memory of the universe.* This is a remarkable development, for *the new paradigm* offers the best-ever basis for the long sought *integral theory of everything* [his italics]."

Pushing monological reductionism into everything is indeed a grand project. But for somebody who is engaged in a similar subtle reductionism, Edgar Morin is much the better theorist and philosopher, covering more ground with more insight. Laszlo does wonderfully when he discusses zones that actually use methodology #8—namely, systems theory in all its classical and recent forms, dynamic to chaos to complexity. There, as usual, Laszlo is a master. But when he pushes his imperialism into the other 7 zones, the results are less than happy. As you can tell, I am particularly disappointed (and hence a tad irritated) with Laszlo's type of approach, because it does so much damage to so many areas, all the while claiming to be integral.

The Book of Secrets: Unlocking the Hidden Dimensions of Your Life, by Deepak Chopra. Serious writers accuse Deepak of being "spirit lite." I think this is unfair; he is a fine scholar with a searching intellect and superb writing skills. What the intellectuals resent, I think, is Deepak's capacity to write simply and accessibly for wide audiences, which has made his books very popular and often best-sellers (which is usually enough to get you disbarred by the *intelligentsia*). My concern, rather, is similar to that expressed about the others in this appendix: Deepak's lack of understanding (or at least use) of zones #2 and #4 leaves him with a modernist epistemology (namely, empirical or phenomenological, and particularly the scientific versions of such), which he attempts to extend into interiors à la William James—which, again, is fine as far as it goes, but brutal when it goes no further. Deepak ends up trying to prove *premodern metaphysics* with *modern physics*, and the results are a theoretical shambles, I'm afraid.

The second concern I have with some of these approaches is that, precisely because they are often blind to zone-#2 stages, they are blind to how those stages might be operating in them and in their writing. They often present the values of one of these stages and don't even realize that what they are saying is true merely for one of a dozen or so stages of values development. (Further, they may be caught in the dysfunctional forms of these stages and not even know it, as witness boomeritis.) Deepak has a fine understanding of some of the types of phenomenal or *trained state-stages* that can occur in zone #1 (as he showed in *How to Know God*), but because he does not incorporate an understanding of zone #2 or its stages, he himself often comes solely from the green altitude, and all of his zone-#1 stages are therefore looked at from that single zone-#2 values stage.

A rampant confusion of spirituality with the green-wave of values, norms, and cognition is widespread in this culture, due to the influence, it seems, of the green Cultural Creatives, some 20% of the population. (The most widespread form of this green-wave worldview is "the 415 Paradigm.") Not only is this a massive Level/Line Fallacy, it has made the work of the more popular spiritual writers open to extensive boomeritis.

A third major problem with these general approaches is that they are completely blind to the truth-power-knowledge complex. This is another aspect of postmodernism that seems to have passed these theorists by. A sensitivity to intersubjective realities also sensitized most postmodernists to the abuses that come from a claim to have "truth" and "knowledge"—there are simply no such things divorced from power relations. Even (or especially) somebody claiming to have spiritual truth is somebody who is wielding power and attempted power; there is simply no way to avoid this completely for any form of knowledge or truth, and so the best one can do is acknowledge it and attempt to be self-critical about it. Failing that, you have what both modernists and postmodernists always claimed metaphysics was all about: it's all about power, so watch out. The move from metaphysics to post-metaphysics is an attempt to foreground the truth-power-knowledge complex and deal with it consciously, unlike metaphysics, which simply wields it.

Finally, let's note what we can no longer do: we can no longer simply say things like, "We are combining body, mind, soul, and spirit—and heart and community—to produce a truly integral approach." Because that isn't integral (or it isn't AQAL integral), because somebody at magenta or red or blue (etc.) can embrace those tenets. The simple fact is that including the various components of a human being ("body and mind and soul and spirit and community," etc.), *without also* including the zone-#2 and zone-#4 levels and lines (and genealogical worldspaces), will result not just in a fractured human being, but one that can be deeply immoral as well—all the while imagining that he or she is "integral."

If you haven't seen it, I highly recommend that you get a copy of the Discovery Channel documentary video *Nazis: The Occult Conspiracy.* Hitler and his inner circle—particularly folks like Goebbels and Himmler (head of the SS)—were deeply into the practice of mysticism and mystical states of consciousness. They used astrology before battles, used psychic pendulums to locate Allied warships, encouraged daily practice of meditation, deliberately selected occult symbols and myths, traced what they felt were their own reincarnations, fully supported "body, mind, soul, and spirit," and had numerous and profound experiences of *unio mystica.* That's exactly what you get when you promote horizontal states and not also vertical stages (particularly in ethics, cognition, and interpersonal perspectives).

What the Bleep Do We Know!? The startling success of this indie film shows just how starved people are for some sort of validation for a more mystical, spiritual worldview. But the problems with this film are so enormous it's hard to know where to begin. *What the Bleep* is built around a series of interviews with physicists and mystics, all making ontological assertions about the nature of reality and about the fact that—yes, you guessed it—"you create your own reality." But you don't create your own reality, psychotics do. There are at least 6 major schools of modern physics, and not one of them agrees with the general and sweeping assertions made by this film. No school of physics believes that a human being can collapse the Schroedinger wave equation in 100% of the atoms of an object so as to "qwaff" it into existence. The physics is simply horrid in this film, and the mysticism is not much better, being that of an individual ("Ramtha") who claims to be a 35,000-year-old warrior from Lemuria. None of the interviewees are identified while they speak, because the film wishes to give the impression that these are well-known and well-respected scientists. The net result is New Age mysticism (of the "your ego is in charge of everything" variety) combined with wretched physics (all in a type of 415-Paradigm mush; even IF a human mind were necessary to qwaff an object into existence—and even David Bohm disagreed with this loopy notion!—but even if, the point would be that Big Mind is instantaneously qwaffing ALL of manifestation into existence moment to moment—and not just selectively qwaffing one thing into existence instead of another, such as getting a new car, a job, or a promotion—which is exactly what this film says; again, this is the philosophy of the subject on steroids, aka boomeritis).

Bad physics and fruit-loop mysticism, and people are starving for this kind of stuff, bless them. Between modernism (and scientific materialism) and postmodernism (and its denial of depth), there is nothing left to feed the soul, and thus *What the Bleep* would be received with fevered appreciation. I'm sorry to be so harsh about this, because clearly the intentions are decent; but this is exactly the kind of tripe that gives mysticism and spirituality a staggeringly bad name among real scientists, all postmodernists, and anybody who can read without moving their lips.

Heterologies: Discourse on the Other, by Michel de Certeau. I include this as an example of a different problem: understanding intersubjectivity and jettisoning the myth of the given, but only up to the level of green altitude in any line, and thus being *stuck with multiplicities* that are forever incommensurable and incommunicable, a world of fragments and fractures never reaching fractals (i.e., never reaching vision-logic commonalities and communions). This is classic arrested development at the (postmodern) pluralistic wave.

This classic limitation shows up especially in postmodernism's incapacity to escape the hermeneutic circle, which it absolutizes (i.e., quadrant absolutism—in this case, the LL, and then only up to green). This is captured in its claim that there are no extra-linguistic realities, a claim that AQAL categorically rejects (along with Habermas and other more integral thinkers).

This postmodern-pluralistic (green) wave has, of course, dominated academic humanities for the last 3 decades. It has increasingly hardened into its own dysfunctional forms, resulting in pluralitis and boomeritis, as out come the Green Inquisitors (see *The Shadow University* by Kors and Silverglate, a chilling account of these Inquisitors in action in American universities).

But this is also the deconstructive version of the postmodern worldview that is now dying down, as the Integral Age begins, according to sociologist Jeffrey Alexander. But the green-wave still owns the humanities in academia, owns the 2nd culture, and it will fight to the death, more or less literally, because, as is now common knowledge, old paradigms die when the believers in old paradigms die. The knowledge quest proceeds funeral by funeral. . . .

Jewish Renewal: A Path to Healing and Transformation, by Michael Lerner. Wonderfully driven by a keen spiritual intelligence, but interpreted and enacted at a green center of gravity, with the net effect of trying to force green values on the world, even via a constitutional amendment (this is subtle imperialism in the political arena). As we saw, perhaps the most difficult thing for green to understand is that its values—peace, harmony, healing, transformation, sharing, feeling, embodiment—are values shared only by green. They are not values shared by magenta, red, amber, orange, teal, turquoise, indigo, or violet. If I want to transform the world, implicit in that desire is the assumption, "You are screwed up, but I know what you need." This imposition of my values on you is a subtle violence of values. Second tier, on the other hand, understands that people are where they are, and that you have to let red be red, and let amber be amber, and let orange be orange, and so on. Of course we can work for the growth and development of all humans, but not by forcing my one set of values on everybody. The real question facing an enlightened society is not how to make everybody green, but how to create **stations of life** reflecting the various **stages**, among other things, and not make one station the domineering monad of the group. I have had 3-hour conversations with Michael on why his view is green, and while he cognitively gets it and even agrees, his center of gravity just won't hold it. His latest book, *The Left Hand of God*, is even more polarized and more intensely green than usual, so in my opinion, this is not looking promising.

The Rebirth of Nature: The Greening of Science and God, by Rupert Sheldrake. This is another of my favorite authors dismissed by postmodernists and humanities professors because his epistemologies are basically an extension of the mirror of nature, or the reflection paradigm (which, we saw, are yet other names for the monological myth of the given). So many of Rupert's early books are right on the money, involving issues that simply have not been answered or even addressed by conventional science, none of which is more important than the development of form or structure in living systems (hence his use of Waddington's notion of *morphogenetic fields*, or morphic fields, which happens to be a completely viable scientific hypothesis). This got Sheldrake rejected by both modernists—who found that his work threatened their established worldviews—and postmodernists—because Sheldrake proposed all of this using merely modernist (monological) epistemologies, which is enough to get some extremely important ideas rejected outright, when a slight shift would take the same ideas and simply reframe them in more contextual ways.

As a secondary issue, and possibly because of his rejection by both modernists and postmodernists, Rupert as of late has increasingly retreated to a retro-Romantic worldview, which is unnecessary and unfortunate, in my opinion, because it confuses states and stages (and thus equates childhood states with advanced stages), eulogizes pre-rational as trans-transrational, and loses discriminating capacity when it comes to the difference between, say, preconventional magenta and postconventional turquoise. Rupert has always been a brilliant, quintessential turquoise thinker, who now is embracing magenta perhaps out of exasperation. But in either case, the postmodern notions of contextualism, constructivism, and aperspectivism have not yet permeated his thought to a sufficient degree to get him a hearing in postmodern worlds, which is deeply unfortunate.

The Future of the Body, by Michael Murphy. Some of the same problem—the myth of the given, or the failure to address postmodern intersubjectivity—also affects the equally profound work of Michael Murphy, whose "natural history of meta-normal phenomena" is surely the most important treatment of that topic. But it is marred—and equally dismissed by the postmodernists (and hence virtually all of academic humanities)—because of its failure to take into account the constitutive nature of intersubjectivity. The "natural history" Murphy gives is not the simple objectivist account he imagines, but is a view seen only from turquoise or higher, by an educated-Western-white male, acknowledging and using three particular injunctions, whose own para-normal and meta-normal and transpersonal states and stages enact and bring forth a perceptual capacity that can disclose phenomena that reside in those specific worldspaces—and *then*, and *only then*, can Murphy's data be seen. And that data, those facts, are definitely real. But they aren't just lying around out there waiting for a universal, objective, natural historian to stumble on them and objectively report them. Assuming otherwise has gotten his entire corpus dismissed by postmodernists, which is tragic. Integralists, of course, include his magnificent work, but that's not the issue.

This is a brilliant work of a true pioneering genius, mandatory reading for integral. But synoptic empiricism is a synoptic myth of the given—or a vastly expanded and still monological phenomenology, as is a natural history of meta-normal and super-normal phenomena. This is easily remedied, as so many of the approaches in this appendix are. In the meantime, this is simply using expanded modernist epistemologies to support premodern metaphysics, and both the "modernist" and the "metaphysics" are in need of overhauling to take into account Spirit's postmodern turn. This research will never get the respect it richly deserves in academic circles until this epistemological and methodological partialness (not wrongness) is addressed. This is truly tragic, in my opinion, because for what it does, it is a crucial ingredient of any integral worldview.

Living Buddha, Living Christ, by Thich Nhat Hanh. Perhaps nobody better symbolizes the ambiguity and ambivalence of the spiritual traditions in the post/modern world than Thich Nhat Hanh. The positive aspects are not in doubt: the great heart, the noble intentions, the good that can come from meditation and contemplation. But if the traditions were integral in the premodern world, they are not so in the modern and postmodern world, and thus in today's world, sooner or later, they begin to tear the soul apart, leaving fragments and fractures where wholeness was supposed to be. The spiritual traditions rely for their theoretical aspects on metaphysics, which, as we have often seen, is shot through with a failure to grasp intersubjectivity, among other inadequacies. And for their practical aspects, the traditions have always relied on meditation and contemplation, which embody the myth of the given and monological phenomenology.

These series of partialities and inadequacies do not add up to wholeness. The soul is thus increasingly left with a handful of profound spiritual experiences housed in a fragmented worldview, with a broken framework and a reductionistic attitude. As discussed in chapter 5, this is indeed a prescription for a person to become both deeper and narrower, deeper and narrower, deeper and narrower. . . .

THE PSYCHOACTIVE FRAMEWORK

As we also saw in chapter 5, all of this is salvageable, and without changing any of the basics of the spiritual traditions. A few things need to be added, not subtracted, in order for the great wisdom traditions to become more integral, or capable of embracing Spirit's premodern and modern and postmodern turns. We summarized these changes as **supplement,** and in the Upper Left, we especially emphasized the 3 S's: **shadow, states,** and **stages.**

Perhaps the most important of all supplementations is adopting a more integral Framework. Whatever type of Framework you use, if it is truly integral, it will itself begin to reverse the damage, allowing the strengths of the traditions to shine through while contextualizing and curtailing their limitations. The cognitive line is necessary but not sufficient for all permanent growth and transformation. Whatever cognitive View you have, it sets the entire space of possibilities for the other intelligences as well.

A truly Integral or AQAL Framework is not an inert map, it's a **psychoactive map.** It is a psychoactive system that goes through your entire bodymind and begins to activate any potentials that are not presently being used. Once you download AQAL (or IOS—Integral Operating System), it simply and almost automatically begins looking for areas that the integral map suggests you possess but that you might not have consciously realized—any quadrant, level, line, state, or type. The AQAL Framework activates them, lights them up, makes you realize that you have all of these possibilities in your own being. If you have read this far, the integrative process is already activated in you, and you likely understand just what this means.

Simply learning AQAL sets this psychoactive Framework in motion in your own system. This raises the bar for all the other intelligences as well, because the cognitive line, the co-gnosis line, is necessary but not sufficient for all of them. Because the AQAL Framework is originating at indigo (and higher), it sets up a resonance in your own system, which acts like an indigo magnet helping to pull the other lines up as well. Of course, any of those other lines can and should be practiced, too, but they can only grow into the space of possibilities set by the cognitive line, so set those possibilities as high as you can, download an Integral Operating System, and let the greater possibilities of your own tomorrow begin to unfold, grounded in the great traditions, but moving forward into Spirit's own modern and postmodern flowering. . . .

On the Way to Integral

Not supplementing is no longer something that is without its effects and consequences. Not supplementing—not making one's spiritual practice into an integral spiritual practice—can slowly kill you, more or less literally, or worse: figuratively, because what it kills is the soul struggling to be reborn into today's integral age, struggling to be reborn into its own highest estate of Freedom and Fullness, struggling to acknowledge the Spirit that embraces the entire Kosmos whole, with love and charity, valor and compassion, care and consciousness, interiority and identity, radiance and luminosity, ecstasy and clarity, all at once, and once and for all. In the very deepest part of you, you know You, and I know I-I, and We know This: your very Self is the Self of all that is and all that ever shall be, and the history of the entire Kosmos is the history of Your very own Being and Becoming, you can feel it in Your bones because You *know* that is what You are, in the deepest parts of you when you stop lying to yourself about who and what You really are.

And what You are is the great Unborn, timeless and eternal, in its 1st-person perspective as the great I-I, the great Self, the Witness of this page, and this room, and this universe, and everything in it, witnessing it All with a passionate equanimity that leaves you alone as the Unmoved Mover. You are likewise the great Unborn, timeless and eternal, in its 2nd-person perspective as the Great Thou, the Great Other, before whom you bow in an infinite act of complete release and savage surrender and ecstatic submission, and receive in return the entire Kosmos as your blessing and your forgiveness and your eternal grace. You are likewise the great Unborn, timeless and eternal, in its 3rd-person perspective as the Great Perfection, the Holy Spirit, the great Web of Life in all its infinite perfection and dynamic chaos, its pulsating pulsars and exploding nebulae, its stars and galaxies and planets and oceans, through which runs the common blood and beats the single heart of an Eros seeking its own higher wholeness, and always finding it, and seeking yet again, and always finding it yet once more, because You always know that You are here, don't You? And so in fun and sport and play and delight, and remorse and terror and agony and respite, You throw yourself out to start the play all over again, in this, the deepest part of You that gives birth to galaxies within Your heart, lets the stars light up as the neurons in Your brain, sings songs of love and delight to the submission and surrender of Your own good night, and all of this within the space that is You, the space that You feel as Your own I-I, or this ever-present Witness of the forms of Your own play.

And in the great I-I, as You witness the Forms of Your own play as the entire Kosmos—in that very moment, which is this timeless Now, a Now that has no beginning and no end, there is *simultaneously* Spirit in its 1st-person and 2nd-person and 3rd-person forms, the Great I and We and It *feel each other*, and in that unitary seamless sizzling Now, which is this very moment before you do anything at all, it is, quite simply, over.

Which means, it has, quite simply, begun.

Index

Books by Ken Wilber

The Spectrum of Consciousness (1977). An introduction to the full-spectrum model, the first to show, in a systematic way, how the great psychological systems of the West can be integrated with the great contemplative traditions of the East. Wilber's first book, and still a favorite.

No Boundary: Eastern and Western Approaches to Personal Growth (1979). A simple and popular guide to psychologies and therapies available from both Western and Eastern sources; designated by Wilber as reflecting the "Romantic" phase of his early work.

The Atman Project: A Transpersonal View of Human Development (1980). The first psychological system to suggest a way of uniting Eastern and Western, conventional and contemplative, orthodox and mystical approaches into a single, coherent framework.

Up from Eden: A Transpersonal View of Human Evolution (1981). Drawing on theorists from Joseph Campbell to Jean Gebser, Wilber outlines humankind's evolutionary journey—and "dialectic of process"—from its primal past to its integral future.

The Holographic Paradigm and Other Paradoxes: Exploring the Leading Edge of Science (1982). An anthology of contributions by prominent scientists and thinkers (including Karl Pribram, Stanley Krippner, Renée Weber, William Irwin Thompson, David Bohm, and Marilyn Ferguson) on the dialogue between science and religion.

A Sociable God: Toward a New Understanding of Religion (1983). A scholarly introduction to a system of reliable methods by which to adjudicate the legitimacy and authenticity of any religious movement.

Eye to Eye: The Quest for the New Paradigm (1983). An examination of three realms of knowledge: the empirical realm of the senses, the rational realm of the mind, and the contemplative realm of the spirit. Includes important papers such as "The Pre/Trans Fallacy" and "A Mandalic Map of Consciousness."

Quantum Questions: Mystical Writings of the World's Great Physicists (1984). An anthology of nontechnical excerpts selected from the work of great physicists, including Heisenberg, Schroedinger, Einstein, de Broglie, Jeans, Planck, Pauli, and Eddington.

Transformations of Consciousness: Conventional and Contemplative Perspectives on Development, by Ken Wilber, Jack Engler, and Daniel P. Brown (1986). Nine essays exploring the full-spectrum model of human growth and development, from prepersonal to personal to transpersonal.

Spiritual Choices: The Problem of Recognizing Authentic Paths to Inner Transformation, edited by Dick Anthony, Bruce Ecker, and Ken Wilber (1987). Psychologists and spiritual teachers contribute to this study of religious movements, aimed at answering the dilemma of how to distinguish spiritual tyranny from legitimate spiritual authority.

Grace and Grit: Spirituality and Healing in the Life and Death of Treya Killam Wilber (1991). The moving story of Ken's marriage to Treya and the five-year journey that took them through her illness, treatment, and eventual death from breast cancer. Ken's wide-ranging commentary is combined with excerpts from Treya's personal journals.

Sex, Ecology, Spirituality: The Spirit of Evolution (1995). The first volume of the Kosmos Trilogy and the book that introduced the 4-quadrant model. This tour de force of scholarship and vision traces the course of evolution from matter to life to mind (and possible higher future levels), and describes the common patterns that evolution takes in all three domains. Wilber particularly focuses on how modernity and postmodernity relate to gender issues, psychotherapy, ecological concerns, and various liberation movements.

A Brief History of Everything (1996). A short, highly readable version of *Sex, Ecology, Spirituality*, written in an accessible, conversational style, without all the technical arguments and endnotes; perhaps his most popular book, and the place to begin for readers new to his work.

The Eye of Spirit: An Integral Vision for a World Gone Slightly Mad (1997). Essays explore the integral approach to such fields as psychology, spirituality, anthropology, cultural studies, art and literary theory, ecology, feminism, and planetary transformation. Includes a historical summary of Wilber's own work and responses to his critics.

The Marriage of Sense and Soul: Integrating Science and Religion (1998). Takes on the centuries-old problem of the relationship between science and religion. After surveying the world's great wisdom traditions and extracting features they all share, Wilber offers compelling arguments that not only are these compatible with scientific truth, they also share a similar scientific method.

The Essential Ken Wilber: An Introductory Reader (1998). Brief passages from Wilber's most popular books, imparting the essence and flavor of his writings for newcomers to his work. Compiled by Shambhala Publications.

One Taste: The Journals of Ken Wilber (1999). A lively and entertaining glimpse into a year in the life of Ken Wilber—as well as a thought-provoking series of short essays on current trends in spirituality and psychology, daily reflections, meditation experiences, and advice to spiritual seekers.

The Collected Works of Ken Wilber. The first eight volumes of this ongoing series were published in 1999–2000.

Volume 1: *The Spectrum of Consciousness, No Boundary,* and selected essays.

Volume 2: *The Atman Project* and *Up from Eden.*

Volume 3: *A Sociable God* and *Eye to Eye.*

Volume 4: *Transformations of Consciousness, Integral Psychology,* and selected essays.

Volume 5: *Grace and Grit,* with a new introduction.

Volume 6: *Sex, Ecology, Spirituality.*

Volume 7: *A Brief History of Everything* and *The Eye of Spirit.*

Volume 8: *The Marriage of Sense and Soul* and *One Taste.*

Integral Psychology: Consciousness, Spirit, Psychology, Therapy (2000). A landmark study introducing the first truly integral psychology. This model includes waves of development, streams of development, states of consciousness, and the self, and follows the course of each from subconscious to self-conscious to superconscious. Charts correlating over a hundred psychological and spiritual schools from around the world include Kabbalah, Vedanta, Plotinus, St. Teresa, Aurobindo, Theosophy, and modern theorists such as Piaget, Erikson, Loevinger, Kohlberg, Carol Gilligan, Neumann, and Gebser.

A Theory of Everything: An Integral Vision for Business, Politics, Science, and Spirituality (2000). A compact summary of the Integral Approach as a genuine "world philosophy," noteworthy because it includes many real-world applications in various fields. A popular choice for introductory reading; compact, succinct, with many hands-on examples.

Boomeritis: A Novel That Will Set You Free (2002). The story of a grad student's journey to self-discovery, combining brilliant scholarship with wicked parody. The novel targets one of the most stubborn obstacles to realizing the integral vision: a disease of pluralism plus narcissism that Wilber calls "boomeritis" because it seems to plague the baby-boomer generation most of all.

The Simple Feeling of Being: Embracing Your True Nature (2004). A collection of inspirational, mystical, and instructional passages drawn from Wilber's publications, compiled and edited by some of his senior students.

Integral Spirituality: A Startling New Role for Religion in the Modern and Postmodern World (2006). A theory of spirituality that honors the truths of premodernity, modernity, and postmodernity—including the revolutions in science and culture—while incorporating the essential insights of the great religions. Critics have hailed this book for its revolutionary view of the nature and role of religion and spirituality.

The Integral Vision: A Very Short Introduction to the Revolutionary Integral Approach to Life, God, the Universe, and Everything (2007). An accessible book for anyone who wants an easy introduction to Ken Wilber's thought and its practical applications, both personal and global. The key components of his Integral Approach—a tool for "making sense of everything"—are distilled here into a simple and elegant full-color presentation.

Integral Life Practice: A 21st-Century Blueprint for Physical Health, Emotional Balance, Mental Clarity, and Spiritual Awakening (2008, with Terry Patten, Adam Leonard, and Marco Morelli). At last, a complete guide showing how to use Ken Wilber's acclaimed Integral Approach to design a personal program of transformational practice. With its combination of exercises, explanations, theory, examples, personal stories, and illustrations, *Integral Life Practice* will be the bible of a truly integrated approach to practice for years to come.